Canada Revenue Agency Tax Return Preparation with ProFile® Professional Tax Software: T1 General

2010 Federal Edition

General Income Tax and Benefit Guide 2009
using ProFile® Professional Tax Software

COMPREHENSIVE USER GUIDE

Michael B. Ford

BRADFORD, ONTARIO, CANADA

Copyright © The Ford Group, 2009
All rights reserved.
The Ford Group
PO Box 1123
Bradford, ON L3Z 2B5

Trademarks
The Ford Group, The Ford Group logo, Ford Bookkeeping & Taxation, among others, are trademarks or registered trademarks of The Ford Group in Canada.
Other parties' marks are the property of their respective owners.

Trademarks
Canada Revenue Agency, CRA
www.cra.gc.ca
5000-G - General Income Tax and Benefit Guide – 2009, plus other CRA Guides, Forms and Publications were used as reference for this guide.

Trademarks
Intuit, the Intuit logo, ProFile, and QuickBooks, among others, are trademarks or registered trademarks of Intuit in Canada and other countries. Other parties' marks are the property of their respective owners.
Screen shots © Intuit Inc. All rights reserved
Content © Intuit Inc. All rights reserved

All rights reserved®. No Part of this publication may be reproduced, transmitted or otherwise used in any form or manner or stored in any data base or retrieval system without prior written permission of the publisher.

Much care has been taken to trace ownership of copyrighted material contained in this publication however, the publisher will welcome any information that enables it to rectify any reference or credit for subsequent editions,

The material in this publication is provided for informational purposes only. Laws, regulations, policy and procedures regarding this subject are continuously changing and the information and examples are intended as general guidelines only. This publication is sold with the understanding that neither the publisher nor the author are engaged in rendering professional advice and it is recommended that such advice be obtained before acting on any information herein.

Users of this publication are responsible for their own actions and outcomes. The publishers and author therefore expressly disclaim all and any liability to any person in respect of anything and any consequence. Any examples in this book are factitious and any resemblances to actual people or circumstances are purely coincidental.

Canada Revenue Agency Tax Return Preparation with ProFile® Professional Tax Software: T1 General, is an independent publication and has not been authorized, sponsored, or otherwise approved by Intuit Inc., nor as having been made in affiliation with, or with the endorsement of, the CRA.

For permission to reproduce the information in this publication, please email info@thefordgroup.ca

For additional copies of this publication, please contact:
The Ford Group
PO Box 1123
Bradford, ON L3Z 2B5
Tel. (local): 289-464-1001
Email: info@thefordgroup.ca
Website: www.thefordgroup.ca

This publication is available upon request in accessible formats.
This publication is also available online at www.thefordgroup.ca

ISBN Number: 978-0-9865258-0-3
http://www.collectionscanada.gc.ca

Table of Contents

Chapter 1 17

Using ProFile T1 17

    ProFile T1 Help 18

    New user 18

    T1 module options 19

    Adding forms to the Jump bar 19

    Coupling returns 20

    Merging and separating - data flow when coupling and uncoupling returns 20

    Family returns 21

    Linking family returns 21

    Working with linked files 22

    Printing linked files 23

    Saving linked files 23

    Sharing income between spouses 23

    Sharing data between family members 23

    Special cases 24

    Completing a deceased taxpayer's return 24

    Early-filing a deceased return 24

    Completing a bankruptcy return 25

    Early-filing a bankruptcy return 26

    Information for Non-Residents and Deemed Residents of Canada 26

    Grouping business statement sets 29

    Sharing business income with spouses or partners 29

    Selecting a Standard Industry Code (SIC) 30

    Applying auto expenses to a business 30

    Converting a business to a December 31st year-end 31

Electing to keep a non-calendar year-end 31

Claiming the Employee and Partner GST rebate (GST-370) 32

Claiming medical expenses 32

Optimizations 33

Optimizing medical expenses 33

Optimizing charitable donations 34

Pension income splitting 34

Comparing returns with the "Jump to previous year" feature 37

Foreign income 37

Calculating foreign exchange rates 37

Claiming RRSP Contributions 38

Planning RRSP contributions 38

RRSP tax planning method one: Using window tiling 38

RRSP tax planning method two: Using the data monitor 39

RRSP tax planning method three: Using snapshot variance 39

Summaries: Other income, deductions and credits 39

Calculating installment payments 40

Understanding the T1 assessment process 40

Planning for the following tax year 41

Using next year's rates for tax planning 42

Claiming auto expenses 43

QuickBooks Integration 44

Set up ProFile T1 to QuickBooks billing 44

Create invoice in QuickBooks 44

Chapter 2 47

T1 Forms 47

CarryFWD: Carry forward Summary 48

Dependant: Dependant information 48

Disability/Infirmity 49

Caregiver 50

Disability supplement 50

Transfers from dependants 50

Info: Personal information 51

Residency status 51

EFILE this return? 52

Is return discounted? 52

Use rates for tax year 52

Date of death 52

Joint salutation / client salutation 52

Use joint client letter/invoice? 52

Provincial information - Quebec 53

Taxpayer information 53

Spousal information section 53

Foreign: Foreign employment, pension and investment income 53

Description (Foreign Income) 54

Name of Foreign Country 54

S3Details: Capital gains entry 54

Slips: Slip summary 54

T3 - Statement of Trust Income Allocations and Designations 54

T4 - Statement of Remuneration Paid 58

T4A - Statement of Pension, Retirement, Annuity and Other Income 64

T4A(OAS) - Statement of Old Age Security 68

T4A(P) - Statement of CPP benefits 69

T4A-RCA - Statement of Distributions From a Retirement Compensation Arrangement (RCA) 71

T4E - Statement of Employment Insurance benefits 73

T4PS - Statement of Profit Sharing Payments 75

T4RIF - Statement of RRIF Income 76

T4RSP - Statement of RRSP Income 78

T5 - Statement of Investment Income 81

Entering T101 (Statement of resource expenses) slips 83

T2202/T2202A - Tuition, Education, and Textbook Certificate 85

T5006: Labour-sponsored funds tax credit 88

T5007 - Statement of benefits 89

T5008 - Statement of securities transactions 90

T5013 - Statement of partnership income 94

RC62 - Universal Child Care Benefit (UCCB) statement 101

Chapter 3 103

Income 103

Asset details forms 104

Exempt from 50% rule? 104

Historical information 105

Asset list forms 105

CCA forms and summaries 105

CEC forms 106

Five year comparative summaries 107

Farming inventory adjustment 107

AgriStability and AgriInvest forms 107

Other Income: Other income 108

Rental: Summary of rental income 108

Self Employ: Summary of self-employment income 108

Rental income guide 110

T1139 - Reconciliation of Business Income for Tax Purposes 114

T1170 - Capital gains on gifts of certain capital properties 120

T1212 - Statement of Deferred Stock Option Benefits 121

T2017 - Summary of Reserves on Dispositions of Capital Property 122

T2042, Statement of Farming Activities 123

T2091#: Designation of a property as a principal residence 123

T2091WS#: Principal residence work sheet 124

T2121 Fishing Income and Expenses 124

Business and professional income 124

Form T2205, Calculating Amounts From a Spousal RRSP or RRIF to Include in Income 129

Chapter 4 131
Deductions 131

Allowable business investment loss (ABIL) 132

T777Auto#: Motor vehicle expenses 133

Allocation of expenses 134

Business Auto: Vehicles owned by a business 134

Capital Cost Allowance for motor vehicles 135

LossLPP: Listed personal property losses 136

LossNetCap: Net capital losses 136

LossNonCap: Non-capital losses 136

Other Deduct: Other deductions 137

Resource: Resource income and expenses 137

RPP: Registered pension plan deduction 137

RRSP: RRSP deduction 137

RRSPLimit: Next year's RRSP deduction limit 138

RRSPTransfer: Income eligible for transfer to RRSP 138

Support: Support payments 138

T1M - Moving expenses deduction 138

T657 - Capital Gains Deduction Calculation 142

T746 - Calculating Your Deduction for Refund of Unused RRSP Contributions 143

T777 - Statement of employment expenses 146

T777Details: Employment expenses 147

T777Other: Other deductions 147

Form T778 - Child Care Expenses 147

T929 - Disability Supports Deduction for 2004 and later years 150

T936 - Calculation of Cumulative Net Investment Loss (CNIL) 153

T1223 - Clergy Residence Deduction 154

T1229 - Statement of Exploration and Development Expenses and Depletion Allowance 155

T2200 - Declaration of Conditions of Employment 155

T2222 - Northern resident's deductions 156

T5004 - Statement of Tax Shelter Loss or Deduction 160

Transport Employees 162

Chapter 5 167
Tax & Credits 167

CPT20: Election to pay Canada pension plan contributions 168

Gifts and Income Tax 168

FTC#: Foreign tax credits 169

GST 370 - Employee and Partner GST/HST Rebate 172

Medical: Medical expenses 175

Allowable medical expenses 176

Other Credits: Other credits 177

Repay: Social benefits repayment 177

Student Loan: Interest on student loans 178

T626 - Overseas Employment Tax Credit (OETC) 178

T691 - Minimum tax 179

T1032 - Joint Election to Split Pension Income 180

Form T1172 - Additional Tax on Accumulated Income Payments from RESPs 181

T1198: Statement of qualifying retroactive lump-sum payment 182

T1206: Tax on split income 183

T2036 - Calculation of Provincial Foreign Tax Credits 183

T2038 - Investment Tax Credit (Individuals) 185

T2201#: Disability tax credit certificate 188

T2203: Tax calculation for multiple jurisdictions 189

T2204 - Employee Overpayment of CPP Contributions and EI Premiums 189

T2209 - Federal Foreign Tax Credits 190

Chapter 6 193
T1 Jacket & Schedules 193

T1 Elective return identification 194

T1 Identification 194

T1 Province of residence 194

T1 Province of self-employment 194

T1 Date of entry or departure 194

T1 Date of death 194

T1 Marital status 194

T1 Elections Canada 194

T1 GST/HST credit application 194

T1 Foreign property question 194

T1 Guide: Line 101 - Employment income - Line 101 195

T1 Guide: Line 102 - Commissions 196

T1 Guide: Line 104 - Other employment income 196

T1 Guide: Line 113 - Old Age Security Pension 198

T1 Guide: Line 114 - Canada or Québec Pension Plan benefits 199

T1 Guide: Line 115 - Other pensions or superannuation 199

T1 Guide: Line 119 - Employment Insurance Benefits 202

T1 Guide: Line 120 - Taxable amount of dividends (eligible and other than eligible) from taxable Canadian corporations 202

T1 Guide: Line 121 - Interest and other investment income 203

T1 Guide: Line 122 - Net partnership income (limited or non-active partners only) 205

T1 Guide: Line 125 - Registered disability savings plan (RDSP) income 206

T1 Guide - Lines 126 and 160: Rental income 207

T1 Guide: Line 127 - Taxable capital gains 207

T1 Guide - Lines 128 and 156: Support payments received 209

T1 Guide: Line 129 - Registered retirement savings plan (RRSP) income 209

T1 Guide: Line 130 - Other income 212

T1 Guide: Lines 135 and 162 - Self-employment income - Business income 213

T1 Guide: Lines 137 and 164 - Self-employment income - Professional income 215

T1 Guide: Lines 139 and 166 - Self-employment income - Commission income 216

T1 Guide: Lines 141 and 168 - Self-employment income - Farming income 217

T1 Guide: Lines 135 to 143 - Self-employment income 218

T1 Guide: Line 144 - Workers' Compensation benefits 220

T1 Guide: Line 145 - Social assistance payments 220

T1 Guide: Line 146 - Net federal supplements 221

T1 Line 147: Net federal supplements 221

T1 Line 150: Total income 221

T1 Guide: Line 152 - Disability benefits included on line 114 221

T1 Guide: Line 206 - Pension adjustment 222

T1 Guide - Line 207: Registered pension plan (RPP) deduction 222

T1 Guide: Line 208 - RRSP deduction 223

T1 Guide: Line 209 - Saskatchewan Pension Plan (SPP) deduction 224

T1 Guide: Line 210 - Deduction for elected split-pension amount 225

T1 Guide: Line 212 - Annual union, professional, or like dues 227

T1 Guide: Line 213 - Universal Child Care Benefit (UCCB) repayment 227

T1 Guide: Line 214 - Child care expenses 228

T1 Guide: Line 215 - Disability supports deduction 228

T1 Guide: Line 217 and line 228 - Business investment loss 229

T1 Guide: Line 219 - Moving expenses 229

T1 Guide: Line 220 and 230 - Support payments made 233

T1 Guide: Line 221 - Carrying charges and interest expenses 234

T1 Guide: Line 222 - Deduction for CPP or QPP contributions on self-employment and other earnings 235

T1 Guide: Line 223 - Deduction for provincial parental insurance plan (PPIP) premiums on self-employment income 236

T1 Guide: Line 224 - Exploration and development expenses 236

T1 Guide: Line 229 - Other employment expenses 237

T1 Guide: Line 231 - Clergy residence deduction 238

T1 Guide: Line 232 - Other deductions 238

T1 Line 233 240

T1 Guide: Line 234 - Net income before adjustments 240

T1 Guide: Line 235 - Social benefits repayment 241

T1 Guide: Line 236 - Net incomes 242

T1 Guide: Line 244 - Canadian Forces personnel and police deduction 242

T1 Guide: Line 248 - Employee home relocation loan deduction 243

T1 Guide: Line 249 - Security options deductions 243

T1 Guide: Line 250 - Other payments deduction 243

T1 Guide: Line 251- Limited partnership losses of other years 244

T1 Guide: Line 252 - Non-capital losses of other years 244

T1 Guide: Line 253 - Net capital losses of other years 245

T1 Guide: Line 254 - Capital gains deduction 245

T1 Guide: Line 255 - Northern resident's deductions 245

T1 Guide: Line 256 - Additional deductions 246

T1 Line 257 247

T1 Line 260: Taxable income 247

T1 Guide: Line 421 - CPP contributions payable on self-employment and other earnings 247

T1 Guide: Line 422 - Social benefits repayment 247

T1 Guide: Line 428: Provincial or territorial tax 248

T1 Line 435: Total payable 248

T1 Guide: Line 437 - Total income tax deducted 248

T1 Guide: Line 438 - Tax transfer for residents of Québec 249

T1 Line 439 249

T1 Guide: Line 440: Refundable Québec abatement 249

T1 Guide: Line 448 - CPP overpayment 250

T1 Guide: Line 450: Employment insurance overpayment 250

T1 Guide: Line 452 - Refundable medical expense supplement 251

T1 Guide: Line 453 - Working income tax benefit (WITB) 252

T1 Guide: Line 454 - Refund of investment tax credit 253

T1 Guide: Line 456 - Part XII.2 trust tax credit 253

Line 457: Employee and partner GST/HST 370 rebate 253

T1 Line 460: Direct deposit 254

T1 Line 461: Direct deposit 254

T1 Line 462: Direct deposit 254

T1 Line 463: Direct deposit 254

T1 Line 465: Donation to the Ontario Opportunities Fund 255

T1 Guide: Line 479 - Provincial or territorial credits 255

T1 Line 482: Total credits 256

T1 Refund or balance owing 256

T1 Guide: Line 484 - Reimbursement 256

T1 Guide: Line 485 - Balance owing 256

T1 Guide: Line 486 - Amount enclosed 258

T1 Line 490: Preparer information 258

Schedule 1 - Federal tax and non-refundable tax credits 258

Schedule 1: Line 300 - Basic personal amount 259

Schedule 1: Line 301 - Age amount 259

Schedule 1: Line 303 - Spouse or common-law partner amount 260

Schedule 1: Line 305 - Amount for an eligible dependant 261

Schedule 1: Line 306 - Amounts for infirm dependants age 18 or older 262

Schedule 1: Line 308 - CPP or QPP contributions through employment 263

Schedule 1: Line 310 - CPP or QPP contributions on self-employment and other earnings 265

Schedule 1: Line 312 - Employment Insurance premiums 265

Schedule 1: Line 313 - Adoption expenses 266

Schedule 1: Line 314 - Pension income amount 267

Schedule 1: Line 315 - Caregiver amount 268

Schedule 1: Line 316 - Disability amount for self 269

Schedule 1: Line 318 - Disability amount transferred from a dependant 270

Schedule 1: Line 319 - Interest paid on your student loans 272

Schedule 1: Line 323 - Tuition, education, and textbook amounts 272

Schedule 1: Line 324 - Tuition, education, and textbook amounts transferred from a child 275

Schedule 1: Line 326 - Amounts transferred from your spouse or common-law partner 275

Schedule 1: Line 330 - Medical expenses for self, spouse or common-law partner, and your dependent children 276

Schedule 1: Line 331- Allowable amount of medical expenses for other dependants 280

Schedule 1 - Line 332: Allowable amount of medical expenses 282

Schedule 1 - Line 335: Non-refundable tax credit calculation 282

Schedule 1 - Line 338: Non-refundable tax credit calculation 282

Schedule 1: Line 349 - Donations and gifts 282

Schedule 1 - Line 350: Total non-refundable tax credits 283

Schedule 1: Line 363 - Canada employment amount 283

Schedule 1: Line 364 - Public transit amount 284

Schedule 1: Line 365 - Children's fitness amount 285

Schedule 1: Line 367 - Amount for children born in 1992 or later 286

T1 Guide: Line 405 - Federal foreign tax credit 287

Schedule 1: Lines 409 and 410 - Federal political 287

Schedule 1: Line 412 - Investment tax credit 288

Schedule 1: Lines 413 and 414 - Labour-sponsored funds tax credit 288

Schedule 1: Line 415 - Working Income Tax Benefit (WITB) advance payments 289

T1 Guide: Line 418 - Additional tax on RESP accumulated income payments 290

Schedule 1 - Line 420: Net federal tax 290

T1 Guide: Line 424 - Federal tax on split income 290

Schedule 1: Line 425 - Federal dividend tax credit 291

Schedule 1: Line 426 - Overseas employment tax credit 291

Schedule 1: Line 427 - Minimum Tax Carryover 292

Schedule 2 - Federal Amounts Transferred From Your Spouse or Common-Law Partner 292

Schedule 3 - Capital gains (or losses) 293

Schedule 4 - Statement of Investment Income 295

Schedule 5 - Details of Dependant 296

Schedule 6 - Working Income Tax Benefit 297

Schedule 7 - RRSP Unused Contributions, Transfers and HBP or LPP Activities 299

Schedule 8 - CPP contributions on self-employment and other earnings 302

Quebec Schedule 8 - QPP Contributions on Self-Employment and Other Earnings 303

Schedule 9 - Donations and Gifts 303

Schedule 10 - Employment Insurance (EI) and Provincial Parental Insurance Plan (PPIP) Premiums 304

Schedule 11 - Federal Tuition, Education, and Textbook Amounts 304

Eligible tuition fees and educational institutions 306

Schedule 12 - Home renovation expenses 308

Schedule A - Statement of World Income 309

Schedule B - Allowable amount of non-refundable tax credits 312

Schedule C - Electing Under Section 217 of the Income Tax Act 312

SD: Information about your residency status 313

Chapter 7 315

Filing 315

Bankruptcy: Bankruptcy information 316

DC905: Bankruptcy identification form 316

RC59: Business consent form 316

RC71: Statement of discounting transaction 316

RC72: Notice of the actual amount of the refund of tax 317

RC210: Working Income Tax Benefit advance payment received 317

T1A - Request for Loss Carry back 317

T1ADJ - T1 Adjustment Request 318

Direct deposit 319

T7DRA: Payment form 320

T183: Information return for electronic filing 320

T1013: Consent form 320

T1132: Alternative address authorization 321

Form T1135 - Information Return Relating to a Foreign Property 321

T1141: Information return - transfers or loans to non-resident trust 327

T1142: Information return in respect of ... non-resident trust 327

T1153: Consent and request form 327

T1158#: Registration of family payments 328

T1161: List of properties by an emigrant of Canada 328

T1162A: Pre-authorized payment plan 328

T1243: Deemed disposition of property by an emigrant of Canada 328

T1244: Election, under subsection 220(4.5) of the Income Tax Act, to defer the payment of tax on income relating to the deemed disposition of property 328

TX19: Asking for a clearance certificate 329

Chapter 8 331
Clients 331

Client 332

Billing 332

Client letters and invoices 332

CCTB: Canada Child tax benefit 332

GST/HST credit application 333

Paying Your Tax by Instalments (Instalment Worksheet) 334

Notes 338

Plan#: Tax planner 338

Optimize - Split pension Income 339

Summaries 340

T1EFILE: EFILE information 340

Appendix   343

Teaching Taxes Program – Student Workbook 2009

Chapter 1

Using ProFile T1

2009 Tax Year

ProFile T1 Help

ProFile T1 software is reliable, easy-to-use and offers sophisticated features that will make the tax season more productive for even the experienced T1 tax professional. ProFile T1 can capture the data from past year returns created using certain competitors' software. Whether you carry forward individual client files, or carry files forward in batches, you will find the process quick and convenient.

Using our WYSIWYG (what you see is what you get) **forms, you can view and edit federal T1 and Québec TP1 forms in French or English. When it comes time to** print a return, you can print the forms in either language or both, at the click of a button.

Tip: In the ProFile dialog boxes you will not find any module tab for ProFile TP1. The TP1 return is packaged with our ProFile T1 software. When you enter a valid TP1 license code, you will have access to the additional forms and features of the TP1 product. ProFile TP1 is tightly integrated with ProFile T1.

New user

If you are a first time ProFile T1 user, follow this checklist to set up the program and get ready for using the software.

1. Configure tax preparer information
   Enter your preparer information under Options > Environment > Preparer. If you are a discounter, complete the information in Options > Environment > Trustee.
2. Review ProFile options and database settings
   Under Options > Module > T1, you'll find items that relate specifically to working with T1 returns (such as file management settings, a disclaimer that appears on some forms and a form header that will print on all forms). Under Options > Database, you'll find settings related to the database.
3. Carry forward data from last year's tax software
   Look under Options > Module > T1 for specific carry forward features.
4. Decide to print joint (husband and wife) or individual client letters and invoices
   If you do not want to print letters and invoices addressed to both husband and wife together, go to Options > Module > T1 > General > Options and clear those options. Otherwise, ProFile will print joint client documentation. You can also decide if you wish to have formal (for example, Dear Mr. Smith :) or casual (for example, Dear John :) salutations.
5. Review other options
   Take some time to review the other options found under the Options menu. The software ships with the most popular options selected, so unless you have different preferences, the defaults should be acceptable.
6. Set up tax return defaults
   When you create new tax returns, you may wish to have certain fields default to your usual values - for example, the province of residence. Just follow the instructions for creating a file based on default settings.
7. Set up EFILE using the EFILE > Options Wizard
   If you EFILE your returns, you'll need to configure your EFILE > Options. You can easily do this by running the EFILE > Options > Wizard that guides you through the setup process.
8. Run the tutorials

We know you are anxious to get started, but we recommend you take the time to go through the tutorials (in the main menu). These will demonstrate many of the basic concepts of ProFile.

Note: If you are setting up ProFile T1 to use on a network, refer to the 'Network' section of the ProFile in product help. Here you will find instructions for setting up your files in shared server directories.

T1 module options

There are several module options unique to ProFile T1 under the Options > Module menu. For example, you can set the colour of the forms separately in T1 current and past year modules. This makes it easy to tell at a glance which type of file you are viewing in the Edit window.

Attention: A file template can complete common fields in all your new client files. When you create new files using the carry forward process, a file template will never override past year data, but will complete blank fields automatically. The template applies only to the client file and not to the spouse file.

On the General tab, here are some useful options:

- Carry forward options include slip descriptions, donation descriptions and free form notes. Decide which of these you want to maintain when you carry files forward.
- Select your New file options before you create your current year files using File > New or by carry forward. ProFile can automatically include the T1013 Authorization form for each new file, and the choice to default all your new returns to discounted status.
- Formal or casual client salutation determines what greeting appears at the start of a template letter.
- Choose options that automatically complete in each file: preparer information, current signing date and line 6509. You can also select to use the joint client letter and joint client invoice for coupled files.
- Calculation options instruct ProFile to automatically calculate the maximum OAS claim for taxpayers who are 66 or older at the end of the tax year. You will need to override this calculation on the OAS form for clients who meet the age requirement, but who did not receive the maximum OAS during the year. In addition, you will have to enter the payments received by taxpayers who turned 65 during the year, because they most likely will not receive OAS for the entire year.

Adding forms to the Jump bar

To add forms to the Jump Bar:

1. Open a form using the Form Explorer <F4>.
2. Click on the Jump Bar and hold your selection to drag the Jump Bar under the other toolbars. This will let you see all the icons that are on the bar (you can move it back later).

   Note: The Jump Bar is located in the grey toolbar area and usually shows a handful of commonly used forms. (By default, you should see shortcuts to the T1, TP1, T1Summary, T4 and T5.)

3. With your cursor, click and hold the icon on the tab of the form you would like to see displayed in the Jump Bar.

4. Drag the cursor with the white square onto the Jump Bar and let go of the mouse button.

The icon of the form you selected should now appear on the Jump Bar. Repeat these steps for other forms to which you require quick access.

Coupling returns

Attention: If you have already saved the file before coupling the returns, the file name will include only the client's name. Both returns remain stored in that file. You can rename the file during the coupling process to include the spouse's name in the file name.

To couple two returns:

1. Open or create the file for the client.
2. On the Info form, select either "Married" or "Living common-law" for the marital status.
3. Press <F5>, the function key to switch between spouse returns.
4. Choose whether to create a new return for the spouse, or couple the file to an existing return.
    o Select, Create a new return for spouse, to open a new return for the spouse. Attention: You must close the existing return before you can select to couple it to another.
    o Select , Open an existing return, to browse to a file on your hard drive and select it.

   Note: After combining the data, ProFile will ask if you want to delete the original file for the spouse. Delete the file to avoid duplication or possible confusion of the original spouse's file and the same return in the new coupled file.
5. Select File > Save. ProFile saves both spouses' tax returns in the same data file. This allows you to keep the tax returns together as you perform file operations on the tax return file, such as backing up to a disk.

Once returns are coupled, press <F5> to switch back and forth between the returns.

On the database dialog (Other filter tab), select Show spouse in list to show both the client and the spouse's names. Clear this checkbox to show only the client's name for each coupled file.

Merging and separating - data flow when coupling and uncoupling returns

ProFile handles the coupling and uncoupling process automatically. However, ProFile must make certain assumptions when merging data from two files. We recommend you review your files thoroughly after coupling or uncoupling returns. The situations below are examples of how ProFile handles information upon coupling or uncoupling returns.

Dependants' last name

If you couple two returns, each containing dependant information, ProFile changes the dependants' last name in the spouse's return to the taxpayer's last name.

Example

Jason Travis has two sons, Joey Travis and Joachim Travis. Jason married Joanne Curtis who has her own daughter, Marla Curtis. When you couple the returns, ProFile merges Jason and Joanne's Dependant

> worksheets and gives them all Jason's last name - Travis. In the coupled file, the Dependant worksheet lists Joey Travis, Joachim Travis and Marla Travis. You can override Marla's last name directly on the Dependant worksheet to Marla Curtis, if need be.

When you uncouple a return with dependants, all dependants appear in both uncoupled files. ProFile automatically gives them the same last name as the taxpayer.

> **Example**
>
> Jason Travis and Joanne Curtis divorced. They have three children: Joey, Joachim and Marla. When you uncouple their returns, Jason Travis's Dependant worksheet shows Joey Travis, Joachim Travis and Marla Travis. Joanne Curtis's Dependant worksheet lists Joey Curtis, Joachim Curtis and Marla Curtis. You can override any of their last names.
>
> ProFile retains any overrides of the dependant's last name when you couple or uncouple returns.

Dependants with the same first name and date of birth

If you couple two files, each containing a dependant with the same first name and date of birth, ProFile considers these dependants as one person and only keeps the dependant originally found in the taxpayer's file.

Amounts transferred to a spouse

Amounts transferred to a spouse remain in the return after you uncouple the file. Remember to review your file thoroughly after uncoupling returns.

> **Example**
>
> In a TP1 return, the TP1 Schedule B showed an amount on line 58 (amount transferred to spouse for family tax reduction); that amount remains on line 58 even after you uncouple the returns.

Family returns

A number of file management features make it easy to work with linked T1 or T1/TP1 files for members of the same family:

Linking family returns

Data only transfers when the linked files are open in the ProFile Edit window at the same time. After you close a file, the link is no longer active, but the exchanged data remains with each file.

To create a link, the SIN (or the dependant's first name and birth date) on the Personal Information worksheet in a dependant's file must match data on the Dependant worksheet in the file of the supporting taxpayer.

Family linking optimizes transfer credits between data files for members of a family. If you are completing both taxpayer and dependant returns, ProFile can share data between those files.

Follow the steps below to see how family linking works:

1. Open or create a file that requires dependant information. To watch the transfer most easily, close the spouse return if the file is coupled.
2. Open or create a file for a dependant of this taxpayer.

> Note: You can right-click on a completed dependant column in the taxpayer file to create a new file for that dependant.

3. From the Window menu or using the toolbar button, select Tile horizontally to display the two files together, one above the other. You do not have to tile windows to link files, but this feature will allow you to watch the results.
4. In the dependant file, open the Personal Information worksheet (Info).
5. In the file of the supporting taxpayer, open the Dependant worksheet.

When the dependant's SIN (or name and birth date) match in both the dependant and taxpayer files, linking occurs. You can drag-and-drop these details if you haven't already entered them on both forms. Transferred amounts appear immediately, and in purple.

- Enter all dependant information directly on the Dependant worksheet for the supporting taxpayer. There is no limit to the number of dependants you can include.
- If the dependant has credits that are not needed to reduce taxable income to nil, ProFile automatically transfers eligible amounts to the tax return of the supporting taxpayer or spouse (as needed). Amounts not required by the taxpayer or spouse transfer back to carry forward in the dependant's return.
- Once you enter dependant information on the taxpayer's Dependant form, ProFile provides a right click option to create a tax return file for that dependant. Alternately, if you open files already created for the members of a family, you can link these from the Dependant form in the taxpayer's file by selecting the SIN of the dependant using the drop-down list.

Attention: The Dependant form has additional fields in a T1/TP1 tax return file. Scroll to the bottom of the form to provide provincial information. You can also allocate between spouses the percentage claim for Schedules A and H.

Working with linked files

A number of file management features make it easy to work with linked T1 or T1/TP1 files for members of the same family.

Attention: To deactivate the Family file-handling features, clear the checkbox Options > Module > T1/TP1 > General > Allow family linking.

- Once you link family files, you can open and close these files together as you work on the returns. When you open all family files together, ProFile optimizes transfer credits among the different returns. If you prefer to work with family files open together, open them all together when you first begin working on a set of family files. As long as you close all the files together, <Ctrl+Q> or File > Close family, ProFile will always open the returns together. If you close the file for one family member separately, automatic opening of all family files together will not occur until after the next time you open all the files at once.
- Use the toolbar icon, the Form menu or the Window menu to switch between open files for members of a family.
- When you select File > Print for a linked file, the Print Selection dialog will display a tab for each family member whose file is currently open so you can print returns for the whole family at once.
- You can also view the File Properties details for all family files open together, and listed in the Window menu of ProFile.

Printing linked files

Select File > Print to print one or all of the linked family files.

In the print dialog, you can select to print returns for all or some of the members of the family. Simply select or deselect the checkbox next to the family member's name.

Saving linked files

When you save one return from a group of family files, ProFile asks you to confirm that you wish to save all of the linked files.

You can choose whether or not to save any of the files, by selecting or deselecting client names in the confirmation dialog.

Sharing income between spouses

When sharing income slips such as T3s and T5s between spouses, you'll enter the slip (and the slip will display) on one return only. Both spousal returns will show the amounts from the shared slip(s) on Schedule 4. This schedule indicates the percentage allocated, gross amount on the slip and the portion to be taxed in the hands of each spouse.

Attention: **Hint:** On Schedule 4 ProFile splits the different kinds of income into the appropriate areas.

Thus, there may be more than one line on Schedule 4 for an individual slip, depending on whether or not the slip reported more than one kind of income.

> **Example**
>
> Jane has a T5 with interest of $10,000. She wishes to claim 75% herself and allot the remaining 25% to her husband. Enter this information on the ProFile T5 slip in her return and complete the percentage her spouse will report. You can see this slip in several places in Jane's return: the T5 slip, the Slip Summary and Schedule 4. Schedule 4 shows the slip name along with the percentage allotted, the $10,000 before allocation and her $7,500 portion.
>
> His return will show the slip only on Schedule 4 but will have the same details as hers: name of the slip, percentage of allocation, the $10,000 before allocation and his $2,500 portion of the slip.

Sharing data between family members

Family linking optimizes federal transfer credits between data files for members of a family including the disability tax credit and tuition tax credit. Data transfer takes place only when two or more linked files are open in the ProFile Edit window at the same time.

To create the link, the Social Insurance Number (SIN) on the Info form in a dependant's file must match data on the Dependant form in the file of the supporting taxpayer. ProFile will also transfer data if the dependant's first name and birth date match these same fields on the supporting taxpayer's Dependant information worksheet (for dependants without a SIN).

When deciding where to transfer credits, ProFile evaluates a number of circumstances, such as the optimization of available credits between the taxpayer and spouse.

After you close a file, the link is no longer active, but the exchanged data remains with each file. Follow the steps below to see how family linking works.

1. Open or create a file that requires dependant information. To watch the transfer most easily, close the spousal return if the file is coupled.
2. Open or create a file for a dependant of this taxpayer.
3. From the Window menu (or using the toolbar button), select Align horizontally to display the two files together, one above the other.

    Note: You do not have to tile windows to link files, but this feature will let you watch the results.
4. In the dependant file, use the Form Explorer to open the Personal Information (Info) form.
5. In the file of the supporting taxpayer, open the Dependant form.
6. Click and drag the dependant's Social Insurance Number from the Personal Information form into the SIN field on the Dependant form. You'll see that data immediately transfers from the dependant file to the file of the supporting taxpayer. Transferred amounts appear in purple, like carry forward amounts. If the dependant does not have a SIN, you can create the link using the dependant's first name and birth date on the Dependant form instead.

Special cases

ProFile T1 supports a number of different tax returns to accommodate taxpayer circumstances. In cases where residency status requires a special return, the software will automatically select the correct T1 jacket based on information you provide on the Personal information (Info) worksheet.

The note field at the top of the T1 jacket will be blank for most taxpayers. When necessary, you can enter the special status of a return in this field. For example, you might need to enter the type of optional return for a deceased taxpayer.

Completing a deceased taxpayer's return

To complete a return for a deceased taxpayer who is single, enter the date of death in the Production section of the Info form.

To complete a return for a deceased taxpayer who is married, enter the following information:

1. Enter the date of death in the Production section of the deceased taxpayer's Info form.
2. On the surviving taxpayer's Info form, change the marital status to widow.
3. Enter the date that the taxpayer's marital situation changed. This is the date of death of the taxpayer's spouse or common-law partner.

    Note: When you carry forward a coupled file in which one spouse files a deceased return for the previous taxation year, ProFile automatically only carries forward the return for the surviving taxpayer.

Early-filing a deceased return

The CRA will process individual income tax returns that you file early. This means you can promptly file year-of-death returns for the interval from January 1 to the date or death.

To create a return for a taxpayer with an upcoming taxation year date of death:

1. Create a new current-year T1 return.
2. Enter the taxpayer's personal information on the Info form. (Do not yet save the return).
3. Enter the taxpayer's date of death on the Info form. (Do not yet save the return).
4. Select the upcoming taxation year rates in the Use rates for tax year drop-down list, under the Type of return section of the Info form. If forms for the year of death are not yet available, the CRA requires that you indicate the year for the return that you are filing at the top of the T1 jacket. Either enters the taxation year in the description field at the top of the jacket before you print the return, or print the return then cross out the current year and write the following year.
5. Save the return. As with current year deceased returns, ProFile automatically adds (D) to the file name to help you distinguish between deceased and regular tax returns. When you use the upcoming year rates, ProFile also adds a (YYYY rates) to the file name. For example, if you create an early-file deceased return for Thomas Spurgeon who passed away on March 13, 2005, the default file name would be Spurgeon, Thomas (D) (2004 rates).04T.

Thoroughly review the return before filing.

Completing a bankruptcy return

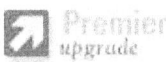

ProFile T1 includes two forms that relate to bankruptcy. The first is called Bankruptcy. Use this form to indicate the type of bankruptcy return and to provide some amounts that are used in calculating non-refundable tax credits.

The second is DC905 where you complete the bankruptcy identification, including trustee and client information. Complete the fields on Options > Environment options under the Trustee tab. ProFile will automatically transfer this information to form DC905.

To prepare a return for a bankrupt client, you must complete two tax returns: a pre-bankruptcy return and post-bankruptcy return. A trustee's return may also be required.

1. On the Bankruptcy form, indicate the type of bankruptcy return you are preparing.
    You will need to save at least two returns for a client claiming bankruptcy. By default, ProFile includes (Pre), (Post) or (Trustee) in the name of the file.
    Attention: ProFile can automatically include the bankruptcy return type in the file name, to help you distinguish between multiple returns for the same client. To use this feature, complete the Info form and Bankruptcy form before you save the new client file. Otherwise, you can change the file name to reflect the bankruptcy type later.
2. Enter the date of bankruptcy. This date is used to prorate the appropriate credits (based in # of days before and after bankruptcy).
3. Enter amounts from the associated pre-bankruptcy or post-bankruptcy return in the table. These amounts are used for the appropriate bankruptcy calculations (such as summing pre and post net income for the purpose of the age amount on form Other Credits).

Form DC905 will complete automatically based on the information you've entered in the tax return, in Options > Environment options > Trustee and on the Bankruptcy form.

ProFile indicates the type of bankruptcy return in a field at the top of the T1 jacket.

When you print the return, ProFile prints form DC905 first by default. This is because you must submit the returns with form DC905 as the cover sheet.

Bankruptcy returns require some manual calculation. For both pre- and post bankruptcy returns, you must calculate the applicable portion of income and deductions, based on the portion of the calendar year covered by each return.

For example, you do not enter the complete T5 information for the year. Rather, enter the portion of that income attributed to the pre- and post-bankruptcy return. ProFile then calculates the non-refundable tax credits based on those amounts.

Early-filing a bankruptcy return

The CRA will process early-filed individual income tax returns. This means you can file pre-bankruptcy returns for the period from January 1 to the day before the date of assignment in bankruptcy.

To create a pre-bankruptcy return for a taxpayer who declared bankruptcy in the following taxation year:

1. Create a new T1 return.
2. Enter the taxpayer's personal information on the Info form.

      Note: Do not yet save the return.

3. Select the following year in the Use rates for tax year drop-down list, under the 'Type of return' section of the Info form.

      Note: Do not yet save the return.

4. Go to the Bankruptcy form and select Pre-bankruptcy as the type of bankruptcy return.

      Note: Do not yet save the return.

5. Enter the date the taxpayer declared bankruptcy.
6. Now save the return.

As with current year pre-bankruptcy returns, ProFile automatically adds (Pre) to the file name to help you distinguish between the different types of bankruptcy tax returns. When you use the following-year rates, ProFile also adds a (XXXX rates) to the file name.

If you create an early-file pre-bankruptcy return for Jennifer Moody who declared bankruptcy on January 1, 2008, the file name would be Moody, Jennifer (Pre) (2008 rates).07T. Thoroughly review the return before filing.

Information for Non-Residents and Deemed Residents of Canada

Completing returns for non-residents

If the T1 jacket is already open in the Edit window, close the form using the <Esc> key before following the steps below.

ProFile includes T1 returns for non-residents. To complete a return for a non-resident:

1. Open the Personal Information worksheet (Info)
2. Under the Residency section, select the appropriate non-resident status from the 'Province of residence' field drop-down menu. Options in this drop-down menu include: non-resident, deemed resident, non-resident S.216, non-resident S.217
3. Open the T1 jacket (using the Form Explorer or by clicking the T1 icon on the jump bar).

 Note: If you've selected the status 'Non-resident S.216', you will see T1159 - Income Tax Return for Electing Under Section S216, instead of the usual T1 jacket in the Form Explorer. The T1159 will open whenever you type 'T1' in the Form Explorer.

ProFile will display the Income Tax and Benefit Return for Non-Residents and Deemed Residents of Canada (or the T1159, tax return for non-residents filing under section 216) rather than the usual T1 Jacket.

The Canada Revenue Agency says... *Non-residents and Income Tax Guide (T4058)*

Were you a non-resident in 2009?

You were a non-resident for tax purposes if you did not have residential ties in Canada, and:

- you stayed in Canada for less than 183 days in the tax year (including the days you arrived and left); or
- you lived outside Canada throughout the tax year (except if you were a deemed resident).

Were you a deemed resident?

Generally, you were a deemed resident of Canada for tax purposes in 2009 if you did not have residential ties in Canada (otherwise a non-resident), but you temporarily stayed in Canada for 183 days or more in the tax year, and under a tax treaty, you were not considered a resident of another country.

To calculate the number of days you stayed in Canada in the tax year, include each day or part of a day that you stayed in Canada, including:

- the days you attended a Canadian university or college;
- the days you worked in Canada; and
- any days or weekends you spent on vacation in Canada.

If you lived in the United States and commuted to work in Canada, do not include commuting days in the calculation.

Do you have to file a return?

You have to file a return for 2009 if any of the following applies to you:

- You have to pay tax for 2009.
- We sent you a request to file a return.
- You disposed of capital property in 2009 (for example, if you sold real estate or shares) or you realized a taxable capital gain (for example, if a mutual fund or trust attributed amounts to you, or you are reporting a capital gains reserve you claimed on your 2008 return).

- You filed Form NR5, Application by a Non-Resident of Canada for a Reduction in the Amount of Non-Resident Tax Required to Be Withheld, for 2009 and we approved it. If this is your situation, you have to file a return electing under section 217 of the Income Tax Act.
- You filed Form NR6, Undertaking to File an Income Tax Return by a Non-Resident Receiving Rent From Real Property or Receiving a Timber Royalty, for 2009 and CRA approved it. If this is your situation, you have to file a return electing under Section 216 of the Income Tax Act.
- You filed an application for a reduction in the amount of non-resident tax required to be withheld on income earned from acting in a film or video production in Canada for 2009 and we approved it. If this is your situation, you have to file a return electing under section 216.1 of the Income Tax Act. If this is your situation, you have to file a return electing under Section 216.1 of the Income Tax Act.

Even if none of these requirements applies, you may still want to file a return if any of the following applies:

- You want to claim a refund.
- You want to carry forward or transfer the unused portion of your tuition, education, and textbook amounts (see line 323 and line 324).
- You want to report income for which you could contribute to an RRSP, in order to keep your RRSP deduction limit for future years up to date.

Which tax and benefit package should you use?

- If you are reporting only income from employment in Canada or from a business carried on through a permanent establishment in Canada (including a non-resident actor electing to file a return under section 216.1, see page 7 for details), use the and related forms book for the province or territory where you earned the income. The forms book includes the return you will need.
- If you are also reporting other types of Canadian-source income (such as scholarships, fellowships, bursaries, research grants, or capital gains from disposing of taxable Canadian property), you will need Form T2203, Provincial and Territorial Taxes for 2009 - Multiple Jurisdictions , to calculate your tax payable.
- If you are reporting only Canadian-source income other than from employment in Canada, from a business with a permanent establishment in Canada (including a non-resident actor electing to file a return under section 216.1), from rental income or timber royalties, or if you are filing an elective return under section 217 of the Income Tax Act, use the for Non-Residents and Deemed Residents of Canada. It includes the return you will need.
- If you received rental income from real property in Canada or timber royalties on a timber resource property or a timber limit in Canada, and you are electing to file a return under section 216 of the Income Tax Act, use guide T4144, called Income Tax Guide for Electing Under Section 216. It includes the return you will need.

What income should you report?

Non-residents and deemed non-residents: Report your 2009 income from Canadian sources such as the taxable part of your scholarships, fellowships, bursaries, net research grants, income from a business without a permanent establishment in Canada, and taxable capital gains from disposing of taxable Canadian property, as indicated under the income lines applicable to non-residents in the guide.

Deemed residents: Report your 2009 world income. World income is income from all sources both inside and outside Canada.

Additional references

Additional references For more information about non-residents and deemed residents, get the following CRA publications:

- T4058, Non-residents and Income Tax
- 5013-G, for Non-Residents and Deemed Residents of Canada
- T4131, Canadian Residents Abroad (Factual residents)
- T4056, Emigrants and Income Tax (Canadian Forces overseas school staff)

Grouping business statement sets

Each new copy of a form appears on its own tab on the Edit window and has its own unique description in the Form Explorer. The ProFile business statements all belong to sets, identified by the set number. For example, T2125#1 will belong to set #1 that includes the related forms, T2125CCA#1 and T2125CEC#1.

Capital Cost Allowance (CCA) and Cumulative Eligible Capital (CEC)

Each of the business statements has additional schedules for CCA and CEC. For example, for the T2125, the additional forms are called T2125CCA and T2125CEC.

When you create a new business statement, ProFile will automatically create new CCA and CEC schedules related to that business statement. The CCA and CEC forms for a second business T2125#2 would be called T2125CCA#2 and T2125CEC#2.

Other business related forms

There may be additional forms associated with certain types of business statements. These are also included in the same numbered set. For example, there are inventory adjustments for farming operations, and additional automobile worksheets for Quebec TP1 business statements. All related forms will share the same set number in the Form Explorer name column. The Form Explorer descriptions of all related forms also include the business name.

Note: Revenu Quebec does not have a form for fishing or farming business income. However, ProFile includes the TP1Farming# and TP1Fishing# worksheets to correspond with the federal T2042# and T2121# forms.

Deleting business statement sets

If you delete any form in a business statement set, ProFile deletes all the related forms in the same set. ProFile will automatically select for printing any of the business statement forms that are used. Unused forms in a set have no impact on your tax return filing.

If you simply want to clear a particular form in the set, open that form in the Edit window, go to the Form menu and select Clear form. This option does not impact other forms in the same set.

Sharing business income with spouses or partners

In a coupled file, the business statements number in sequence without duplication. If the client has a business statement T2125#1, then a new business statement created in the spouse file will be T2125#2. A second business statement for the client in this same file would be T2125#3. Unless there is a spousal share in the business, you cannot use the <F5> jump to switch between spousal returns when you are working on the business statements. ProFile will display a message that there is no corresponding business statement in the spousal file.

You will see a form with the same number in both client and spouse returns only if they are co-owners or partners in the business. So the client might have T2125#1 and T2125#3, while the spouse has a separate business, T2125#2. If the spouse is also a co-owner in the business identified on the client's T2125#2, then T2125#2 will appear in both returns and you will be able to switch between the spousal returns using <F5> from that business statement. This method of handling multiple business statements reduces possible confusion when switching between the spouses.

When a taxpayer has multiple business statements, you can select which statements to share with the spouse. By specifying a percentage in the partnership area of the form, you tell ProFile to share income for only that business. ProFile will only automatically share information between the spouses when you have entered a spousal partnership %.

You can only use <F5> to jump between business statements that have income allocated to both spouses. When the spouse has no corresponding business statement, ProFile will jump to the Info form instead. When you print the file, the business statements will print for client and spouse only if both have a share in the business.

Near the bottom of the business statement (e.g. T776, T2125), you can designate income allocation to partners, including the spouse. By specifying a percentage in the partnership area of the form, you tell ProFile to share income for the business identified on that form. ProFile will share business statement information between the spouses only when you enter a partnership %.

You can see the client's share of the income at the top of the statement. Do not override here. This field updates automatically depending on how you allocate income at the bottom of the form.

Selecting a Standard Industry Code (SIC)

The CRA requires a SIC code (Standard Industry Code) on business statements. To select a SIC code from the list, right click on the Industry Code field and choose "SIC Codes" from the context-sensitive menu. You can also press <F6> to see the SIC codes.

Enter keywords to narrow your selection. For example, to find the SIC code for your client in the nightclub business, you could type in "bar." One of the items in the list will be "Tavern, bar or nightclub." Another item in the list would be "Barber."

Applying auto expenses to a business

To apply the auto expense to a business:

1. Create a business statement.
2. On the Business Auto form, select your business statement from the Allocation of expenses drop down menu. (If you have not yet opened a business statement, the drop down list will be empty.)
3. Enter a percentage into the Allocation of Expenses table on the form.

The expenses transfer to the Expenses section of the relevant business statement.

Converting a business to a December 31st year-end

To convert a business from an alternate fiscal year-end to December 31st ProFile:

1. Open one of the following related business statements: (your selection will depend on the type of business)
    - T2042#: Farming activities
    - T2121#: Fishing activities
    - T2125#: Business or professional activities
2. Enter the start of the fiscal period.

     Note: If you carried forward the file from a previous year, the start, end and type of fiscal period will already appear. ProFile will calculate the year end
3. Select Convert - first period from the drop-down list
4. Enter the revenue and deductions for the first period.
ProFile automatically creates a second business statement to treat the stub period.
If the first business statement was a T2125#1 - Business activities for Harold's business, ProFile creates a second "stub" business statement (T2125#2) with the description of Stub: Business activities for Harold's business. Both business statements appear in the Form Explorer.
5. Go the Form Explorer and open the "stub" business statement.
ProFile automatically completed the stub fiscal period in the Identification section of the form and selected Convert - stub period from the drop-down list.
ProFile posts unused UCC, business use of home expenses and reserves to the stub period statement.
6. Enter the revenue and deductions for the stub period.

ProFile automatically completes Part 1 of the T1139.

The taxpayer must sign and date the T1139 when they convert to a December 31st year-end.

Electing to keep a non-calendar year-end

To elect to use a non-calendar year-end in ProFile:

1. Depending on the type of business, open one of the following related business statements:
    - T2042#: Farming activities
    - T2121#: Fishing activities
    - T2125#: Business or professional activities
2. Enter the start of the fiscal period in the Identification section of the business statement. ProFile automatically calculates the fiscal year-end.
3. Select Elect non-calendar year-end from the drop-down list. ProFile automatically completes Part 2 of the T1139 form.

The taxpayer must sign and date the T1139 when they first elect to have alternate year-end.

Taxpayers can revoke the election to have an alternative fiscal year-end at any time and change the fiscal period end to December 31st of the year in which they file the revocation. See Converting a business to a December 31st year-end to revoke the election to have an alternative fiscal year-end.

Claiming the Employee and Partner GST rebate (GST-370)

ProFile can automatically calculate the GST rebate for employees on form GST-370. To do so:

1. Open the T777 - Statement of employment expenses form and answer "Yes" to the question Do you qualify for a GST rebate?
2. Open the T777Auto worksheet.
3. If you are claiming the GST rebate, enter expense amounts (including GST) under the 'GST' column (or 'HST' column, if applicable) of the "Calculation of allowable motor vehicle expenses" section.
4. If you are not claiming the GST rebate, enter the total receipt amounts (including GST), in the 'Non-Eligible' column.

The amounts from the T777 and T777Auto forms automatically post to the GST-370 for further calculations.

Claiming medical expenses

Use line 330 of the T1 return to claim medical expenses for the taxpayer, his/her spouse (or common-law partner) and dependent children born in 1987 or later.

Use line 331 to claim medical expenses for other dependants.

Medical expenses from lines 330 and 331 must be paid during the same 12 month period.

Medical expenses - line 330

On the Medical expenses form, line 330 section, enter ONLY the unused medical expenses from the previous and the current year. ProFile optimizes medical expenses to claim the most advantageous 12-month period and carries forward unused eligible medical expenses from the current year to the following year.

The Medical expenses form automatically shares information between the coupled returns.

To optimize medical expenses, answer 'Yes' to the question "Optimize medical expenses?" at the top

of the form. ProFile will determine which taxpayer should claim the deduction at lines 330 and 331, according to the lowest net income (as long as the taxpayer can claim all expenses).

 Note: The Optimize question will only display for coupled returns.

If you want to decide yourself which spouse should claim the deduction, answer 'No' next to the question "Optimize medical expenses?" and answer 'Yes' to the question: "Are you claiming medical expenses?". To allocate a percentage to each spouse, select 'Percentage' and enter it in the corresponding field for the current return. The spouse's return will automatically reflect the remaining percentage.

Allowable amount of medical expenses for other dependants - line 331

If you entered the names of the dependants on the Dependant information form, select the name of the other dependant from the drop-down list. The dependant's net income will automatically transfer to the Net Income field of the Medical Expense form.

If you answered 'No' to the question "Optimize medical expenses?" at the top of the form, you will need to answer the question: "Are you claiming medical expenses for this dependant?" for each of the taxpayer's other dependants.

The allowable amount of medical expenses will be limited to $10,000 per other dependant.

The allowable amount of expenses for each other dependant will be calculated by the difference of the total medical expenses and 3% of the dependant's net income (to a maximum of $2,011).

If the amount of medical expenses for a dependant in this section is such that more than one supporting person can claim the maximum $10,000 for that dependant, and the spouse is one of them, you will need to split the expenses between the taxpayer and spouse. To do so:

1. For each spouse, in the appropriate provincial credits worksheet (such as ON Credits), split the amounts in column A Amount of medical expenses between the spouses as needed. The total of both spouses' Box A amounts for a specific dependent should equal the total claimable medical expenses for that dependent, before taking the dependant's income into account.
2. In the spouse's return, on the Medical worksheet, override the "Allowable amount of medical expenses (maximum $10,000)" field with the amount to be allocated to the spouse. This amount is calculated in column D on the provincial credits worksheet.

Optimizations

ProFile provides seamless, invisible optimizations, and savvy audit messages designed to achieve the best results for your clients. In addition to the optimizations described here, there are foreign tax credit optimizations, advantageous caregiver and infirm dependant claims between spouses, smart disability credit transfer, and intelligent transfer of tax credits between taxpayers and their dependants.

Optimizing medical expenses

The Medical Expense form automatically shares information between coupled returns.

To optimize medical expenses, answer 'Yes' to the question "Optimize medical expenses?" at the top of the form. ProFile will determine which taxpayer should claim the deduction at lines 330 and 331, according to the lowest net income (as long as the taxpayer can claim all expenses).

 Note: The Optimize question will only display for coupled returns.

If you want to decide yourself which spouse should claim the deduction, answer 'No' next to the question

"Optimize medical expenses?" and answer 'Yes' to the question: "Are you claiming medical expenses?" To allocate a percentage to each spouse, select 'Percentage' and enter it in the corresponding field for the current return. The spouse's return will automatically reflect the remaining percentage.

When should you split medical expenses?

You can claim only enough medical expenses to reduce your tax payable to zero. If the lower income spouse only needs a small portion of the expenses to reduce his or her taxes payable to zero, using all the medical expense credit will not be of any benefit. In this situation, you can split the medical expenses between spouses.

Medical expenses must exceed 3% of net income or $2,011 before they produce a tax credit. If splitting them between spouse's results in one of you not reaching the threshold, you should claim them on one return.

When should the higher income spouse claim medical expenses?

If line 435, total payable, on the lower income spouse's T1 General is nil (0.00) before or after claiming medical expenses, then you should consider having the higher income spouse claim them.

You can claim only enough medical expenses to reduce your tax payable to zero. If the lower income spouse already has enough personal tax credits and deductions to eliminate all taxes payable, using the medical expense credit will not benefit that spouse.

If both spouses have a net income over 60,000, then it likely doesn't matter which spouse claims the expenses. Either spouse would get the same refund for the medical expenses.

Note: If you answered 'No' the question "Optimize medical expenses?" at the top of the form, you will also need to answer the question: "Are you claiming medical expenses for this dependant?" for each of the taxpayer's other dependants.

12 month medical optimization

When you right-click on a claim amount on the Medical expenses-line 330 or line 331 sections, you will see the following two options:

- o Optimize and sort expenses - this option sorts the medical expenses by payment dates and selects the optimum 12-month period for the expenses.
- o Optimize expenses without sorting - this option selects the optimum 12-month period for the expenses without sorting the medical expenses by payment dates (maintaining the order in which you entered the expenses).

Optimizing charitable donations

ProFile optimizes the donation claim by using only the amount required to reduce federal tax to zero. The balance is carried forward according to the table found at the bottom of the Charitable Donations form.

On the Donations worksheet, right-click on the list of donations to:

- Sort donations alphabetically.
- Transfer all donations, or a single donation, to the spouse's return.
- Remove 'Zero' lines.
  This function is useful if you checked the feature Options > Module > T1 > Carry forward > Donation descriptions. ProFile will carry forward the names of the charitable organization from last year's return but not the amounts (to serve as a checklist reminder for you when entering this year's donations). There may be some organizations the taxpayer chose not to donate to again. You can right click and select Remove 'Zero' lines to clear these unused descriptions.

Pension income splitting

Canadian residents who received eligible pension income during the taxation year may be able to allocate up to half of their eligible pension income to their spouse (or common-law partner) for income tax purposes.

Which pension income can be split?

Not all pension income is eligible for splitting with your spouse or common-law partner. It depends on the type of pension income (column 5), and the category of the person receiving the pension (column 6).

The table below outlines which pension amounts are eligible and which are not. For the purpose of this table, categories are defined as:

- **Category 1** - Persons 65 and over on December 31
- **Category 2** - Persons under 65 on December 31, and receiving benefits due to death of a spouse or common-law partner
- **Category 3** - Persons under 65 on December 31, and not receiving benefits due to death of a spouse or common-law partner

Federal		Québec		Type	Category (see above)	Pension splitting
T-slip	Box #	Relevé slip	Box #			
T3	22	RL-16	B	Lump-sum pension benefits	1, 2, 3	Not eligible
	31		D	Qualifying pension income	1, 2, 3	Eligible
T4A	16	RL-2	A	Pension or superannuation	1, 2, 3	Eligible
	18		C	Lump-sum payments	1, 2, 3	Not eligible
	24		B	Annuities	1, 2	Eligible
					3	Not eligible
	28 code 33		B	Variable pension benefits	1, 2	Eligible
					3	Not eligible
T4RIF	16	RL-2	B	RRIF annuity	1, 2	Eligible
					3	Not eligible
	18		E	Deemed received on death	1, 2, 3	Not eligible
	20		G	Deemed received on deregistration	1, 2	Eligible
					3	Not eligible
	22		H	Other income	1, 2	Eligible
					3	Not eligible
T4RSP	16	RL-2	B	Annuity payments	1, 2	Eligible

Federal		Québec		Type	Category (see above)	Pension splitting
T-slip	Box #	Relevé slip	Box #			
					3	Not eligible
	18, 20, 22, 26, 28, 34		D, F, C, G, H, E	Other RRSP payments	1, 2, 3	Not eligible
T5	19	RL-3	J	Accrued income annuities	1, 2	Eligible
					3	Not eligible
Foreign slip	N/A	N/A		Foreign pension	1, 2, 3	See note*
T4A(OAS)	All boxes	N/A		Old Age Security pension	1, 2, 3	Not eligible
T4A(P)	All boxes	RL2	C	CPP/QPP benefits	1, 2, 3	Not eligible

* Note: Some foreign pensions may be eligible except any portions that are exempt under a tax treaty and U.S. IRAs

Potential tax savings from pension income splitting can depend on a number of factors, such as federal and provincial income level and tax brackets of the taxpayer and his/her spouse. We have provided additional factors and considerations below; however, they do not represent an exhaustive list of all considerations.

When should you consider Pension Income Splitting?

- If the transfer of pension income reduces the combined total taxes payable for a married or common-law couple.
- If one spouse is in a higher tax bracket (page 2 of Schedule 1). At a minimum, you will save the difference in the tax rates between each spouse's tax bracket.
- If one spouse is not fully using the Pension credit amount (line 314 of Schedule 1).
- If the spouse with eligible pension income can avoid or reduce OAS claw back (line 235 of the T1 General) after pension income splitting.
- If the spouse with eligible pension income can increase the age credit amount (line 301 of Schedule 1) after pension income splitting.

When will Pension Income Splitting not benefit the taxpayer?

- If both spouses have eligible pension income, are fully using the Pension income amount and are in the same tax bracket, there may be no benefit to pension splitting.
- If neither spouse's income is taxable, pension splitting will not be beneficial.

Other points to consider

- Pension income does not have to be split equally (50/50).

You can choose the most beneficial amount to split, as long as it does not exceed 50% of the eligible pension income.
- Future year income tax installment. The spouse who is receiving pension income may be required to pay installments; on the other hand, the spouse transferring income may be required to pay less or no installments.
- Pension splitting can impact tax credits and calculations and you should review these claims before and after transferring pension income:
    - Age amount (line 301 of Schedule 1)
    - Medical expenses (line 330 of Schedule 1)
    - Donations and gifts (line 349 of Schedule 1)
    - Social benefits repayment (OAS claw back) (line 235 of T1 General)
    - Spouse or Common-law partner amount (line 303 of Schedule 1)
    - Pension income amount (line 314 of Schedule 1)
    - Amounts transferred from your spouse or common-law partner (line 326 of Schedule 1)
    - Other discretionary deductions/credits (such as non-capital losses)

Comparing returns with the "Jump to previous year" feature

Since ProFile allows you to keep tax returns for multiple years in memory for a single taxpayer, a handy feature is the ability to jump directly from a line number on this year's return to the related line number on last year's return. Try the following procedure to quickly compare this year's return to last year's (this assumes you've already carried forward the tax return):

1. Right-click on a field in the current year return and select Previous year's return from the context-sensitive menu. ProFile will open last year's tax return and display the related field.
2. Select Window > Tile horizontally from the main menu.

Each return is displayed in its own window.

Review each of them independently.

Foreign income

ProFile has several features that make entering foreign income and subsequent foreign tax credit calculations easy.

Income may be denominated in a foreign currency. On an applicable form (i.e. T5 slip, T3 slip, Foreign income slip), select the name of the foreign currency.

ProFile automatically includes the correct conversion rate for the income. The converted Canadian income transfers to the appropriate form. For example, ProFile multiplies the investment income by the conversion rate, and posts the converted amount to Schedule 4.

In coupled returns, the % reported by spouse amount flows from the applicable slip to both the taxpayer's and the spouse's Schedule 4 (in combination with foreign income conversions), according to the percentage entered. Since this feature shares income from a single slip, the slip details appear ONLY in the return of the slip recipient.

Calculating foreign exchange rates

ProFile T1 includes integrated foreign exchange rates for more than 70 countries on the T3, T5, T5008 and Foreign slips.

To choose a rate, click the down arrow next to the Currency field on these slips. With the keyboard, press <Alt+down arrow> to display the list. Then, use the arrow keys and <Enter> to select a currency.

Attention: For Quebec residents, foreign exchange rates appear on RL-3 and RL-16. These exchange rates transfer from the corresponding federal forms.

ProFile will automatically calculate the currency exchanges and post amounts accordingly.

Claiming RRSP Contributions

In the expandable table at the top of the form RRSP, enter a line for each RRSP contribution slip the taxpayer received. You can easily double check your RRSP contribution entries if you use a separate line for each slip.

- To enter the 'Contribution period,' click on the down arrow beside the field or press <Alt+down arrow>. Select from the drop-down list of different periods.
- Repayments and withdrawals from the Home Buyer's plan are also handled on the RRSP form.
- ProFile calculates next year's deduction limit on form RRSP Limit.
- Enter eligible transfers to an RRSP on RRSPTransfer. Eligible retiring allowances transfer automatically from the appropriate slips (for example, T4A) to this form.

Planning RRSP contributions

During the first 60 days of the year, your clients may ask you about the impact of their RRSP contribution on their tax payable. There are several ways you can see the impact.

The first two planning methods, method one - window tiling or method two - Data Monitor, allow you to immediately see the impact of the RRSP contributions on the tax payable. The third method allows you to see the impact of RRSP contributions throughout the tax return. This method uses the snapshot variance and auditor features of ProFile.

RRSP tax planning method one: Using window tiling

The goal of this method is to display both the RRSP worksheet and the last page of the T1 jacket on the screen at the same time. Then, when you enter data on the RRSP form, you'll immediately see the impact on tax payable.

1. Go to form RRSP and enter a 'Tax planning RRSP' for the first 60 days of the year.

   Note: You may want to check the field with an 'X' review mark or attach a memo to make sure you don't file the return with the amount until you confirm it.
2. Right-click on the form and select "New window." Under the main menu Window, you'll notice there are two windows now. Both refer to the same tax return.
3. Select Window > Tile horizontally. Your newly created window will display on half of the screen and the original window in the other half.

4. In the original window, open the T1 form and scroll until you see line 485 - Balance owing. The changes you make on the RRSP form in the top window will show on the T1 jacket in the bottom window.

RRSP tax planning method two: Using the data monitor

The Data Monitor can display any four fields at the bottom of the Edit window. You can watch the totals for these fields change as you work on different forms in the software.

At the bottom of the screen you will see a status indicator and four Data Monitor cells. By default, the software monitors several key fields in the client file. In ProFile T1, the first is Balance/Refund. If you do not see this field, right click on the data monitor and select "Default monitors."

When you make a change to the RRSP contribution, you'll immediately see the effect on tax payable in the data monitor.

RRSP tax planning method three: Using snapshot variance

Snapshot variance allows you to take a "snapshot" of the current return, change the RRSP amount and have the Active Auditor automatically detect the changes between the new return and the return in the snapshot.

Attention: Only those fields with the CRA line numbers will be included in the variance comparison.

1. Open the taxpayer's return, and view the RRSP deduction worksheet, but do not enter any RRSP planning amount.
2. Select Audit > Snapshot / Variance.
3. Enter new data, such as an RRSP contribution.

    Note: You may want to attach a review mark or a memo so you do not inadvertently file with planning data in the return.
4. From the Audit menu, choose your snapshot to compare current values with the original data. Fields that differ from those in the snapshot have a light orange background. Press <F9> or click the toolbar icon to display the Active Auditor.
5. Click on the Variance tab Press <F9> repeatedly. The Active Auditor will take you to every change caused by the data you entered in step 3. Keep in mind that variance analysis depends on the thresholds you have configured under Options > Module > T1 > Variance.

Summaries: Other income, deductions and credits

There are several lines from the tax return that accumulate data from different ProFile worksheets. For example, line 104: Other employment income can include amounts from several sources.

ProFile gathers data from these worksheets on three convenient forms: Other Income, Other Deduct and Other Credits. This makes it easy to enter, review and print breakdown information for the line number. From these summary forms, the totals flow to the Jacket and schedules.

You can use the Form Explorer to open these forms. However, the easier way is to right-click on a field (for example, line 104 on the T1 jacket) and jump to the 'Other' form using the context-sensitive menu.

Calculating installment payments

ProFile T1 and ProFile T1/TP1 calculate federal installment payments required for the next taxation year. Installment payments are calculated on projected income, or on a combination of prior and current year tax returns. This combination reflects the fact that payments early in the calendar year may be due before the CRA has processed the current tax return.

Installments 1 and 2

ProFile calculates the first two installments based on net tax owing from the preceding year's tax return. If you have carried forward the return, this is automatic. Alternately, you can supply past year information to the Installments worksheet.

Installments 3 and 4

The third and fourth installments are based on amounts that flow to the Installments form from other sections of this tax return file.

To determine the amounts for the third and fourth installments, ProFile subtracts the first two installment amounts from the total tax owing on this tax return. The balance of tax payable is split between the third and fourth installments.

If there are no amounts available for the preceding taxation year, the third and fourth installment payments will equal the full tax payable.

Attention: Like the federal Installments form, the TP1026 estimates installments required from self-employed tax payers during the next taxation year. Quebec provincial installment payments follow the same formula used for federal installments. As long as taxpayers make payments according to the installment notices from Revenu Quebec, they will not be subject to penalties.

Note:
- If you know that tax payable will be higher in the next year, you can base installment payments on estimated income.
- Keep in mind that taxpayers will not be subject to any penalties provided they make payments according to the installment notices from the CRA.

Understanding the T1 assessment process

Canada Revenue Agency (CRA) may conduct a review of a tax return prior to or after the initial assessment of the return. According to the CRA "all returns, whether filed electronically or on paper, are subject to the same selection process for verification both before and after assessment." They also state that less than 5% of returns are subject to a post-assessment review.

Pre-Assessment

The CRA may conduct a review of the return prior to the initial assessment to verify certain claims, such as disability amount. If a return was submitted by EFILE, #2139 will appear beside the client's surname on the 'Accepted Records Acknowledgement File' to indicate that the return has been selected for pre-assessment review.

Supporting documentation may be requested during this review. The CRA handles requests for documentation as follows:

Paper return - the CRA mails the request letter to the address on page 1 of the tax return.

EFILE return - the CRA directs the request letter based on the tax preparer's preferred method of contact for pre-assessment reviews. The method of contact is specific to each taxpayer. The choices are:

- Contact with tax preparer by FAX.
- Contact with tax preparer by mail.
- Contact with the client only.

Assessment

The CRA processes a return using the identification information from the T1 jacket and business statements and numeric fields from the T1 jacket, schedules and other CRA forms. The numeric fields that are captured by their system are generally identified on a CRA form by a three or four digit line number.

In the case of an return submitted by EFILE, the CRA requests some additional details that are not found on the CRA forms. In ProFile, these details are included on the EFILE worksheet. The CRA provides a list of all of the fields used for EFILE in the Electronic Filers Manual, which is available on their website.

The Notice of Assessment is issued to the taxpayer's address on the return unless an Alternative Address Authorization has been completed. This authorization is provided on Form T1132 for a paper-filed return and Form T183 for a return submitted by EFILE. The authorization can also apply to any tax refund. By default, any tax refund is provided to the taxpayer via cheque or direct deposit.

Post-Assessment

A post-assessment review occurs after the initial assessment of a return. The initial contact for a request for supporting documentation is a letter from the CRA:

- **Paper return** - the CRA contacts the taxpayer based on the address on page 1 of the return.

    Note that the authorizations provided on Forms T1013 or T1132 are not used by the CRA to determine who they contact.
- **EFILE return** - if the taxpayer authorized the electronic filer to represent him or her (Part E of Form T183), then the letter is directed to the electronic filer; otherwise, the CRA contacts the taxpayer based on the address on page 1 of the return.

The T183 EFILE authorization is specific only to the current year. If such an authorization has been granted and the CRA does not receive a response from the tax preparer regarding the request, they will contact the client directly.

If a reassessment results from the post-assessment review, the Notice of Reassessment is always mailed to the taxpayer's address on page 1 of the return.

Planning for the following tax year

The current T1 module includes a tax planner to help you prepare your clients for the coming year. The tax planner form, Plan #, is in the Client category of the Form Explorer. Plan# is an unlimited form, so you can create as many plans as you require for each client. Just right-click on the form and select "New form" to add another plan to the file.

Attention: For more complex scenarios, or a more detailed plan, see the topic: Using next year's rates for tax planning.

If you are working on a coupled file that contains tax returns for a client and spouse, ProFile will create pairs of the Plan form. Create a new Plan in one return, and a matching Plan form appears in the spousal return. Each set of Plan forms (e.g. Plan#1 for client, Plan#1 for spouse) shares information to correctly handle spousal amounts and transfers.

For your convenience, ProFile can automatically transfer amounts from the existing tax return into a plan. To copy the amounts from the T1 jacket, right-click on any field on the Plan form and select 'Copy T1 return'. In most cases, the amounts will copy directly from the T1 jacket or the appropriate schedule. In some cases, the Plan form will use calculated amounts that are available for carry forward. This function is a one-time copy. Subsequent changes to the T1 return will not be reflected in the Plan form (unless you 'Copy T1 return' again). Since a tax plan is a snapshot representing a particular set of circumstances, ProFile does not update any Plan amounts with automatic data flow from other forms.

ProFile module options include data locking to secure your completed tax return files so that you don't accidentally change a return after filing. The Tax Planner is not included in the data locking, so there's no need to change a file status to work with the tax planner.

The planner calculates the fields that appear in blue, so these do not transfer from the T1 return.

Attention: The tax planner may not be available in ProFile T1 versions at the start of the tax season. We wait until the government announces the budget for the coming year before updating this form.

Additional information regarding the Plan form

- If you answer 'Yes' to 'Calculate Installments', ProFile T1 will print the installment schedule when the tax owing is more than $2,000. If you answer 'No,' the Installment section will not print with the Plan.
- Right-click on the form (not on a field) to jump to a specific section of the Plan form.
- Answer 'Yes' to the question 'Include lines with zero amounts ...?' to print all of the detail. Select 'No' if you just want to print lines that have amounts in them. The Minimum Tax calculation will only print when it applies.
- You can create any number of Plans. In the Edit window, right-click on an existing Plan and select "New Form". ProFile will add a new Plan to the client's return (and a corresponding Plan in the spouse return of a coupled file).
- Right-click on any field and select 'Copy T1 Return' to transfer the contents of the current client and spouse returns to the current copies of the Plan form.

Using next year's rates for tax planning

The Plan worksheet is a simple and effective tool for testing scenarios for the next taxation year. However, it does not take into account more complex tax scenarios. In such cases, you can select rates on the Info form to plan for the following year. It is like preparing a brand new tax return, with all the rates and calculations required to analyze the next year's return.

To create a planning return from a current-year T1 file:

1. Open the client file.
2. Select File > Save as and rename the file so you can easily distinguish between the planning return and the actual return filed with the CRA.

    Note: We recommend adding the year in brackets after the client name. In fact, ProFile will automatically add the year in brackets to any new return if you apply upcoming-year rates before you first save the file.
3. Go to the 'Type of return' section of Info form and select 2010 in the Use rates for tax year dropdown list.
4. Go to the T1 jacket. You will note that ProFile automatically inserts the description. For 2009 planning purposes only at the top of the T1 jacket.

You now have a file containing the amounts you entered for the current year, but calculated using the following year's rates. You can begin modifying amounts to create different scenarios for the upcoming taxation year.

Review messages in the Active Auditor. ProFile indicates when rates and calculations are not handled automatically.

To test different scenarios, simply save the file again under a descriptive new name and change amounts to reflect a different tax situation.

Attention: Remember that even with projected rates and data, ProFile will still treat the file as a current-year tax file. There is no carry forward from a current-year file to a file using next year's rates. You cannot open a current-year file that uses next year's rates as a tax file in the following year module of ProFile T1. You will need to carry forward from your original tax return file when we release carry forward processes for the upcoming tax season.

Claiming auto expenses

Claiming auto expenses for employees

To calculate motor vehicle expenses used to earn employment income, you will need to use the T777Auto expense worksheet. ProFile allocates 100% of the automobile expenses entered on the T777Auto to the T777, Employment Expense form. However, ProFile will only select this form to print if you have entered employment expense information directly on the form.

Claiming auto expenses used for business

The Business Auto worksheet begins with a table listing all the business statements that, if used, allow the client to allocate automobile expenses to different business statements within the client file.

Therefore, the Business Auto worksheet does not belong to a particular business form set that may appear

in the taxpayer's file. The Business Auto worksheets are only linked to the business statements through the allocation table at the top of each worksheet.

   Note: Both the T777Auto and Business Auto worksheets are designed as an unlimited form, so that you can provide details for any number of automobiles the taxpayer may have.

QuickBooks Integration

Do you use QuickBooks to manage your small-business accounting? Do you also use ProFile T1 to prepare tax returns for your clients? Would you like to transfer the ProFile T1 billing and invoicing information into a QuickBooks invoice? If so, try the ProFile T1 "Create an invoice in QuickBooks" feature!

Simply set up your QuickBooks options under Options > Integration and then right-click on the Billing form for a particular client to transfer the billing information into your QuickBooks file.

Attention: This feature does not work with QuickBooks Basic 2004.

Set up ProFile T1 to QuickBooks billing

To configure ProFile T1 QuickBooks invoice:

1. Open (in QuickBooks) the QuickBooks file that will accept ProFile T1 billing information.
2. In ProFile, go to Options > Integration and click on the QuickBooks Invoice Transfer option in the left-hand panel.
3. Browse for the QuickBooks file where you want to transfer ProFile T1 billing data.

    Note: If this is the first time you access this file through ProFile, QuickBooks may ask you to give ProFile access to the QuickBooks file. If you see this screen, click [Yes, Always].
    ProFile populates the drop-down boxes with information from the QuickBooks file. Which options you see depends on how you have set up your QuickBooks file.
    - **Account**: Select the Accounts Receivable account in which to create the new invoice.
    - **Class:** Select the Class to enter on the QuickBooks Invoice. If class tracking is turned on, this lets you track income and expenses by department, business office or location, separate properties you own, or any other meaningful breakdown of your business.
    - **Item:** Select the name of the item you want to enter on the invoice. This includes Service items only.
    - **Terms:** Select the term when you expect to receive payment from a customer, or when a vendor expects to receive payment from you. Terms show the number of days (or date) by which payment is due, and can include a discount for early payment.
    - **Tax Code:** Select the tax code that will apply to the transaction. QuickBooks uses this to determine what taxes apply. ProFile transfers the pre-tax amount to the QuickBooks invoice. Then, QuickBooks calculates the tax.
    - Customer Message: Select the customer message to print at the bottom of the invoice.

    Attention: If you go into QuickBooks and add new accounts, new classes or change the file while you are setting these options, click [Refresh] to update the drop-down lists you see on screen.
4. For couples, select a joint or separate invoice:
    - Select Include Spouse's Amount to add both the client and spouse balance owing to the invoice.
    - To invoice the client and spouse separately, clear this box and create an invoice in QuickBooks from the client's Billing form and then from the spouse's Billing form.
5. Click [OK] to save your options.

Create invoice in QuickBooks

Attention: This feature does not currently function when you use French regional settings in Windows®. To use create an invoice in QuickBooks, select English regional settings in Windows®. Refer to Windows® Help for instructions on how to change the regional settings.

Additionally, this feature does not work with QuickBooks Basic 2004 (you must use the premier or Pro versions).

To create an invoice in QuickBooks:

1. Set up the QuickBooks options under Options > Integration See Set up ProFile T1 for QuickBooks billing.
2. Set up your ProFile billing options under Options > Pricing.
3. Open a ProFile T1 client file.
4. Open the Billing worksheet.
5. Right-click on the Billing worksheet and select Create invoice in QuickBooks. ProFile lists all of the customers entered in QuickBooks.
6. Apply the invoice to a customer in the QuickBooks file
    - **If the customer exists in the QuickBooks file,** ProFile automatically selects the name from the list. Click [OK] to confirm this selection.
    - **If the customer does not exist in the QuickBooks file,** click [Add Customer] to create a new customer in the QuickBooks file. Enter the customer name and click [OK]. ProFile transfers address and contact information to QuickBooks and indicates that it successfully created a new customer. If you want to specify additional options for the customer, go to QuickBooks and edit the customer there.
    - **To apply the invoice to a different customer in the QuickBooks file,** select an alternate customer from the list and click [OK].

ProFile indicates that it was successful in creating a new invoice in QuickBooks. ProFile attaches a memo to the Invoice # field on the Billing form to tell you the invoice number assigned within QuickBooks.

Chapter 2

T1 Forms

2009 Tax Year

CarryFWD: Carry forward Summary

We provide the Carry forward Summary to help you review key amounts that will affect next year's return. To keep the worksheet manageable for our users, this is a summary and not a comprehensive list of every amount that will carry forward. When we release software for a subsequent year, we include the carry forward process that creates new files based on prior year data. Data carries forward from all the source forms in the tax return. We do not carry data forward from the Carry forward Summary. To review all carry forward amounts, display the Active Auditor <F9> and select the Carry forward tab. This is your complete review of all amounts that we have included from the prior year.

This form summarizes the amounts that can be carried forward from the previous year to the current year (Beginning balance column) and the amounts that may be carried forward to next year (End balance column). The Beginning balance column data pertains to the returns that you created using the Carry forward function.

You can right-click on most of the fields to go to the form where ProFile uses or calculates that carry forward amount.

Some carry forwards require schedules, for example, Minimum tax carry-overs and donations that can be carried forward for several years. You can find these carry forward schedules on the related forms (i.e. Donations, T657 and T691).

Consider using ProFile variance features and the Active Auditor to review data that carried forward from a previous year's return.

Use the right-click menu option to open the previous year's return when you are working with information carried forward.

Dependant: Dependant information

You can enter all dependant information directly on this form. There is no limit to the number of dependants you can include. The form includes an expanding table, so once you use the last column for a dependant, a new column appears immediately.

To find out more about how coupling and uncoupling returns affects the dependant information see Merging and separating - data flow when coupling and uncoupling returns.

The Dependant form includes disability information, caregiver and transfers from dependants. The following fields have field specific help:

- Disability/Infirmity
- Caregiver
- Disability supplement
- Transfers from dependants

Tip: The Dependant worksheet is dynamic and will display additional sections for taxpayers whose province of residence is Québec or Nova Scotia.

Child Tax Benefit

By default, ProFile answers "Yes" to the question Are you eligible to receive the Child Tax Benefit? On the taxpayer's return (and not on the spouse's if the returns are coupled). ProFile automatically determines which of the two spousal returns should show the claim. If the gender question on the form Info is answered, ProFile sets the Female return to "Yes" in a couple of scenarios. ProFile calculates the estimated Child Tax Benefit for the spouse(s) on form CTB. Answer "No" if you do not wish ProFile to calculate this amount.

Child care expenses

Enter child care expenses for each child at the bottom of this form. As soon as you enter an expense, ProFile adds a line to the table for more entries. ProFile automatically calculates the claim on form T778. The expense detail table also appears on form T778 so you can enter it in either location. ProFile automatically claims the amount on the appropriate spouse's return.

If you have entered payments eligible for the child care expense amount, but there is no claim on line 214 of the jacket or on T778, check the dependant information on T778 and on the Dependant form.

ProFile compares the claim information with the personal information you provided on the Dependant form. In the table for expenses, enter only the first name of the child, exactly as it appears on the Dependant form. If the child name on the Dependant schedule is Robert, you cannot use the name Bobby in the child care expense area. ProFile will not claim for him because it cannot match these two together for dependants' income and other details. If the two names match, ProFile will verify eligibility for the claim based on the birthdates and other dependant information you have provided.

Disability/Infirmity

Tip: If this is the first time anyone has claimed the disability amount for this person, you must submit a completed and certified T2201: Disability tax credit certificate.

This section of the Dependant worksheet handles credits for disability or infirmity of a dependant.

Qualify for disability amount?

You can choose to claim the disability amount for this dependant by entering "Yes" in this field. If the dependant file is linked to with the taxpayer, the answer to this question flows from the answer to the Claim disability amount? question on the dependants Info form and the text in this field will be purple.

If the dependant is under 18, ProFile automatically calculates the disability supplement for dependants under 18 when you select "Yes" in this field.

Mentally or physically infirm?

When you select "Yes" in the disability amount field, the answer to this field automatically becomes"; Yes" and the field turns blue, because a person with a disability is by nature mentally or physically infirm. However, if you select "No" in the disability amount field, you can still indicate that a person is mentally or physically infirm.

For dependants 18 and over, ProFile uses this information to calculate line 306 of the T1 jacket based on the information you provide in this section.

Percent and amount claimed on Schedule 5

Once ProFile calculates the Amount for infirm dependants on Schedule 5, the amount shows up on the Dependant form. ProFile automatically decides whether to claim the amount on the spouse or on the taxpayer's return in order to produce the best results. However, you can modify the percent claimed by the taxpayer or spouse in this section. If the taxpayer claims 100% of the credit, the spouse claims none and vice versa.

Caregiver

ProFile calculates the caregiver amount for the dependant on Schedule 5, which is then claimed on line 315 of the T1 jacket.

If, at any time in 2009, you (either alone or with another person) maintained a dwelling where you and one or more of your dependants lived, you may be able to claim a maximum amount of $4,198 for each dependant. Each dependant must have been one of the following individuals:

- you or your spouse's or common-law partner's child or grandchild; or
- you or your spouse's or common-law partner's brother, sister, niece, nephew, aunt, uncle, parent, or grandparent who was resident in Canada. You cannot claim this amount for a person who was only visiting you.

In addition, each dependant must meet all of the following conditions. The person must have:

- been 18 years of age or over at the time he or she lived with you;
- had a net income in 2009(line 236 of his or her return, or the amount that it would be if he or she filed a return) of less than $18,534; and
- been dependent on you due to mental or physical impairment or, if he or she is your or your spouse's or common-law partner's parent or grandparent, born in 1944 or earlier.

Did the dependant live with you?

The dependant must have lived with you at any time during the taxation year for you to claim the caregiver amount. If the dependent did not live with you, select "No" in this field and ProFile calculates the Amount for infirm dependants age 18 or older, if applicable.

Percent and amount claimed on Schedule 5

Once ProFile calculates the Amount for infirm dependants on Schedule 5, the amount shows up on the Dependant form. ProFile automatically decides whether to claim the amount on the spouse or on the taxpayer's return in order to produce the best results. However, you can modify the percent claimed by the taxpayer or spouse in this section. If the taxpayer claims 100% of the credit, the spouse claims none and vice versa.

Disability supplement

If the dependant was under 18 at the end of the year, the taxpayer can claim the disability supplement on behalf of this dependant. Child care expenses and attendant care expenses you or someone else claimed for the dependant may reduce this claim.

Transfers from dependants

This section treats non-refundable amounts transferred from dependants whose taxable income does not permit them to claim them on their own return. In linked files, these amounts flow directly from the dependant's return (see table below). For files that are not linked, you can enter the amounts directly in this section.

Field	Source
Tuition fees	Box A of the dependant's T2202A.
Month's of part-time education	Box B of the dependant's T2202A.
Month's of full-time education	Box C of the dependant's T2202A.
Unused tuition/education	Line 1 on the dependant's Schedule 11, or carried forward from previous year.
Net income	Net income field at the top of the form.
Deductions from net income	Lines 248 to 256 of the T1 jacket.
Taxable income	Calculated by ProFile
Non-refundable amounts	Total of lines 303 to 315 of the dependant's Schedule 1

Info: Personal information

Use this form to enter the basic processing information for the taxpayer(s). ProFile uses data from the Info form (among others) for calculations and to determine which other forms to include in a return for the client. Make sure you complete all fields here, particularly province of residence, birth date and marital status.

If you are processing a taxpayer and spouse together, you'll need to couple the returns. To do this, enter the taxpayer's information first. Then, select "Married" or "Living Common Law" as the marital status. Finally, press <F5> to switch between spousal returns. ProFile will ask you if you wish to create a new return for the spouse. ProFile stores both the taxpayer and the spouse in the same data file.

Tip: If you select Quebec as the province of residence, the Provincial information - Quebec section appears at the bottom of the form.

Residency status

The "Residency status" field on the Info worksheet allows calculation of provincial tax for non-residents. Select the province where the income is to be taxed as the "Province of residence." The "Residency status" defaults to resident or non-resident based on the "Province of residence." If the taxpayer is a non-resident with employment or business income in a particular province, override this field to Non-resident.

EFILE this return?

This question will default to "Yes" if you've entered an EFILE On-Line Number under EFILE > Options.

Is return discounted?

This question will default to "Yes" if you select the checkbox under Options > Module > New File > Default to discount.

Use rates for tax year

The Use rates for tax year drop-down list, in the Type of return section of the Info form allows you to use rates for the upcoming taxation year. You can use this option to:

- early-file a deceased return;
- early-file a bankruptcy return; or
- help your clients plan for the following taxation year.

Additional considerations

When you apply upcoming-year rates in a current-year ProFile file, remember:

- The forms you see on screen and in print are all current-year certified forms even though the rates applied in the background are for the upcoming year.
- When you use upcoming-year rates in a current-year client file, you will not be able to convert the data into the following year's tax return once the new ProFile T1 module becomes available. For example, there is no functionality to open a 2007 return prepared using 2008 rates as a ProFile T1 2008 file. We recommend that you create a copy of your current-year file for planning purposes. You can then change amounts without affecting the electronic copy of the return as filed, and you can carry forward next season from the original file.
- We recommend you thoroughly review any return you are filing early.

Date of death

Enter the date of death on the Info worksheet and ProFile transfers this information to the T1 jacket and to the appropriate field on the spouse's return (if required).

Joint salutation / client salutation

Set the default type of salutation under Options > Module > T1 > General > Salutation. You can choose between Formal (such as, Dear Mr. and Mrs.) or Casual (i.e. Dear John and Shirley:). ProFile will address the mailing label to both spouses only if the returns are coupled.

Use joint client letter/invoice?

This question will default to" Yes" if you've selected the corresponding options under Options > Module > T1 > General.

Of course, you can set default values or text for any field by creating a default tax return under Options > Module > T1 > File Template.

Provincial information - Quebec

You must select Quebec as the province of residence on the Info form before ProFile will calculate TP1 forms (if Quebec is a jurisdiction on the T2203 ProFile will also calculate TP1 forms).

If you select Quebec as the province of residence, the 'Provincial information Quebec' section appears at the bottom of the form.

Taxpayer information

In this section, you can claim the credit for individuals living alone.

Additionally, it is important that you correctly answer the "Prescription Drug Insurance Plan" questions. Select the applicable code and situation from the drop-down menu to indicate that the taxpayer is not required to complete a Schedule K and therefore does not have to pay prescription drug plan premiums.

A taxpayer who does not fall under one of the listed situations must pay prescription drug plan premiums. When this is the case, ProFile automatically calculates the premium amount and completes Schedule K.

Make sure you indicate whether the taxpayer is paying their spouse's premium. If they are, go to the spouse's Info form and select code 20. If you do not do this, the premium will appear on line 447 of the spouse's return.

Spousal information section

If necessary, enter the date of death in this section. If you are preparing coupled returns, ProFile transfers amounts from lines 220, 293 and 295 of the spouse's return to this section.

If you are preparing a return for married or common-law taxpayers and you are not coupling the returns, you must enter the amounts from line 220, 293 and 295 so that ProFile calculates the spousal amount.

Foreign: Foreign employment, pension and investment income

In the fields of the Foreign Income form, enter the taxpayer's employment, social security, pension and investment income from foreign sources.

Currency

This field has a drop-down list of the more common currencies. Click on the status box or press <Alt+Down Arrow> to choose from the list. If you choose a currency, the exchange rate appears automatically.

Exchange rate

ProFile will multiply amounts on the foreign slips by the conversion amount before posting to the appropriate form. For example, if you enter $1,000 as investment income with a conversion rate of 1.20, ProFile will post a description like "1,000.00 * 1.2" and the amount of $1,200.00 to part II of Schedule 4.

Foreign income and tax paid

If a slip shows foreign income and/or foreign tax paid, complete the Name of foreign country field.

ProFile will automatically generate the FTC, T2209 and T2036 forms with the applicable calculations.

Description (Foreign Income)

Enter a description of the source of the foreign income on the Foreign slips worksheet. If the taxpayer has multiple sources of foreign income, be sure to enter a description that allows you to distinguish between each income source.

Name of Foreign Country

Complete the Name of Foreign Country field on the Foreign worksheet so that ProFile can generate the applicable FTC , T2209 and T2036 forms.

S3Details: Capital gains entry

Use this ProFile worksheet to enter details of capital gains.

S3Details, like other slips, is an expandable table that allows unlimited entries. Use the scroll bar along the top of the slip to scroll through gains reported. The worksheet uses a feature called the Slip Sidebar, which is handy if you have a larger number of entries. To jump directly to a particular slip without scrolling, you can also select a capital gain description in the sidebar to the left of the slips.

S3Details allows you to enter full data for each capital gain, and automatically assigns gains to the correct rate period based on the date of disposition.

Information flows from S3Details to Schedule 3.

Slips: Slip summary

This form summarizes all the slips you have entered into the current tax return. Only those slips that contain information will appear on the summary. If you haven't entered any slips yet, this form will be blank.

You can use the form to check data entry against the actual slips for the client.

T3 - Statement of Trust Income Allocations and Designations

T3: Statement of trust income

The T3 slip is the statement of trust income allocations and designations. Enter the amounts from the taxpayer's T3 slip into the corresponding fields of the T3 form.

Some T3s report amounts that are shared between spouses. If you are preparing a coupled return, enter the percent that the spouse will report. ProFile will not create a T3 slip for the spouse since there is only one slip. Instead, ProFile will transfer the percent and the spouse's share of the amounts to the related forms. For example, if you enter a value of $20,000 for "Taxable amount of dividends" from the ABC Bank, with 30% reported by the spouse, Schedule 4 for the taxpayer will show the description as "ABC Bank

(70.0% of 20,000)" and an amount of $14,000 Schedule 4 for the spouse will show the description as "ABC Bank (30.0% of 20,000)" and an amount of $6,000.

If there is foreign income and/or foreign tax paid amounts on the slip, enter a description for the foreign country. ProFile will automatically generate the FTC, T2209 and T2036 forms for the country with the applicable calculations.

You can enter an exchange rate to convert foreign amounts to Canadian currency. Use the down arrow in the status box for the currency field to select a foreign currency. ProFile includes average exchange rates as determined by CRA. Select a currency and the average exchange rate for the current year appears automatically.

 **The Canada Revenue Agency says...**

Box	Title	Description
Box 21	Capital gains	This is the full amount of capital gain or loss. Enter a loss as a negative number (e.g. -800).
		The portion not eligible for the capital gains deduction (the amount in box 21 minus the amount in box 30) is transferred to line 176 on Schedule 3.
		All or part of this amount may be foreign non-business income, which will be footnoted. The foreign non-business income is transferred to Form FTC, Foreign Tax Credits Worksheet and from there included in your credit on line 433 of Schedule 1.
Box 22	Lump-sum pension benefits	This amount is transferred to line 130 of your T1 General. You may be able to transfer this amount to an RRSP or RPP.
Box 23	Actual amount of dividends	This amount is on the T3 slip for your information only.
Box 24	Foreign business income	This amount is transferred to Form T2125 and Form T2209, and is included in line 135.
Box 25	Foreign non-business income	
	- Investment	This amount is transferred to Section II of Schedule 4 and is included on line 121 of your T1 General.

		- Other	This amount is included on line 130 of your T1 General.
Box 26	Other income		This includes income from retiring allowances or severance pay, and certain trust income. This amount is included on line 130 of your T1 General. Any amount in Box 31 is subtracted from this amount. If this amount includes any Death Benefits, a portion of it may be non-taxable; see box 35 (below) for more information.
Box 30	Capital gains eligible for deduction		The Qualified Small Business Corporation Shares (QSBCS) amount is included on line 107 of Schedule 3. Qualified Farm Property (QFP) is included on line 110 of Schedule 3. Your capital gains deduction is calculated on Form T657 and is shown on line 254 of your T1 General.
Box 31	Qualifying pension income		This amount is included on line 115 of your T1 General. It is used in calculating your pension income tax credit on line 314 of Schedule 1.
Box 32	Taxable amount of dividends		This amount is transferred to Section I of Schedule 4 and included to line 120 of your T1 General.
Box 33	Foreign business income tax paid		This amount is used in calculating your federal foreign tax credit on Form T2209.
Box 34	Foreign non-business income tax paid		This amount is used in calculating your federal foreign tax credit on Form T2209.
Box 35	Eligible death benefits		You may not have to pay tax on up to $10,000 of this amount (see Death Benefits for more information). This amount is included in Box 26 (Other Income).
Box 37	Insur. segregated fund losses		This amount is transferred to line 176 of Schedule 3.
Box 38	Part XII.2 tax credit		This amount is included on line 456 of your T1 General.
Box 39	Federal Dividend		This amount is on the T3 slip for your information only.

	Tax Credit	You do not need to enter this amount. The software calculates it for you (using the amount in box 11) and transfers it to line 425 of Schedule 1.
Boxes 40 and 41	Investment tax credit	
-	Box 40 - Investment cost or expenditures	Include this amount on Form T2038(IND), Investment Tax Credit (Individuals). The investment code should be identified as a footnote on this slip.
-	Box 41 - Investment tax credit	Investment tax credits are included on line 412 of Schedule 1.
Boxes 42 and 45	Other amounts	
-	Box 42 - Amount resulting in cost base adjustment	This amount represents a distribution or return of capital from the trust. Follow the instructions in the footnote area and adjust the cost base of the property at the end of the tax year. For more information, see Information Sheet RC4169, *Tax Treatment of Mutual Funds for Individuals*.
-	Box 45 - Other credits	Include the footnoted amount on Form T1129 for Newfoundland and Labrador or Form T1232 for Yukon, whichever applies.
Box 46	Pension income - minor	This amount is already included in box 26. For more information, see the guide RRSPs and Other Registered Plans for Retirement.
Box 47	Income eligible for transfer	Any footnote for this box showing income eligible for a transfer is already included in box 26. The footnote identifies the type of income, and the type of plan to which you can transfer the income. See Transfers for further information.
Box 48	Charitable donations	.
	- Charitable	These amounts are used to calculate your Donations and Gifts tax credit on Schedule 9 - Donations and Gifts. Any footnote showing a charitable

	donations	donation or gift identifies its type. Your donations tax credit is shown on line 349 of Schedule 1.
	- Cultural and ecological gifts	These amounts used to calculate your Donations and Gifts tax credit on Schedule 9 - Donations and Gifts. Any footnote showing a charitable donation or gift identifies its type. Your donations tax credit is shown on line 349 of Schedule 1.
Boxes 49, 50 and 51	Eligible dividends	
-	Box 49 - Actual amount of eligible dividends	This is the amount you actually received.
-	Box 50 - Taxable amount of eligible dividends	This is the amount you have to report as income - it is included on line 120 of your return.
-	Box 51 - Dividend tax credit	This is the federal dividend tax credit to which you are entitled - it is included on line 425 of Schedule 1.
(%)	Your percentage	

T4 - Statement of Remuneration Paid

T4: Statement of remuneration paid

The T4 is the Statement of remuneration paid. Enter the amounts from the taxpayer's T4 slips into the corresponding fields of the T4 form.

ProFile automatically calculates EI insurable and CPP/QPP pensionable earnings (boxes 24 and 26) based on the employment income entered on line 14. Override box 24 or 26 if the amount that appears on the T4 slip is different than the amount calculated by ProFile. DO NOT override box 24 or 26 if the corresponding box on the T4 slip is blank, unless you are a Québec resident on December 31st. In this case, override the amount in box 26 on the T4 form, so that it corresponds to the amount in box G of the Relevé.

If you contributed more than the maximum amount for CPP/QPP and/or EI, ProFile will automatically calculate and transfer the overpayment to the T1 jacket or if applicable, to the Quebec provincial return.

Some of the taxable employment benefits are already included in employment income in box 14, however there are certain taxable benefits that are eligible for deductions (employee home relocation loan deduction and stock option and shares deductions).

Some boxes on the T4 slip do not appear on the T4 form. These amounts are for notification only and have no affect on the calculation of the tax return.

Status Indians

If you are a status Indian receiving taxable salary or wages, your employment income is reported in Box 14 of the T4 slip. Non-taxable salary or wages is reported in Box 71 and is excluded from pensionable employment (CPP) but is subject to EI.

Emergency volunteers

The Income Tax Act provides an exemption of up to $1,000 on amounts an individual receives from a government, municipality, or public authority.

This exemption applies to the following individuals:

- volunteer firefighters;
- volunteer ambulance technicians; and
- emergency service volunteers who help in the search or rescue of individuals or in other emergency situations and disasters.

The $1,000 exemption only applies if the amount paid for the duties that the individual performs is a nominal amount in comparison to what it would have cost in the same circumstances to have the same duties performed by a regular full-time or part-time individual.

The $1,000 exemption does not apply if the individual was employed in the year by the same public authority for the same or similar duties (i.e. a full-time firefighter who from time to time acts as a volunteer firefighter or rescue worker for the municipality that employs him or her would not be eligible for the exemption).

The non-taxable portion of the payment must be included in calculating the earned income for the federal child care expenses deduction and for the Quebec tax credit for child care expenses. ProFile automatically includes the non-taxable amount in the earned income calculation when you enter a value in the box "Volunteer allowance (non-taxable)" on the T4 form.

Clergy housing allowance

If you received a housing allowance as a member of the clergy, the allowance may be included in box 14 of your T4 slip. If so, enter the amount of the allowance on the T4 form in the box Clergy housing allowance. From the Transfer clergy housing allowance drop-down list, select the T1223#: Clergy residence deduction form to which the allowance applies.

ProFile will automatically subtract the amount of the allowance from the amount in box 14 and will include the difference as employment income on line 101. ProFile will also include the allowance as other employment income on line 104. You may also be entitled to claim a clergy residence deduction on line 231.

Employment income not reported on slips

The box "Employment income not reported on slips" allows you to enter employment income which has not been reported on a T4 slip, such as tips and occasional earnings, and keeps all the employment income amounts on one form. ProFile posts these amounts as employment income on line 104 of the T1 jacket.

> **? Frequently Asked Questions**

What is reported on T-4 slips?

T4 - Statement of remuneration paid - definition

T4 slips report the wages, salary, and commission income paid to you by your employer. They also show employer-paid taxable allowances and benefits such as low-interest or interest-free loans, health care premiums, stock option benefits, and profit-sharing.

 The Canada Revenue Agency says...

 Note: An asterisk (*) indicates that the amount is included in box 14.

Box	Title	Description
Box 14	Employment income	This amount is transferred to line 101 of your T1 General.
Box 16 / 17	Employee's CPP/ QPP contributions	This amount is transferred to line 308 of Schedule 1. If you overpaid CPP or QPP, the excess is calculated on Form T2204 and, if you were a resident of Québec, Line 452 of your TP1.
Box 18	Employee's EI premiums	This amount is transferred to line 312 of Schedule 1. If you overpaid EI premiums, the excess is calculated on Form T2204.
Box 20	RPP contributions	Usually, the total of these amounts is transferred to line 207 of your T1 General.
Box 22	Income tax deducted	This amount is included on line 437 of your T1 General.
Box 24 / 26	EI Insurable earnings CPP/QPP pensionable earnings	These amounts are used to determine if you have overpaid your CPP or EI premiums. They are not taxable. These amounts are typically the same as the income amount reported in box 14. Do not be concerned if your T4 slip has no

		amounts in box 24 or 26.
Box 28	CPP/QPP, EI, or PPIP Exempt?	An **X** under CPP/QPP, EI, or PPIP in box 28 of your T4 slip indicates that your earnings are exempt from these withholdings. The majority of taxpayers are **not** exempt, so the default here is **No**.
Box 30*	Housing, board, and lodging	This is the taxable amount of the housing, board, or lodging benefit provided by your employer. This amount is already included in box 14. It is not added again to your total income.
Box 31	Special work site	This amount is for the Northern Residents Deduction.
Box 32*	Travel in a prescribed zone	Employer-provided amount for travel assistance for an employee living in a prescribed zone. This amount is already included in box 14. It is not added again to your total income.
Box 33	Medical travel	Employer-provided amount for medical travel assistance for an employee living in a prescribed zone.
Box 34*	Personal use of employer's automobile	Employer-provided automobile for the personal use of an employee. This amount is already included in box 14. It is not added again to your total income.
Box 36*	Interest free and low interest loans	This amount is already included in box 14. It is not added again to your total income.
Box 37	Employee home relocation loan deduction	This is a deduction related to the benefit in box 36, if the loan was for an eligible home relocation. This amount is transferred to line 248 of your T1 General.
Box 38*	Stock options benefits	This amount is already included in box 14. It is not added again to your total income.
Box 39	Stock option deductions	This amount is transferred to line 249 of your T1 General.
Box 40*	Other taxable allowances	These are employer-provided taxable allowances or benefits not shown elsewhere on the T4 slip. This amount is already included

	and benefits	in box 14. It is not added again to your total income.
Box 41	Stock option deductions	This amount is transferred to line 249 of your T1 General.
Box 42*	Employment commissions	This amount is already included in box 14. The amount is transferred to line 102 of your T1 General but is not added to your total income.
Box 43	Canadian forces personnel and police allowance	This amount is transferred to line 244 of your T1 General.
Box 44	Union Dues	This amount is transferred to line 212 of your T1 General.
Box 46	Charitable donations and gifts	This amount is transferred to Schedule 9. Your allowable credit is transferred to line 349 of your Schedule 1.
Box 52	Pension adjustment	This amount is transferred to line 206 of your T1 General but is not included as income nor as a deduction. It is used in determining your maximum RRSP deduction.
Box 53	Deferred security option benefits	This amount shows a taxable benefit that is deferred until the disposition of the eligible securities. This amount is transferred to line 6520 of Form T1212, Statement of Deferred Stock Option Benefits.
Box 55	Employee's PPIP Premiums	Provincial Parental Insurance Plan (PPIP) Residents of Quebec, this amount is shown at 375 of your Schedule 1. Residents of provinces or territories other than Quebec, this amount is shown at line 312 of your Schedule 1.
Box 56	PPIP Insurable Earnings	This amount is used to determine if you have overpaid your PPIP premiums, and is not taxable. This amount is typically the same as the income amount reported in box 14. Do not be concerned if your T4 slip has no amounts in box 24 or 26.

Box 70	Municipal officer's expense allowance	A municipal corporation or board paid an expense allowance to an elected officer to perform the duties of that office.
Box 71	Status Indian employee	Employer paid non-taxable salary or wages to a status Indian. This indicates your wages were non-taxable.
Box 72 / 73	Section 122.3 income (employment outside Canada) and the number of days outside Canada	This is income earned from employment outside of Canada and the amount of time spent outside Canada. These amounts are used to calculate the Overseas Employment Tax Credit for line 426 of Schedule 1. You should review Form T626, Overseas Employment Tax Credit to see if you qualify for this credit.
Box 74 / 75	Pre-1990 past-service RPP contributions	These are pre-1990 past-service contributions made to a registered pension plan either while you were a contributor (box 74) or while not a contributor (box 75). They are transferred to line 207 of your T1 General.
Box 77	Workers' compensation benefits repaid to the employer	This amount is transferred to line 229 (Other employment expenses) of your T1 General.
Box 78	Fishers - Gross earnings	The earnings of a fisher are the amount paid to the fisher from the proceeds of a catch. These earnings do not include amounts paid for a catch made by persons who were not members of the crew.
Box 79	Fishers - Net partnership amount	This is the amount in box 78, minus the amount in box 80, multiplied by your percentage of a partnership agreement. It is included in box 24.
Box 80	Fishers - Share person amount	This is the amount paid to the fisher from the proceeds of a catch based on the sharing arrangement agreed to prior to embarking on the fishing trip. It is included in box 24 and box 78.
Box 81	Placement or employment agency	Enter your information in the space provided as well as on *T2125 - Statement of Business or Professional Activities*.

	workers	
Box 82	Drivers of taxis and other passenger-carrying vehicles	Enter your information in the space provided as well as on *T2125 - Statement of Business or Professional Activities*.
Box 83	Barbers or hairdressers	Enter your information in the space provided as well as on *T2125 - Statement of Business or Professional Activities*.
Box 84	Public transit pass	You can claim the cost of monthly public transit passes or passes of longer duration such as an annual pass for travel within Canada on public transit during the year. These passes must permit unlimited travel on local buses, streetcars, subways, commuter trains or buses, and local ferries. For more information see Line 364 - Public transit amount.
Box 85	Employee-paid premiums for private health services plans	You can claim on line 330 the total eligible medical expenses you or your spouse or common-law partner paid for: • yourself; • your spouse or common-law partner; or • you or your spouse's or common-law partner's child born in 1992 or later and who depended on you for support. Medical expenses for other dependants must be claimed on line 331. For more information see Line 330 - Medical expenses for self, spouse or common-law partner, and your dependent children.

T4A - Statement of Pension, Retirement, Annuity and Other Income

T4A: Statement of pension, annuity and other income

The T4A is the Statement of Pension, Retirement, Annuity, and Other Income. Enter the amounts from the taxpayer's T4A slips into the corresponding fields of the T4A form.

Box 24: Annuities

If you answer "Yes" to the field "Box 24 received due to death of spouse?," ProFile will transfer the amount in Box 24 to line 115 of the T1 jacket (the amount is eligible for pension amount). If you answer "No", ProFile will transfer the amount to line 130.

Box 26: Retiring Allowances

If you enter an amount in Box 26: Retiring allowances (Eligible for RRSP Transfer), ProFile will automatically transfer the amount into the RRSP transfer form. This sets up the allowable transfer amount. In order to claim the RRSP deduction, you must enter the contributions into the RRSP deduction form.

Box 28: Other income

Note that Box 28 includes several different line items, all of which transfer to the Other Income form to be summed before posting to line 104 of the T1 jacket.

Frequently Asked Questions

What is reported on T4A slips?

T4A - Statement of pension, retirement, annuity and other income - definition

T4A slips show income received from pension plans, annuities, retirement allowance (including severance pay), death benefits, accumulated income payments, wage-loss replacement plans, research grants, scholarships, bursaries, lump-sum payments from deferred profit-sharing plans, medical premiums, and self-employed commission income.

The Canada Revenue Agency says...

Box	Title	Description
Box 16	Pension or superannuation	This amount is transferred to line 115 of your T1 General. If eligible, your pension amount credit is included on line 314 of your Schedule 1.
Box 18	Lump-Sum payments	This amount is included on line 130 of your T1 General.
Box 20	Self-employed commissions	This amount is transferred to Form T2125 - Statement of Business or Professional Activities.
Box 22	Income tax deducted	This amount is included on line 437 of your T1 General.
Box 24	Annuities	This amount is transferred to line 115 of your T1 General if: • you were 65 or older at the end of the year, or • the amount was received due to the death of your spouse or common-law partner (see the box below).

		If neither of the above applies, this amount is included on line 130 of your T1 General.
	Rec'd due to spouse's death	
Box 26	Eligible retiring allowances	This amount is included on line 130 of your T1 General. You may be able to transfer this amount to an RRSP or RPP and claim a deduction. For more information, see Transfers to Registered Plans or funds and annuities.
Box 27	Non-eligible retiring allowances	This amount is transferred to line 130 of your T1 General. You cannot transfer this amount to an RRSP or RPP.
Box 28	Other Income	Find the code in the footnote area of your slip (box 38) and see below.
	- Code 04, Research grants	The taxable amount is included on line 104 of your T1 General.
	- Code 05, scholarships, bursaries, fellowships, artists' project grants, and prizes	Enter the full amount of the scholarships, fellowships, bursaries and artists' project grants you received. The taxable amount is included on line 130 of your T1 General. Prizes and awards you receive as a benefit from your employment or in connection with a business are fully taxable - do not enter them here.
	- Code 06, Death benefits from employer	You may not have to pay tax on up to $10,000 of this amount (see Death benefits for more information). Enter the total benefit here. The taxable portion is included on line 130 of your T1 General.
	- Code 07, Wage-loss insurance programs	These are payments from a wage-loss replacement plan. The net amount is included on line 104 of your T1 General.
	- Code 16, Medical Travel	This shows amounts paid by your employer for medical travel. This amount is transferred to line 130 of your T1 General.

	- Code 17, Loan benefit	This amount is transferred to line 130 of your T1 General.
	- Code 18, Medical premium benefits	This amount is included in line 104 of your T1 General.
	- Code 19, Group life insurance premiums	This amount is the taxable benefit for premiums paid to cover you under a group term life-insurance plan. This amount is transferred to line 104 of your T1 General.
	- Code 23, Payments from a revoked DPSP	This amount is transferred to line 130 of your T1 General.
	- Code 25, Disability benefits from pension	This amount is transferred to line 130 of your T1 General.
	- Code 27, Veterans' benefits	This amount is transferred to line 104 of your T1 General.
	- Code 29, Tax deferred cooperative share	This amount is transferred to line 130 of your T1 General.
	- Code 30, Apprenticeship incentive grant	This amount is transferred to line 130 of your T1 General.
	- Code 31, Registered disability savings plan	This is transferred to line 125
	- Code 32, Wage Earner Protection Program	This amount is transferred to line 104 of your T1 General.
	- Code 33, Variable pension benefits	This amount is transferred to line 130 of your T1 General.
	- Other income - Code OI (Other income)	Enter all other box 28 amounts here. This amount is transferred to line 130 of your T1 General.
Box 30	Patronage allocations	Split the total between the amount for business purchases and the amount for personal purchases. The business portion is

			included in line 130 of your T1 General.
Box 32	Registered pension plan contributions (past service)		Pre-1990 past-service contributions (code 26) will be shown in the footnote codes area of your slip. Your allowable deduction is included in line 207 of your T1 General. For more information, see Registered Pension Plans.
Box 34	Pension adjustment		This amount is neither income nor a deduction. It is used in determining your maximum RRSP deduction. The amount is included on line 206 of your T1 General.
Box 40	RESP accumulated Income Payments		This amount is included on line 130 of your T1 General and Form T1172, Tax on Accumulated Income Payments from RESPs.
Box 42	RESP educational assistance		This amount is transferred to line 130 of your T1 General.
Box 46	Donations and gifts		This amount is transferred to Schedule 9. Your allowable claim is included on line 349 of Schedule 1.

T4A(OAS) - Statement of Old Age Security

T4A(OAS): Statement of Old Age Security

The T4A(OAS) is the Statement of Old Age Security. Enter the amounts from the taxpayer's T4A(OAS) slips into the corresponding ProFile fields of the T4A(OAS) form.

You may have to repay all or a part of your OAS pension (line 113) or net federal supplements (line 146) if your net income before adjustments (line 234) is more than $66,335.

If your net income before adjustments (line 234) is $66,335 or less, you can claim a deduction on line 250 for the net federal supplements on line 146. If line 234 of your return is more than $66,335 and you reported net federal supplements on line 146, you may not be entitled to claim the whole amount on line 147.

ProFile calculates the claw back and the net federal supplements deduction on the Repay form.

Frequently Asked Questions

What is reported on T4A(OAS) slips?

T4A(OAS) - Statement of Old Age Security – definition

T4A(OAS) slips show pension income received from Old Age Security benefits.

The Canada Revenue Agency says...

Tell me about the boxes on my T4A(OAS) slip

Box	Title	Description
Box 18	Taxable pension paid	This is the portion of your pension that is considered to be taxable. This amount is transferred to line 113 of your T1 General.
Box 19	Gross pension paid	This is the gross (total) amount of Old Age Security pension you received in the year.
Box 20	Overpayment recovered	This is the amount recovered from the gross Old Age Security pension amount because of an overpayment you received in a previous period. This amount is included on line 232 of your T1 General.
Box 21	Net Supplements Paid	This is the net amount of any Allowance, Allowance for the Survivor, or Guaranteed Income Supplement you received in the year. If the amount in box 21 is negative, enter 0. This amount is transferred to line 146 of your T1 General. The program also claims an offsetting deduction on line 250 of your T1 General if you qualify.
Box 22	Income tax deducted	This amount is included on line 437 of your T1 General.
Box 23	Québec Income Tax Deducted	If you were a resident of Québec, this amount is reported on your Québec return. If you were not a resident of Québec at the end of the year, this amount is transferred to line 437 of your T1 General.

T4A(P) - Statement of CPP benefits

T4A(P): Statement of Canada Pension Plan benefits

The T4A(P) is the Statement of Canada Pension Plan benefits. Enter the amounts from the taxpayer's T4A(P) slip into the corresponding fields of the T4A(P) form.

If you have retirement or disability benefits (box 14 or 16), complete field 21 to show the number of months you received these benefits. This will prorate the CPP contributions on Schedule 8 and the T2204 form.

If you qualify to claim the disability amount, you need to answer "Yes" to the question "Claim disability amount?" on the Info form. ProFile does not make the claim automatically when you enter an amount in box 16.

Frequently Asked Questions

What is reported on T4A(P) slips?

T4A(P) - Statement of Canada Pension Plan Benefits - definition

T4A(P) slips show income received from the Canada Pension Plan, including lump-sum benefits, disability benefits, retirement benefits, survivor benefits, death benefits, and child benefits received because you were the child of a deceased or disabled contributor.

The Canada Revenue Agency says...

Tell me about the boxes on my T4A(P) slips

Box	Title	Description
Box 20	Taxable CPP benefits	This amount is calculated as the sum of boxes 14 through 18. This amount is transferred to line 114 of your T1 General. It also includes any recovery of CPP overpayments or payments for arrears. If the benefits include a lump-sum payment, see line 114 for more information.
Box 21	Number of months	This is the number of months that you did not have to make CPP contributions. For example, if you started receiving benefits during the year, it should show the number of months you received CPP benefits. This will affect CPP payable on Schedule 8, as well as the calculation of overpayments on Form T2204.
Box 22	Income tax deducted	This amount is included on line 437 of your T1 General.

Note: The amounts in boxes 14 through 18 are added to calculate the amount for box 20. Enter all the amounts from boxes 14 through 18 in the

Box		Description
Box 14	Retirement benefit	This amount is your basic CPP retirement pension.
Box	Survivor	This the pension paid to the legal spouse or common-law partner of a deceased CPP

15	benefit	contributor.
Box 16	Disability benefits	These are CPP or QPP disability benefits. This amount is transferred to line 152 of your T1 General. This amount is already included in the amount in box 20. It is used in the calculation of your RRSP deduction limit.
Box 17	Child benefits	These are payments made to the child of a deceased or disabled contributor. This is income of the child, no matter who actually received the payment. If you received an amount but you are not the child, you may have to adjust the amount you report in box 20.
Box 18	Death benefit	If you received this amount and you are a beneficiary of the deceased person's estate, you can choose to include it either on line 114 of your own return, or on a *T3, Trust Income Tax and Information Return*, for the estate. Do not report it on the deceased person's individual return. If you choose to report this amount on a T3 Trust return for the estate of the deceased instead of line 114 of your T1 General, you may have to adjust the amount you report in box 20.

T4A-RCA - Statement of Distributions From a Retirement Compensation Arrangement (RCA)

T4A(RCA): Statement of Amounts Paid from a RCA

The T4A(RCA) is the Statement of Amounts Paid from a Retirement Compensation Agreement.

Enter the amounts from the taxpayer's T4A(RCA) slip into the corresponding fields of the T4A (RCA) form.

ProFile adds boxes 14 through 20 and transfers them to line 130 of the T1 jacket.

If you include an amount from box 14, 16, or 20 in your income, you may be eligible to claim a deduction online 232 of your income tax return.

If you include an amount in box 18 and you made non-deductible contributions to this RCA, or you had previously purchased an interest in this RCA, you may claim a deduction on line 232 of your income tax return.

To claim the deduction, enter the amount on the Other Deduct form under Other deductions - line 232.

❓Frequently Asked Questions

What is reported on T4A-RCA slips?

T4A-RCA - Statement of Distributions From a Retirement Compensation Arrangement - definition

The T4A-RCA slip shows payments made to you from an RCA trust.

What is an RCA?

A retirement compensation arrangement (RCA) is a plan or an arrangement under which an employer, former employer, and in some cases an employee makes contributions to a person or partnership, referred to as a custodian.

The custodian holds the funds in trust with the intent of eventually distributing them to the employee, former employee or other beneficiary on, after, or in contemplation of:

- an employee's retirement;
- an employee's loss of an office or employment; or
- any substantial change in the services the employee provides (for example, a senior corporate director who, after termination, is retained on a part time basis to teach a management course to new trainees).

An employer or former employer may acquire an interest in a life insurance policy (including an annuity) to fund benefits on, after, or in contemplation of an employee's retirement, an employee's loss of an office or employment, or any substantial change in the services the employee provides. In this case, we consider this interest to be the property of an RCA and the employer to be the custodian of the RCA.

 The Canada Revenue Agency says...

Box	Explanation of box and instructions
Box 12	This is an amount refunded to the employer. If the amount received represents a contribution the employer made to the RCA that was deductible under paragraph 20(1)(r) of the Income Tax Act, the employer has to include the amount in computing income from a business or property in the year the amount is received from the RCA.
Box 14	This is a refund of contributions that you or another beneficiary made. You have to include this amount on line 130 of your income tax and benefit return.
Box 16	This is an amount paid as benefits from the RCA. If the amount in box 16 relates to your employment, you have to report the amount on line 130 of your income tax and benefit return. If the amount relates to another person's employment, you have to include this amount in your income if that other person: • died, and this amount was not reported on the final return of the deceased; or • became a non-resident.
Box 18	This is the amount you received for selling an interest in the RCA. You have to include this amount on line 130 of your income tax and benefit return.
Box 20	You have to report this amount on line 130 of your income tax and benefit return. This amount results from certain RCA trust transactions. For more information about this amount, contact the trust's custodian.
Box	Enter this amount on line 437 of your income tax and benefit return

22	
Box 24	This is your social insurance number.

T4E - Statement of Employment Insurance benefits

T4E: Statement of employment insurance and other benefits

The T4E is the Statement of Employment Insurance and other benefits. Enter the amounts from the taxpayer's T4E slip into the corresponding fields of the T4E form.

For ProFile to calculate the claw back on the Repay form, you must enter a repayment rate in box 7 and an amount in box 15.

 The Canada Revenue Agency says...

Tell me about the boxes on my T4E slip

Box	Title	Description
Box 7	Repayment rate	If the rate is 30%, and your net income before adjustments is more than $51,375, the software a Social Benefits Repayment on line 422 and the corresponding deduction on line 235 of your T1 General.
Box 14	Total benefits paid	This amount may include benefits earned in the previous year but paid in the year shown on this slip. Box 14 includes the amounts shown in boxes 15, 17, 18, 33, and 36. This amount is transferred to line 119 of your T1 General. If your net income exceeds $51,375, see box 7 (above).
Box 15*	Regular and other benefits paid	This box includes work-sharing benefits paid, and the income benefits under section 25 of the *Employment Insurance Act*. This amount is used to calculate Social Benefits repayment, if required.
Box 17*	Employment benefits & support measures paid	This box includes EI-funded financial assistance paid while you were taking part in an approved employment program (that is not already included in Box 15).

		This amount is already included in box 14.
Box 20*	Taxable tuition assistance	This amount is included in box 17 or 33, and also in box 14. However, you may be able to claim the tuition, education, and textbook amount tax credit (see line 323 for more information). Enter the amounts from your T2202 or T2202A slips in the T2202/A entry window.
Box 21*	Non-taxable tuition assistance	This amount is included as a deduction on line 256 of your T1 General.
Box 22	Federal income tax deducted	This amount is transferred to line 437 of your T1 General.
Box 23	Québec income tax deducted	This amount is transferred to line 437 of your T1 General, or, if you live in Québec, to your Québec provincial return.
Other information		
Box 24	Non-resident tax deducted	This amount is transferred to line 437 of your T1 General.
Box 26	Overpayment recovered or repaid	The amount recovered because of an overpayment, or repaid either in cash, or as a returned warrant. It is already included in box 30.
Box 27	Reversal of federal tax deducted	This is a reversal of federal tax deducted from an amount which was directly repaid. It is already included in box 30.
Box 30	Total repayment	The amount in Box 30 is the total of boxes 26 and 27. It is claimed as a deduction on line 232 of your T1 General.
Box 33*	Consolidated revenue fund	This amount is already included in box 14.
Box 36*	Provincial Parental Insurance Plan	This amount is already included in box 14.

| | benefits | |

T4PS - Statement of Profit Sharing Payments

T4PS: Statement of employee profit-sharing plan allocations and payments

The T4PS is the Statement of Employee Profit-Sharing Plan Allocations and Payments. Enter the amounts from the taxpayer's T4PS slips into the corresponding fields of the T4PS form.

If there is foreign income and/or foreign tax paid amounts on the slip, provide the "Name of foreign country." ProFile will automatically generate the FTC, T2209 and T2036 forms with the applicable calculations.

 The Canada Revenue Agency says...

Tell me about the boxes on my T4PS slip

Box	Title	Description
Box 30	Actual amount of dividends	This is the actual amount of dividends allocated to you. This amount does not have to be entered - only the taxable amount (box 31) needs to be entered.
Box 31	Taxable amount of dividends	This amount is transferred to Section I of Schedule 4 and included to line 120 of your T1 General. This is the amount in box 30 multiplied by 125%.
Box 32	Federal dividend tax credit	You do not need to enter this amount. The software calculates it for you (using the amount in box 11) and transfers it to line 425 of Schedule 1.
Box 34	Capital gains (or losses)	This amount is transferred to line 174 of Schedule 3. If this amount has brackets around it (showing a loss), enter the amount as a negative number.
Box 35	Other income	This amount is transferred to line 104 of your T1 General.
Box 36	Total amount forfeited due to withdrawal	This amount is entered on line 229 of your T1 General and reduces your total income.

	from plan	
Box 37	Foreign non-business income	This amount is already included in box 35. It is used to calculate your foreign tax credit on Form T2209, *Federal Foreign Tax Credit*.
Box 38	Foreign capital gains or losses	This amount is already included in box 34. It is used to calculate your foreign tax credit on Form T2209, Federal Foreign Tax Credit. Do not include it on Schedule 3 since it is already included in box 34.
Box 39	Foreign non-business income tax	This amount is used to calculate your foreign tax credit on *Form T2209, Federal Foreign Tax Credit*.

T4RIF - Statement of RRIF Income

T4RIF: Statement of income from a RRIF

The T4RIF is the Statement of Income from a RRIF (Registered Retirement Income Fund). Enter the amounts from the taxpayer's T4RIF slips into the corresponding fields of the T4RIF form.

If you answer "Yes" to the field "Received due to death of spouse?" ProFile will transfer the amounts in box 16 and box 20 to line 115 of the T1 jacket (the total is eligible for the pension amount). If you answer "No", ProFile will transfer the amounts to line 130.

 The Canada Revenue Agency says...

Tell me about the boxes on my T4RIF slip

Box	Title	Description
Box 16	Taxable amounts	This amount is transferred to line 115 of your T1 General if: • you were 65 or older at the end of the year, or • the amount was received due to the death of your spouse or common-law partner (see the box below). If neither of the above applies, this amount is transferred to line 130 of your T1 General.
Y/N	Rec'd due to spouse's death?	Enter Yes if the amount in the box just above it was received due to the death of your spouse or common-law partner.

Box 18	Deemed received (by the annuitant) on death	This is the fair market value of all the property held by the RRIF at the time of the annuitant's death. This amount is transferred to line 130 of your T1 General.
Box 20	Deemed received (by the annuitant) on deregistration	This is the fair market value of all the property held by the RRIF just before the RRIF became an amended fund. This amount is transferred to line 115 of your T1 General and to Form PENSION if: • you were 65 or older at the end of the year, or • the amount was received due to the death of your spouse or common-law partner (enter Yes in the box below box 20). If neither of the above applies, this amount is transferred to line 130 of your T1 General. If your spouse or common-law partner made contributions for you, see also Boxes 26 and 32
Y/N	Rec'd due to spouse's death?	Enter Yes if the amount in the box just above it was received due to the death of your spouse or common-law partner.
Box 22	Other income or deductions	Enter amounts shown in brackets as a negative amount. This deduction is then included on line 232 of your T1 General. For a positive amount (i.e. income): • If you receive this income from a deceased annuitant's RRIF and you are either 65 years of age or over, or the beneficiary spouse or common-law partner of the deceased, the amount is transferred to line 115 of your T1 General. • If neither of the above applies, this income is included on line 130 of your T1 General.
Y/N	Rec'd due to spouse's death?	Enter Yes if the amount in the box just above it was received due to the death of your spouse or common-law partner.
Box 24	Excess amount	This is the taxable part of amounts received in the year that is more than the minimum amount. This amount is shown for

		information only and is already included in box 16.
		If your spouse or common-law partner made contributions for you, see also Boxes 26 and 32.
Boxes 26 and 32	Spousal/common-law partner RRIF?	If box 26 of your slip indicates YES, or if the SIN of the spouse or common-law partner who made the contribution is shown in box 32, enter Yes in box 26 of the entry window. The software determines how much of any amount in box 20 or 24 is attributable to you and transfers it to line 129 of your return. If you are preparing a coupled return, the amount that your spouse or common-law partner has to claim is transferred to his or her return.
Box 28	Income tax deducted	This amount is included on line 437 of your T1 General.
Box 35	Transfers on breakdown of marriage or common-law partnership	This is the amount directly transferred on breakdown of a marriage or common-law partnership. This amount is not included in income.
Box 36	Tax paid amount	The legal representative needs this amount to determine the amount to report on the deceased annuitant's final tax return. This requirement applies only to trustee RRIFs.

T4RSP - Statement of RRSP Income

T4RSP: Statement of RRSP income

The T4RSP is the Statement of Registered Retirement Savings Plan income. Enter the amounts from the taxpayer's T4RSP slips into the corresponding fields of the T4RSP form.

? Frequently Asked Questions

What is reported on T4RSP slips?

T4RSP - Statement of RRSP income - definition

T4RSP slips show income from RRSPs, commutation payments on an RRSP annuity, and withdrawals under the Lifelong Learning Plan (LLP).

 The Canada Revenue Agency says...

Tell me about the boxes on my T4RSP slip

Box	Title	Description
Box 16	Taxable amounts	This amount is transferred to line 115 of your T1 General if: • you were 65 or older at the end of the year, or • the amount was received due to the death of your spouse or common-law partner (see the box below). If neither of the above applies, this amount is transferred to line 130 of your T1 General.
Y/N	Rec'd due to spouse's death?	Enter Yes if the amount in the box just above it was received due to the death of your spouse or common-law partner.
Box 18	Deemed received (by the annuitant) on death	This is the fair market value of all the property held by the RRIF at the time of the annuitant's death. This amount is transferred to line 130 of your T1 General.
Box 20	Deemed received (by the annuitant) on deregistration	This is the fair market value of all the property held by the RRIF just before the RRIF became an amended fund. This amount is transferred to line 115 of your T1 General and to Form PENSION if: • you were 65 or older at the end of the year, or • the amount was received due to the death of your spouse or common-law partner (enter Yes in the box below box 20). If neither of the above applies, this amount is transferred to line 130 of your T1 General. If your spouse or common-law partner made contributions for you, see also Boxes 26 and 32
Y/N	Rec'd due to spouse's death?	Enter Yes if the amount in the box just above it was received due to the death of your spouse or common-law partner.
Box 22	Other income or deductions	Enter amounts shown in brackets as a negative amount. This deduction is then included on line 232 of your T1 General. For a

		positive amount (i.e. income):
		<ul><li>If you receive this income from a deceased annuitant's RRIF and you are either 65 years of age or over, or the beneficiary spouse or common-law partner of the deceased, the amount is transferred to line 115 of your T1 General.</li><li>If neither of the above applies, this income is included on line 130 of your T1 General.</li></ul>
Y/N	Rec'd due to spouse's death?	Enter Yes if the amount in the box just above it was received due to the death of your spouse or common-law partner.
Box 24	Excess amount	This is the taxable part of amounts received in the year that is more than the minimum amount. This amount is shown for information only and is already included in box 16. If your spouse or common-law partner made contributions for you, see also Boxes 26 and 32.
Boxes 26 and 32	Spousal/common-law partner RRIF?	If box 26 of your slip indicates YES, or if the SIN of the spouse or common-law partner who made the contribution is shown in box 32, enter Yes in box 26 of the entry window. The software determines how much of any amount in box 20 or 24 is attributable to you and transfers it to line 129 of your return. If you are preparing a coupled return, the amount that your spouse or common-law partner has to claim is transferred to his or her return.
Box 28	Income tax deducted	This amount is included on line 437 of your T1 General.
Box 35	Transfers on breakdown of marriage or common-law partnership	This is the amount directly transferred on breakdown of a marriage or common-law partnership. This amount is not included in income.
Box 36	Tax paid amount	The legal representative needs this amount to determine the amount to report on the deceased annuitant's final tax return. This requirement applies only to trustee RRIFs.

T5 - Statement of Investment Income

T5: Statement of investment income

The T5 is the Statement of Investment Income. Enter the amounts from the taxpayer's T5 slips into the corresponding fields of the T5 form.

Percent reported by spouse

Some T5s report amounts that are shared between spouses. If you are preparing a coupled return, enter the percent that the spouse will report. ProFile will not create a T5 slip for the spouse since there is only one slip. Instead, ProFile will transfer the percent and the spouse's share of the amounts to the related forms. For example, if you enter a value for "Taxable amount of dividends" from the Royal Bank, with 30% reported by the spouse, Schedule 4 for the taxpayer will show the description as "Royal Bank (70.0% of 20,000)" and an amount of $14,000. Schedule 4 for the spouse will show the description as "Royal Bank (30.0% of 20,000)" and an amount of $6,000.

Currency

This field has a drop-down list of the more common currencies. Click on the status box or press <Alt+Down Arrow> to choose from the list. If you choose a currency, the exchange rate appears automatically.

Exchange rate

ProFile will multiply the amounts on the T5 slip by the exchange rate before posting it to the appropriate form. For example, if you enter $1,000 for "Taxable amount of dividends" with an exchange rate of 1.20, ProFile will post the description as "1000.00 * 1.2" with an amount of $1,200 to Schedule 4.

Foreign income and tax paid

If there is foreign income and/or foreign tax paid amounts on the slip, provide the "Name of foreign country". ProFile will automatically generate the FTC, T2209 and T2036 forms with the applicable calculations.

Canada savings bonds

Financial institutions no longer issue T600s for Canada Savings Bonds (CSBs). Instead they issue T5 slips to report the interest income earned.

 The Canada Revenue Agency says...

Box	Title	Description
Box 10	Actual amounts of dividends	This shows the amount of dividends received. You do not need to enter this amount.

| Box 11 | Taxable amount of dividends | This is the amount that you report as income.

This amount is transferred to Section I of Schedule 4 and included to line 120 of your T1 General. |
|---|---|---|
| Box 12 | Federal dividend tax credit | You do not need to enter this amount. The software calculates it for you (using the amount in box 11) and transfers it to line 425 of Schedule 1. |
| Box 13 | Interest from Canadian sources | This amount is transferred to Section II of Schedule 4 and to line 121 of your T1 General. |
| Box 14 | Employment income | This amount is transferred to line 101 of your T1 General. |
| Box 15 | Foreign income | This amount is transferred to Section II of Schedule 4 and to line 121 of your T1 General. |
| Box 16 | Foreign tax paid | This amount is transferred to Form FTC and is used to calculate your foreign tax credit. This credit is included in Other deductions on line 232 of your T1 General. |
| Box 17 | Royalties from Canadian sources | Click this box to open the secondary data-entry window. Click Other boxes to go to the secondary data-entry screen.

If the royalties are from a work or invention, the amount is transferred to line 104 of your T1 General. Otherwise it is transferred to line 121. |
| Box 18 | Capital gains dividends | This amount is transferred to line 174 of Schedule 3. |
| Box 19 | Accrued income annuities | The general annuity earnings are included on line 115 of your T1 General. You may qualify for a credit at line 314 if:

- you were 65 or older at the end of the year, or
- the amount was received due to the death of your spouse or common-law partner (see box 20, below).

If neither of the above applies, this amount is included on line 130 of your T1 General. |

	Received due to spouse's death?	Enter Yes if the amount in box 19 was received due to the death of your spouse or common-law partner.
Box 20	Eligible resource allowable deduction	You may be able to claim 25% of the amount in box 20 as a resource allowance deduction. This calculation is done on Form T1229, and the resulting deduction is transferred to line 224 of your T1 General. This amount is included in box 17.
Box 21	Report code	The code in this box indicates that the slip is the original ("0") or an amended ("1") slip.
Box 22	Recipient identification number	If you are an individual (other than a trust), the number in this box is your SIN. In all other cases, the number is your Business Number.
Box 23	Recipient type	The code in this box indicates if the amount was paid to an individual ("1"); a joint account ("2"); a corporation ("3"); an association, trust, club, or other ("4"); or a government ("5").
Source country	Source country of foreign income	

Entering T101 (Statement of resource expenses) slips

T101: Statement of renounced resource expense

The T101 slip is the statement of renounced resource expense. Enter the amounts from the taxpayer's T101 slips into the corresponding fields of the T101 form.

The CEE, CDE and COGPE expenses are additions to the pools for the current year. ProFile posts these to the appropriate place on the Resource summary.

❓ Frequently Asked Questions

What is reported on T101 slips?

What is reported on T101 slips?

A T101 slip is completed for each person who owns flow-through shares for which a renunciation of Canadian resource expenses, an adjustment to an amount previously renounced, or an allocation of assistance has been made.

The renunciation must be made in the name of the shareholder and not the agent. Only the original shareholder is entitled to the renunciation. Expenses are deemed to be incurred on the effective date of renunciation by the person to whom they are renounced, and never to have been incurred by the corporation.

 **The Canada Revenue Agency says...**

Most of the amounts on the T101 are transferred to Form T1229, Statement of exploration and development expenses and depletion allowance.

Box	Title	Description
Box 10	Actual amounts of dividends	This shows the amount of dividends received. You do not need to enter this amount.
Box 11	Taxable amount of dividends	This is the amount that you report as income. This amount is transferred to Section I of Schedule 4 and included to line 120 of your T1 General.
Box 12	Federal dividend tax credit	You do not need to enter this amount. The software calculates it for you (using the amount in box 11) and transfers it to line 425 of Schedule 1.
Box 13	Interest from Canadian sources	This amount is transferred to Section II of Schedule 4 and to line 121 of your T1 General.
Box 14	Employment income	This amount is transferred to line 101 of your T1 General.
Box 15	Foreign income	This amount is transferred to Section II of Schedule 4 and to line 121 of your T1 General.
Box 16	Foreign tax paid	This amount is transferred to Form FTC and is used to calculate your foreign tax credit. This credit is included in Other deductions on line 232 of your T1 General.
Box 17	Royalties from Canadian sources	Click this box to open the secondary data-entry window. Click Other boxes to go to the secondary data-entry screen. If the royalties are from a work or invention, the amount is transferred to

		line 104 of your T1 General. Otherwise it is transferred to line 121.
Box 18	Capital gains dividends	This amount is transferred to line 174 of Schedule 3.
Box 19	Accrued income annuities	The general annuity earnings are included on line 115 of your T1 General. You may qualify for a credit at line 314 if: • you were 65 or older at the end of the year, or • the amount was received due to the death of your spouse or common-law partner (see box 20, below). If neither of the above applies, this amount is included on line 130 of your T1 General.
	Received due to spouse's death?	Enter Yes if the amount in box 19 was received due to the death of your spouse or common-law partner.
Box 20	Eligible resource allowable deduction	You may be able to claim 25% of the amount in box 20 as a resource allowance deduction. This calculation is done on Form T1229, and the resulting deduction is transferred to line 224 of your T1 General. This amount is included in box 17.
Box 21	Report code	The code in this box indicates that the slip is the original ("0") or an amended ("1") slip.
Box 22	Recipient identification number	If you are an individual (other than a trust), the number in this box is your SIN. In all other cases, the number is your Business Number.
Box 23	Recipient type	The code in this box indicates if the amount was paid to an individual ("1"); a joint account ("2"); a corporation ("3"); an association, trust, club, or other ("4"); or a government ("5").
Source country	Source country of foreign income	

T2202/T2202A - Tuition, Education, and Textbook Certificate

T2202A: Tuition and education credit certificate

The T2202A is the Tuition and education credit certificate. Enter the amounts from the taxpayer's T2202A slips into the corresponding fields of the T2202A form.

Complete Schedule 11, Federal Tuition and Education Amounts, to calculate the federal amount you can claim on line 323 of Schedule 1.

If you resided in Newfoundland and Labrador, PEI, Nova Scotia, Ontario, Saskatchewan, Alberta, British Columbia, Northwest Territories or Nunavut on December 31, also complete the provincial or territorial Schedule (S11), Provincial (or Territorial) Tuition and Education Amounts, to calculate the amount you can claim on line 5856 of Form 428.

Frequently Asked Questions

What is reported on T2202 and T2202A slips?

T2202/2202A - Tuition, Education, and Textbook Amounts Certificate - definition

This certificate shows a student's educational institution, program or course, dates of registration, eligible tuition, and qualifying months for the education amount.

What are eligible fees and programs?

Eligible tuition fees and programs

Qualifying courses

Generally, a course qualifies if it was taken in the calendar year, and:

- it was taken at the post-secondary level or
- it develops or improves skills in an occupation, you were 16 or over at the end of the year, and the educational institution has been certified by Human Resources and Social Development Canada.

Tuition fees paid to any one institution have to be more than $100 in a calendar year.

Things you can claim

The following are eligible tuition fees and expenses:

- admission fees;
- charges for laboratory or library facilities;
- examination fees;
- application fees (but only if you later enroll in the institution);
- charges for a certificate, diploma, or degree;
- mandatory computer service fees;
- academic fees;
  the cost of any books that are included in the total fees for a correspondence course taken through a post secondary educational institution in Canada; and
- fees, such as athletic and health services fees, paid to a university, college, or other educational institution in addition to your tuition for post-secondary courses, when such fees are required to be paid by all students. The amount of eligible fees is limited to $250 if the fees do not have to be paid by all students.

Things you can't claim

The following fees and expenses are not eligible tuition expenses. You cannot claim:

- cost of books (other than books that are included in the total fees for a correspondence course). However, you may be entitled to the textbook amount.
- student association fees;
- medical expenses;
- transportation and parking;
- meals and lodging.
- goods of lasting value that you will keep, such as a computer, microscope, uniform, or an academic gown;
- initiation or entrance fees to a professional organization;
- private elementary or secondary school tuition (e.g., grade 1 through grade 12), preschool, play school, or camp fees (although you might be able to claim these as a child care expense;
- high school upgrade courses as a prerequisite to university or college entrance;
- private tutoring;
- summer school programs (unless they are part of a post-secondary program, such as a college summer semester);
- music, art, drama, or dance lessons (unless in conjunction with a post-secondary educational program, such as a Bachelor of Fine Arts or teaching certificate);
- driver's education.

 The Canada Revenue Agency says...

About the boxes on T2202 or TL11A or TL11C slips

	Eligible tuition fees	Enter your eligible tuition fees from column A of your T2202A. These amounts are transferred to the federal Schedule 11 and to line 323 of Schedule 1 (if it is needed to reduce your tax owing). For those provinces that offer a tuition and education amount, these amounts are also transferred to the provincial Schedule 11 and to line 5856 of your provincial Form 428.
B	Number of part-time months	Enter the total number* of part-time months from column B of your T2202, T2202A, TL11A or TL11C slip. TL11B and TL11D slips do not show the number of months and are not eligible for the education amount.
C	Number of full-time months	Enter the total number* of full-time months from column C of your T2202, T2202A, TL11A or TL11C slip. TL11B and TL11D slips do not show the number of months and are not eligible for the education amount.

 Notes

*You can only count any month once. For example, if you were in program A at the beginning of June, and in program B at another institution at the end of June, make sure you do not include June twice when you enter the number of months.

Student's authorization to transfer tuition, education, and textbook amounts

Tax Tip: You may not need all of your education amount to reduce your federal and/or provincial income tax to zero. In this case, you may be able to transfer all or part of your tuition, education, and textbook amount to a parent or grandparent (including in-laws) or to your spouse or common-law partner. See Tuition, education, and textbook amounts transferred - line 324 and Amounts transferred from your spouse - line 326 for details.

T5006: Labour-sponsored funds tax credit

A taxpayer may invest in a federal or provincial labour-sponsored fund. A T5006, Statement of Labour Sponsored Funds Tax Credit, is issued for investments in federal funds. For investments in provincial funds, a provincial slip is issued.

In ProFile, the T5006 works like other slips in ProFile; each slip has its separate column. Enter the amounts from the provincial/territorial slips in the Provincial funds section. ProFile then calculates the provincial credit and the corresponding federal credit. When the contribution is for a registered fund that is only registered federally, enter the amounts in the Federal funds section.

For residents of Ontario, if the labour-sponsored investment fund qualifies as a research-oriented investment fund (ROIF), you can claim an additional provincial credit of 5% of the cost of the shares. The maximum amount of the credit you can claim is $250. To claim the additional provincial credit, go to the Ontario row under Provincial funds answer "Yes" to the question "ROIF eligible".

For residents of Saskatchewan, if you invested in a labour-sponsored venture capital corporation that is registered in Saskatchewan, the maximum provincial credit you can claim is $1,000. Enter this contribution in the Provincial funds section. If you invested in a labour-sponsored venture capital corporation that is only registered federally, the maximum provincial credit you can claim is $525. Enter this contribution in the Federal funds section. The total maximum provincial labour-sponsored venture capital tax credit you can claim is $1,000. The total maximum federal labour-sponsored venture capital tax credit you can claim is $750.

Federal credit details transfer to lines 413 and 414 of the federal Schedule 1. Provincial credit details transfer to the provincial forms of the taxpayer's province of residence.

RRSP contributions

If the investment in the Labour-Sponsored Fund is made from an RRSP, enter the amounts in the RRSP contribution table at the bottom of the form. Typically, in this case, you will receive both a T5006 and an RRSP contribution slip for the amount. ProFile will automatically transfer the RRSP contribution to the RRSP deduction worksheet. To avoid double-counting, do not enter the RRSP contribution on the RRSP deduction form.

If a spousal RRSP makes the investment to a labour-sponsored fund, the tax credit is available to either the taxpayer or the spouse.

T5007 - Statement of benefits

T5007: Statement of benefits

The T5007 is the Statement of Benefits. Enter the amounts from the taxpayer's T5007 slip into the corresponding fields of the T5007 form.

If you received workers' compensation benefits and/or social assistance payments, report each of these amounts as income. However, you do not pay tax on them, since you can claim a deduction on line 250 that equals the amount you report as income. CRA includes the amounts in net income for the calculation of provincial credits.

For federal purposes, ProFile posts the information entered on the T5007 slips to the T1 jacket as income on lines 144 and 145> and as a deduction on line 250.

Workers' compensation benefits

You may have repaid salary or wages originally paid to you by your employer in a previous year, in anticipation of workers' compensation benefits you would receive. This amount should be shown in box 77 of your T4 slips. In this situation, you may be able to claim a deduction on line 229.

Social assistance payments

For federal purposes, if you lived with your spouse or common-law partner when you received the social assistance payments or provincial or territorial supplements, the spouse or common-law partner with the higher net income has to report all of the payments, no matter whose name is on the slip. If you and your spouse or common-law partner have the same net income, the person whose name is on the T5007 (or the prestataire on the federal part of the Relevé 5) slip has to report this amount. The spouse or common-law partner who reports this amount as income can claim an equivalent deduction on line 250.

ProFile does not transfer the social assistance payments to the spouse or common-law partner with the higher net income. Instead a diagnostic notifies the preparer that the social assistance income should be reported on the spouses return.

 The Canada Revenue Agency says...

Box 10	Workers' compensation benefits	This amount is transferred to line 144 and included as a deduction on line 250 of your T1 General.
Box 11	Social assistance payments / provincial or territorial supplements	If you did not live with a spouse or common-law partner when you received these payments, enter the amount from box 11 of your slip. This amount is transferred to line 145 and included as a deduction on line 250 of your T1 General.
Box	Manitoba Credit Fraction	For Manitoba residents, the amount from box 14 is transferred to line

| 14 | (Manitoba only) | 6130 of the Manitoba Tax Credits Form MB479. |

T5008 - Statement of securities transactions

T5008: Statement of securities transactions

The T5008 is the Statement of securities transactions. Enter the amounts from the taxpayer's T5008 slip into the corresponding fields of the T5008 form.

The disposition of shares and other securities usually gives rise to a capital gain or loss whereas bearer debt obligations usually give rise to interest income.

If you select "Shares and other securities" from the drop-down list, enter the proceeds of disposition, the adjusted cost base and any outlays and expenses related to the disposition, on the T5008 form. ProFile will automatically calculate the capital gain or loss and will post it to Schedule 3.

If you select "Bearer debt obligations" from the drop-down list, enter the proceeds of disposition, the adjusted cost base and any outlays and expenses related to the disposition on the T5008 form. ProFile will automatically calculate the net investment income and will post it to Part II of Schedule 4.

Percent reported by spouse

Some T5008 slips report amounts that are shared between spouses. If you are preparing a coupled return, enter the percent that the spouse will report. ProFile will not create a T5008 slip for the spouse since there is only one slip. Instead, ProFile will calculate the spouse's share of capital gains/losses and net investment income and will transfer these amounts to the related forms. For example, if your T5008 slip shows a capital gain of $4,700 of which 30% will be reported by the spouse, the Schedule 3 for the taxpayer will show a capital gain of $4,700 * 70% = $3,290 at line 174. The Schedule 3 for the spouse will show a capital gain of $4,700 * 30% = $1,410 at line 174.

Currency

This field has a drop-down list of the more common currencies. Click on the status box or press <Alt+Down Arrow> to choose from the list. If you choose a currency, the exchange rate appears automatically.

Exchange rate

ProFile will multiply the amounts on the T5008 slips by the exchange rate before posting it to the appropriate form. For example, if you enter $1,000 as "Bearer debt obligations" with an exchange rate of 1.20, ProFile will post the description as "1,000 * 1.2" with an amount of $1,200 to the Schedule 4.

Frequently Asked Questions

What is reported on T5008 slips?

This slip reports the amount paid or credited to you for securities you disposed of or redeemed during the year indicated. These transactions may show interest income (shown on Schedule 4) or capital gains (shown on Schedule 3).

The Canada Revenue Agency says...

Box 14	Date (mmdd)	This is the date on which the transaction was complete (settlement date). If there were multiple transactions throughout the year, the date shown is 1231 (December 31). Enter the date in format **dd/mm/yyyy**.
Box 16	Quantity of securities	This is the number of securities involved in the transaction. For gold, this represents ounces. For capital types of income, this information is transferred to Schedule 3, Capital Gains or Losses. Enter to two decimal places.
Box 17	Identification of securities	This shows a description of the securities (e.g., Treasury Bill, banker's acceptance, shares of XYZ Corporation, debt obligation in bearer form). For capital types of income, this information is transferred to Form S3 SUPP, Schedule 3 Supplemental Statement and Schedule 3, Capital Gains or Losses.
Box 20	Cost or book value	This is the cost or book value of the securities involved in the transaction (i.e. the amount you paid for the securities). The software subtracts this amount from the proceeds of settlement. For capital types of income, it is transferred to Form S3 SUPP, Schedule 3 Supplemental Statement and Schedule 3, Capital Gains or Losses under Adjusted Cost Base. If this amount is greater than the amount in box 21, the software calculates a **loss** on Schedule 3 and line 127.
Box 21	Proceeds or settlement amount	This is the total amount of money received by or credited to the recipient in exchange for the securities. You have to prepare a T5008 slip for all reportable transactions, regardless of the amount of proceeds. There is no administrative limit for reporting securities transactions. Enter, in dollars only, the total proceeds received by or credited to the recipient in exchange for the securities. This is used in calculating the net investment income or capital gain/loss. For capital types of income, this is transferred to Form S3 SUPP, Schedule 3 Supplemental Statement and Schedule 3, Capital Gains or Losses under Proceeds of Disposition.

	Outlays and expenses	These are amounts that you incurred to sell a capital property, and include finders' fees, commissions, brokers' fees, legal fees, and transfer taxes.
		This amount is subtracted from the proceeds of settlement. For capital types of income, it is transferred to Schedule 3 under Outlays and Expenses.

The following boxes are shown on your T5008 slip **for information purposes**, and are not required by the software.

	Year	Indicates the year when the security transaction sale occurred. Report transactions in the tax year in which they occur.
Box 10	Report Code	Indicates whether slip is Original (**0**), amended (**A**), or cancelled (**C**).
		Be sure to report the same transaction **only once**. If you have an original and an amended T5008 slip for the same transaction, **only** report the amended slip, and not the original. However, keep both slips for your records.
		Do not report a cancelled slip.
Box 11	Recipient type	Indicates the type of person or account.
		1 = individual
		2 = joint account
		3 = corporation
		4 = other, e.g., association, trust (fiduciary-trustee, nominee, or estate), club, or partnership.
Box 12	Recipient identification number	When the recipient type in box 11 is an individual ("1") or joint account ("2"), this shows the SIN of the first individual identified as a recipient on the slip.
		When the recipient type in box 11 is a corporation ("3") or other ("4"), this shows the first nine digits of the recipient's Business Number (BN).
Box 13	Foreign currency	This indicates the foreign currency in which the proceeds of disposition (box 21) were received.
		If the transaction was in Canadian funds, this box is blank.
Box 15	Type code of securities	Indicates the type of security.

		BON - Bonds
		BO1 - A bulk transaction in bonds for which the quantity cannot be determined
		DOB - Debt obligations in bearer form
		DO1 - A bulk transaction in debt obligations in bearer form for which the quantity cannot be determined
		FUT - Futures
		MET - Precious metals
		MFT - Units in a mutual fund trust or investment fund trust
		MSC - Miscellaneous
		OPC - Option contracts
		PTI - Publicly traded interest in a trust or partnership
		RTS - Rights
		SHS - Shares
		UNT - Units (e.g., a unit consisting of a bond and a warrant)
		WTS - Warrants
Box 18	ISIN/CUSIP number	This is the CUSIP number (Committee on Uniform Securities Identification Procedures) or ISIN number (International Securities Identification Number).
Box 19	Face amount	For bonds and other debt obligations, this is the nominal value that appears on the face of the document (i.e., the amount to be repaid at maturity).
		This box is blank if the security does not have a face amount (e.g., shares or commodities).
Boxes 22, 23, and 24	Securities received on settlement	In some securities transactions, securities are received instead of proceeds of disposition. This usually happens in exchange or conversion transactions. You should complete boxes 22, 23, and 24 only when you cannot readily determine the value of the securities received on settlement. Do not report any monetary values in these boxes. Report in box 21 any part of the proceeds that is credited in money.

T5013 - Statement of partnership income

T5013/T5013A: Statement of partnership income

The T5013/T5013A is the Statement of Partnership Income. Enter the amounts from the taxpayer's T5013/T5013A slip into the corresponding fields of the T5013/T5013A form. The ID information in the first several fields of the T5013/T5013A form is required for EFILE.

Industry code

To choose the Standard industry classification from a list of available codes, press <F6> or right click and select SIC codes from the context-sensitive menu.

Source of net income (loss)

If the slip shows an amount entered in boxes 20 to 23, 30, 35, 37, 39, 41 or 43, select the appropriate box from the drop-down list from the Source of net income (loss) row. Enter the amount for this box on the row immediately below labeled Net income (loss) - Total. For example, if your slip shows an amount of $10,000 in box 35, you should select 35: (135) Business income as your source of net income (loss) and enter $10,000 as your Net income (loss) - Total.

If the slip shows amounts entered in more than one of the aforementioned boxes, complete a separate slip for each income source.

Amounts entered on the T5013 automatically flow through to the related business statements.

Foreign income and tax paid

If the slip shows foreign income and/or foreign tax paid, complete the Name of foreign country field. ProFile will automatically generate the FTC, T2209 and T2036 forms for the selected country with the applicable calculations. If the slip shows foreign income and/or foreign tax paid from more than one country, complete a separate slip for each country.

Resource expenses

The CEE, CDE and COGPE expenses (lines 39, 40 and 41) are additions to the pools for the current year. ProFile posts these amounts to the appropriate lines of the Resource form.

 The Canada Revenue Agency says...

Boxes are listed here in numerical order; they may appear in a different order on your paper slip.

Box	Description	Reporting Instructions
	Partnership information	Enter the Partnership's name, Business number, Fiscal period start and end dates, and Industry code. If this is the partnership's final fiscal year, enter **Yes** next to this question.
		If you're unsure of your industry code, see Industry Codes and click on your business type or profession for a complete list of

		codes.
02 to 03	Partnership's filer ID number/Tax shelter ID number	CRA uses this information for identification purposes. If the partnership is a Tax Shelter, see also Form T5004. Your partnership identification number is **9 characters long (2 letters followed by 7 digits)**. Enter all 9 characters in the space provided. Your tax shelter ID is **8 characters long (always the letters TS followed by 6 digits**.
08	Member code	This shows the partner's membership status within the partnership: "0" is a limited partner, "1" is a specified member who is not a limited partner, and "2" is a general partner. Code "3" is for a limited partner's exempt interest. If box 08 is code 2, then the amount in box 18 (business income) will go to one of line 126, 130, 135, 137, 139, 141, or 143 of your tax return (depending on the code in box 05). If Box 09 is code 0, 1, or 3, or if the codes entered in box 05 or box 09 are not valid, the amount from box 18 will go to line 122 - Limited Partnership Income.
10	Partner's share (%) of partnership income (loss)	Enter your percentage share of the partnership. This is for information purposes, and does not affect calculations the software makes with the amounts entered on this screen. Most amounts shown on the T5013 slip represent **only your share** of the total partnership income (or loss).
11 & 12	Recipient's identification number; Complex sharing arrangements	These are for information purposes only and do not need to be entered.
20	Limited partnership farming income (loss)	This income is included at line 141 of your return.
20.1	Agricultural income stabilization (CAIS)	This income is included on the T1163 - Statement A, CAIS Program Information and Statement of Farming Activities for Individuals or T1273 - Harmonized CAIS Program Information and Statement of Farming Activities for Individuals, whichever applies to you.
21	Limited partnership fishing income (loss)	This income is included at line 143 of your return.
22	Limited partnership	This income is included on Schedule 4 and shown at line 135 of

	business income (loss)	your return.
22.1	Limited partner's at-risk amount	If there is no amount in this box, you cannot claim any losses shown in boxes 20, 21, 22, and 26.
23	Limited partnership rental income (loss)	This amount is transferred to Form T776 and included on line 126 - Rental Income.
24	Limited partnership loss available for carry forward	This is the part of your current-year limited partnership loss that you **cannot** deduct on the current year's T1 return. You can only deduct it from the same partnership's income in future years if you have a positive at-risk amount after applying paragraph 111(1)(e) of the Act. You can carry it forward indefinitely.
25	Previous loss carry forward eligible in the current year	This is the limited partnership loss from previous years that you can claim in the current year. It is shown at line 251 of your T1 General.
26	Canadian and foreign net rental income (loss)	This amount is entered on Form T776 and included on line 126 - Rental Income.
26.1	Foreign rental income that is exempt from Canadian tax due to a tax convention or agreement	This amount is included in line 26 and is used to calculate your foreign tax credit for the country named. This credit is shown at line 405 of Schedule 1.
30	Other income	This amount is included at line 130 of your T1 General.
34	Partnership's total gross income	This is the total gross income for the partnership from all sources. This amount is shown at line 162 (business), 164 (professional), 166 (commission), 168 (farming), or 170 (fishing) of the T1 General.
35	Business income (loss)	This is your **net** income from business. It is shown on your T2125 - *Statement of Business or Professional Activities* and at line 135 of your T1 General.
35.1	Foreign business income that is exempt from Canadian tax due to a tax convention or agreement	This amount is included in box 35. It is used to calculate your foreign tax credit for the country named. This credit is shown at line 405 of Schedule 1.
37	Professional income (loss)	This is your **net** income from professional activities. It is shown on your Form 2125, *Statement of Business or Professional Activities* and at line 137 of your T1 General.
39	Commission income (loss)	This is your **net** income from commission. It is shown on your T2125 - *Statement of Business or Professional Activities* and at line 139 of your T1 General.

41	Farming income (loss)	This is your **net** income from farming. It is shown on your T2042 - Statement of Farming Activities, T1163 - CAIS Program Information and Statement of Farming Activities for Individuals, or T1273 - Statement A - Harmonized CAIS Program Information and Statement of Farming Activities. It is also shown at line 141 of your T1 General. You could have a restricted farm loss.
43	Fishing income (loss)	This is your **net** income from fishing. It is shown on your T2121 - Statement of Fishing Activities and at line 143 of your T1 General.
50	Interest from Canadian sources	This amount is shown at line 121 of Schedule 4.
51.1	Taxable non-eligible dividends	This is the taxable amount of dividends (**other than eligible dividends**) for partners that are individuals resident in Canada (other than a trust that is a registered charity), including partnerships and trusts that are eligible for the federal dividend tax credit. These amounts are shown at line 180 of Schedule 4.
52.1	Taxable eligible dividends	This is the taxable amount of **eligible** dividends for partners that are individuals resident in Canada (other than a trust that is a registered charity), including partnerships and trusts that are eligible for the federal dividend tax credit. These amounts are shown at line 120 of Schedule 4.
55	Foreign dividend and interest income	This amount is shown at line 121 of Schedule 4.
55.1	Foreign investment income that is exempt from Canadian tax due to a tax convention or agreement	This amount is included in line 54 and is used to calculate your foreign tax credit for the country named. This credit is shown at line 405 of Schedule 1.
56	Business investment loss	This amount is your gross business investment loss. It is calculated and shown at line 228 of your T1 General.
57	Dividend rental arrangement compensation payments	This amount is shown at line 221 of Schedule 4.
58	Other investment income	This amount is shown in Area II (line 121) of Schedule 4.

59	Carrying charges	This amount is your share of the carrying charges for earning all investment income. It is shown at line 221 of your T1 General.
70	Capital gains (losses)	Click the Box 70 button to enter amounts shown in boxes 70-1 through 70-18 on your paper slip. This amount is included at line 174 of Schedule 3 - Capital Gains (or Losses) and at line 127 of your T1 General.
71	Capital gains reserves	Click the Box 71 button to enter amounts shown in boxes 71-1 through 71-8 on your paper slip. This amount is used to complete Form T2017 - Summary of reserves on dispositions of capital property. The result is included on Schedule 3 and at line 127 of your T1 General.
80	Income tax deducted	This amount is included at line 437 of your T1 General.
81	Foreign tax paid on non-business income	This amount is used to calculate your foreign tax credits on your foreign non-business income. This credit is shown at line 405 of Schedule 1.
82	Foreign tax paid on business income	This amount is used to calculate your foreign tax credits on your foreign business income. This credit is shown at line 405 of Schedule 1.
90	Canadian exploration expenses (CEE)	This amount is used to calculate your allowable deduction for your cumulative Canadian exploration expense (CCEE) pool on Form T1229 - Statement of Exploration and Development Expenses and Depletion Allowance. This amount is included at line 224 of your T1 General
91	Canadian development expenses (CDE)	This amount is used to calculate your allowable deduction for your cumulative Canadian development expense (CCDE) pool on Form T1229 - Statement of Exploration and Development Expenses and Depletion Allowance. This amount is included at line 224 of your T1 General
92	Canadian oil and gas property expenses (COGPE)	This amount is used to calculate your allowable deduction for your cumulative Canadian oil and gas property expenses (CCOGPE) pool on Form T1229 - Statement of Exploration and Development Expenses and Depletion Allowance. This amount is included at line 224 of your T1 General.
93	Foreign exploration and development expenses	This amount is added to your development expense pool in Area III of Form T1229 - Statement of Exploration and

	(FEDE)	Development Expenses and Depletion Allowance.
94	Recapture of earned depletion	This is your share of the recapture of earned depletion that the partnership used to arrive at the net income (loss) shown in boxes 30, 35, 37, 41, and 43. It is calculated on Form T1229 and included in line 224 of your T1 General.
95	Amount eligible for a resource allowance deduction	This is your share of the resource profits that the partnership used to arrive at the net income (loss) shown in box 35. It is calculated on Form T1229 and included in line 224 of your T1 General.
96	Assistance for Canadian exploration expenses	This amount is used to calculate your allowable deduction for your cumulative Canadian exploration expense (CCEE) pool on Form T1229 - Statement of Exploration and Development Expenses and Depletion Allowance. This amount is included at line 224 of your T1 General
97	Assistance for Canadian development expenses	This amount is used to calculate your allowable deduction for your cumulative Canadian development expense (CCDE) pool on Form T1229 - Statement of Exploration and Development Expenses and Depletion Allowance. This amount is included at line 224 of your T1 General
98	Assistance for Canadian oil and gas property expenses	This amount is used to calculate your allowable deduction for your cumulative Canadian oil and gas property expense (CCOGPE) pool on Form T1229 - Statement of Exploration and Development Expenses and Depletion Allowance. This amount is included at line 224 of your T1 General.
103	Eligible amount of charitable donations and government gifts	This amount is included in line 1 on Schedule 9 - Donations and Gifts. The donation credit is calculated and shown at line 349 of Schedule 1.
104	Eligible amount of cultural and ecological gifts	This amount is included in line 342 on Schedule 9 - Donations and Gifts. The donation credit is calculated and shown at line 349 of Schedule 1.
105	Eligible amount of federal political contributions	This amount is included in the political tax credit calculated at line 409 of Schedule 1.
106	Eligible amount of provincial and territorial	This amount is included in the political tax credit calculated on the provincial form.

		political contributions	
107		Investment tax credit	This amount is used to complete Form T2038 - Investment Tax Credit (Individuals) and line 412 of your T1 General.
108		Excess ITC captures	Excess ITC captures are shown on Form T2038 - Investment Tax Credit (Individuals).
120 to 125		CEE or CDE renunciation and assistance	This is your share of renunciation or assistance for Canadian exploration expenses (CEE) or Canadian development expenses (CDE). The amounts reported here depend on whether you are a general or a limited partner. These amounts are transferred to Area I of Form T1229 - Statement of Exploration and Development Expenses and Depletion Allowance.
130		Portion of expenses or reduction subject to an interest-free period (CEE)	This is your share of the reduction that is available for the interest-free period. These amounts are transferred to the bottom of Area I on Form T1229.
128		Expenses qualifying for an ITC	This is your share of any Canadian exploration expenses (surface exploration in the mining sector only) that qualify for ITC. This amount is transferred to Area I of Form T1229.
141 to 145		Expenses qualifying for a provincial tax credit	This is your share of any Canadian exploration expenses (mining only) that qualify for a provincial tax credit. You may be eligible for a provincial tax credit on qualifying expenditures. See Provincial tax and credits for more information. The provincial credit is also transferred to Area IV of Form T1229.
162		Gross business income (loss)	This amount is shown at line 162 of your T1 General.
164		Gross professional income (loss)	This amount is shown at line 164 of your T1 General.
166		Gross commission income (loss)	This amount is shown at line 166 of your T1 General.
168		Gross farming income (loss)	This amount is shown at line 168 of your T1 General.
170		Gross fishing income (loss)	This amount is shown at line 170 of your T1 General.
Other Information		Source Country of foreign income	This indicates the country where the income shown was generated or earned. Use Country #2 and Country #3 as temporary placeholders to represent source countries other

		than the U.S.A.

RC62 - Universal Child Care Benefit (UCCB) statement

UCCB - Universal Child Care Benefit

Since July 2006, if you are an eligible individual responsible for the care of a child under 6 years of age, you are eligible to receive $100 per month for each qualified dependant. You do not need to apply for the UCCB if either of the following situations applies to you. The benefit will be sent to you automatically if:

- you already receive the CCTB or CDB (if applicable) for your children under 6 years of age; or
- you have applied for the CCTB or CDB (if applicable) for your children under 6 years of age, and do not receive it (perhaps because your family income is too high).

If neither of these situations applies to you, then you will have to apply for the UCCB by completing Form * RC66, Canada Child Tax Benefit Application.

The UCCB slip in ProFile allows you to enter the amount shown in box 10 of your RC62 slip. (Enter UCCB in the Form Explorer to activate the slip).

While the UCCB is taxable in the hands of the spouse or common-law partner with the lower net income, it will not be taken into account in calculating your GST/HST credit, your CCTB payments and any related provincial or territorial benefit, social benefits repayment (line 235), and the refundable medical expense supplement (line 452).

If you had a spouse or common-law partner on December 31, the one with the lower net income must report the UCCB. Otherwise you have to report the UCCB you received.

The UCCB amount that you enter in ProFile will display on both the taxpayer's and the spouse's UCCB slips. However, ProFile will automatically determine which spouse reports the amount (based on the lower net income) and include it in the total income on line 150.

Note: Form RC66 is only available in ProFile FX.

Universal Child Care Benefit (UCCB) repayment

In 2009", a taxpayer (or his/her spouse or common-law partner) may have repaid an amount that was included in his/her income for 2008. The spouse who reported the UCCB income for the previous year may deduct the repayment amount.

Enter the amount in box 12 (taxpayer or spouse line, as applicable) of form RC62. ProFile will automatically transfer this amount to line 213 - Universal Child Care Benefit repayment on the T1 Jacket of the person deducting the repayment amount.

Note: In coupled returns the amounts will flow between the spousal returns; if returns are prepared individually, enter the data on both returns, but make sure to enter the amount on the appropriate lines of box 12.

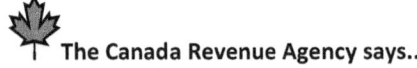 **The Canada Revenue Agency says...**

Box 10, Total benefit paid	This is the total benefit paid minus any repayment for the current year (including any lump sum payment). • If you did not have a spouse or common-law partner at the end of the year, enter this amount on line 117 of your return. • If you had a spouse or common-law partner at the end of the year, the spouse or common-law partner with the lower net income has to report this amount on line 117 of his or her return regardless of which person received the benefit. • If you are the spouse or common-law partner with the higher net income, enter the amount from box 10 in "Information about your spouse or common-law partner" area on page 1 of your return.
Box 12, Repayment of previous-year benefits	This is the total amount of benefits repaid for previous years. Enter this amount on line 213. • The person (you or your spouse or common-law partner) who reported UCCB income for the previous year(s) must claim this amount on line 213.

Chapter 3

Income

2009 Tax Year

Asset details forms

Asset details forms are part of the business-statement set. For each business statement, ProFile creates a corresponding Asset details and Asset list form. For example, when you create a T2125#1, ProFile creates the T2125Asset#1 and T2125AssetList#1.

Use Asset details and Asset list forms to track business and rental assets. Enter asset information on the Asset details form. ProFile automatically transfers this information to the corresponding Asset list form. The Asset list form displays all assets in a single table that you can print. You cannot print the Asset details form.

To enter asset information:

1. Complete a separate entry for each asset. A list of assets appears in the panel on the left of the Asset details form. Click on one of these items to display the asset details for a particular asset. To enter information in a blank column, click on <New>. ProFile automatically numbers each asset as you enter the information and creates a blank entry for the next asset.
2. Enter details for each asset under the Federal / Quebec headings. ProFile automatically calculates the net cost or proceeds and transfers the amount to the CCA form to calculate the capital cost allowance (CCA), recapture or terminal loss.
3. Use one of two methods to enter an addition for an asset acquired during the year
   - Create a separate class for the asset. If the addition has the same class number as an existing asset, you may wish to create a separate class for this asset. Most depreciable properties are grouped together with others of the same class. However, you are required to place certain assets in a separate class (for example, rental properties costing $50,000 or more) and you may elect to place certain assets in a separate class (for example, class 10 computer equipment costing $1,000 or more). Placing an asset in a separate class ensures that the recapture or terminal loss is calculated as soon as the asset is disposed of, rather than when all assets in that same class are disposed of. To create a separate class for an asset, select "New" from the drop-down list in the "Link asset to:" field.
   - Enter the asset as an addition to an existing asset. ProFile adds the cost of the addition and the cost of the existing asset together in the Historical Information section when you carry forward the return to the following year.

Attention: For ProFile to correctly apply the special rules for Class 13 assets, always create a separate class for each Class 13 addition. For more information on entering Class 13 items, see CCA forms and summaries.

Exempt from 50% rule?

In the year you acquire a depreciable property, you can usually claim CCA only on one-half of your net additions to a class. This is known as the 50% rule. ProFile follows this rule for new additions.

 Note that you can usually only claim CCA if the property is available-for-use.

What properties are not subject to the 50% rule?

Some properties in classes 12, 13, 14, 23, 24, 27, 29, and 34, as well as some properties obtained in a non-arm's length transaction are not subject to this 50% rule. For details, see the CRA Interpretation Bulletin IT-285, Capital Cost Allowance - General Comments.

What if a property is not subject to the 50% rule?

If you want to claim the maximum CCA, you can choose to manually calculate the CCA for the class to which the exempt property belongs.

Manually calculate the CCA for the entire class on the applicable ProFile business statement. On the corresponding CCA form, enter the CCA for the year (from column 9 of the business statement) next to "CCA for the year". You will have to override (F2) the ProFile calculation to do this.

Historical information

Use the Historical information section of the Asset detail forms to enter the capital cost of an asset purchased in a prior year and to enter its acquisition date. ProFile uses this information to determine the proceeds of disposition when you dispose of an asset. For CCA purposes, the proceeds of disposition are equal to the lesser of the capital cost and the net proceeds received for the asset.

When you enter historical information on the Asset details form, ProFile calculates the proceeds of the disposition and transfers it to the CCA form.

When you do not enter historical information on the Asset details form, ProFile does not calculate the proceeds of disposition. Either enter the historical information on the Asset details form or override the proceeds of disposition on the CCA form.

Asset list forms

Asset list forms are part of the business-statement set. For each business statement, ProFile creates corresponding Asset list and Asset details forms. For example, when you create a T2125#1, ProFile creates the T2125Asset#1 and T2125AssetList#1.

Use Asset list and Asset details forms to track business and rental assets. Enter asset information on the Asset details form. ProFile automatically transfers this information to the corresponding Asset list form. The Asset list form displays all assets in a single table that you can print. You cannot print the Asset details form.

When you dispose of an asset, you can enter the type of disposition and the proceeds of disposition on the Asset list form or on the Asset details form. If the disposition produces a capital gain, ProFile transfers the appropriate amounts to Schedule 3 to calculate the capital gain.

Data flow in Quebec returns

When you dispose of an asset, make sure you enter the information on the federal Asset details or Asset list forms. As with other forms in ProFile T1/TP1, the data flows from the federal to the Quebec form. Overriding the amount on the Quebec form will not transfer that information back to the federal form.

CCA forms and summaries

Capital Cost Allowance (CCA) forms and summaries are part of the business statement set. For each business statement, ProFile creates a corresponding CCA and CCASummary form. For example, when you create a T2125#1, ProFile creates the T2125CCA#1 and T2125CCASummary#1 forms.

Business statements

- if you have business income, professional income or commission income, use Form T2125, Statement of Business or Professional Activities.
- if you have farming income, and do not participate in CAIS, use Form T2042, Statement of Farming Activities.
- if you have farming income, and participate in CAIS, use the T1163-4 CAIS Program Information form or the T1273-4 Harmonized CAIS Program Information form.
- if you have fishing income, use Form T2121 Statement of Fishing Activities.
- if you have rental income, use Form T776 Statement of Real Estate Rentals.

Entering CCA information

Forms with the CCA suffix allow you to enter and view each CCA item individually.

Complete a separate column for each CCA item, including Class 13 (leaseholds) and Class 14 (patents, franchises, concessions and licenses) items. ProFile automatically numbers each item as you enter information and creates a blank column for the next item. If you enter assets on the Asset details form, the asset information transfers directly to the corresponding CCA form.

A list of CCA items appears in the panel on the left of the form. Click on one of these items to display the CCA details for a particular asset. To enter information in a blank column, click on 'New'.

Class 13

So that ProFile applies the special rules for Class 13 items, always create a separate class for each addition. When applicable and if there is more than one Class 13 asset, ProFile automatically calculates an adjustment to the UCC (UCC reduction).

To create a separate class for a Class 13 addition, enter the details for the asset on the Asset details form. ProFile then automatically links the asset to a new CCA class on the CCA form.

In order for ProFile to properly calculate the annual CCA, enter start and expiration dates of the lease:

- Enter the start date for existing Class 13 assets in the Historical Information section on the Asset details form. If you do not enter the lease start date, the amortization period defaults to the maximum amortization period of 40 years.
- Enter the lease expiry date on the CCA form. If you do not enter the lease expiration date, the amortization period defaults to the minimum amortization period of 5 years.

CCASummary forms

Forms with the CCASummary suffix group and display CCA items by category in a table similar to the one distributed by CRA to help you calculate CCA.

CEC forms

Cumulative Eligible Capital (CEC) forms are part of the business-statement set. For each business statement, ProFile creates a corresponding CEC form. For example, when you create a T2125#1, ProFile creates a T2125CEC#1 form. Forms with the CEC suffix calculate the Cumulative Eligible Capital for the business.

Eligible capital expenditures are capital expenditures of an intangible nature incurred for the purpose of earning business income. They do not qualify as depreciable property or permit the immediate deduction of the expenditure. For example, goodwill and customer lists are eligible capital expenditures.

The maximum amount you can deduct on the business statement is 7% of the cumulative eligible capital for the business at the end of the year. The CEC consists of:

- 75% of eligible capital expenditures
- minus 75% of the proceeds of disposition for eligible capital property
- minus all deductions previously claimed

The disposition of eligible capital property may create a positive or negative CEC balance:

- **If the CEC balance is negative**, the negative amount is included in business income.
- **If the CEC balance is positive**, you can claim the usual 7% deduction.

For a taxpayer who ceases to carry on business the balance of the cumulative eligible capital is deducted in the business statement.

Five year comparative summaries

Five year comparative summaries are part of the business-statement set. For each business statement, ProFile creates a corresponding five year comparative summary form. For example, when you create a T2125#1, ProFile creates the T2125Comparative#1 form. Use this form to compare up to five years of business statement information.

ProFile automatically carries forward previous-year business statement information from the previous year to this form. Enter any additional information directly in the summary.

If you create a new return rather than carrying forward an existing return, enter the prior year information directly on the comparative summary. ProFile will then carry forward this information in the following year.

Farming inventory adjustment

The farming inventory adjustment forms are T1163-T1273Inv and T2042Inv.

AgriStability and AgriInvest forms

The AgriStability and AgriInvest programs replace the Canadian Agricultural Income Stabilization program (CAIS).

The AgriStability and AgriInvest form set in ProFile includes the following forms: T1163-T1273 Statement of farming Inventory, T1163-T1273CCASummary, T1163-1273CEC, T1163-T1273Asset, T1163-T1273AssetList, T1163-T1273CCA, T1163-T1273Inv, T1163-T1273Comparative, T1273Crop, T1273Livestock and T1273Other.

At the top of the T1163-T1273 Statement of farming Inventory, you will need to select whether to use the T1163-4 AgriStability and AgriInvest Program Information form or the T1273-4 Harmonized AgriStability and AgriInvest Program Information form. AgriStability and AgriInvest program participants in British Columbia, Saskatchewan, Manitoba, New Brunswick, Nova Scotia, Newfoundland and Labrador, and Yukon must use the harmonized T1273/T1274 forms to report income (or losses) from farming. Individuals who farm in Alberta, Ontario, Quebec and PEI should use the T1163/T1164 forms.

ProFile allows you to have any number of T1163-1273 forms.

Complete the T2042 forms to report income (or losses) from farming for taxpayers who are not participants of the AgriStability and AgriInvest Program.

Other Income: Other income

The Other Income form gathers income amounts from a variety of slips, and calculates the totals to the corresponding lines of the T1 jacket. On this form you can also enter various income amounts that do not have full supporting schedules, but that you must report on the T1 jacket.

The sections are organized according to the line numbers on the jacket. Each section has an expanding table where you can enter an unlimited number of income sources.

A section that does not include any amounts will not appear on the printed form.

Foreign amounts

If you enter amounts for foreign income/pension (and corresponding tax paid), ProFile will automatically calculate the applicable foreign tax credits and include T2209 and T2036 forms for the specified countries. The software summarizes foreign tax credits for each country on the form FTC.

Rental: Summary of rental income

This form summarizes all the amounts from rental income. The name of the rental property (or its address), gross income and net income transfer from the T776 form(s). You cannot enter that information directly on the summary. The summary tables will expand as required to accommodate all the T776 forms with information for the current return.

If you do not see information transferred from a T776 form to this summary, chances are you did not enter "Your % of ownership" on the T776 for the current taxpayer.

Self Employ: Summary of self-employment income

This form summarizes all the amounts from self employment forms, slips and resource income.

The name of business, gross income and net income transfer to this form from the relevant forms. You cannot enter the details directly on the summary. The summary tables will expand as required to accommodate all of the forms with information for the current return.

If you do not see information transferred from a business statement to this summary, chances are you did not enter a "% of the partnership" on the business statement for the current taxpayer.

How to calculate your restricted farm loss

If farming was not your chief source of income and you had a net farm loss, the loss you can deduct depends on the amount of your net farm loss.

When your net farm loss is $15,000 or more, you can deduct $8,750 from your other income. The rest of your net farm loss is your restricted farm loss.

When your net farm loss is less than $15,000, the amount you can deduct from your other income is the lesser of:

A) your net farm loss for the year; or
B) $2,500 plus 50% × (your net farm loss minus $2,500).

The amount remaining is your restricted farm loss.

Note: When the farm loss you deduct is different from your actual farm loss because of the restricted farm loss calculation, you should indicate this on your income tax and benefit return on the line called "Farming income." For example, you can do this by noting "restricted farm loss," "RFL," or "Section 31" to the left of line 168.

Example

Sharon ran a cattle farm with the intention of making a profit. However, farming was not her chief source of income in 2009. In 2009, she had employment income and a net farm loss of $9,200, which she calculated on line 9946 of Form T2042.

The part of Sharon's net farm loss she can deduct from her other income in 2009 is either amount A or B, whichever is less:

- A) $9,200; or
- B) $2,500 plus 50% × ($9,200 - $2,500)

    = $2,500 plus 50% × $6,700

    = $2,500 + $3,350

    = $5,850

    Therefore, B = $5,850.

Because Sharon can only deduct either A or B, whichever amount is less, she enters $5,850 on line 141 of her income tax and benefit return and deducts this amount from her other income in 2009. Her restricted farm loss is the amount that remains, which is $3,350 ($9,200 minus $5,850). Sharon prints "Section 31" to the left of line 168 on her income tax and benefit return to show that the loss she is deducting is the result of a restricted farm loss calculation.

Applying your 2009 restricted farm loss

You can carry back your 2009 farm loss for up to 3 years. You can also carry it forward up to 20 years. The amount you deduct in any year cannot be more than your net farming income for that year. If you have no net farming income in any of those years, you cannot deduct any restricted farm loss.

If you choose to carry back your 2009 farm loss to your 2006, 2007, or 2008 income tax and benefit returns, complete Form T1A, Request for Loss Carry back, and file one copy of the form with your 2009 income tax and benefit return. Do not file an amended return for the year to which you apply the loss.

If you answer "Yes" to the question "Add back: Restricted farm loss?" on the Self Employ form, ProFile will automatically calculate the allowable claim.

Rental income guide

T776#: Rental income

Rental income can be either income from property or income from business. Income from rental operations is usually income from property. Use this form only if you have rental income from property.

Type of ownership

If you own a rental property together with one or more persons, you need to determine whether you are a co-owner or a member of a partnership. These terms are not defined in the Income Tax Act. In the Rental Income Guide, CRA indicates that most situations are considered to be co-ownerships. The guide further advises that you should refer to provincial partnership law to determine if you are in a partnership.

CCA for co-owners and partners in rental operations

In a co-ownership, CCA is calculated independently for each co-owner after the calculation of that co-owner's share of net income. In ProFile, if you indicate "co-ownership" and a rental or business statement is shared between spouses, you must enter the CCA details on each spouse's CCA statement in proportion to the share of ownership.

In a partnership, CCA is calculated for the partnership and is allocated to each partner as part of his/her share of net income. In ProFile, if you indicate "partnership" and the rental statement is shared with a spouse, you must enter 100% of the CCA for the partnership on the CCA statement for one of the spouses. ProFile will automatically transfer amounts to the CCA statement for the other spouse.

Note: The detail of land additions and dispositions in the year does not transfer to the Calculation of CCA chart. Land is not considered a depreciable property.

Foreign properties

If the rental property is in a foreign country, enter the foreign address on the T776 form and enter the foreign rental income and expenses in Canadian dollars. Use the exchange rate that was in effect on the day you received the income or paid the expense. If the amount was paid at various times throughout the year, use the average annual rate.

Frequently Asked Questions

Rental Operations - Property or Business Income?

 The Canada Revenue Agency says...

To determine whether your rental income is from property or from business, consider the number and kinds of services you provide for your tenants.

In most cases, you are earning income from property if you rent space and provide basic services only. Basic services include heat, light, parking, and laundry facilities. If you provide additional services to tenants, such as cleaning, security, and meals, you may be carrying on a business. The more services you provide, the greater the chance that your rental operation is a business.

For more information on whether your rental income is income from property or income from business, get Interpretation Bulletin IT-434, Rental of Real Property by Individual, and its Special Release.

Note: If your rental operation is a business, do not use the rental guide. Instead, see Business and Professional Income. Rental income is reported on T776 - Statement of real estate rentals.

The Canada Revenue Agency says... *Rental Income Guide (T4036)*

What's new for 2009?

My Payment

> My Payment is a new payment option that allows individuals and businesses to make payments online, using the Canada Revenue Agency's Web site, from an account at a participating Canadian financial institution.

My Business Account

> You can now transfer payments and credits from one interim period to another interim period or to an amount owing within the same account. You will be able to see the results immediately, including up-to-date account balances and interest, if applicable. Go to the "Account balance and activities" service to access the "Transfer Payments" option.

Class 52 (100%)

> Class 52 includes general-purpose electronic data-processing equipment (commonly called computer hardware) and systems software for that equipment, including associated data processing equipment, acquired after January 27, 2009, and before February 2011. The capital cost allowance (CCA) rate is 100% and the half-year rule will not apply.

Line 9974 - GST/HST rebate for partners received in the year

> If you received a GST/HST rebate for partners related to your rental property partnership, report the amount of the rebate that relates to eligible expenses other than CCA on line 9974 of Form T776, Statement of Real Estate Rentals, in the year you receive it.

General information

Rental income is income you earn from renting property that you own or have use of. You can own the property by yourself or with someone else. Rental income includes income from renting:

- houses
- apartments
- rooms
- space in an office building
- other real or movable property

Rental income can be either income from property or business. Income from rental operations is usually income from property. Use this guide only if you have rental income from property.

Keeping records

Keep detailed records of all the rental income you earn and the expenses you incur. You have to support your purchases and operating expenses with:

- invoices;
- receipts;
- contracts; or
- other supporting documents.

Do not send us these records when you file your return. Keep them in case we ask to see them. We may disallow all or part of your expenses if you do not have receipts or other documents to support them.

Generally, you must keep your records for six years from the end of the tax year to which they relate. For more information about keeping records, see Guide RC4409, Keeping Records.

Calculating your rental income or loss

If you received income from renting real estate or other real property, you have to file a statement of income and expenses. You can use Form T776, Statement of Real Estate Rentals, to help you calculate your rental income and expenses for income tax purposes. Although we accept other types of financial statements, we encourage you to use Form T776.

Form T776 includes areas for you to enter your gross rents, your rental expenses, and any capital cost allowance. To calculate your rental income or loss, complete the areas of the form that apply to you.

Note: Rental losses are not allowed if your rental operation is a cost-sharing arrangement rather than an operation to make a profit.

If you are a sole proprietor, complete all the areas and lines on Form T776 that apply to you.

Form T776, Statement of Real Estate Rentals

Expenses you can deduct

- Prepaid expenses
- Advertising - Line 8521
- Insurance - Line 8690
- Interest - Line 8710
- Maintenance and repairs - Line 8960
- Management and administration fees - Line 8871
- Motor vehicle expenses - Line 9281
- Office expenses - Line 8810
- Legal, accounting, and other professional fees - Line 8860
- Property taxes - Line 9180
- Salaries, wages, and benefits - Line 9060
- Travel - Line 9200
- Utilities - Line 9220

- Landscaping costs (Line 9270 - Other expenses)
- Lease cancellation fees
- Vacant land

Expenses you cannot deduct

- You cannot deduct land transfer taxes when you purchase your property. Add these amounts to the cost of the property. If you later dispose of the property, these taxes will reduce the capital gain, or increase the capital cost.
- Mortgage principal
- Penalties
- Value of your own labour
- Total personal portion of expenses - Line 9949

Deductible expenses

Your deductible expenses equal your total expenses minus your personal portion.

Net income (loss) before adjustments - Line 9369

> Enter the gross income minus the deductible expenses (line a minus line b). This amount is the net rental income of all co-owners or partners before any claim for capital cost allowance.

Co-owners - Your share of line 9369

> If you are a co-owner, enter your share of the amount from line 9369 on line c. This amount is based on your share of ownership of the rental property.

> If you are a co-owner or partner, also complete the area called "Details of other co-owners and partners" on Form T776.

Other expenses of the co-owner - Line 9945

> Enter the amount of deductible expenses you have as a co-owner that you did not deduct elsewhere on Form T776.

Recaptured capital cost allowance - Line 9947

> If you had a recapture of capital cost allowance (CCA), enter it on this line. If you are a co-owner, enter your share of the amount.

Terminal loss - Line 9948

> Enter any terminal loss you had on the sale of rental property on this line. If you are a co-owner, enter your share of the amount.

Capital cost allowance

> Enter the amount of your capital cost allowance (CCA) as calculated in Area A on the back of Form T776.

> If you are a partner of a partnership that does not need to issue you a T5013 or T5013A slip, enter the total CCA allocated on the financial statements the partnership gave you.

Do not use this line if you are a member of a partnership that has to file Form T5013 Summary, Information Return of Partnership Income. Your CCA amount is already included in box 26 of your T5013 or T5013A slip.

Net income (loss)

Enter on line d your net income (or loss) after subtracting your claim for CCA on line 9936.

Partnerships - Your share of line d

If you are a member of a partnership, enter your share of line d.

Other expenses of the partner - Line 9943

Enter the amount of deductible expenses you have as a partner that you did not deduct elsewhere on Form T776.

Your net income (loss)

Enter this amount on line 126 of your return. If you have a rental loss, show the loss in brackets.

Rental losses

You have a rental loss if your rental expenses are more than your gross rental income. If you incur the expenses to earn income, you can deduct your rental loss against your other sources of income.

Renting below fair market value

You can deduct your expenses only if you incur them to earn rental income. In certain cases, you may ask your son or daughter, or another relative living with you, to pay a small amount for the upkeep of your house or to cover the cost of groceries. You do not report this amount in your income, and you cannot claim rental expenses. This is, in fact, a cost-sharing arrangement, so you cannot claim a rental loss.

If you lose money because you are renting a property to a relative for a lower rate than you would rent it to other tenants, you cannot claim a rental loss. When your rental expenses are consistently more than your rental income, you may not be allowed to claim a rental loss because your rental operation is not considered to be a source of income. However, you can claim a rental loss if you are renting the property to a relative for the same rate as you would charge other tenants and you reasonably expect to make a profit.

Other

- Capital Cost Allowance - Rental Operations
- Classes of depreciable properties
- Changes in use
- Principal residence

T1139 - Reconciliation of Business Income for Tax Purposes

T1139#: Reconciliation of business income

While self-employed individuals usually use a December 31st year-end for their business, in certain circumstances, they may be allowed to keep a fiscal period that does not end of December 31.

ProFile automatically handles electing to keep a non-calendar year-end and converting a business to a calendar year-end.

Use the T1139 to elect to use a non-calendar year-end or to revoke that election. You must submit a T1139 when you first elect to follow a non-calendar year-end, every year that you file a business statement with a non-calendar year-end; and the year you convert to a December 31st calendar yearend.

This form has two parts:

- **Part 1** deals with calculating your business income if you change or have already changed your fiscal period end to December 31st.
- **Part 2** deals with calculating your business income if you elect or have already elected to keep a fiscal period that does not end on December 31.

If you have more than one business with fiscal periods that do not end on December 31, ProFile may complete both Part 1 and Part 2 of the T1139 for you. Use form T1139 only for businesses carried on in Canada.

The Canada Revenue Agency says... *Reconciliation of Business Income for Tax Purposes (RC4015)*

Generally, you have to report your business income from a business carried on in Canada on a calendar-year basis. This rule affects sole proprietorships, professional corporations that are partners of a partnership, and partnerships (in which at least one partner of the partnership is an individual, professional corporation, or another affected partnership).

You may be able to use an alternative method of reporting your business income that is available on a business-by-business basis. This alternative method, which allows you to have a fiscal period that does not end on December 31, applies to individuals and partnerships in which all the partners are individuals. An individual who is a partner of a partnership that includes a professional corporation as a partner cannot use the alternative method. Also, partnerships that are partners of other partnerships cannot use the alternative method.

If you are an eligible individual (including an individual who is a partner of an eligible partnership) who wants to have a fiscal period that does not end on December 31, you will have to file an election with your income tax return to keep that period. If you filed an election in previous years for a business, you do not have to file an election for the 2009 taxation year for that particular business.

You have to use Form T1139, Reconciliation of 2009 Business Income for Tax Purposes, to file your election on or before the filing due date of your income tax return. A partner who has authority to act for a partnership can make a valid election for a partnership. All the partners of the partnership must complete a copy of this form and include it with their income tax returns to reconcile their share of the net business income (loss) for the 2009 taxation year.

Note: If you are a goods and services tax/harmonized sales tax (GST/HST) registrant, your decision about your fiscal period end for income tax purposes may affect your GST/HST reporting periods, as well as your filing and balance due dates.

Filing and balance due dates

You may have self-employment income or you may be the spouse or common-law partner of someone who does. If so, you have until June 15, 2010, to file your income tax return and Form T1139, unless the expenditures made to carry on the business are mainly the cost or capital cost of tax shelter investments. However, you have to pay any tax owing by April 30, 2010.

Note: If any of the dates mentioned above fall on a Saturday, Sunday or statutory holiday, you have until the next business day to file your return or make your payment.

Completing Form T1139 - Reconciliation of Business Income for Tax Purposes

Existing businesses - Started before current year

If you filed Form T1139 with your 2008 income tax return, you also have to file this form with your 2009 income tax return to calculate your additional business income in Part 2. Complete the part that applies to your situation by following the instructions in this chapter.

You have to complete Form T1139 for the 2009 taxation year if you started your business in 2008 and you're first fiscal period ended in 2009 but you did not elect to complete Part 2 of Form T1139 and report business income in 2008.

Identification area

Enter your social insurance number (SIN) in the appropriate area. Enter your 15-digit Business Number (BN) in the appropriate area. If you have more than one BN, enter the number for your proprietorship.

Part 1 - Converting to a December 31 fiscal period end

Part 1 applies only to existing businesses that started before 2009 and completed Form T1139 last year.

Complete this part if you elected to keep a year-end other than December 31 and you now want to convert it to December 31. If you choose this option, you have to report your business income on a calendar-year basis in later years. Part 1 will help you calculate the amount of business income to report on the appropriate line of your 2009 income tax return.

Line A - Net income (loss) for your first fiscal period ending in 2009

Line A applies only to existing businesses that started before 2009 and that are converting to a December 31 year-end in 2009.

The amount on line A represents the net income (loss) of your first fiscal period ending in 2009. For example, if your fiscal period began July 1, 2008, and ended June 30, 2009, the amount to enter on line A is the net income (loss) for the fiscal period ending June 30, 2009.

Note: If you have more than one fiscal period that does not end on December 31 for the same business, the net income (loss) of your first fiscal period above is the total of the net income (loss) of these fiscal periods.

For each business, enter on line A the amount of your net income (loss) from your income and expense statement. This is the amount reported on line 9946 of the following forms:

- T2125 - Statement of Business or Professional Activities;
- T2121 - Statement of Fishing Activities;
- T2042 - Statement of Farming Activities;

- T1163 - Statement A: AgriStability and AgriInvest Programs Information and Statement of Farming Activities for Individuals;
- T1164 - Statement B: AgriStability and AgriInvest Programs Information and Statement of Farming Activities for Additional Farming Operations;
- T1273 - Statement A: Harmonized AgriStability and AgriInvest Programs Information and Statement of Farming Activities for Individuals;
- T1274 - Statement B: Harmonized AgriStability and AgriInvest Programs Information and Statement of Farming Activities for Additional Farming Operations.

If you are a partner of a partnership, enter on line A your share of the partnership's net business or professional income (loss) for the first fiscal period ending in 2009. If you have deductible expenses from your share of the net partnership business income, subtract these amounts before entering your share of the net partnership income (loss) on line A. For more information on expenses deductible from your share of the net partnership income (loss), see "Other amounts deductible from your share of net partnership income (loss)" in the guide that applies to your type of business income.

If you are a partner of a partnership and you received either a T5013 slip - Statement of Partnership Income or a T5013A slip - Statement of Partnership Income for Tax Shelters and Renounced Resource Expenses, enter on line A the amount from box 35 or 37 for your share of business or professional income for the period ending December 31, 2009.

Form T1139 can accommodate more than one business. If you have more than two businesses, attach a separate sheet listing the net income (loss) for each additional business.

Line B - Net income (loss) for the period ending December 31, 2009

This line applies to existing businesses that started before 2009 and the year-end was converted to December 31 in 2009. In this case, enter on line B the net income (loss) of your fiscal period ending December 31, 2009.

For example, if you're first 2009 fiscal period ended on June 30, 2009, the amount to enter on line B is the net income (loss) for the period July 1, 2009, to December 31, 2009. You will have to prepare an income and expense statement for this period for each business.

Your net income (loss) is the amount on line 9946.

Additional information for line B if you are converting to a December 31 fiscal period end in 2009

Generally, you calculate the income and expenses of your fiscal period ending on December 31, 2009, in the same way as your previous fiscal period ending in 2009. However, you have to consider the following items:

- Reserves;
- Opening inventory and closing inventory;
- Work-in-progress (WIP);
- Capital cost allowance (CCA);
- Business-use-of-home expenses;

For more information see Guide T4002 Business and Professional Income.

Line C - Subtotal (line A plus line B)

Enter on line C the total of the amounts on lines A and B. Calculate this total for each business. If you have more than two businesses and you attached a separate sheet, remember to subtotal each business on line C.

Line D - Last year's additional business income

If you converted to a December 31 fiscal period end in 2009, enter on line D last year's additional business income from line H on last year's Form T1139.

Line E - Net income (loss) for each business

Enter on line E the amount of line C minus line D. Calculate this total for each business. If you have more than two businesses and you attached a separate sheet, remember to do the same calculation for each business.

Enter the amount(s) on line E on the appropriate line(s) of your income tax return.

Part 2 - Electing to have a fiscal period that does not end on December 31 (alternative method)

This election, which is available on a business-by-business basis, applies to individuals and partnerships in which all the partners are individuals. However, partnerships that are partners of another partnership cannot use the alternative method. Also, you cannot use the alternative method for a business if the expenditures made in the course of carrying on the business are primarily the cost or capital cost of tax-shelter investments.

Part 2 applies to businesses that started before 2009 and elected to keep a fiscal period that does not end on December 31.

If you started your business in 2009 and your first fiscal period ends in 2010, you can elect to complete Part 2 and report business income in 2009. For more information, see "New businesses starting in 2009 with a first fiscal period" below.

Part 2 will help you calculate the amount of business income to report on the appropriate line of your 2009 income tax return.

Line F - Net income (loss) for your fiscal period(s) ending in 2009

This is the net income (loss) for your fiscal period(s) ending in 2009. For example, if your fiscal period began June 1, 2008 and ended May 31, 2009, the amount to enter on line F is the net income (loss) for the fiscal period ending May 31, 2009.

Note: If you have more than one fiscal period that does not end on December 31 for the same business, the net income (loss) of your fiscal period(s) on line F is the total of the net income (loss) of these fiscal periods. For example, if you had a regular fiscal period ending on May 31, 2009 and then ceased to do business and retired on July 31, then you would have a second fiscal period ending July 31, 2009. For each business, enter on line F the amount of your net income (loss) from your income and expense statement. This is the amount on line 9946 of the following forms:

- Form T2125, Statement of Business or Professional Activities;
- T2121 - Statement of Fishing Activities;
- T2042 - Statement of Farming Activities;

- T1163 - Statement A: AgriStability and AgriInvest Programs Information and Statement of Farming Activities for Individuals;
- T1164 - Statement B: AgriStability and AgriInvest Programs Information and Statement of Farming Activities for Additional Farming Operations;
- T1273 - Statement A: Harmonized AgriStability and AgriInvest Programs Information and Statement of Farming Activities for Individuals;
- T1274 - Statement B: Harmonized AgriStability and AgriInvest Programs Information and Statement of Farming Activities for Additional Farming Operations.

If you are a partner of a partnership, enter on line F your share of the partnership's net business or professional income (loss) for the fiscal period ending in 2009. If you have incurred expenses during the fiscal period of the partnership that are deductible from your share of the net partnership business income, subtract these amounts before entering your share of the net partnership income (loss) on line F. For more information on these expenses, see "Other amounts deductible from your share of net partnership income (loss)" in the guide that applies to your type of business income.

If you are a partner of a partnership and you received either a T5013 slip, Statement of Partnership Income or a T5013A slip, Statement of Partnership Income for Tax Shelters and Renounced Resource Expenses enter on line F the amount of business or professional income from box 35 or 37 of your slip.

Form T1139 can accommodate more than one business. If you have more than two businesses, attach a separate sheet listing the net income (loss) for each additional business.

Line H - Subtotal (line F plus line G)

Enter on line H the total of the amounts on lines F and G. Calculate this total for each business. If you have more than two businesses and you attached a separate sheet, remember to subtotal each business on line H.

Line I - Last year's additional business income

For each business, enter on line I the amount included on line H of last year's Form T1139.

Line J - Net income (loss) for each business

Enter on line J the result of line H minus line I. Calculate this amount for each business. If you have more than two businesses and you attached a separate sheet, remember to do the same calculation for each business.

Enter the amount(s) of line J on the appropriate line(s) of your tax return.

Death of a partner or proprietor in the year

If an individual who uses the alternative method dies after the end of the regular fiscal period of the business, the legal representative can elect to file an optional income tax return (optional return), including Form T1139, to report the business income from the end of the regular fiscal period until the date of death (short fiscal period). This means that the legal representative will complete two income tax returns (including two T1139 forms) for the 2009 year as follows:

- a final income tax return (including Form T1139) that reports business income for the regular fiscal period as well as all other income; and

- an optional income tax return (including Form T1139) for the business income from the short fiscal period.

For more information about filing returns for deceased persons, see our Guide T4011Preparing Returns for Deceased Persons.

Election

If you completed Part 2, you have to sign and date the election portion on the prescribed Form T1139 unless you already made this election. However, an election for a partnership is valid if it is made for all the partners of the partnership by a partner who has authority to act for the partnership. If you are a partner of a partnership, all the partners of the partnership have to complete this form and include it with their income tax returns.

If you started your business in 2009 and your first fiscal period ends in 2010, you have to file an election with your 2010 income tax return.

You can revoke your election at any time and change your fiscal period end to December 31 of the year in which you file the revocation. However, once you change your fiscal period end to December 31, you cannot change back.

T1170 - Capital gains on gifts of certain capital properties

T1170: Capital gains on gifts of certain capital property

Do not include any gains reported on this form on Schedule 3. However, if you have a capital loss on

gifts of capital property, report it on Schedule 3. You may be able to use the capital loss to reduce other capital gains.

 The Canada Revenue Agency says... *Gifts and Income Tax Guide (P113)*

If you donated certain types of capital property to a registered charity or other qualified donee, in 2009, you may not have to include in your income any amount on capital gain realized on such gifts. You may be entitled to an inclusion rate of zero on any capital gain realized on such gifts.

Note: For donations of ecologically sensitive land to a private foundation, the inclusion rate of zero does not apply.

The inclusion rate of 25% or zero applies if you donate the following property:

- a share, right, or debt obligation listed on a prescribed stock exchange;
- a share of the capital stock of a mutual fund corporation;
- a unit of a mutual fund trust;
- an interest in a related segregated fund trust;
- a prescribed debt obligation;
- ecologically sensitive land (including a covenant, an easement, or in the case of land in Québec, a real servitude) donated to a qualified donee other than a private foundation;
- a share, debt obligation, or right listed on a designated stock exchange.

In cases where the exchanged property is a partnership interest (other than prescribed interests in a partnership), the capital gain will generally be the lesser of:

- the capital gain otherwise determined; and
- the amount, if any, by which the cost to the donor of the exchanged interests (plus any contributions to partnership capital by the donor) exceeds the ABC of those interests (determined without reference to distributions of partnership profits or capital).

If there is no advantage received in respect of the gift, the full amount of the capital gain is eligible for the inclusion rate of zero. However, if there is an advantage in respect of the gift, only a portion of the capital gain is eligible for the inclusion rate of zero. The rest is subject to an inclusion rate of 50%.

The amount subject to the inclusion rate of zero is calculated using the following formula:

A x (B / C)

Where:

A = the capital gain

B = the eligible amount of the gift

C = the proceeds of disposition

Report all donations of these properties on Form T1170, Capital Gains on Gifts of Certain Capital Property, whether the inclusion rate is 50% or zero. Report the amounts calculated on this form on line 132, line 153, and line 193 of Schedule 3, Capital Gains (or Losses).

Note: The capital gain realized on an exchange of partnership interests for publicly listed securities that are then donated should not be reported on Form T1170. Instead, it should be reported directly on line 174 of Schedule 3.

T1212 - Statement of Deferred Stock Option Benefits

T1212: Statement of deferred stock option benefits

Consult the CRA guide information below for details regarding this form.

The Canada Revenue Agency says...

Use this form to keep track of the benefits you have deferred as a result of exercising a security option after February 27, 2000, to acquire eligible securities as a result of your employment. Eligible securities are common shares of a class listed on a prescribed stock exchange in or outside Canada, and units of mutual fund trusts.

The deferred benefits have to be included in your employment income for the year in which you dispose of the security, become a non-resident, or die.

You have to file this form with your tax return each year you have a balance of deferred security option benefits outstanding. You have to do this whether or not you have deferred any security option benefits in the year, or disposed of any securities in the year relating to a security option benefit that was previously deferred.

Income from stock options and ESPP plans

T2017 - Summary of Reserves on Dispositions of Capital Property

T2017 - Summary of Reserves on Dispositions of Capital Property

Consult the guide information below for details regarding this form.

 The Canada Revenue Agency says...

Use this form if you are an individual (other than a trust) who is

- reporting a reserve you claimed on your 2008 return; or
- claiming a reserve on dispositions of capital property (including gifts of certain securities) in 2009.

To determine if you are eligible to claim a reserve in 2009, see the section "Claiming a reserve" in the Capital Gains guide.

Form T2017 provides a summary of the following reserve amounts:

- Dispositions of qualified farm property (QFP).
- Dispositions of qualified fish property (QFP).
- Dispositions of qualified small business corporation (QSBCS) shares.
- Dispositions of property (other than QFP and QSBCS) to your child.
- Dispositions of other property.
- Dispositions of capital property before November 13, 1981.

What is a reserve?

When you sell a capital property, you usually receive full payment at that time. However, this is not always the case. Sometimes the amount is spread over a number of years. In this type of situation, you can claim a reserve. Usually, a reserve allows you to defer reporting a portion of the capital gain to the year in which you receive the proceeds. For more details, including gifts of non-qualifying securities, see Capital gains reserves and the CRA Interpretation Bulletin IT-236, Reserves Disposition of Capital Property.

How do you calculate a reserve?

The amount of a reserve you can claim in a taxation year depends on when you disposed of the property, and the type of property you disposed of.

Note that you do not have to claim the maximum reserve in the taxation year. You can claim any amount up to the maximum. However, the amount you claim in a later year for the disposition of a particular property cannot be more than the amount you claimed for that property in the immediately preceding year. To determine your maximum reserve for 2009, use the calculation that applies to your situation.

For further details, see Capital gains reserves.

Dispositions of capital property before November 13, 1981

If you sold property before November 13, 1981, use the calculation below to determine your reserve. You should also use the calculation for property that you sold, or are considered to have sold, after November 12, 1981, if the disposition occurred under the terms of an offer or a written agreement made or entered into before November 13, 1981, or as a result of the property having been stolen, destroyed, or expropriated before November 13, 1981.

Capital gain x (Amount payable after the end of the year / Proceeds of disposition).

What other forms do you complete?

Related forms that you may have to complete are as follows:

- Schedule 3 - Capital Gains (or Losses)
- T657 - Capital Gains Deduction Calculation
- T936 - Cumulative Net Investment Loss (CNIL)

T2042, Statement of Farming Activities

T2042#: Farming activities

Use this form if you earned income as a self-employed farmer or as a member of a farm partnership.

If you are participating in the Canadian Agricultural Income Stabilization (CAIS) program, you have to use the CAIS forms provided in ProFile.

To claim a restricted farm loss, answer "Yes" to the question "Add back: Restricted farm loss?" on the Self Employ form.

 The Canada Revenue Agency says...

Use Form T2042 - Statement of Farming Activities if you earned income as a self-employed farmer or as a partner in a farm partnership. It will help you calculate the farming income you will report on your 2009 income tax and benefit return.

If you are participating in the AgriStability and AgriInvest programs, you have to use the applicable guide:

- If you are an AgriStability and AgriInvest participant in Quebec, use this guide for your income tax and benefit return and contact La Financière agricole du Québec at 1 800-7493646 regarding AgriStability and AgriInvest participation.
- If you are a AgriStability and AgriInvest participant in Alberta, Ontario, or Prince Edward Island, use Guide RC4060, Farming Income and the AgriStability and AgriInvest Programs and complete Form T1163, Statement A - AgriStability and AgriInvest Programs Information and Statement of Farming Activities for Individuals.
- If you are an AgriStability and AgriInvest participant in the rest of Canada, use Guide RC4408, Farming Income and the AgriStability and AgriInvest Programs Harmonized Guide and complete Form T1273, Harmonized AgriStability and AgriInvest Programs Information and Statement of Farming Activities for Individuals.

T2091#: Designation of a property as a principal residence

Use this form to designate a property as a principal residence and to calculate the capital gain for the year if you:

- disposed of, or were considered to have disposed of, your principal residence or any part of it, or
- granted some an option to buy your principal residence or any part of it.

For more information, check the instructions on the form.

T2091WS#: Principal residence work sheet

Use the principal residence worksheet along with form T2091 to calculate a reduction as a result of the capital gains election.

T2121 Fishing Income and Expenses

T2121#: Fishing activities

Consult the CRA guide information below for details regarding this form.

 The Canada Revenue Agency says... *Fishing Income Guide (T4004)*

Fiscal Period

Complete this form if you engaged in any self-employed fishing activities during 2009. You may also have to make CPP contributions on your self-employment income. See line 222 and Schedule 8 for details.

If you have more than one fishing business, use a separate T2121 form to report each operation.

You now generally have to report your business income on a calendar year basis. For further information on non-calendar year-ends, see Reconciliation of Business Income for Tax Purposes.

Business and professional income

T2125#: Statement of business or professional activities

Complete a separate T2125 for each business or profession.

File each completed T2125 with your T1 Income Tax and Benefit Return.

For more information on how to complete this form, see guide T4002, Business and Professional Income.

 Tip: When entering Capital Cost Allowance information for business auto expenses, use Chart C-Capital Cost Allowance for motor vehicles in the Bus Auto form.

Frequently Asked Questions

Am I employed or self-employed?

You may need to determine your status, for example, if you work on contract. Generally, the degree of control over the work you perform is a determining factor in deciding whether you are an employee or self-employed.

You are likely considered an employee if your employer:

- decides where, when, and how the work is to be done;
- establishes your working hours;
- determines your salary amount;
- supervises your activities; and
- assesses the quality of your work.

As an employee, you could be entitled to receive certain benefits such as sick leave, paid statutory holidays, and vacation pay. Also, you will probably be subject to Canada Pension Plan (CPP) or Quebec Pension Plan (QPP), and Employment Insurance (EI) deductions. You should receive a T4 slip from your employer.

You are likely considered self-employed if you:

- control the time, place, and manner of performing your activities;
- supply your own equipment and tools, and assume the rental and maintenance costs;
- make a profit or incur a loss, and cover operating costs; and
- integrate your client's activities into your own business activities.

As a self-employed worker, you might be entitled to claim expenses incurred to earn business income. Generally, you are not entitled to receive EI benefits. In addition, you will have to remit both the employer's and employee's shares of CPP (QPP in Quebec) contributions, and pay your income tax in quarterly instalments.

For more information, get the guide RC4110, Employee or Self-Employed?

The Canada Revenue Agency says... *Business and Professional Income Guide (T4002)*

What's new for 2009?

Reporting business income

Business income includes income from a profession, calling, or trade (including farming and fishing), a manufacture, an undertaking of any kind, and an adventure or concern in the nature of trade. You report your business income on a fiscal period basis. A fiscal period is the time covered from the day your business starts its business year to the day your business ends its business year. For an existing business, the fiscal period is usually 12 months. A fiscal period cannot be longer than 12 months. However, it can be shorter than 12 months in some cases, such as when a new business starts or when a business stops.

Self-employed individuals generally have to use a December 31 year-end. If you are an eligible individual, you may be able to use an alternative method of reporting your business income which allows you to keep a fiscal period that does not end on December 31.

If your fiscal year-end is not December 31, use Form T1139 - Reconciliation of 2009 Business Income for Tax Purposes to calculate the amount of business income to report on your 2009 income tax return. If you filed Form T1139 with your 2008 income tax return, generally you have to file that form again for 2009.

In most cases as a self-employed individual, you report business income, by using the accrual method of accounting.

If you are a self-employed commission salesperson, you can use the cash method of reporting your income and expenses as long as it accurately shows your income for the year.

Are you self-employed?

Use this guide if you are a self-employed businessperson (which includes a self-employed commission salesperson) or a professional.

A business is an activity that you intend to carry on for profit and there is evidence to support that intention. A business includes:

- a profession;
- a calling;
- a trade;
- a manufacture;
- an undertaking of any kind; and
- an adventure or concern in the nature of trade

Note: For the purpose of this guide and other reporting purposes, professional activities will be discussed as a separate category of business.

Business income includes income from any activity you do for profit. For example, income from a service business is business income. However, you do not include employment income as business income.

Note:

- Include all your income when you calculate it for tax purposes. If you fail to report all your income, you may be subject to a penalty of 10% of the amount you failed to report after your first omission.
- A different penalty may apply if you knowingly or under circumstances amounting to gross negligence participate in the making of a false statement or omission on your income tax return. This penalty is 50% of the tax attributable to the omission or false statement (minimum $100).

Income from a business

If you are a sole proprietor, complete all the applicable areas and lines on Form T2125, Statement of Business or Professional Activities.

If you are a member of a partnership, see Partnerships for more information.

Income from a business includes:

- Sales, Gross Revenue
- Reserves deducted last year
- Other income
- Recapture of capital cost allowance

Cost of goods sold and gross profit

Complete this part if you have a business and your business buys goods for resale or makes goods for sale. Claim the cost of the goods you buy or make for sale in the fiscal period in which you sell them. Enter only the business part of the costs on the form.

To calculate your cost of goods sold, you need to know the following:

- the value of your inventory at the start and end of your fiscal period;
- the cost of your purchases (net of discounts) for the fiscal period;
- direct wage costs; and
- sub-contracts.

Income from a profession

Tick the box in Part 2 to indicate that you have professional income.

You should complete this part only if you have professional income. If you have business income, leave this part blank and complete Part 1. If you have both professional and business income, you must complete a separate Form T2125 for each.

Professional activities are business activities. Usually, you calculate your income from professional activities using the same rules as for a business. However, some aspects of professional activities are different from those of other types of businesses. Some of these differences are discussed below.

Line D - Professional fees

Your professional income includes all fees you receive for goods or services you provide, whether you receive or will receive money, something the same as money (such as credit units that have a notional monetary value), or something from bartering. Bartering occurs when two people agree to exchange goods or services without using money. For more information, see Interpretation Bulletin IT-490, Barter Transactions.

As a professional, your income generally includes the value of your work-in-progress (WIP). WIP is goods or services that you have not yet completed at the end of your fiscal period.

Your professional fees for the current year are the total of:

- all amounts you received during the year for professional services, whether you provided the services before or during the current year or after your current year-end;

plus

- all amounts receivable at the end of the current year for professional services you provided during the current year; and
- the value of your WIP at the end of your current year for which you have not received any amount during the year;

minus

- all amounts receivable at your previous year-end; and
- the value of your WIP that was included in professional fees at the end of your previous year.

The result is the amount you enter at line D.

If you usually deduct GST and PST, or HST directly from your professional fees when you earn them, you can show your net professional fees (after GST, PST, or HST) on line D. Then, do not enter the GST, PST, or HST deducted on the following line. If GST, PST, or HST are not deducted directly from your professional fees, show GST, PST, or HST separately on the appropriate line.

Note:

If you elected to use the quick method option to calculate your GST/HST remittances, complete the following calculation:

- First enter the professional fees including work in-progress (WIP) (net of GST/HST collected or collectible) on line D.
- Next subtract any PST included in the fees and WIP at the end of the year if you elect to exclude it.
- Then add the WIP for the start of the year if excluded at the end of last year to arrive at your adjusted professional fees on line F.

Report the 1% credit on eligible professional fees (maximum $300) that you claimed on line 107 of Form GST34, Goods and Services Tax/Harmonized Sales Tax Return for Registrants, on line 8230 in Part 3 of Form T2125.

For more information about the quick method and examples of how it works, see Guide RC4058, Quick Method of Accounting for GST/HST.

Deductible expenses

As a rule, you can deduct any reasonable current expense you incur to earn business income. The expenses you can deduct include any GST/HST you incur on these expenses. However, since you cannot deduct personal expenses, enter only the business part of expenses on the form.

You cannot claim expenses you incur to buy capital property and depreciable assets.

Renovations and expenses that extend the useful life of your property or improve it beyond its original condition are usually capital expenses. However, an increase in a property's market value because of an expense is not a major factor in deciding whether the expense is capital or current. To determine whether an expense is a current or capital expense, see the chart Current or capital expense.

Note: When you claim the GST/HST you paid on your business expenses as an input tax credit, reduce the amounts of the business expenses you show on Form T2125 by the amount of the input tax credit. Do this when the GST/HST for which you are claiming the input tax credit was paid or became payable. Similarly, subtract any other rebate, grant, or assistance from the expense to which it applies. Enter the net figure on the proper line. Any such assistance you claim for the purchase of depreciable property used in your business will affect your claim for capital cost allowance. If you cannot apply the rebate, grant, or assistance you received to reduce a particular expense, or to reduce an asset's capital cost, include the total on line 8230, Other income, on Form T2125. See Grants, subsidies, or other incentives or inducements.

For information on expenses see Expenses.

Prepaid expenses

A prepaid expense is an expense you pay for ahead of time. Under the accrual method of accounting, claim any expense you prepay in the year or years in which you get the related benefit. For example, suppose your fiscal year-end is December 31, 2009. On June 30, 2009, you prepay the rent on your store for a full year (July 1, 2009 to June 30, 2010). You can only deduct one-half of this rent as an expense in 2009. You deduct the other half as an expense in 2010.

For more information, see Interpretation Bulletin IT-417, Prepaid Expenses and Deferred Charges.

Form T2205, Calculating Amounts From a Spousal RRSP or RRIF to Include in Income

T2205: Amounts from a spousal RRSP or RRIF

A spouse may have to report some or all of the taxpayer's income from RRSPs or RRIFs if he or she contributed to these funds in the current taxation year, or either of the two previous taxation years. A T4RSP will usually indicate the spouse's name or social insurance number when this is the case. Include this form for both spouses if you paper file the returns. Only the RRSP or RRIF annuitant can claim the income tax deducted (i.e. the individual to whom the slips are issued).

If the spouses were living apart because of a breakdown in the relationship when one spouse withdrew funds from an RRSP or RRIF, that spouse must report the entire amount shown on the T4RSP slip.

 The Canada Revenue Agency says...

Who should complete this form?

Complete this form if you meet both of the following conditions:

- you received an amount from a spousal or common-law partner RRSP or RRIF; and
- your spouse or common-law partner made a contribution to a spousal or common-law partner RRSP for you in the year you received the amount or in the two preceding years.

By completing this form, you will calculate how much of the amount to include in your income on your own return, and how much your spouse or common-law partner has to include in income.

If you're RRSP or RRIF has been deregistered, we consider that you received an amount from it in the year it was deregistered. The amount we consider that you received is the fair market value of the plan or fund calculated immediately before it was deregistered. This requirement does not apply to deregistered RRIFs that were established before March 1986, unless they were amended after February 1986.

Do not complete this form if any of the following apply:

- the amount you received is a periodic annuity payment from an RRSP;
- the amount you received is a minimum amount payment from a RRIF; or
- your spouse or common-law partner died in the year.

Do not complete this form if, when you received the amount or when the RRSP or RRIF was deregistered, either of the following applied:

- you and your spouse or common-law partner were living separate and apart because of your relationship breakdown;
- you or your spouse or common-law partner was a non-resident; or

In any of the situations listed above, include the amounts in your own income.

Spousal or common-law partner RRSP and RRIF

An RRSP or RRIF is a spousal or common-law partner plan or fund if it meets any of the following conditions:

- Your spouse or common-law partner contributed an amount to the RRSP while you were the annuitant.

- It is an RRSP that has received a payment or a transfer of property from a spousal or common-law partner RRSP or RRIF.
- It is a RRIF that has received a payment or a transfer of property from a spousal or common-law partner RRSP or RRIF.

For more details, see "Amounts from a Spousal or Common-law Partner RRSP or RRIF" in Chapter 4 of the income tax guide called RRSPs and Other Registered Plans for Retirement.

Lines 5 and 16

If your spouse or common-law partner made more than one contribution to your RRSPs in the two preceding years, he or she has to include the contributions in income in the order they were contributed.

Example:

James makes the following contributions to Tania's RRSP.

- 2006: $3,000
- 2007: $8,000
- 2008: $ 0
- 2009: $ 0

Tania made the following withdrawals from her spousal RRSP.

- 2008: $5,000
- 2009: $4,000

James had to include $5,000 in income for 2008. That $5,000 represented, in order, $3,000 from 2006, and $2,000 from the year 2007 contribution of $8,000.

When Tania completes this form for 2009, the amount on line 5 will be $2,000 (the amount James included in income for the year 2007 contribution).

Unused contributions

Part of the amount your spouse or common-law partner includes in income for the year, based on this completed form, may be for RRSP contributions that were not deducted for any year. Your spouse or common-law partner may be able to claim a deduction on his or her return to offset the amount included in income. To determine the deductible amount, your spouse or common-law partner can complete Form T746, Calculating Your Deduction for Refund of Unused RRSP Contributions.

Tax deducted

Only the person who is shown as the annuitant on the T4RSP or T4RIF slip can claim the income tax deducted. The amount of tax deducted is shown in box 30 of the T4RSP or box 28 of the T4RIF slip.

Chapter 4

Deductions

2009 Tax Year

Allowable business investment loss (ABIL)

ABIL: Allowable business investment loss

Consult the CRA guide information below for details regarding the allowable business investment loss.

 The Canada Revenue Agency says... *Capital Gains Guide (T4037)*

If you had a business investment loss in 2009, you can deduct 1/2 of the loss from income. The amount of the loss you can deduct from your income is called your allowable business investment loss (ABIL). Complete Chart 6 on page 37 to determine your ABIL and, if applicable, your business investment loss reduction. Claim the deduction for the ABIL on line 217 of your return. Enter the gross business investment loss on line 228 of your return.

What is a business investment loss?

A business investment loss results from the actual or deemed disposition of certain capital properties. It can happen when you dispose of one of the following to a person you dealt with at arm's length:

- a share of a small business corporation; or
- a debt owed to you by a small business corporation.

For business investment loss purposes, a small business corporation includes a corporation that was a small business corporation at any time during the 12 months before the disposition.

You may also have such a loss if you are deemed to have disposed of, for nil proceeds of disposition, a debt or a share of a small business corporation under any of the following circumstances:

- A small business corporation owes you a debt (other than a debt from the sale of personal-use property) that is considered to be a bad debt at the end of the year.
- At the end of the year, you own a share (other than a share you received as consideration from the sale of personal-use property) of a small business corporation that:
    - has gone bankrupt in the year;
    - is insolvent, and a winding-up order has been made in the year under the Winding up Act ; or
    - is insolvent at the end of the year and neither the corporation, nor a corporation it controls, carries on business. Also, at that time, the share in the corporation has a fair market value of nil, and it is reasonable to expect that the corporation will be dissolved or wound up and will not start to carry on business*.

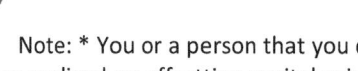 Note: * You or a person that you do not deal with at arm's length will be deemed to have realized an offsetting capital gain if the corporation, or a corporation it controls, carries on business within 24 months following the end of the year in which the disposition occurred. You or that person will have to report the capital gain in the tax year the corporation starts to carry on business. This applies if you or the person owned the share in the corporation at the time the business started.

You can elect to be deemed to have disposed of the debt or the share of the small business corporation at the end of the year for nil proceeds of disposition, and to have immediately reacquired the debt or the share after the end of the year at a cost equal to nil. To do this, you have to file an election with your return. To make this election, attach to your return a letter signed by you. State that you want subsection 50(1) of the Income Tax Act to apply.

What happens when you incur an ABIL?

You can deduct your ABIL from your other sources of income for the year. If your ABIL is more than your other sources of income for the year, include the difference as part of your noncapital loss for the year. You can carry a non-capital loss back three years and forward seven years.

You can now carry a non-capital loss arising in tax years ending after March 22, 2004, back three years and forward ten years.

Although you can generally carry a non-capital loss arising in tax years ending after 2005, back three years and forward 20 years, this extension does not apply to a non-capital loss resulting from an ABIL. Instead, an ABIL that has not been used within ten tax years will continue to become a net capital loss in the eleventh year.

To carry a non-capital loss back to 2006, 2007, or 2008, complete Form T1A, Request for Loss Carry back, and include it with your 2009 return. Do not file an amended return for the year to which you want to apply the loss.

If you cannot deduct your ABIL arising in 2003 or prior years as a non-capital loss by the end of the seventh year, the unapplied part becomes a net capital loss. You can use this loss to reduce your taxable capital gains in the eighth year or any year after.

For example, Cathy had an ABIL in 1997 that became a non-capital loss and that she was not able to deduct in the three years before 2000 or the seven years after 2000. She can now use the loss to reduce her taxable capital gains in 2009 or any year after.

The unapplied part of your non-capital loss resulting from an ABIL arising in 2004 or future years will become a net capital loss in the eleventh year.

Note

Any ABIL that you claim for 2009 will reduce the capital gains deduction you can claim in 2009 and in future years.

T777Auto#: Motor vehicle expenses

Use this form to calculate automobile expenses related to earning employment income.

Create a new T777Auto worksheet for each automobile and then complete the expense details for the automobile. You can create any number of copies of the form. Simply right-click on the form and select New form from the context-sensitive menu.

Click on of the following link to see information on calculating CCA for motor vehicles:

Capital Cost Allowance for motor vehicles

Claiming the GST/HST rebate on the GST370 for auto expenses

For amounts allocated to the T777, you can automatically claim the GST/HST Rebate on the form GST370. To do this, go to the T777 and answer "Yes" to the question, Do you qualify for a GST rebate? at the top of the form. ProFile will automatically complete and calculate the rebate for the form GST370.

Sharing automobile expenses between spouses

ProFile does not automatically share the details of motor vehicle expenses with the spouse's return. If both spouses have expenses related to an automobile, they will each have to have their own T777Auto form.

Tip: To save time, once you have entered motor vehicle details in one of the spouse's returns, go to Edit > Copy Form, then toggle to the spouse's return (F5) and open a new T777Auto. Select Edit > Paste Form. Don't forget to adjust amounts and percentages accordingly!

Note: For information on how to apply auto expenses to a business, refer to the information related to the Business Auto form.

Allocation of expenses

Remember to allocate the auto expenses to the appropriate business statement at the top of the Business Auto worksheet. These automobile expenses always transfer to the expense section of the business statement. If a business statement is shared between spouses, ProFile automatically prints the Business Auto worksheet for both the taxpayer's and the spouse's return.

As you create and enter data in other business statements (such as the T2125), ProFile adds these forms to this list. The Business Auto form allows you to allocate expenses to multiple business statements. As you enter data in the fields in the last available row, ProFile will add another blank row to the table.

Business Auto: Vehicles owned by a business

Use the Business Auto worksheet to treat motor vehicle expenses used for business purposes (related to the T2125, T2121, T2042 and Quebec business statements)

From the Allocation of expenses drop down menu, select your business statement (if you have not yet opened a business statement, the drop down list will be empty). The data you enter on the Business Auto form will flow to the selected business statement(s).

In the case of the T2125, T2121 and T2042 business statements, ProFile transfers automobile expenses to different areas on the statements depending on the taxpayer's percentage of ownership of the business:

- If the business is a sole proprietorship (% ownership = 100%), then the automobile expenses are transferred to the expense section of the business statement (line 9281 or 9819, depending on the business statement).
- If the business is a partnership, the expenses are transferred to line 9943, "Other amounts deductible from your share of net partnership income (loss)".

As you complete the Business Auto worksheet, ProFile automatically transfers the required information to the related Quebec business auto form (for example, TP80Auto, TP1FishingAuto).

Capital Cost Allowance (CCA)

Chart C of the Business Auto worksheet lets you calculate the Capital Cost Allowance (CCA) Chart C of the Business Auto worksheet lets you calculate the CCA amounts are transferred to the business statement's CCASummary or the CCA (assets owned by partner) table of the relevant business statement, depending on whether or not the vehicle is owned by the business. This is specified in the Owned by business? column of the >Allocation of expenses table. For vehicles owned by a partner in a business, ensure that Owned by business? is set to No for the related business statement.

Sharing automobile expenses between spouses

ProFile does not automatically share the details of motor vehicle expenses with the spouse's return. If both spouses have expenses related to the business use of an automobile, they will each have to create their own Business Auto form.

Capital Cost Allowance for motor vehicles

Be sure to select the appropriate CCA class for your vehicle. Motor vehicles can belong to either class 10 or class 10.1. Select class 10 unless your vehicle meets the following class 10.1 condition: The vehicle was purchased in the current or previous taxation year and cost more that $30,000.

T777Auto (expenses related to earning employment income)

Enter the capital cost allowance information for the vehicle in the Capital Cost Allowance for motor vehicles section of the T777Auto form.

Class 10 vehicle

> Using the drop-down arrow next to the line pertaining to Class, select class 10.
>
> Enter the date acquired and complete the data entry fields that display in this section (fields in black).

Class 10.1 vehicle

> Using the drop-down arrow next to the line pertaining to Class, select class 10.1.
>
> Enter the date acquired and complete the data entry fields that display in this section (fields in black). Remember, a vehicle purchased in the current year must cost more than $30,000 to be included in class 10.1.

Business Auto (vehicles owned by business or a partner in a business)

For vehicles owned by a business, enter the CCA information on Chart C of the Business Auto form. Using the drop-down arrow next to the line pertaining to Class, select the applicable class 10 or 10.1.

If the taxpayer owns less than 100% of the partnership (as indicated in the Details of other partners section of the business statement), you must fill in the "Owned by business?" column in the Allocation of expenses table of the Business Auto form.

- When you select Yes, the asset will transfer to the business statement's CCASummary (for example: T2125CCASummary, T2121CCASummary).
- When you select No, the asset will transfer to the CCA (assets owned by partner) table of the relevant business statement.

Proration of class 10 and 10.1 vehicles

ProFile prorates the CCA for class 10 and class 10.1 if the automobile is allocated 100% to a business with a short business year.

LossLPP: Listed personal property losses

Use this form to calculate your listed personal property losses.

You can deduct capital losses on listed personal property (LPP) against other listed personal property gains of the year, however, you cannot claim a capital loss on the disposal of personal use or listed personal use property against other income. If you dispose of LPP in 2009:

- you can only deduct LPP losses from any gains you had from selling other LPP;
- the total amount of LPP losses you deduct in the year cannot be more than the total LPP gains for that year; and
- you cannot use this loss to reduce any capital gains you had from selling other types of property.

Report these dispositions on line 159 of Schedule 3.

To determine the value of many listed personal property (LPP) items, you can have them appraised by a dealer. You can also refer to catalogues for the value of the properties.

Note: LPP gains do not include gains from selling or donating certified Canadian cultural property to a designated institution. For more information, see "Selling or donating certified Canadian cultural property."

Because LPP is a type of personal-use property, the capital gain or loss on the sale of the LPP item is calculated the same way as for personal-use property.

If your 2009 gains from dispositions of LPP are more than your 2009 losses from such dispositions, you can use unapplied LPP losses from 2002 and later years to reduce your 2009 gains. If you want to do this, do not enter these losses on line 253 of your return. Instead, subtract the unapplied LPP losses of previous years from your 2009 LPP gains. You should only complete the "Listed personal property" area of Schedule 3 if, after doing these calculations, you still have a net LPP gain in 2009.

If your 2009 losses from dispositions of LPP are more than your 2009 gains from such dispositions, the difference represents your LPP loss for the year. Keep a record of your LPP losses that have not expired so you can apply these losses against LPP gains in other years. An unapplied LPP loss expires when you do not use it by the end of the seventh year after you incurred it.

LossNetCap: Net capital losses

A net-capital loss occurs when the total of capital losses exceeds the total of capital gains on Schedule 3 of your tax return. This type of loss may only be deducted from net capital gains in of the previous 3 years or in any of the following years.

Use this form to calculate a capital loss when you sell, or are considered to have sold, a capital property for less than the total of its adjusted cost base plus the outlays or expenses you incurred to sell the property.

LossNonCap: Non-capital losses

On this form you can enter your non-capital losses reported on your returns for the previous seven years. You can also report unapplied farming or fishing losses from the previous ten years.

Other Deduct: Other deductions

This form gathers deduction amounts entered on a number of other ProFile forms. In addition, the form includes fields to enter deductions that do not have full supporting schedules. This allows you to review all your deduction information on a single form.

Each section has an expanding table where you can enter an unlimited number of deductions. Any section that does not have amounts will not appear on the printed form.

Resource: Resource income and expenses

These resource forms allow you enter resource income and expenses: Resource, RA# and ResourceCCA Resource is the summary form. Amounts from the RA forms, ResourceCCA, T101 and 102 slips and T5013 slips transfer to the Resource form.

The RA (Resource Activity) form lets you detail resource activity from a single source. You can create any number of copies of the RA form for any sources of resource activity you need to report.

The ResourceCCA form allows you to reduce net income using capital cost allowance in your resource expense calculation.

RPP: Registered pension plan deduction

Use the RPP form to enter RPP contributions for which no slips were issued and un-deducted contributions from prior years. This form also gathers information from a number of other ProFile slips and performs calculations to determine the current year RPP deduction for line 207 of the T1 jacket.

With the exception of your T4, T4 Short, and T4A slips, do not include your receipts with your paper return. If you are using EFILE, verify the slips.

Note: Generally, you cannot claim contributions to pension plans in foreign countries.

RRSP: RRSP deduction

Enter a single line for every RRSP contribution receipt the taxpayer has. The table expands to accommodate any number of entries. Select the contribution period - ProFile will decide which contributions to use first and will carry forward any allowable amounts.

Make sure you complete either Option 1 or Option 2 in the section "RRSP Deduction Limit." If you do not complete either option, ProFile will not claim any RRSP deduction amount.

EFILE error 2197 - RRSP contributions do not match CRA amounts

If the client's RRSP contributions do not match those from the CRA (EFILE error 2197), check the entry for unclaimed amounts in the first 60 days of the current taxation year. Make sure you select "First 60 days (Reported)" for amounts reported on a previous year's tax return.

If the amount was contributed in the first 60 days of the current taxation year was NOT reported on the prior year's tax return, select "First 60 days (NOT Reported)."

RRSPLimit: Next year's RRSP deduction limit

The form calculates next year's anticipated RRSP limit based on earned income calculations from this year. This form is for your information only. Each taxpayer receives a Notice of Assessment that includes the exact RRSP limit as calculated by CRA.

RRSPTransfer: Income eligible for transfer to RRSP

Use this form to enter amounts eligible for transfer to an RRSP, outside of the normal contribution limits. Since these amounts are added to the normal contribution limits on form RRSP, you will need to go to that form to enter the date of contribution and the actual contribution amount.

Support: Support payments

Use this ProFile worksheet to enter amounts of support payments received or support payments made. Both sections of the worksheet provide an expandable table so that you can list any number of payments.

The totals of payments received (gross and taxable amounts) flow to lines 156 and 128 of the T1 jacket.

The totals of payments made (gross and taxable amounts) flow to lines 230 and 220 of the T1 jacket.

Support payments

A support payment is an amount a payer is required to pay to a recipient for the maintenance of the recipient, children of the recipient, or both. There are two types of support payments. The tax rules are different depending on the type.

1. Support for a spouse or common-law partner means support payments made under an order or agreement that are only for the recipient's maintenance.
2. Support for a child means any support payment that is not identified in the order or agreement as being only for the recipient's maintenance. Therefore, if an order or agreement provides for a global amount of support to be paid for a spouse or common-law partner and a child, the full amount is considered support for a child.

In all cases, the payer and the recipient must live apart because of a breakdown in the relationship when the payments are made. For an amount to be considered a support payment, it must meet certain conditions, detailed in Support Payments.

T1M - Moving expenses deduction

T1M#: Moving expenses

Complete this form to determine what portion of your moving expenses you can deduct.

Choosing simplified or detailed moving expenses calculation

Radio buttons in the 'Calculation of allowable moving expenses' section of form T1M allow you to choose either the simplified or detailed method of calculation for moving expenses. If you enter in detailed amounts on screen, only certain fields appear on the printed forms. If you switch to the simplified method after entering detailed amount, ProFile retains the detailed amounts in the background so that you can choose the method that is most beneficial to the taxpayer.

 The Canada Revenue Agency says... *Form T1M - Moving Expense Deduction*

Use this form to calculate your moving expenses deduction. Complete a separate form for each move. Do not attach this form, or the receipts and documents supporting your claim, to your return. Keep them in case we ask to see them. If you are using EFILE, show them to your EFILE service provider.

Can you deduct moving expenses?

You can deduct eligible moving expenses from employment or self-employment income you earn at your new location if you move and establish a new home to be employed or carry on a business. You can also deduct moving expenses if you move to study courses as a full-time student at a college, university, or other institution offering post-secondary education. However, you can only deduct moving expenses from the part of your scholarships, fellowships, bursaries, certain prizes, and research grants required to be included in your income.

Your new home must be at least 40 kilometres (by the shortest usual public route) closer to the new place of work or educational institution. You must establish your new home as the place where you ordinarily reside. For example, you have established a new home if you have sold or rented (or advertised for sale or rent) you're old home.

Generally, your move must be from one place in Canada to another place in Canada. For information and conditions regarding moves to or from Canada, or between two locations outside Canada, see below.

Are you employed or self-employed?

If you are employed or self-employed, you can deduct eligible moving expenses from employment or self-employment income you earn at the new location.

If your moving expenses that you paid in the year of the move are more than the net eligible income earned at the new location in the year you move, you can carry forward and deduct the unused part of those expenses from employment or self-employment income earned at the new location in the following years. You cannot deduct your moving expenses from any other type of income, such as investment income or Employment Insurance benefits, even if you receive this income at the new location.

Did you receive a reimbursement, or an allowance that is not included in your income, for eligible moving expenses (see "Expenses you can deduct" below)? If yes, you can only deduct moving expenses if you include the amount you received in your income or if you reduce your moving expenses by the amount reimbursed. You may be asked to provide a letter from your employer stating that you were not reimbursed for the moving expenses you are claiming.

Expenses you can deduct

You can deduct reasonable amounts that you paid for moving yourself, your family, and your household effects. Not all members of your household have to travel together or at the same time.

Eligible moving expenses include:

- transportation and storage costs (such as packing, hauling, in-transit storage, and insurance) for household effects, including items such as boats and trailers;

- travelling expenses, including vehicle expenses, meals, and accommodation, to move you and members of your household to your new residence (you can choose to claim vehicle and meal expenses using the simplified method (see the note below);
- costs for up to 15 days for meals and temporary accommodation near either residence for you and the members of your household (you can choose to claim meal expenses using the using the simplified method (see the note below); and
- the cost of cancelling a lease for your old residence, except any rental payment for the period during which you occupied the residence.

When your old residence is sold as a result of your move, eligible moving expenses also include:

- legal or notaries fees for the purchase of the new residence, as well as any taxes paid (other than GST/HST or property taxes) for the transfer or registration of title to the new residence, if you or your spouse or common-law partner sold the old residence; and
- the cost of selling your old residence, including advertising, notaries or legal fees, real estate commission, and mortgage penalty when the mortgage is paid off before maturity.

If you moved after 1997, and your moving expenses were paid in a year after the year of your move, you may be able to claim them on your return for the year you paid them against employment or self-employment income earned at the new location. The same possibility is also extended to students reporting a taxable amount of scholarships, fellowships, bursaries, certain prizes, and research grants. You can carry forward any unused amounts and deduct them only against such income earned at the new location in the following years.

This may apply if your old residence did not sell until after the year of your move. If this is the case, you may be asked to submit this form with the receipts and explain the delay in selling your home.

The simplified method for claiming expenses

> Instead of claiming your actual expenses (the detailed method), you can choose the simplified method of claiming vehicle and meal expenses. Although you do not have to submit detailed receipts for actual expenses if you choose to use the simplified method, we may still ask you to provide some documentation to establish the duration of temporary lodging.

Expenses you cannot deduct

Moving expenses that you cannot deduct include:

- expenses for work done to make your former residence more saleable;
- any loss from the sale of your home;
- expenses for house hunting trips before you move;
- the value of items movers refused to take, such as plants, frozen food, ammunition, paint, and cleaning products;
- expenses for job hunting in another city (such as travelling expenses);
- expenses to clean or repair a rented residence to meet the landlord's standards;
- expenses to replace personal-use items such as tool sheds, firewood, drapes, and carpets;
- mail-forwarding costs (such as with Canada Post);
- costs of transformers or adaptors for household appliances; and
- costs incurred in the sale of your old home if you delayed selling for investment purposes or until the real estate market improved.

Generally, you cannot deduct the cost of moving a mobile home. However, if you have personal effects in a mobile home when it is moved, you can deduct the amount it would have cost to move those personal effects separately.

Did you move from Canada?

Provided you met all other conditions and requirements described above under "Can you deduct moving expenses?", you can claim expenses for a move from Canada if:

- you are a full-time student (including a co-operative student), or a factual resident or a deemed resident; and
- you moved from the place where you ordinarily resided to live in another place where you ordinarily reside.

You cannot claim moving expenses if you rent an apartment in another country where you are working temporarily and you maintain residential ties in Canada (for example, your spouse and children remain in your home in Canada), because your home in Canada is where we consider you to ordinarily reside.

Did you move to Canada?

Provided you met all other conditions and requirements described above under "Can you deduct moving expenses?", you can claim eligible expenses for a move to Canada if you are a fulltime student (including a co-operative student), or a factual resident or deemed resident.

Did you move between two locations outside Canada?

Provided you met all other conditions and requirements described above under "Can you deduct moving expenses?", you can claim eligible expenses for a move between two locations outside Canada if you are a factual resident or deemed resident and you moved from the place where you ordinarily resided to live in another place where you ordinarily reside.

What can students deduct?

You can only deduct moving expenses if you move to study courses as a full-time student, student at a college, university, or other institution offering post-secondary education. However, you can only deduct these expenses from the part of your scholarships, fellowships, bursaries, certain prizes, and research grants required to be included in your income.

If you're eligible moving expenses are more than the scholarships, fellowships, bursaries, certain prizes, and research grants income you report for the year, you can deduct the unused part of those expenses from the same type of income you receive and report on your return for the following years.

You can claim moving expenses you incur at the beginning of each academic period when you move to the educational institution, as long as you meet the 40-kilometre limitation outlined and have income earned at the new location. You can also claim moving expenses when you move back after a summer break, or a work semester if you have income earned at the new location.

The rules that apply to an employed or self-employed person (see "Are you employed or self-employed?") apply to you if you move to a new location in Canada to work (including a summer job) or to run a business. Complete a separate Form T1-M for each move and enter the total of all amounts from line 20 on line 219 of your return.

If you need more information, see Interpretation Bulletin IT-178, Moving Expenses.

T657 - Capital Gains Deduction Calculation

T657: Capital gains deduction

Use this form to calculate the capital gains deduction. If you have investment income or investment expenses from prior years, you will also have to complete form T936: Cumulative net investment loss (CNIL).

 Tip: Claiming a capital gains deduction is not mandatory. In other words, you can claim any amount you want to in a year, from zero up to the maximum.

Carry-forward information section

Using a drop down list in ProFile, select the years for which you need to enter eligible taxable capital gains, losses and capital gains deductions.

Select only the years that apply to the client for whom you are preparing a return. The table grows automatically as you enter data, giving you extra blank rows as you need them.

To prevent errors, once you have entered carry-forward information for a particular year, the year will then disappear from the drop-down list to ensure that it is not re-used a second time. You can also quickly sort by year of ascendance by right clicking on the last 4 columns of the chart and selecting Sort by year.

The Canada Revenue Agency says...

Use this form if you disposed of qualified farm property or qualified small business corporation shares in 2009 or a previous year, or disposed of qualified fishing property after May 1, 2006.

For information about business investment losses, see also Business investment loss - Line 217 and 228.

Note: Any capital gains realized from the disposition of qualified farm property, qualified fishing property or qualified small business corporation shares while you were a non-resident of Canada are not eligible for the capital gains deduction.

You have to be a resident of Canada throughout 2009 to be eligible to claim this deduction. For the purposes of this deduction, CRA also considers you to have been a resident throughout 2009 if you were a resident of Canada for part of 2009, and you were a resident of Canada throughout 2008 or 2010.

Deferred capital gains from the disposition of qualified small business corporation shares do not qualify for the capital gains deduction.

If you have investment income or investment expenses in 2009, you have to complete Form T936, Calculation of Cumulative Net Investment Loss (CNIL) before you complete this form. Form T936 lists what is considered to be investment income and expenses.

What is the capital gains deduction limit?

For 2009, if you disposed of qualified small business corporation shares, qualified farm property, or qualified fishing property, you may be eligible for the $750,000 LCGE. Because you only include one-half of the capital gains from these properties in your taxable income, your cumulative capital gains deduction is $375,000 (1/2 of $750,000).

The total of your capital gains deductions from 1985 to 2009 for all types of capital property cannot be more than your cumulative deduction of $375,000. For more information, see Claiming a capital gains deduction.

Qualified farm property and qualified fishing property

When you dispose of qualified farm property or fishing property and have a capital gain, you can claim a capital gains deduction in 2009 that is equal to the lowest of the following amounts:

- your annual gains limit for 2009;
- your cumulative gains limit for 2009;
- your net taxable capital gains in 2009 from dispositions of qualified farm property after 1984 or of qualified fishing property after May 1, 2006; or
- your maximum capital gains deduction available for 2009.

Qualified small business corporation shares

When you dispose of qualified small business corporation shares and have a capital gain, you can claim a capital gains deduction in 2009 equal to one of the following amounts, whichever is lowest:

- your annual gains limit for 2009, minus any capital gains deduction for qualified farm or fishing property claimed in 2009;
- your cumulative gains limit for 2009, minus any capital gains deduction for qualified farm or fishing property claimed in 2009;
- your net taxable capital gains in 2009 from dispositions of qualified small business corporation shares after June 17, 1987; or
- your maximum capital gains deduction available for 2009.

There is an election available to you if you own shares of a qualifying small business corporation that stops being a small business corporation because:

- a class of its shares is listed on a prescribed stock exchange; or
- after 1999, a class of another corporation's shares is listed on a prescribed stock exchange.

This election will allow you to report a capital gain on your return and claim the $375,000 capital gains deduction, even though you did not actually sell your shares. The deduction applies to any gains you have on these shares to the date the shares are listed. To make this election, complete Form T2101, Election for Gains on Shares of a Corporation Becoming Public.

What other forms do you complete?

Related forms that you may have to complete are as follows:

- Schedule 3 - Capital Gains (or Losses)
- T936 - Cumulative Net Investment Loss (CNIL)
- T2017 - Reserves on Dispositions of Capital Property

T746 - Calculating Your Deduction for Refund of Unused RRSP Contributions

T746: Deduction for refund of unused RRSP contributions

If you did not use all your RRSP contributions in the year you contributed them, in the year after you contributed them or in the year you were sent a Notice of Assessment for the year you contributed them, you may be able to withdraw these contributions and claim a deduction against your income.

Use the T746 to calculate the amount you can deduct for the withdrawing unused RRSP contributions.

**The Canada Revenue Agency says...**

Overview

You may be able to claim a deduction if you withdraw unused contributions you made to your own or your spouse's or common-law partner's RRSPs after 1990 or withdraw from a RRIF to which you transferred property from the RRSP. Unused contributions are contributions that you did not deduct from your income. You include the amount you withdrew in your income on your return, and then claim a deduction at line 232 of your return if you meet certain conditions. Use this form to calculate the deduction you can claim.

If you do not want to withdraw the unused contributions, you can leave them in the plan and carry them forward to deduct in a future year by filing Schedule 7, RRSP Unused Contributions, Transfers and HBP or LPP Activities.

If you made, or CRA considers you to have made, RRSP contributions in a calendar year after 1990 that you could not deduct for the year contributed or for the previous year, you may have to pay a tax on those undeducted contributions. If you have to pay the tax, you have to send CRA a T1-OVP return. For more details, see Tax on over contributions. Amounts withdrawn or repaid under the Home Buyers Plan do not generally increase or reduce the RRSP contributions that are subject to tax.

See also Unused contributions.

To qualify for this deduction, it has to be reasonable for CRA to consider that one of the following conditions, or both, apply:

- you expected to be able to fully deduct the RRSP contributions for the year you contributed them or for the previous year; or
- you did not make the unused RRSP contributions with the intention of later withdrawing them and deducting an offsetting amount.

To claim a deduction at line 232 of your return, you have to meet all of the following conditions.

You or your spouse or common-law partner must have received the undeducted contributions:

- in the year you contributed them;
- in the following year; or
- in the year CRA sent you a Notice of Assessment or Notice of Reassessment for the year you contributed them, or in the following year.

In addition, all of the following must apply:

- You have not deducted, for any year, the unused contributions that you made to your RRSPs or to your spouse or common-law partner's RRSPs.

- You have not designated the withdrawal of the unused RRSP contributions as a qualifying withdrawal to have your past-service pension adjustment (PSPA) certified. If you want to know about qualifying withdrawals, see Past -service pension adjustments (PSPAs).
- No part of the withdrawn contribution was a lump-sum payment from an RPP, or certain DPSP amounts that you transferred directly to an RRSP. For more information, see Direct transfer of an excess RPP lump-sum payment.
- No part of the withdrawn contribution was a lump-sum payment from the Saskatchewan Pension Plan that you transferred directly to an RRSP.

Attach a completed copy of this form, and the T4RSP or T4RIF slips that show the amounts withdrawn, to your tax return for the year in which you or your spouse or common-law partner withdrew the contributions.

If you receive unused RRSP contributions that apply to more than one year after 1990, complete a separate Form T746 for each year.

Note

Do not use this form to claim a deduction for unused RRSP contributions received if those contributions arose because of an excess lump-sum transfer from a registered pension plan (RPP). Instead, use Form T1043, Deduction for Excess Registered Pension Plan Transfers You Withdrew From Your RRSP or RRIF.

Do not use this form if you received a refund of your RRSP from completing Form T3012 Tax Deduction Waiver on the Refund of your unused RRSP Contributions. Instead, when you complete your return for the year you receive the refund, enter on line 129 "RRSP income" and line 232 "Other deductions," the total unused contributions that you made to your own or your spouse's or common-law partner's RRSPs that were refunded. You will find this total in box 20 of your own or your spouse or common-law partner's T4RSP slips. Attach to your return those T4RSP slips and copy 2 of the Form T3012A that you used to designate that amount as a refund.

Deduction for Amounts Withdrawn by Spouse or Common-Law Partner

If your spouse or common-law partner received a withdrawal of unused contributions from an RRSP or RRIF to which you were a contributor, complete Form T2205. Enter the amount you must report as income (from line 8 of your spouse or common-law partner's Form T2205) on line 9 of form T746. On your T1 General, report the RRSP amount on line 129 and the RRIF amount on line 130.

Deduction for Amounts Withdrawn from RRIF

On line 8, enter the amount shown in box 24 of your T4RIF slip that represents amounts you received in 2009 from a RRIF to which the unused RRSP contributions were transferred. Also report this amount on line 130 of your return.

Total unused contributions

If you made the unused RRSP contributions in more than one year, complete lines 1 through 4 of a separate Form T746 for each year. Enter the total line 4 amounts for all years on line 4 of the form for the most recent year. Then complete the rest of the form for the most recent year.

Note: If CRA allows the deduction for the unused RRSP contributions you or your spouse or common-law partner received, such contributions are not considered to be RRSP contributions, and you cannot deduct them for any year.

T777 - Statement of employment expenses

T777: Employment expenses

Use form T777 to calculate your allowable employment expenses. There are four forms related to employment expenses: T777, T777Details, T777Other and T777Auto. Enter employment expenses for commission and non-commission employees on T777Details. Enter expenses for musicians, forestry workers and apprentice mechanics on T777Other. Use form T777Auto to calculate automobile expenses related to earning employment income

What expenses can I claim?

That depends on whether you are a salaried or commission employee. It also depends on whether your employer requires you to pay the expenses to earn employment income. In that case, salaried employees can claim accounting and legal fees, allowable motor vehicle expenses, parking costs, supplies, travelling expenses, work space in the home, salaries paid to a substitute or assistant, and office rent. In addition, commission employees can claim advertising and promotion expenses, capital cost allowance, entertainment, food, beverages, and lodging. Special rules apply to forestry workers, transport employees, musicians, artists, and tradespersons (apprentice vehicle mechanics).

See T777 - Statement of employment expenses for more details.

GST Rebate

If you answer "Yes" to the question Do you qualify for a GST rebate? at the top of the form, ProFile will automatically complete and calculate form GST370: Employee and partner GST rebate.

**The Canada Revenue Agency says...** *Employment Expenses Guide (T4044)*

Use this guide if you are an employee and your employer requires you to pay expenses to earn your employment income.

If you are self-employed, see Business and Professional Income instead for more information.

What's new for 2009?

Meal expenses of long-haul truck drivers

> Meal and beverage expenses of long-haul truck drivers are deductible at a higher rate than the 50% permitted for other transportation employees. During eligible travel periods in 2009, meal and beverage expenses incurred are deductible at a rate of 70%. This rate will increase by 5% each year until the maximum rate of 80% is reached in 2011. For more information, see Transportation employees.

My Payment

My Payment is a new payment option that allows individuals and businesses to make payments online, using the Canada Revenue Agency's Web site, from an account at a participating Canadian financial institution.

T777Details: Employment expenses

Use form T777Details to enter employment expenses for commission and non-commission employees. Enter expenses for musicians, forestry workers and apprentice mechanics on T777Other. Amounts from this form flow back to the T777.

GST rebate

If you answer "Yes" to the question at the top of the form Do you qualify for a GST rebate?, ProFile will automatically complete and calculate form GST370: Employee and partner GST rebate.

Commission and non-commission expenses

The Expenses and Commission expense sections show the two options for calculating employment expenses. ProFile automatically chooses the calculation method that produces the best results.

T777Other: Other deductions

Enter expenses for musicians, forestry workers and apprentice mechanics on T777Other. Use form T777Details to enter employment expenses for commission and non-commission employees. Amounts from this form flow back to form T777.

GST rebate

If you answer "Yes" to the question Do you qualify for a GST rebate? at the top of form T777Other, ProFile will automatically complete and calculate form GST370: Employee and partner GST rebate.

Tracking the cost of tools

Track the cost of tools in the Apprentice Mechanic section. Enter a description and the cost of each tool in the beginning of this section. This section contains an expandable table so that you can enter as many tools as you need. As soon as you enter information in the blank line, ProFile adds a new blank line to the table.

ProFile takes the cost of all the tools purchased in the taxation year and calculates the maximum allowable deduction.

This form also tracks the disposition of the tools in the table at the bottom of the section. When you dispose of a tool, enter the proceeds of the disposition in this table. ProFile then calculates the adjusted cost and the additional income for each tool separately. ProFile will carry forward any unused amounts to the following year.

Form T778 - Child Care Expenses

T778: Child care expenses

To make your claim, attach a completed form T778 to your return. ProFile will transfer the total claim from the T778 to line 214 of the T1 jacket.

Note that section G is for information only and will not appear on the printed copy of the form.

 Tip: When entering the children's names in the child care expense details area you can get a list of dependants you have already entered on the Dependant schedule. Press and hold the Ctrl key and press the down arrow while in the "Name of child" cell of the table <Ctrl+DnArrow>. Alternately, you can click on the black bar at the end of the "Name of child" cell to display the names. This will reduce entry errors and ensure correct sharing of information with the Dependant schedule.

Child care expense amount not being claimed

If you have entered payments eligible for the child care expense amount, but there is no claim on line 214 of the jacket or on T778, check the dependant information on T778 and on the Dependant worksheet.

ProFile compares the claim information with the personal information you provided on the Dependant worksheet. In the table for expenses, enter only the first name of the child, exactly as it appears on the Dependant form. If the child name on the Dependant schedule is Robert, you cannot use the name Bobby in the child care expense area. ProFile will not claim for him because it cannot match these two together for dependants' income and other details. If the two names match, ProFile will verify eligibility for the claim based on the birth date and other dependant information you have provided.

The Canada Revenue Agency says... *Form T778, Child Care Expenses Deduction*

Who can claim child care expenses?

If you are the only person supporting the child, you can claim child care expenses you incurred while the eligible child was living with you.

However, there may have been another person who lived with you at any time in 2009 and at any time during the first 60 days of 2010 who was:

- the eligible child's parent;
- your spouse or common-law partner, if you are the father or the mother of the child; or
- an individual claiming an amount for the eligible child on line 305, 306, 315 or 367 of their Schedule 1.

If there is another person, the person with the lower net income (including zero income) must claim the child care expenses unless one of these situations applies.

If there is another person, and one of these situations applies, the child care expenses can be claimed by the person with the higher net income, or in part by both the person with the higher net income and the person with the lower net income. In any such situation, the person with the higher net income must calculate the claim first.

If there is another person and you have equal net incomes, you have to agree on which one of you will claim the expenses.

If you got married or began living common-law in 2009, you and your spouse or common-law partner have to consider your net incomes for the whole year. Include child care expenses you both paid for the whole year.

What payments can you claim?

You can claim payments for child care expenses made to:

- caregivers providing child care services;
- day nursery schools and daycare centres;
- educational institutions for the part of the fees that relate to child care services;
- day camps and day sports schools where the primary goal of the camp is to care for children (an institution offering a sports study program is not a sports school); or
- boarding schools, overnight sports schools, or camps where lodging is involved to a maximum of:
    - $175 per week per eligible child who was born in 2003 or later for whom the disability amount cannot be claimed;
    - $250 per week for an eligible child who was born in 2009 and earlier for whom the disability amount can be claimed; and
    - $100 per week for any other child born in 1993 to 2002 (or born in 1992 and earlier with a mental or physical infirmity for whom the disability amount cannot be claimed).

Advertising expenses and placement agency fees paid to locate a child care provider may also qualify as child care expenses. For more details, see Interpretation Bulletin IT-495, Child Care Expenses.

When the child care services are provided by an individual, the individual cannot be:

- the child's father or mother;
- another person;
- a person for whom you or another person claimed an amount on line 305, 306, 315, or 367 of Schedule 1; or
- a person under 18 who is related to you.

Note: A related person is someone connected by a blood relationship, marriage or common-law partnership, or adoption, such as your or your spouse's or common-law partner's child, brother, sister, brother-in-law, or sister-in-law. However, nieces, nephews, aunts, and uncles are not considered related persons.

Receipts

The individual or organization who received the payments must give you a receipt showing information about the services provided. When the child care services are provided by an individual, you will need the social insurance number of the individual. Do not send receipts with your return, but keep them in case we ask to see them. If you file your return electronically using EFILE, show your receipts to your EFILE service provider.

Notes

You may have paid an amount that would qualify to be claimed as child care expenses and the children's fitness amount (line 365). If this is the case, you must first claim this amount as child care expenses. Any unused part can be claimed for the children's fitness amount as long as the requirements are met. If you paid an individual to provide child care in your home, you may have some responsibilities as an employer. If you are not sure of your situation, contact us.

What payments can't you claim?

You cannot claim payments for medical or hospital care, clothing, or transportation costs.

For payments made to an educational institution, you cannot claim the part of the fees that relate to education costs, such as tuition fees of a regular program or a sports study program. Also, you cannot claim fees paid for leisure or recreational activities, such as tennis lessons or the annual registration fees paid for Scouts.

Note

Although some expenses may not be eligible to deduct as child care expenses, they may qualify for the children's fitness amount as long as the requirements are met to claim an amount at line 365.

You cannot claim expenses for which you or another person received, or is entitled to receive, a reimbursement of the child care expenses or any other form of assistance not included in income. If your employer paid the child care expenses on your behalf, you can claim the part of the expenses included in your income for the year.

Other situations

When completing the return of a person who died in 2009, claim eligible child care expenses that were paid while that person was living with the child as if he or she was the only person supporting the child. However, if there was another person, that person is also considered the only person supporting the eligible child and can claim eligible child care expenses paid while living with the child, as long as the expenses were not claimed on the return of another person.

If you lived outside Canada for part or all of 2009, and we consider you to be a factual or deemed resident of Canada, you can claim child care expenses that you paid to a non-resident person for services provided outside Canada. For information on other circumstances in which you can claim child care expenses paid for services provided outside Canada (e.g., commuters to the United States), please contact us.

If you immigrated to or emigrated from Canada in 2009, you can claim child care expenses for the period you were in Canada, as long as you otherwise qualify.

T929 - Disability Supports Deduction for 2004 and later years

T929: Disability supports deduction

Use this form to calculate the allowable deduction for expenses you paid to an attendant. ProFile transfers the total from this form to line 215 of the T1 jacket.

Do not include your receipts or form T929 with your paper return. If you EFILE, verify the taxpayer's receipts. In either case, instruct the taxpayer to keep the receipts in case CRA asks to see them.

The Canada Revenue Agency says... *T929 Disability Supports Deduction*

You can claim a disability supports deduction if you paid expenses that no one has claimed as medical expenses, and you paid them so you could:

- be employed or carry on a business (either alone or as an active partner);
- do research or similar work for which you received a grant; or
- attend a designated educational institution or a secondary school where you were enrolled in an educational program.

You cannot claim amounts that were reimbursed by a non-taxable payment such as insurance. Expenses must be claimed in the same year they are paid.

If you lived outside Canada for part or all of the year and we consider you to be a factual or deemed resident of Canada, you can claim disability supports expenses that you paid to a non-resident person for services provided outside Canada.

Do not attach this form or your receipts to your return, but keep them in case we ask to see them.

Note 1 - Allowable disability supports services or devices

You can claim amounts you paid for any of the following disability supports services or devices that you used because of your impairment:

- **Attendant care services** provided in Canada and used by a person with a mental or physical impairment. Amounts paid for attendant care services provided by the person's spouse or common-law partner, or to someone less than 18 years of age, cannot be claimed. Full-time attendant care services may be claimed if the person with the impairment qualifies for the disability amount (Form T2201, Disability Tax Credit Certificate, required) or a medical practitioner certifies in writing that this expense is necessary and that the impairment is likely to be indefinite. Part-time attendant care services may only be claimed if the person with the impairment qualifies for the disability amount (Form T2201 required).
- **Bliss symbol boards** or similar devices used by a person who has a speech impairment to help the person communicate by selecting the symbols or spelling out words (for 2005 and later years) - prescription required.
- **Braille note-takers** used by a person who is blind to allow that person to take notes (that can be read back to them, printed, or displayed in Braille) with the help of a keyboard prescription required.
- **Braille printers** or similar devices, including synthetic speech systems and large-print on-screen devices designed exclusively to be used by a person who is blind in the operation of a computer - prescription required.
- **Deaf-blind intervening services** used by a person who is both blind and profoundly deaf when paid to someone in the business of providing such services.
- **Devices or software** designed to be used by a person who is blind or has a severe learning disability to enable them to read print - prescription required.
- **Electronic speech synthesizers** that enable a person who is unable to speak to communicate using a portable keyboard - prescription required.
- **Job coaching services** (other than job placement or career counselling services) provided to a person with a severe and prolonged mental or physical impairment and paid to someone in the business of providing such services (for 2005 and later years) A medical practitioner must certify in writing that this expense is necessary.
- **Note-taking services** used by a person with a physical or mental impairment and paid to someone in the business of providing such services. A medical practitioner must certify in writing that this expense is necessary.

- **Optical scanners** or similar devices designed for use by a person who is blind to enable them to read print - prescription required.
- **Page-turning devices** to help a person turn the pages of a book or other bound document when they have a severe and prolonged impairment that markedly restricts their ability to use their arms or hands - prescription required.
- **Reading services**, provided to a person who is blind or has a severe learning disability and paid to someone in the business of providing such services. A medical practitioner must certify in writing that these services are necessary.
- **Real-time captioning services or sign-language interpretation services** used by a person with a speech or hearing impairment and paid to someone in the business of providing such services.
- **Talking textbooks** for a person who has a perceptual disability and is enrolled in a secondary school in Canada or a designated educational institution. A medical practitioner must certify in writing that the expense is necessary.
- **Teletypewriters** or similar devices that enable a person who is deaf or unable to speak to make and receive phone calls - prescription required.
- **Tutoring services** used by, and which are supplementary to the primary education of, a person with a learning disability or an impairment in mental functions, and paid to someone in the business of providing such services who is not related to that person. A medical practitioner must certify in writing that these services are necessary.
- **Voice-recognition so**ftware used by a person who has a physical impairment. A medical practitioner must certify in writing that this expense is necessary because of a physical impairment.

Note 2 - Earned income

For the purposes of line 6 of Form T778 - Child care expenses, and Form T929 - Disability supports, your earned income is the total of:

- employment income (including tips and gratuities, and the non-taxable part of an allowance received as an emergency volunteer);
- net self-employment income, either alone or as an active partner (excluding losses);
- the taxable portion of scholarships, bursaries, fellowships and similar awards, and net research grants;
- any earnings supplement received under a project sponsored by the Government of Canada to encourage employment or sponsored under Part II of the Employment Insurance Act or any similar program;
- disability benefits received from the Canada Pension Plan or the Quebec Pension Plan; and
- apprenticeship incentive grants received under the Apprenticeship Incentive Grant program administered by Human Resources and Skills Development Canada;
- apprenticeship completion grants received under the Apprenticeship Incentive Grant program administered by Human Resources and Skills Development Canada.

Note 3 - Net income

Net income is your total income from all sources minus these deductions:

- Line 206 - Pension adjustment
- Line 207 - Registered pension plan (RPP) deduction
- Line 208 - RRSP deduction

- Line 209 - Saskatchewan Pension Plan (SPP) adjustment
- Line 212 - Annual union, professional, or like dues
- Line 214 - Child care expenses
- Line 215 - Disability supports deduction
- Line 217 - Business investment loss
- Line 219 - Moving expenses
- Line 220 - Support payments made
- Line 221 - Carrying charges and interest expenses
- Line 222 - Deduction for CPP or QPP contributions on self-employment and other earnings
- Line 224 - Exploration and development expenses
- Line 229 - Other employment expenses
- Line 231 - Clergy residence deduction
- Line 232 - Other deductions, such as certain legal fees, repayments of income from some government programs, and refunds in special RRSP and RPP situations
- Line 235 - Social benefits repayment

T936 - Calculation of Cumulative Net Investment Loss (CNIL)

T936: Cumulative net investment loss (CNIL)

This is a form that ProFile calculates using values that you enter on other slips or forms in the client file. There are also fields where you can enter additional investment income and expenses that do not have full supporting schedules.

The Canada Revenue Agency says...

- Use this form if you had any investment income or investment expenses for 2009.
- Your CNIL reduces the amount of your cumulative gains limit for the year and may affect the allowable amount of your capital gains deduction.
- Even if you are not claiming a capital gains deduction in 2009, you should still complete this form if you had any investment income or expenses in 2009.
- Because the balance in your CNIL account is a cumulative total, you may need this information in a future year. Keep a copy for your records and attach another to your return.
- If you need more information, contact us at 1-800-959-8281.

Note: If you have capital gains other than from the disposition of qualified farm or fishing property or qualified small business corporation shares in 2009, you should start by completing Chart A on the back of this form to determine if you have additional investment income to include when you calculate your CNIL.

Other investment expenses (for line 6808)

Other investment expenses include:

- repayments of inducements
- repayments of refund interest

- the uncollectible portion of proceeds from dispositions of depreciable property (except passenger vehicles that cost more than $30,000)
- sale of agreement for sale or mortgage included in proceeds of disposition in a previous year under subsection 20(5)
- foreign non-business tax under subsections 20(11) and 20(12)
- life insurance premiums deducted from property income
- capital cost allowance claimed on certified films and videotapes
- farming or fishing losses claimed by a non-active partner or a limited partner.

Does not include:

- expenses incurred to earn business income
- repayment of shareholders' loans deducted under paragraph 20(1)(j)
- interest paid on money borrowed to:
    - buy an income-averaging annuity contract;
    - pay a premium under a registered retirement savings plan;
    - make a contribution to a registered pension plan; or
    - make a contribution to a deferred profit-sharing plan.

Other property income (for line 6810)

Other property income includes:

- amounts from insurance proceeds for the recapture of capital cost allowance (other than amounts already included on line 9)
- home insulation or energy conversion grants under paragraph 12(1)(u)
- payments received as an inducement or reimbursement
- income from the appropriation of property to a shareholder
- farming or fishing income reported by a non-active or a limited partner
- other income from a trust
- allowable capital losses included in partnership losses of other years after 1985
- amounts withdrawn from Net Income Stabilization Account (NISA) Fund 2.

Do not include:

- income amounts that relate to business income
- payments received from an income-averaging annuity contract
- payments received from an annuity contract bought under a deferred profit-sharing plan
- shareholders' loans included in income under subsection 15(2).

T1223 - Clergy Residence Deduction

T1223#: Clergy residence deduction

Complete this form to claim the clergy residence deduction. In order to qualify for this deduction, the taxpayer must be one of the following:

- a member of the clergy or a religious minister, and in charge of or ministering to a diocese, parish, or congregation, or engaged in full-time administrative service; or
- a member of a religious order.

Clergy housing allowance

In the T4 slip, enter the clergy housing allowance (which appears in box 30 of the client's T4 slip) in the Clergy housing allowance field and select the correct T1223# from the Transfer allowance to 1223 drop-down list (that appears below the 'Clergy housing allowance' field). This amount then flows through to part C of form T1223 and to line 104 and line 231 of the T1 jacket. (You may also have to override the CPP or EI earnings.)

The Canada Revenue Agency says...

- You have to complete this form to claim the clergy residence deduction. You complete Part A and Part C, and your employer completes Part B. If you have more than one employer in the year, each employer has to complete a separate Part B. In this situation, you must complete only one Part C calculation by combining the income from all eligible employers.
- You do not have to file this form with your return. However, you have to keep it in case we ask to see it.
- For more information, see Interpretation Bulletin IT-141, Clergy Residence Deduction.

Note

Line 7 - the actual rent and utilities paid or, if residence owned, the fair rental value including utilities must be reduced by all other amounts deducted in calculating your income from a business or from an office or employment in connection with the same accommodation. This could arise, for example, when your spouse or common-law partner claims work-space-in-the home expenses for the same accommodation.

If you received free accommodation (A) for part of the year and owned or rented the residence being claimed (B) for a different part of the year, add amounts (A) and (B) and claim the total amount on line 231 of your return. The amount claimed for the clergy residence deduction can never exceed income from qualifying employment on Line 1 of the above calculation.

T1229 - Statement of Exploration and Development Expenses and Depletion Allowance

T1229: Statement of exploration and development expenses

Amounts in Part I of form T1229 flow from any T101 and T5013 slips.

The Canada Revenue Agency says...

Use this form to calculate your resource expenditure pools, exploration and development expense deduction, expenses renounced in respect of flow-through shares which qualify for investment tax credits and to claim your depletion allowance.

Receipts - Attach your T101, T5013 and T5 slip(s) to the statement. If you do not have any of these slips, attach a statement that identifies you as a participant in the venture. Attach a completed copy of this form to your T1 General Income Tax and Benefit Return.

T2200 - Declaration of Conditions of Employment

T2200: Declaration of conditions of employment

Consult the guide information below for details regarding this form.

The Canada Revenue Agency says... *Employment Expenses Guide (T4044)*

You have to complete Form T2200 if you are deducting employment expenses. Make sure that Part A is complete, then print the form and have your employer complete and sign Part B. If you have more than one employer, have each employer complete and sign a separate form.

You do not have to submit this form with your income tax return. However, keep it in case CRA asks to see it.

For more information, see Statement of Employment Expenses, or get the CRA guide called Employment Expenses, or Interpretation Bulletins IT-352, Employee's Expenses, Including Work Space in Home Expenses, and IT-522, Vehicle, Travel and Sales Expenses of Employees.

T2222 - Northern resident's deductions

T2222: Northern resident's deduction

Use this form if you lived in a prescribed northern zone or in a prescribed intermediate zone for at least six consecutive months beginning or ending in the current taxation year. ProFile transfers the total deduction from this form to line 255 of the T1 jacket.

If you were not allowed these deductions last year, or if you do not receive form T2222 in the mail by the end of February, you can get a copy from the CRA. For a list of the areas that qualify, get form T4039, Northern Residents Deductions - Places in Prescribed Zones.

The Canada Revenue Agency says... *Form T2222 - Northern resident's deductions*

Do you qualify for the northern residents deductions?

To qualify for northern residents deductions, you must have lived, on a permanent basis, in a prescribed northern or intermediate zone for a continuous period of at least six consecutive months. (This period can begin or end in the year specified on the attached Form T2222).

There are two northern residents' deductions:

- a **residency deduction** for having lived in a prescribed zone; and
- a **travel deduction** for taxable travel benefits you received from employment in a prescribed zone.

Publication T4039, Northern Residents Deductions - Places in Prescribed Zones, lists the places in the zones.

Deduction limits

> If you lived in a prescribed northern zone (Zone A), you can claim full northern residents deductions. If you lived in a prescribed intermediate zone (Zone B), you can claim one-half of the full northern resident's deductions.

Deceased individuals

> A person who died in the year qualifies if he or she lived in a prescribed zone for six months or more before the date of death.

Moving

> Your period of residency is not affected if you moved from one place in a prescribed zone directly to another place in a prescribed zone.

Absences from a prescribed zone

> If you lived in a prescribed zone on a permanent basis, absences from a prescribed zone do not usually affect your period of residency. If you lived in a prescribed zone for work-related reasons (while your principal place of residence was not in a prescribed zone), you may have lived in the prescribed zone on a temporary basis only and therefore may not qualify for the deduction.
>
> To determine whether you lived in the prescribed zone on a permanent or a temporary basis, we consider the number of your absences from the prescribed zone and the purpose and length of your absences.

Step 1 - Calculate your residency deduction

Complete Step 1 of Form T2222 for Zone A or Zone B as applicable. There are two parts to the residency deduction:

- **Basic residency amount** - You can claim the number of days in the year that you lived in a prescribed zone; and
- **Additional residency amount** - You can claim an additional amount for those days you used to calculate your basic amount if you maintained and lived in a dwelling in the prescribed zone during that time and you are the only person claiming the basic residency amount for living in that same dwelling for that period.

A dwelling means a self-contained domestic establishment. Generally, this is a complete and separate living unit with a kitchen, bathroom, sleeping facilities, and its own private access. It includes a house, apartment, mobile home, or other similar place of residence in which a person usually sleeps and eats. It does not include a bunkhouse, dormitory, hotel room, or room in a boarding house.

We consider you to have maintained and lived in a dwelling, even if your employer let you live there rent-free and paid all the utility, maintenance, and other costs related to the dwelling. Each taxpayer living in the dwelling can claim the basic residency amount as a deduction on their income tax return. However, if more than one person claims the basic residency amount for a particular period and dwelling, no one in that household can claim the additional residency amount for that period and dwelling.

If only one person in a household claims the basic residency amount for a particular period and dwelling, that person can also claim the additional residency amount. To claim the deduction in the way that most benefits you're household, you should consider the taxable income of all the members of your household when deciding which household member will claim the residency deduction.

You can claim the basic residency amount for living at a special work site in a prescribed zone, when your principal place of residence is not in a prescribed zone. To do so, reduce your residency amount by the amount of board and lodging benefits you received for working at a special work site. The amount of these benefits is shown in box 31 of your T4 slip, or in the footnotes area of your T4A slip. If your slip does not show the value of these benefits, ask your employer for a corrected slip. For more information about special work sites, see Interpretation Bulletin IT-91, Employment at Special Work Sites or Remote Work Locations.

Step 2 - List your trips

Complete the chart in Step 2 of Form T2222 to list your trips. You can claim the deduction for expenses you incurred to travel or the value of travel provided if you meet all of the following conditions:

- you qualify to claim northern residents deductions;
- you are an employee dealing at arm's length with your employer; and
- you have included in your income the taxable travel benefits received from your employment in a prescribed zone.

You can claim a deduction for travel even if you are not claiming a residency deduction. For example, if your spouse or common-law partner claims both the basic and the additional residency amounts, you can still claim a deduction for any taxable travel benefits you received. Taxable travel benefits include:

- travel assistance provided by your employer such as airline tickets or a trip on the company owned airplane; and
- a travel allowance or a lump-sum payment you received from your employer for travel expenses you incurred.

You cannot claim a deduction for travel expenses if:

- you or any member of your household received or was entitled to receive non-taxable amounts as travel assistance, a travel allowance, or as a reimbursement for those expenses; or
- someone else has already claimed the deduction for travel expenses for this trip on their tax return.

If you received a benefit that was not for any particular trip, you have to split it reasonably between the trips you are claiming. To claim the deduction for travel, you must receive the taxable travel benefits in the same year you have the travel expenses. For example, if you take a trip that begins and ends in one year and you are reimbursed the following year, you cannot claim the travel deduction for that trip.

However, you can claim a deduction for travel if you leave on a trip in one year and return the next year. For example, you may leave on a trip in December and come back in January. If you receive non-refundable tickets or travel vouchers, the taxable travel benefit should be included in your T4 or T4A slip for the year the trip begins.

Travel expenses include: air/train/bus fares, vehicle expenses, meals, hotel or motel accommodations, camping fees, and other incidental expenses such as taxis and road/ferry tolls.

Column 1 of the trip list - Who is eligible?

To claim a deduction for travel, you must have included in your income taxable travel benefits (in the same year you have the travel expenses) from your employment in a prescribed zone. You can only claim a deduction for travel for a trip that you or your household members (who lived with you at the time of the trip) actually took and that started from a prescribed zone.

You can claim a deduction for Other Travel if you have an amount in box 32 of your T4 slip or box 28 of your T4A slip showing any taxable travel benefits you received in the year. Other Travel means travel for vacation or family reasons (maximum of two trips per year by each household member).

You can claim a deduction for Medical Travel if you have an amount in box 33 of your T4 slip or box 28 of your T4A slip showing any taxable travel benefits you received in the year. There is no limit on the number of trips for Medical Travel by each family member. The medical services had to be for you or a member of your household and must not have been available where you lived. If you are claiming a medical travel deduction on this T2222 form, no one else can claim it as a medical expense on his or her income tax return.

Column 4 - Methods of calculating expenses

Methods of calculating expenses

To calculate meal and vehicle expenses only, you may choose the detailed or simplified method. Your total travel expenses equal the total of the value of travel assistance provided by your employer and the travel expenses incurred by you. Ensure that you have included any travel costs paid by your employer.

Detailed Method - You must keep your receipts and claim the actual amount that you spent.

Simplified Method - You do not need to keep receipts.

- **Meals** - You can claim a flat rate of $17/meal, to a maximum of $51/day (Canadian or US funds) per person, without receipts.
- **Vehicle Expenses** - You must keep track of the number of kilometres driven during the tax year for the trip. To determine the amount you can claim for vehicle expenses, multiply the number of kilometres by the cents/km rate for the province or territory in which the travel begins.

For information on detailed and simplified travel methods, see travel methods.

About Medical Expenses - In cases of medical travel, if the patient needs an attendant while travelling, the attendant's travel costs are included as part of the patient's total travel expenses, regardless if they are in the form of travel assistance your employer provided or actual expenses you incurred.

- **If the attendant was you or a member of your household**: In Column 5, include the cost of the attendant's lowest return airfare as part of the patient's expense for airfare. In Column 4, include the cost of the attendant's travel expenses (excluding airfare) as part of the patient's travel expenses.
- **If the attendant was not you or a member of your household:** In Column 5, do not include the cost of the attendant's lowest return airfare as part of the patient's expense for airfare. In Column 4, include the cost of the attendant's travel expenses (including airfare) as part of the patient's travel expenses.

Column 5 - Lowest return airfare

lowest return airfare available at the time of the trip means the lowest return airfare for regularly scheduled commercial flights on the date that the travel began. The lowest return airfare to be used to complete Column 5 is the cost quoted for a flight from the airport closest to your residence to the nearest designated city (even if you did not actually travel by air or to that city).

About Medical Expenses - In cases of medical travel, if the patient needs an attendant while travelling, the attendant's travel costs are included as part of the patient's total travel expenses, regardless if they are in the form of travel assistance your employer provided or actual expenses you incurred.

- **If the attendant was you or a member of your household:** In Column 5, include the cost of the attendant's lowest return airfare as part of the patient's expense for airfare. In Column 4, include the cost of the attendant's travel expenses (excluding airfare) as part of the patient's travel expenses.
- **If the attendant was not you or a member of your household:** In Column 5, do not include the cost of the attendant's lowest return airfare as part of the patient's expense for airfare. In Column 4, include the cost of the attendant's travel expenses (including airfare) as part of the patient's travel expenses.

Step 3 - Calculate your travel deduction

The maximum deduction you can claim for each eligible trip is the lowest of the following three amounts:

- the taxable travel benefits you received from your employer for the trip (Form T2222: Step 2 - Column 3);
- the total travel expenses paid for the trip (Form T2222: Step 2 - Column 4); or
- the cost of the lowest return airfare available at the time of the trip between the airport closest to your residence and the nearest designated city (Form T2222: Step 2 - Column 5).

Designated cities	
Vancouver, BC	Ottawa, ON
Calgary, AB	Montréal, QC
Edmonton, AB	Québec, QC
Saskatoon, SK	Moncton, NB
Winnipeg, MB	Halifax, NS
North Bay, ON	St. John's, NL
Toronto, ON	

Attach to your income tax return a completed copy of Form T2222.

Step 4 - Calculate your northern resident's deductions

Add lines 13 (residency deduction) and line 18 (travel deduction) on Form T2222. Enter the amount from line 21 (on Form T2222) on line 255 of your return.

If you have not lived in a prescribed zone for six consecutive months at the time you file your income tax return, you do not yet qualify. File your return without making the claim. When you qualify, you can ask us to adjust your return. To do so, follow the instructions in the under the heading "After you file."

T5004 - Statement of Tax Shelter Loss or Deduction

T5004: Tax shelter loss or deduction

If you are claiming your loss or deduction on an individual income tax return, use the last column in the form's table to indicate the line where you are making your claim. If you are a limited partner of a partnership that invested in a tax shelter, make your claim on line 122, Net partnership income: limited or non-active partners only.

Otherwise, make your claim on the line that corresponds with the type of loss you are claiming: i.e., line 126, Rental income; line 135, Business income; line 141, Farming income; line 143, Fishing income; line 217, Business investment loss; line 221, Carrying charges and interest expenses, line 224, Exploration and development expenses; line 232, Other deductions.

 The Canada Revenue Agency says...

Use this form if you are an investor claiming a loss or deduction, a donation or political contribution deduction, or a tax credit for an interest in a tax shelter. We may verify and adjust your claim.

If you receive a T5003 slip (tax shelter), and a T5013 slip (partnership) or an official donation or political contribution slip for the same tax shelter, do not claim amounts more than once.

Under the Income Tax Act, we can apply a penalty of 50% of the understated tax if you make a false claim knowingly or in circumstances amounting to gross negligence.

Attach a completed copy of this form to your income tax and benefit return together with documents (a copy of your T5003 slip and the tax shelter's statement of earnings, or a copy of your T5013 slip) to support the amount you are claiming as a loss or deduction, a donation or political contribution deduction, or a tax credit.

You have to identify a tax shelter interest you bought after August 31, 1989, with a tax shelter identification number. You have to provide this number on your claim for any investment in the tax shelter you bought after that date.

Tax Shelters

Generally, a tax shelter is:

an **investment in property** (other than a flow-through share or a prescribed property); or

a **gifting arrangement** under which a person entering into the arrangement:

- makes a gift to a qualified donee or makes a monetary contribution to a registered party, a provincial division of a registered party, a registered association, or a candidate as those terms are defined in the Canada Elections Act; or
- incurs a limited-recourse debt that can reasonably be considered to relate to a gift to a qualified donee or to a monetary contribution.

Generally, the investment in property or the gifting arrangement is a tax shelter if it is promoted as offering income tax savings and if it is reasonable to consider, based on statements or representations made or proposed to be made, that within the first four years of buying an investment in the property or entering into the gifting arrangement, the buyer or donor will have losses, deductions, or credits. Further, it has to be reasonable to consider that the losses, deduction, or credits would be equal to or more than the cost of the original investment or of the property acquired under the gifting arrangement, net of any prescribed benefits expected to be received or enjoyed, directly or indirectly, by the person or another person with whom the person does not deal at arm's length.

The tax shelter rules for gifting arrangements generally apply to gifts monetary contributions, and representations made and property acquired under the gifting arrangement after February 18, 2003.

Under the Income Tax Act, a tax shelter promoter has to get an identification number from the Canada Revenue Agency before selling the tax shelter. The number does not indicate that we guarantee any investment, or authorize any resulting tax benefits. We use this number for administrative purposes only. If you own a tax shelter, you have to give its identification number when you file a tax return.

We recognize that legitimate tax shelters are established for valid business reasons. However, we are concerned that some promoters sell tax shelters mainly to help taxpayers avoid paying taxes.

Investors should be cautious when considering a tax shelter investment if they suspect that it has these features:

- a lack of business activity, or an activity with no reasonable expectation of profit;
- unreasonable or inflated expenses, or overvalued assets;
- limited-recourse financing, or financing arrangements that indefinitely defer an investor's payment;
- losses for tax purposes will be more than the amount of the investment that is actually at risk; or
- the promoter or others are making verbal assurances of income tax consequences that are different from, or are not confirmed by, professional opinions contained in the investment documents.

Tax benefits resulting from a tax shelter for a genuine business or investment are acceptable if they are reasonable and all other requirements of the Income Tax Act have been met. However, a tax shelter established only for a tax benefit (e.g., to generate a tax refund) may be unacceptable, and we may apply the general anti-avoidance rule of the Income Tax Act to deny the benefit being sought.

To ensure fairness in the tax system and prevent abuses through aggressive tax shelter promotions, we review and audit tax shelters. When we review a tax shelter, we determine if the tax shelter leads to an abusive application of the rules by letting investors claim deductions or losses that are more than any amounts they will have to pay. If we suspect fraud, we investigate the actions of the parties involved.

For more information on tax shelters and the general anti-avoidance rule, see Information Circular 89-4, Tax Shelter Reporting, and Information Circular 88-2, General Anti-Avoidance Rule - Section 245 of the Income Tax Act.

Transport Employees

TL2#: Claim for meals and lodging expenses

Form TL2 is used by transport employees, such as employees of airline, railway, bus, trucking or other transport companies. You will have to complete form TL2 if you are deducting expenses and your employer's principal business is transporting goods, passengers, or both.

Your employer has to sign the form. Most transport employees will complete form TL2. You do not have to submit this form with your income tax return. However, keep it in case CRA asks to see it.

 **The Canada Revenue Agency says...** *Employment Expenses Guide (T4044)*

You may be able to claim the cost of meals and lodging (including showers) if you are an employee of a transport business, a railway employee, or other transport employee. This cost includes any GST and provincial sales tax, or HST, you paid on these expenses. You may be able to receive a rebate of the GST/HST you paid. See GST/HST rebate for more information.

Employees of a transport business

You can deduct the cost of meals and lodging if you meet all of the following conditions:

- you work for an airline, railway, bus or trucking company, or for any other employer whose principal business is the transport of goods, passengers or both;
- you travel in vehicles your employer uses to transport goods or passengers;
- you regularly have to travel away from the municipality and the metropolitan area (if there is one) where your home terminal is located; and
- you regularly incur meal and lodging expenses while travelling away from the municipality and the metropolitan area (if there is one) where your employer's relevant establishment (home terminal) is located. This means that you must generally be away from home overnight to do your job.

You must reduce your claim for meal and lodging expenses by any non-taxable allowance or reimbursement you received or are entitled to receive from your employer. For information on meal allowances and subsidized meals, see Information Circular 7321, Claims for Meals and Lodging Expenses of Transport Employees.

Railway employees

You can also claim the cost of meals and lodging when you meet one of the following conditions:

- You work away from home for a railway company as a telegrapher or station agent in a relief capacity, or carrying out maintenance and repair work for the railway company.
- You are a railway employee who works away from the municipality and the metropolitan area (if there is one) where your employer's relevant establishment (home terminal) is located. You also work at such a distant location that it is unreasonable for you to return daily to your home, where you support a spouse or common-law partner, or a dependant related to you.

Other transport employees

Even if you do not meet all of the conditions listed in the section called "Employees of a transport business," you may still be able to claim the cost of meals and lodging you incur in the year. For example, you may be an employee whose main duty of employment is transporting goods, but your employer's main business is not transporting goods or passengers.

If you satisfy the conditions listed under the section called "Travelling expenses," you will still qualify to use the simplified method of meal reporting described on this page. For more details about both sets of conditions, see Information Circular 73-21 Claims for Meals and Lodging Expenses of Transport Employees.

If your employer has paid or will pay you for any part of your meal and lodging expenses, subtract that amount from your claim.

How to claim your expenses

Complete Parts 1 and 2 of Form TL2, Claim for Meals and Lodging Expenses, and have your employer complete Part 3 and sign it. Trips that qualify as an eligible trip for long haul- truck drivers should be reported in Part 2B, and all other trips should be reported in Part 2A. Claim your meal and lodging expenses on line 229 of your return. You do not have to send Form TL2 with your return, but keep it in case we ask to see it later.

Below, we explain how to calculate your meal and lodging expenses. For more detailed information about meal and lodging expenses, see Information Circular 73-21, Claims for Meals and Lodging Expenses of Transport Employees.

Meals

To calculate your meal expenses, you may use either the simplified or detailed method, or in certain situations, the batching method. These methods are explained in this section.

The most you can deduct for meal expenses is 50% of your claim (unless you are a long-haul truck driver claiming meals for an eligible trip, as explained in the section called "Meal expenses of long haul truck drivers"). For example, if you use the simplified method, which is based on a daily meal rate of $17 per meal, the most you can deduct is $8.50 ($17 x 50%) for each meal.

Under either the simplified or detailed method, you can claim one meal after every four hours from the departure time, to a maximum of three meals per day. For the purposes of calculating the maximum number of meals allowed, a day is considered to be a 24-hour period that begins at the departure time.

The simplified method

> This is the easiest way to calculate your meal expenses since you do not have to keep receipts for your meals, although you do have to keep a detailed list of the trips you take, in a record or log book. The simplified method is based on a meal rate of $17 for each meal. Multiply the actual number of meals you ate by $17 (to a maximum of three meals per day) and report that amount on Form TL2, Claim for Meals and Lodging Expenses, under the "Meals bought" column of Part 2 - Trip and expense summary.

The detailed method

> If you choose to use the detailed method to calculate your meal expenses, you have to keep a log or record book itemizing each expense. You also have to keep receipts to support the amount you deduct. Report the actual amount you spent on meals on Form TL2 under the "Meals bought" column of Part 2 - Trip and expense summary.

The batching method

> When you are part of a work crew, such as on a train, your employer may provide you with cooking facilities. If you buy groceries and cook meals either by yourself or as a group, each person can claim up to $34 for each day. As long as you do not claim more than this amount, you do not have to keep receipts. Report this amount on Form TL2 under the "Meals bought" column of Part 2 - Trip and expense summary.

Meal expenses of long-haul truck drivers

Meal and beverage expenses for long-haul truck drivers are deductible at a rate higher than the 50% permitted for other transportation employees. During eligible travel periods in 2009, meal and beverage expenses incurred are deductible at 70%. This rate will increase by 5% each year until the maximum rate of 80% is reached in 2011.

You are a long-haul truck driver if you are an employee whose main duty of employment is transporting goods by way of driving a long-haul truck, whether or not your employer's main business is transporting goods, passengers, or both.

A long-haul truck is a truck or tractor that is designed for hauling freight, and has a gross vehicle weight rating of more than 11,788 kg.

An eligible travel period is a period during which you are away from your municipality or metropolitan area for at least 24 hours for the purpose of driving a long-haul truck that transports goods at least 160 kilometres from the employer's establishment to which you regularly report to work.

Lodging and showers

You can deduct your lodging expenses. The costs of showers are also considered to be deductible as part of lodging expenses for transportation employees who may have slept in the cab of their trucks rather than at hotels. You need to keep your receipts to support the amount you deduct.

Trips to the United States

You can claim the meal and lodging expenses you incur while performing your duties as a transport employee in the United States. If you are using the simplified method of reporting meal expenses, you are entitled to US$17 per meal while in the United States. The most you can deduct for meal expenses is 50% of your claim, just as it is for trips within Canada (unless you are a long-haul truck driver, as described in the section called "Meal expenses of long-haul truck drivers" under Meals above).

Calculate the total U.S. dollar amount of both the meal and lodging expenses incurred in the United States and convert these two totals to Canadian dollars by multiplying them by the Bank of Canada average annual U.S. conversion rate.

Provide a summary of your trips to the United States in Part 2 - Trip and expense summary of Form TL2. Attach a more detailed list of these trips to the form.

Chapter 5

Tax & Credits

2009 Tax Year

CPT20: Election to pay Canada pension plan contributions

Complete this form for taxpayers who choose to make additional CCP contributions because they did not contribute to the CPP when earning employment income or contributed less than the allowable amount.

Gifts and Income Tax

Donations: Charitable donations

Use the Donations form to enter charitable donations for the taxpayer. You can enter donations for both Canadian and U.S. organizations. Keep in mind that you need to enter U.S. source income for a U.S. donations claim to calculate.

Any donations that appear on slips will flow automatically to the Donations form. Enter these amounts directly on the related slips (e.g. T4, T3, T2202A, T4A and T5013).

 Tip: You can claim donations that your spouse made as long as your spouse does not claim them.

 Note: A claim for allowable charitable donations and government gifts is subject to different rules than a claim for cultural and ecological gifts.

Member of a religious order

If you are a member of a religious order and you have taken a vow of perpetual poverty, claim your deduction on line 256 of your return.

Complete your claim for charitable donations and government, cultural, and ecological gifts from the calculation on Schedule 9, which includes lines 340 (Allowable charitable donations and government gifts) and 342 (Cultural and ecological gifts). The total flows to line 349 of the T1 jacket.

Carrying forward the donations

The donation carry forwards appear at the bottom of this form. ProFile will automatically claim older donations first to ensure the taxpayer uses these before they expire (you can carry forward charitable donations for up to 5 years).

The Canada Revenue Agency says... *Gifts and Income Tax Guide (P113)*

If you made a gift of money or other property to certain institutions, you may be able to claim federal and provincial or territorial non-refundable tax credits when you file your return, provided that you receive an official receipt from the institution(s). If you lived in Quebec on December 31, claim your provincial tax credit on your Quebec return.

In most cases, a gift is a voluntary transfer of property without valuable consideration. However, for gifts made after December 20, 2002, a transfer of property for which you received an advantage will still be considered a gift for purposes of the Income Tax Act as long as we are satisfied that the transfer of property was made with the intention to make a gift. An intention to make a gift will be presumed when the fair market value (FMV) of the advantage does not exceed 80% of the FMV of the transferred property.

Note: If the amount of the advantage exceeds 80% of the FMV of the transferred property, we may still consider the transfer to be a gift for purposes of the Income Tax Act.

For gifts made after December 20, 2002, it is the eligible amount of the gift that is used to calculate your non-refundable donation tax credits.

The tax consequences of a gift depend on such facts as whether it is:

- a gift to a qualified donee such as a registered charity, the Government of Canada, a province, or a territory;
- a gift of ecologically sensitive land; or
- a gift of certified cultural property to a designated institution or a public authority under the Cultural Property Export and Import Act; or
- a gift of a share, debt obligation or right listed on a designated stock exchange, a share of the capital stock of a mutual fund corporation, a unit of a mutual fund trust, an interest in a related segregated fund trust or a prescribed debt obligation.

It will also depend on whether the property was capital property, listed personal property, or inventory of a business.

For more information see:

- What gifts can you claim?
- Gifts in kind
- Capital gains and losses
- Schedule 9 - Donations and Gifts (Calculating your increased donation limit)

For information on the Cultural Property Export and Import Act, see the complete P113, Gifts and Income Tax guide.

FTC#: Foreign tax credits

This form summarizes foreign income, tax paid and credits for a specified country. As well, the form includes fields where you can enter foreign tax and income that do not have supporting slips. Enter these amounts in the fields for income and tax "not linked to the form."

Foreign income amounts and foreign tax paid flow to the FTC from T3, T5, T4PS and T5013 slips.

ProFile calculates foreign tax credits automatically for any number of countries, using a separate FTC, >T2209 and T2036 for each country. All of these forms allow you to create unlimited copies.

For example, on a T5 form, you can enter the name of the foreign country, the foreign income amount and the foreign tax paid.

ProFile will automatically complete forms FTC, T2209 (Federal foreign tax credits) and T2036 (Provincial foreign tax credits) for EACH foreign country you enter on the slips. These forms appear as separate lines in the Form Explorer "Tax + credits" category with the country name as part of the description.

Definitions of terms on the FTC form

Non-business-income tax paid to a foreign country

Non-business income tax paid to a foreign country (see note below) is the total of non-business income or profits tax you paid to that country or to a political subdivision of that country for the year, minus any part of this tax that is deductible under subsection 20(11) or deducted under subsection 20(12) of the Canadian Income Tax Act. Non-business income tax paid to a foreign country does not include tax that can reasonably be attributed to an amount that:

- any other person or partnership has received, or is entitled to receive from the foreign country;
- relates to employment income from that country, and you claimed an overseas employment tax credit for that income;
- relates to taxable capital gains from that country, and you or your spouse or common-law partner claimed a capital gains deduction for that income;
- was deductible as income exempt from tax under a tax treaty between Canada and that country; or
- was taxable in the foreign country because you were a citizen of that country, and relates to income from a source within Canada.

Note: Any amount of tax you paid to a foreign government in excess of the amount you had to pay according to a tax treaty is considered a voluntary contribution and does not qualify as foreign taxes paid.

Net foreign non-business income

Net foreign non-business income (see note below) is the net amount you calculate when the non-business income you earned in a foreign country is more than the non-business losses you incurred in that country. When you calculate the non-business income and losses, claim the allowable expenses and deductions relating to the foreign income or loss (including foreign resource and exploration and development deductions, as well as deductions claimed under subsections 20(11) or 20(12) of the Act - do not include any deduction you claimed for a dividend you received from a controlled foreign affiliate). Reduce your foreign non-business income by any income from that foreign country for which you claimed a capital gains deduction, and by any income from that country that was, under a tax treaty between Canada and that country, deductible as exempt from tax in Canada or in that country. Also, reduce it by any part of employment income from that country for which you claimed an overseas employment tax credit. If your net foreign non-business income is more than your net income, use your net income in the calculation.

For more information on deductions claimed under subsections 20(11) and 20(12) of the Act, see Interpretation Bulletin IT-506, Foreign Income Taxes as a Deduction from Income.

Note: Include only your foreign non-business income for the part of the year you were a resident of Canada.

Net income

Net income (see note below) is the amount on line 236 of your return (or, if you filed a Form T581 election, the amount on line 8 of that form), minus any:

- amounts deductible as an employee home relocation loan deduction (line 248 of your return);
- amounts deductible as stock option and shares deductions (line 249 of your return);
- amounts deductible as an other payments deduction (line 250 of your return);
- net capital losses of other years you claimed (line 253 of your return);

- capital gains deduction you claimed (line 254 of your return); and
- foreign income deductible as exempt income under a tax treaty, or deductible as net employment income from a prescribed international organization (included on line 256 of your return).

Note: If you were a resident of Canada for part of the year, include the income for the part of the year you were a resident of Canada, and the taxable income you earned in Canada (before deductions in paragraphs 115(1)(d) to (f) of the Income Tax Act) as reported on your Canadian income tax return, for the part of the year you were not a resident of Canada.

Federal tax

Federal tax (see note below) is the amount on line 429 of Schedule 1 or line 12 of Form T2203, plus any:

- overseas employment tax credit (from Form T626 or line 8 of Form T2203);
- dividend tax credit (line 425 of Schedule 1 or line 9 of Form T2203); and
- federal surtax for income you earned outside Canada (from Schedule 1 or line 13 of Form T2203);

and minus any:

- refundable Quebec abatement (line 35 of Form T2203); and
- tax adjustments for CPP/QPP benefits for previous years (included on line 423 of Schedule 1 or line 5 of Form T2203).

Note: If you were a resident of Quebec, federal tax or basic federal tax is the amount on line 429 of Schedule 1 or line 12 of Form T2203, plus any:

- overseas employment tax credit (from Form T626 or line 8 of Form T2203); and
- dividend tax credit (line 425 of Schedule 1 or line 9 of Form T2203);

and minus any:

- federal forward-averaging tax credit (line 13 of Form T581); and
- refundable Quebec abatement (line 440 of your return or line 37 of Form T2203).

Business income tax paid to a foreign country

Business income tax paid to a foreign country (see note 1 below) is the total of business income or profits tax you paid to a country or a political subdivision of a country for the year (see note 2 below). It does not include any part of the business income tax that can be reasonably attributed to an amount that any other person or partnership has received or is entitled to receive from a country, or that was payable on income that was exempt from tax under a tax treaty between Canada and that country.

Note: Any amount of tax you paid to a foreign government in excess of the amount you had to pay according to a tax treaty is considered a voluntary contribution and does not qualify as foreign taxes paid.

Note: If you were a resident of Quebec, multiply this amount by 55%.

Net foreign business Income

foreign business income is the net amount by which the business income you earned in a foreign country is more than the business losses you incurred in that country. When you calculate the business income and losses, claim the allowable expenses and deductions relating to the foreign income or loss, including foreign resource and exploration and development deductions. Also reduce your foreign business income by any income from that country that was, under a tax treaty between Canada and that country, exempt from tax in Canada or in that country. If your net foreign business income is more than your net income, use your net income in the calculation.

Note: Include only your foreign non-business income for the part of the year you were a resident of Canada.

Basic federal tax

Basic federal tax (see note below) is the amount on line 429 of Schedule 1 or line 12 of Form T2203, plus any:

- overseas employment tax credit (from Form T626 or line 8 of Form T2203); and
- dividend tax credit (line 425 of Schedule 1 or line 9 of Form T2203);

and minus any:

- tax adjustments for CPP/QPP benefits for previous years (included on line 423 of Schedule 1 or line 5 of Form T2203).

Note: If you were a resident of Quebec, federal tax or basic federal tax is the amount on line 429 of Schedule 1 or line 12 of Form T2203, plus any:

- overseas employment tax credit (from Form T626 or line 8 of Form T2203); and
- dividend tax credit (line 425 of Schedule 1 or line 9 of Form T2203);

and minus any:

- federal forward-averaging tax credit (line 13 of Form T581); and
- refundable Quebec abatement (line 440 of your return or line 37 of Form T2203).

GST 370 - Employee and Partner GST/HST Rebate

GST370: Employee and partner GST rebate

If you deducted expenses from your income as an employee (lines 212 or 229) or as a partner (lines 135 to 143), you may be eligible for a rebate of the GST/HST you paid on those expenses.

Eligible expenses include the GST/HST, provincial sales tax and tips.

Use form T777 to calculate your allowable employment expenses. If you answer "Yes" to the question "Do you qualify for a GST rebate?", at the top of the form, ProFile will automatically complete and calculate form GST370: Employee and Partner GST Rebate.

What's the difference between the GST 370 rebate and the GST credit?

The GST 370 rebate is based on GST/HST you paid on certain employment-related expenses that you have deducted on your income tax return. This rebate must be reported as income.

The GST/HST credit is a tax-free payment to help lower income individuals and families offset the cost of the GST/HST. It is based on your net family income, and is not taxable.

 The Canada Revenue Agency says... *Employment Expenses Guide (T4044)*

General information

Provincial sales taxes in Nova Scotia, Newfoundland and Labrador, and New Brunswick were harmonized with the goods and services tax (GST) to create the harmonized sales tax (HST). For the rest of this chapter, we call these the participating provinces.

As an employee, you may have incurred expenses in the course of your employment duties. Some of these expenses you paid may have included GST or HST. If you deducted these expenses from your employment income, you may be able to get a rebate of the GST or HST you paid on these expenses. Complete Form GST370, Employee and Partner GST/HST Rebate Application and claim the rebate on line 457 of your income tax return. For more information, see the section called "How to complete Form GST370, Employee and Partner GST/HST Rebate Application."

It is important for you to keep proper records so you can identify the expenses that included GST/HST. For more information, see Guide RC4409, Keeping Records.

How a rebate affects your income tax

When you receive a GST/HST rebate for your expenses, you have to include it in your income for the year you received it. Report the amount on line 104 of your tax return. For example, if in 2009 you received a GST/HST rebate that you claimed for the 2008 tax year, you have to include it on line 104 of your 2009 tax return.

If any part of the GST/HST rebate is for a vehicle or musical instrument you bought, it will affect your claim for capital cost allowance in the year you receive the rebate. If this applies to you, reduce the undepreciated capital cost of your vehicle or musical instrument by the amount of the rebate at the beginning of the year in which you receive the rebate and do not include that part of the rebate on line 104 of your tax return.

Do you qualify for the rebate?

As an employee, you may qualify for a GST/HST rebate if:

- you paid GST or HST on certain employment-related expenses and deducted those expenses on your income tax return; and
- your employer is a GST/HST registrant.

You do not qualify for a GST/HST rebate if your employer:

- is not a GST/HST registrant; or
- is a listed financial institution as defined in the Excise Tax Act (for example, an entity that was at any time during the year a bank, an investment dealer, a trust company, an insurance company, a credit union, or a corporation whose principal business was lending money).

Expenses that qualify for the rebate

You can only apply for a rebate for the GST/HST you paid on expenses that you deducted on your tax return. You must have paid the GST/HST before claiming the rebate. Common examples of eligible expenses are described in Form T777 - Statement of Employment Expenses.

Non-eligible expenses include the following:

- Expenses on which you did not pay GST or HST, such as:
    - goods and services acquired from non-registrants (for example, small suppliers);
    - most expenses you incurred outside Canada (for example, gasoline, accommodation, meals, and entertainment);
    - certain expenses that you do not pay GST or HST on, such as basic groceries
    - expenses that are not subject to GST or HST, including medical underwriting fees, insurance premiums, bonding premiums, mortgage interest, residential rents, interest, motor vehicle licence and registration fees, and salaries.
- expenses you incurred when your employer was not a GST/HST registrant.;
- expenses that relate to an allowance you received from your employer that is not reported in Area C of the GST/HST rebate application - For example, an allowance that was not included in your income as a taxable benefit because it was a reasonable allowance;
- any personal-use portion of an eligible expense;
- 50% of the GST/HST paid on eligible expenses for food, beverages, and entertainment (for long haul-truck drivers, 30% of the GST/HST paid on these expenses that were incurred during eligible travel periods); and
- an expense or part of an expense for which you were reimbursed or are entitled to be reimbursed by your employer.

Capital cost allowance

You can claim a GST/HST rebate based on the amount of capital cost allowance (CCA) you claimed on motor vehicles and musical instruments on which you paid GST or HST. If you claim CCA on more than one property of the same class, you have to separate the portion of the CCA for the property that qualifies for the rebate from the CCA for the other property.

You cannot claim a rebate for CCA claimed on motor vehicles and musical instruments you bought before 1991, since you did not pay GST/HST on them.

In most cases, you cannot claim a GST or HST rebate on the CCA claimed on motor vehicles and musical instruments that relates to any allowance your employer paid you on those properties. However, you can claim a rebate if it relates to an allowance your employer reports in Area C of Form GST370. You cannot claim a rebate on CCA claimed on property for which you received a non-taxable allowance.

If you paid GST when you bought your motor vehicle or musical instrument in 2009, you can claim a rebate of 5/105 of the CCA you claimed on your tax return. If you paid HST, you can claim a rebate of 13/113 of the CCA you claimed on your tax return.

In certain cases, you may have to do an additional calculation if you bought your motor vehicle or musical instrument outside a participating province and brought the property into a participating province. For more information, see the section called "Situation 5 - Property and services brought into a participating province".

Filing deadline

You should file your Form GST370, Employee and Partner GST/HST Rebate Application, with your tax return for the year in which you deduct the expenses.

If you do not file your rebate application with your tax return, send it along with a letter to your tax centre. Include details such as your social insurance number and the tax year to which the application relates.

If you do not file your rebate application with your tax return, send in a letter with the application. Give details such as your social insurance number and the tax year to which the application relates.

Rebate restriction

You can only file one GST370, GST/HST rebate application for each calendar year.

You cannot get a rebate of an amount if:

- we previously refunded, remitted, or credited the tax to you;
- you received or are entitled to receive a rebate, refund, or remission under any other section of the Excise Tax Act or any other act of Parliament for the same expense; or
- you received a credit note, or you issued a debit note, for an adjustment, refund, or credit that includes the amount; or
- the deadline for filing the rebate has passed.

Overpayment of a rebate

If you receive an overpayment of a GST/HST rebate, you have to repay the excess. We charge interest on any balance you owe.

Quebec sales tax rebate

Some of the expenses you paid to earn your employment income may have included Quebec

sales tax (QST). If you deducted these expenses from your employment income, you may be able to receive a rebate of the QST you paid. This rebate also applies to the QST you paid on a musical instrument you use to earn employment income. Claim the QST rebate on line 459 of your Quebec provincial tax return.

If the QST rebate is for your expenses, include the rebate in your income for the year you received it. Report the amount on line 104 of your federal tax return

If the QST rebate is for a vehicle or musical instrument you bought, it will affect your claim for capital cost allowance in the year you receive the rebate. If this applies to you, reduce the capital cost of your vehicle or musical instrument by the amount of the rebate. Do not include the rebate on line 104 of your federal tax return.

For more information about the QST rebate and Form VD-358-V, Québec Sales Tax Rebate Application for Employees and Partners, contact Revenu Québec.

Medical: Medical expenses

TP1 tip! Only enter Quebec Prescription Drug Plan premiums from the previous year on this worksheet. This differs from the provincial worksheet, where you can only claim Quebec Prescription Drug Plan premiums from the current year.

Taxpayers may claim medical expenses for any twelve-month period that ends in the current tax year. You cannot claim expenses already claimed on last year's tax return. Generally, you can claim all amounts paid, even if they were not paid in Canada.

Taxpayers can claim amounts paid for the taxpayer or a relative to learn to care for a relative who has a mental or physical infirmity and who is in the taxpayer's household or is dependent on the taxpayer for support. There is a refundable tax credit for working individuals with low incomes and high medical expenses.

You cannot claim the part of any medical expense for which you have been (or can be) reimbursed. However, you can claim all of the expenses if you include the reimbursement in your income. For example, benefits from a T4 slip, if you did not deduct the reimbursement anywhere else on your return.

Note:

- It may be better for the spouse with the lower income to claim the allowable medical expenses. Compare your credit with the credit your spouse would be allowed. You can make whichever claim you prefer.
- If medical treatment is not available locally, you may be able to claim the cost of travelling to receive treatment elsewhere.

Allowable medical expenses

Your total expenses must be more than either 3% of your net income or $2,011, whichever is less.

This is a list of the more common medical expenses that you can claim, provided you were not reimbursed for them. If your employer or a private insurance or drug plan paid a percentage of the expenses, you can claim the remaining portion that you paid (see examples below).

payments to a medical doctor, dentist, nurse, or certain other medical professionals, or to a public or licensed private hospital;

- payments for prescription medicines and drugs;
- dental services (including x-rays, fillings, extractions, oral surgery, dentures, and tooth straightening);
- prescription eyeglasses, prescription contact lenses, laser eye surgery, ;
- ambulance charges to or from hospital;
- premiums paid to private or non-government health services plans (other than those paid by an employer);
- artificial limbs, aids, and other devices and equipment (including artificial eyes and limbs, iron lung, a rocking bed for poliomyelitis victims, wheelchairs, crutches, spinal braces, a brace for a limb, ileostomy or colostomy pads, a truss for a hernia, laryngeal speaking aids, hearing aids, pacemakers, an artificial kidney machine, and certain prescription medical devices;
- repairs to and replacement batteries for the above;
- laboratory tests;
- hospital services (including anaesthesia, oxygen masks/tents, vaccines, and x-rays);
- amounts paid for attendant care, or care in an establishment, provided no one claimed the disability amount for the person receiving the care;

- devices designed to assist in daily living (for example, to enter or leave a bathtub or shower);
- special telephone devices to help people who are hearing-impaired.
- expenses relating to guide and hearing-ear dogs;
- cost of diabetic testing supplies;
- incremental cost of gluten-free food (compared to the cost of non-gluten-free food) if required due to Celica disease; and
- reasonable travel expenses (such as meals and accommodation), if medical treatment was not available locally.

Note: You cannot claim payments to a provincial health insurance plan (e.g., Ontario Health Insurance Plan (OHIP), Alberta Health Care Insurance Plan (AHCIP), and BC Medical Services Plan (MSP)).

For a complete list of what you can claim as medical expenses, get the CRA publication IT519, Medical Expense and Disability Tax Credits and Attendant Care Expense Deduction.

Ineligible expenses

You cannot claim the following as medical expenses:

- Payments to a provincial health insurance plan (e.g., Ontario Health Insurance Plan (OHIP), Alberta Health Care Insurance Plan (AHCIP), BC Medical Services Plan (MSP), etc.).
- Birth control devices (non-prescription)
- Diet programs, food, and scales for weighing food
- Funeral expenses
- Maternity clothes
- Memberships to health clubs, gyms, and fitness centres
- Non-prescription creams and lotions
- Toothpaste
- Wigs (unless custom-made for victims of abnormal hair loss due to disease or medical treatment)

Other Credits: Other credits

The Other Credits form includes calculations for various credits on the T1 jacket that do not have full supporting schedules. The form also gathers all the credit information from other forms and schedules so that you can review all credits on the same form. If a section does not contain any amounts, it will not print on the form.

ProFile transfers the credits from each area of the Other Credits form to the appropriate line of the T1 jacket.

Please refer to your Provincial Supplement Guide

Repay: Social benefits repayment

Recovery tax:

- is a tax on OAS payments made to higher-income pensioners

- does not apply to any other, non-OAS income you receive
- applies only if your net world income is more than $62,144 for the 2009 tax year.

ProFile automatically calculates what Employment Insurance benefits or Old Age Security payments you are required to repay and enters the amounts on line 235 (as a deduction) and on line 422 (as a part of taxes payable).

The Social benefits repayment form reproduces Chart 1 from the back of the CRA T4E slip and Chart 2 from CRA's federal worksheet.

The calculations on Chart 1 and 2 apply if you have an amount in Box 15 of the T4E slip and the repayment rate in Box 7 is 30%.

Student Loan: Interest on student loans

You can claim an amount for the interest you, or a person related to you, paid in the taxation year on loans for post-secondary education made to you under the Canada Student Loans Act, the Canada Student Financial Assistance Act, or similar provincial or territorial government laws.

Enter the total of the amounts shown on the receipts. If you do not wish to claim these amounts on your current return, you can carry them forward and apply them on any one of the next five years' returns. Complete this form to make the claim.

T626 - Overseas Employment Tax Credit (OETC)

T626: Overseas employment tax credit

The overseas employment tax credit is available to individuals resident in Canada working abroad for six consecutive months in connection with a resource, construction, installation, agricultural or engineering project.

 The Canada Revenue Agency says...

The OETC provides a tax reduction for up to $100,000 of income earned in a full year of employment outside Canada.

You may be able to claim this credit if both of the following apply for 2009:

- You were a resident or deemed resident of Canada at any time in the year.
- You have employment income from certain kinds of work you did in another country.

What employment qualifies for the OETC?

To qualify for the OETC, an individual must:

- be employed by a specified employer (see "Specified employer" below), other than for the performance of services under a prescribed international development assistance program of the Government of Canada;
- be employed in connection with a contract under which the specified employer carried on business outside Canada on a resource, construction, installation, agricultural, engineering or prescribed activity (or for the purpose of obtaining such a contract); and

- have performed all or substantially all the employment duties (done in connection with a contract described in (b) above) outside Canada.

Specified employer

A **specified employer** is:

- a person resident in Canada;
- a partnership in which persons resident in Canada or corporations controlled by persons resident in Canada own more than 10% of the aggregate fair market value of all interests in the partnership; or
- a corporation that is a foreign affiliate (as defined in subsection 95(1)) of a person resident in Canada.

Note: Your employer may need to consult subsection 122.3(1.1) of the Income Tax Act to determine if the income qualifies.

Part 1 of this form must be completed by your employer, and you must meet all of the conditions of the form to qualify for the credit. You will not qualify if your employer answers No to any of the questions in Part 1.

Complete Part 2 of the form after your employer completes Part 1. This amount is transferred to line 426 of your Schedule 1.

Alternative Minimum Tax

Claiming this tax credit may result in you having to pay alternative minimum tax. To determine if minimum tax applies to you, complete Form T691 - Alternative Minimum Tax.

T691 - Minimum tax

T691: Calculation of minimum tax

If you are subject to minimum tax, you will need to complete form T691, Calculation of minimum tax. ProFile automatically determines whether or not a taxpayer is subject to minimum tax based on data from other forms and schedules.

The Canada Revenue Agency says... *General Income Tax and Benefit Guide*

Minimum tax limits the tax advantage you can receive in a year from certain incentives. You have to pay minimum tax if it is more than the federal tax you calculate in the usual manner. When calculating your taxable income for this tax, which does not apply to a person who died in 2009, you are allowed a basic exempt amount of $40,000.

Generally, to find out if you have to pay this tax, add the amounts in section B below and 60% of the amount on line 127 of your return. If the total is $40,000 or less, you probably do not have to pay minimum tax. If the total is more than $40,000, you may have to pay it.

To calculate if you have to pay it, use Form T691, Alternative Minimum Tax. You also have to calculate your additional provincial or territorial tax for minimum tax purposes by completing Form 428.

The most common reasons why you may have to pay minimum tax

- You reported a taxable capital gain on line 127.
- You claimed any of the following:
    - a loss (including your share of a partnership loss) resulting from, or increased by, claiming capital cost allowance on rental properties;
    - a loss from a limited partnership;
    - most carrying charges (line 221) on certain investments;
    - a loss from resource properties resulting from, or increased by, claiming a depletion allowance, exploration expenses, development expenses, or Canadian oil and gas property expenses;
    - a deduction on line 248 for an employee home relocation loan; or
    - a deduction on line 249 for security options.
- You claimed any of the following tax credits on Schedule 1:
    - a federal political contribution tax credit on lines 409 and 410;
    - an investment tax credit on line 412;
    - a labour-sponsored funds tax credit on line 414; or
    - an overseas employment tax credit on line 426.

Tip: You may be able to claim a credit against your taxes for 2009 if you paid minimum tax on any of your returns for 2002 to 2008 (see line 427).

Example

Paul claimed a $50,000 deduction in 2009 for carrying charges. Since this deduction is more than $40,000, Paul will probably have to pay minimum tax. To find out, he should complete Form T691, Alternative Minimum Tax.

T1032 - Joint Election to Split Pension Income

T1032: Joint election to split pension income

Canadian residents who received eligible pension income during the taxation year may be able to allocate up to half of their eligible income to their spouse (or common-law partner) for income tax purposes.

To complete form T1032, simply indicate whether you are the Pensioner (transferring pension income to his/her spouse) or the Pension Transferee (receiving pension income from his/her spouse) at the top of form T1032.

Enter the amount of the elected split pension on Line E of the form. Based on your Pensioner / Pension Transferee selection, the amounts will automatically flow to lines 210 / 116 of each of the spouse's returns. The Optimize - Split Pension Income worksheet can help you determine the optimal transfer amount.

The Canada Revenue Agency says... *Form T1032 - Joint Election to Split Pension Income*

Complete this form if you and your spouse or common-law partner are electing to split eligible pension income received in the tax year and if all of the following conditions are met:

- You and your spouse or common-law partner were not, because of a breakdown in your marriage or common-law partnership, living separate and apart from each other at the end of the year and for a period of 90 days commencing in the year.
- You and your spouse or common-law partner are residents of Canada on December 31 of the year.
- You received pension income in the year that qualifies for the pension income amount (see line 314 in the guide).

Attach a copy of this form with your return. Your spouse or common-law partner must attach a copy of this form to his or her paper return. If you are filing electronically, keep it in case we ask to see it.

Only one joint election can be made for a tax year. This form is to be filed by your filing due date for the year (see the guide for details).

Form T1172 - Additional Tax on Accumulated Income Payments from RESPs

T1172: Additional Tax on Accumulated Income Payments from RESPs

Use this form when you have accumulated income payments from a registered education savings plan(s). The form determines what income is subject to the additional 20% tax and calculates that tax.

T4A slips issued to the recipient of the payments include the RESP accumulated income in box 40. There are two sections to the T1172. Complete Part A if you are a subscriber to an RESP or the surviving spouse of a deceased original subscriber to an RESP, which no longer has a subscriber. Any other recipients of RESP accumulated income payments will complete Part B.

 The Canada Revenue Agency says…

Use this form to calculate the amount of additional tax you have to pay on accumulated income payments (AIPs) you received in 1999 and later years from Registered Education Savings Plans (RESPs).

What are accumulated income payments (AIP)?

These payments are distributions from an RESP other than a refund of contributions, an educational assistance payment, a payment to a designated educational institution in Canada, a transfer to another RESP or a repayment of any amounts under a Canada Education Savings Program or any provincial program. An RESP contract may (after 1997) allow for AIPs if the following conditions are met:

- the payment is made to, or for, a subscriber under the plan who is a resident of Canada;
- the payment is made to, or for, only one subscriber; and
- **Any one** of the following three conditions must also apply:
    o the plan has existed for 10 years and each individual (other than a deceased individual) who is or was a beneficiary has reached 21 years of age and is not currently eligible to receive an educational assistance payment;
    o the plan has existed for 36 years, unless the plan is a specified plan (in general a non-family plan where the beneficiary is entitled to the disability tax credit for the beneficiary's tax year ending in the 32nd year of existence of the plan) in which case the plan has existed for 41 years; or
    o all beneficiaries under the plan are deceased.

How RESP accumulated income payments are taxed

AIPs are reported in box 40 of the T4A slips issued in the name of the recipient. The recipient has to include the total of all AIPs on line 130 of his or her return for the year the payments are received and pay the regular tax. These payments are also subject to an additional tax. However, if you receive an AIP, the amount subject to the additional tax may be reduced or eliminated if all the following conditions are met:

- you are the subscriber of the RESP (this excludes a person who becomes a subscriber because of the death of the original subscriber) or the spouse or common-law partner of a deceased original subscriber under an RESP for which there is no subscriber;
- you contribute an amount equivalent to, or the promoter transfers, all or part of the AIPs to your RRSP or your spouse's or common-law partner's RRSP in the year the AIPs are received or in the first 60 days of the following year; and
- you deduct the amount contributed as an RRSP contribution in the year the payments were received (and your RRSP deduction limit is sufficient to allow you to do so).

Do you have to complete this form?

If you receive AIPs in 1999 or later years, you have to complete this form to calculate the additional tax. Complete either Part A or Part B (whichever applies) and Part C if you are a resident of Quebec.

Attach a copy of this form to your return for the year you received the payments. The additional tax on RESP income is due on the balance due date for that year. In most cases that means April 30 of the year that follows the year in which the payments are received. Where the recipient is a trust, the balance due date is 90 days after the end of the tax year of the trust in which the payments are received. For information about the balance due date in the case of a deceased person, see the guide called Preparing Returns for Deceased Persons.

For more information about AIPs and RESPs, see the Information Sheet RC4092, Registered Education Savings Plans (RESPs).

T1198: Statement of qualifying retroactive lump-sum payment

Enter the breakdown of the principal retroactive lump-sum payment on this form.

What is a qualifying retroactive lump-sum payment (QRLSP)?

A QRLSP is a lump-sum payment paid to an individual (other than a trust) in a year that relates to one or more preceding years throughout which the individual was a resident of Canada. The lump sum payment must have been paid after 1994 from one of the following sources:

- income from an office or employment received under a court judgment, arbitration award, or lawsuit settlement agreement (including damages for loss of office or employment);
- benefits from Unemployment Insurance or Employment Insurance;
- benefits from a superannuation or pension plan (other than non-periodic benefits such as lump-sum withdrawals);
- spousal, common-law partner or child support payments; or
- benefits from a wage-loss replacement plan.

Why provide the breakdown of a QRLSP?

Generally, a lump-sum payment is included in income in the year when the recipient receives it.

This may result in a greater tax liability than if the payment had been received in the year or years to which it related.

A special tax calculation is available to individuals who receive QRLSPs that relate to 1978 and later. The calculation applies if the total of all principal amounts that relate to prior years (after 1977) from all QRLSPs is $3,000 or more.

If you are the payer of a QRLSP, please complete this form to help us determine if the special tax calculation is beneficial to the recipient.

Note: The QRLSP income indicated on this form still has to be reported on the recipient's relevant information slip (e.g., T4, T4A, T4E).

Who should attach this form to their return?

Attach this form to your return for the year of payment to ask for a special tax calculation if the amount shown under "Total principal (prior years only)" is $3,000 or more. If you have more than one QRLSP form, add the amounts shown under "Total principal (prior years only)" on all your forms. If the result is $3,000 or more, attach your QRLSP forms to your return.

What information do I need to provide on this form?

If you are the payer of a QRLSP, please provide the following information on the other side of this sheet:

- the recipient's name and social insurance number, and the year the lump-sum payment was paid;
- a description of the lump-sum payment and the reasons for paying it;
- the total amount of the lump-sum payment including the interest (box 6850), the total principal that relates to all years (box 6851), the total interest that relates to all years, and the total principal that relates to prior years only; and
- the portion of the amount of principal (without the interest) that relates to each applicable year covered by the payment. (Leave the lines blank for the years not covered by the payment.)

Amounts paid for years before 1978 must be allocated to the year the payment was made.

T1206: Tax on split income

Use this form to calculate tax on split income if your client:

- Was born in 1992 or later;
- Was a non-resident at no time during the taxation year
- Has a parent who was resident in Canada at any time during the year; and
- reported on his/her return, split income as described on the form.

T2036 - Calculation of Provincial Foreign Tax Credits

T2036#: Provincial foreign tax credits

ProFile will automatically calculate this form if you enter foreign income or tax paid in other forms (such as the T5). The amount transfers automatically to the FTC form.

The Canada Revenue Agency says... *T2036 - Provincial or territorial foreign tax credit*

Where do I use this form?

Use this form to calculate the non-business foreign tax credit for 2009 that you can deduct from the income tax payable to the province or territory you resided in at the end of the year.

This form does not apply to residents of Quebec. If you are a resident of Manitoba and subject to minimum tax, you cannot claim a provincial foreign tax credit.

Before you complete this form, calculate your federal foreign tax credit by using Form T2209, Federal Foreign Tax Credits. If the amount of federal foreign tax credit you are entitled to deduct is equal to the foreign non-business tax you paid, your provincial or territorial foreign tax credit would be zero. As a result, you do not have to complete this form.

Attach a completed copy of this form to your return. If the non-business income taxes you paid to all foreign countries total more than $200, complete a separate form for each foreign country to which you paid taxes.

Net foreign non-business income

Enter the amount reported as net foreign non-business income in the calculation of line 2 on

Form T2209.

Net income

Enter the amount reported as net income in the calculation of line 2 on Form T2209

If you were a resident of Canada for part of the year, include the income for the part of the year you were a resident of Canada plus any income and losses referred to in paragraphs 115(1)(a) to (c) of the federal Income Tax Act as reported on your Canadian return, for the part of the year you were not a resident of Canada.

If you paid tax to more than one jurisdiction in 2009, calculate this amount according to note (c) of T2209, using the amount allocated to your province or territory of residence in column 4, Part 1 of Form T2203 instead of "line 236 plus the amount on line 4 of Form T1206" in that note.

Provincial or territorial tax otherwise payable

If you were a resident in a province or territory other than Ontario, Alberta, or British Columbia, enter the amount of tax calculated before determining the provincial and territorial foreign tax credit from Form 428 or Section 428MJ of Form T2203 for your province or territory of residence.

If you were a resident of Ontario, calculate this amount by adding the amounts from lines 42 and 43 of Form ON428 to the amount from line 48 and continue the calculation. The amount from line 60 is your "provincial or territorial tax otherwise payable". If you paid tax to more than one jurisdiction in 2009, add the amounts from lines 18 and 19 in Section ON428MJ to the amount on line 29 and continue the calculation. The amount on line 41 is your "provincial or territorial tax otherwise payable".

If you were a resident of Alberta, to calculate your "provincial or territorial tax otherwise payable" add the amounts of lines 34 and 35 to the amount from line 40 of Form AB428 or the total of lines 7, 8, and 26 in Section AB428 of Form T2203.

If you were a resident of British Columbia, your "provincial or territorial tax otherwise payable" is the amount of tax calculated before determining the provincial and territorial foreign tax credit minus any British Columbia additional tax for minimum tax purposes from Form BC428 or Section BC428MJ of Form T2203.

Note:
- If you were a resident of British Columbia and subject to minimum tax, follow the instruction for line 2 as if you were not subject to minimum tax.
- If you are a resident of another province or territory, and are subject to minimum tax for 2009, enter on line 2 the part of the special foreign tax credit (line 87 of Form T691, Alternative Minimum Tax) that relates to non-business income taxes you paid to a foreign country for 2009.

T2038 - Investment Tax Credit (Individuals)

T2038: Investment tax credit

At the top of the T2038 and T2038S is a field to link the form to another ProFile form. Enter the name of the business statement for which CCA will be reduced next year by the ITC claim in the current year. Remember to include the statement number, for example T2038#2, in the link field. The ITC claim for the current year is calculated at the bottom of the T2038S. When you carry forward the file for next year, the amount on this field will flow through to the linked business statement to reduce the CCA.

🍁 **The Canada Revenue Agency says...** *Form T2038 - Investment Tax Credit (Individuals)*

Use this form if:
- you earned an investment tax credit (ITC) during the current tax year or you are claiming a carry forward of ITC from a previous tax year. File one completed copy of Part A of this form with your income tax return for the year in which you acquired a qualified or certified property, made a qualified expenditure (which includes contributions made to agricultural organizations), were allocated renounced Canadian exploration expenses, have paid eligible salary and wages to eligible apprentices, or have created child care spaces in a licensed child care facility for the benefit of your employees' children, or a combination of your employees' children and other children;
- you have a recapture of ITC on a scientific research and experimental development (SR&ED) expenditure and/or a recapture of ITC on a child care spaces expenditure. File one completed copy of Part A of this form with your income tax return for the year in which you recapture an ITC on an SR&ED expenditure and/or for the year in which you recapture an ITC on a child care expenses expenditure; or
- you are requesting an ITC carry back or you are claiming a refund for an ITC earned during the current tax year. File one completed copy of Part B of this form with your income tax return.

Note: You have to file this form no later than 12 months after the filing due date of your income tax return for the tax year in which you acquired the property or made the expenditure.

How to calculate your ITC

The ITC is based on a percentage of the investment cost (the cost of the property you bought and the expenditures you made). If you received, are entitled to receive, or can reasonably expect to receive any reimbursement, inducement, or government or non-government assistance (including grants, subsidies, forgivable loans, or deductions from tax and investment allowances) that we can reasonably consider to relate to the property or expenditure, you have to decrease your investment cost by the amount you received, are entitled to receive, or can reasonably expect to receive. If you repay any of this assistance, add the repayment to the investment cost. Calculate the ITC for any repayment using the same percentage you used for the original investment cost.

Determine your ITC at the end of 2009. If the fiscal year-end of your business is in 2009, include any ITC you earn on the property you buy during the calendar year. Investments and expenditures are eligible for an ITC only when the income from the related business is subject to Part I tax

Properties acquired and SR&ED capital expenditures incurred to acquire property are eligible for an ITC claim only when the properties are considered to be available for use.

Table 1. ITC - Investment or expenditures, percentages, and codes. Review the codes shown below, and use the one that applies to you in Part A of form T2038.

Type of investment or expenditure	Specified percentage	Code
Certain certified property	30%	3A
Qualified expenditures for SR&ED carried out in the following areas: • Newfoundland and Labrador, Prince Edward Island, Nova Scotia, New Brunswick, or the Gaspé Peninsula; Note: For qualified expenditures incurred after 1994, the rate is 20%. However, for the Atlantic Provinces and the Gaspé Peninsula, qualified expenditures incurred under a written agreement entered into before February 22, 1994, will still qualify for the 30% rate.	20%	3B
• or; any other area in Canada.	20%	4B
Contributions made after 2000 to agricultural organizations for SR&ED carried out in Canada	20%	4C

Type of investment or expenditure	Specified percentage	Code
Note: Contributions made on or subsequent to January 1, 2001, qualify for the 20% rate. Enter the amount in box 6715 with a note on the top of the form stating that your claim is for contributions to agricultural organizations.		
Qualified property acquired after 1994 for use in the following specific areas: Newfoundland and Labrador, Prince Edward Island, Nova Scotia, New Brunswick, or the Gaspé Peninsula, or a prescribed offshore region	10%	12
Renounced Canadian exploration expenses	15%	5
Apprenticeship job creation tax credit	10%	6
Investment tax credit for child care spaces	25%	7

How to claim your 2009 ITC

You can use the ITC that you earn in 2009 to reduce your federal tax for a previous year, or to reduce your federal tax for 2009 or for a future year. See "Refund of ITC" below.

Current-year claim

> To calculate your ITC to reduce your federal income tax for 2009, complete Part A of this form. Enter the amount of your credit on line 412 of Schedule 1 of your income tax return. If a partnership or trust made the investments, enter only your share.

Carry back to previous years

> You can carry back the ITC you earn in 2009 for up to three years and use it to reduce your federal tax in those years. To do this, complete Part B of this form.

Carry forward to future years

> Under proposed changes to the Income Tax Act , you can carry forward for up to 20 years credits earned in tax years that end after 1997 and 10 years for credits earned in tax years that end before 1998.

Property bought or expenditures made before 2009

You may be able to apply unused ITCs from expenditures or acquisitions made from 1998 to 2007 on your 2009 income tax return. To do this, complete Part A of this form.

Refund of ITC

If you do not use all of your ITC to reduce your taxes in the year or in the three previous years, we may refund up to 40% of your unused credit to you. You can only claim this refund in the year you buy property or make an expenditure that qualifies for the credit, unless the available for use rules (or other rules deeming the expenditure to have been made in a later year) apply. To claim a refund of ITC, complete Part B of this form. Enter your refund amount on line 454 of your income tax return. If a partnership or trust made the investments, enter only your share of the amount.

Adjustments - Reducing Capital Cost Allowance

The credit you claim or that we refund to you for 2009 reduces the capital cost of the property. Any 2009 credit you carry back to a previous year will also reduce the capital cost of the property. Make this adjustment in 2010. This adjustment reduces the capital cost allowance you can claim for the property. It also affects your capital gain when you dispose of the property. You might have claimed a credit or received a refund for 2009 for a property that you already disposed of. In addition, you might still have other property in the same class. If so, reduce the undepreciated capital cost of the class for 2010 by the amount of the credit you claimed or received as a refund. If, after the disposition, you do not have any property left in the same class, include in your 2010 income the amount of the credit you claimed or received as a refund. Enter the amount as other income on line 9600 if you are filing Form T2042, T1163, T1164, T1273, or T1274. Enter the amount on line 8230 if you are filing Form T2125 (Form T2032 and/or Form T2124 for 2007 and previous tax years).

Other adjustments

A credit deducted or refunded will also reduce the balance in the SR&ED pool, the adjusted cost base (ACB) of an interest in a partnership, and the ACB of a capital interest in a trust in the next tax year.

Partnership

If you are a partner of a partnership, include only your part of the partnership investment or expenditure. An ITC earned by a partnership is usually allocated to a partner. However, an ITC earned on qualified SR&ED expenditures may not be allocated to a specified partner of a partnership. If you received an allocation of ITC from a partnership, use the credit and the rate to calculate your share of the investment cost or expenditure. Enter this cost or expenditure on the line corresponding to the appropriate rate.

For more information, Interpretation Bulletin IT-411, Meaning of Construction, and Information Circular IC78-4, Investment Tax Credit Rates, and its Special Release.

T2201#: Disability tax credit certificate

The disability tax credit provides additional tax assistance for individuals who have a severe and prolonged mental or physical impairment. The credit will reduce your income tax payable if you qualify. If you have no tax payable, you may transfer the credit to your spouse or supporting person.

Not all people with disabilities will be able to claim the disability tax credit. The fact that you receive Canada or Quebec Pension Plan disability payments, Workers' Compensation benefits, or other types of disability or insurance benefits does not necessarily mean you qualify for this credit.

CRA will review your claim for the disability tax credit when your return is filed, to make sure you qualify. In some cases, CRA may ask a medical advisor to review a claim to determine if it meets the eligibility criteria. Therefore, the medical advisor may contact you or the certifying doctor or optometrist to get more information.

Any medical fees related to a request for clarification or additional information are the responsibility of the claimant. Provincial Medicare plans do not cover these fees.

If the impairment is permanent, it is not necessary to file another form T2201 in later years unless the circumstances change, or unless CRA asks you for it. If the impairment is temporary, you have to submit a new form if the period stated on an earlier certificate has ended.

You or your representative must complete Part A of form T2201. Then, ask a licensed medical doctor, or, in the case of vision impairment, a medical doctor or a registered optometrist (authorized to practice as such), who knows about your or your dependant's impairment to complete Part B. In the case of a hearing impairment, a registered audiologist (authorized to practise as such) can also complete Part B.

Please note that if the doctor, optometrist or audiologist does not fully complete Part B or does not provide all the necessary information, CRA may deny your claim. You may also use the disability tax credit certificate to substantiate a claim for a deduction for certain medical expenses, attendant care expenses, or for child care expenses for a child with a disability.

T2203: Tax calculation for multiple jurisdictions

Use the T2203 to calculate provincial or territorial tax if either of the following applies:

- the taxpayer resided in a province or territory on December 31 of the taxation year (if he/she ceased to reside in Canada during the taxation year, use the last day of residence in Canada) and all or part of his/her business income for the year was earned and is allocable to a permanent establishment outside that province or territory, or outside Canada;
- the taxpayer was a non-resident throughout the taxation year carrying on business in more than one province or territory in Canada.

ProFile incorporates the T691 into the T2203 to calculate minimum tax that may apply for income from multiple jurisdictions. If minimum tax applies, provincial taxes are calculated using the basic federal tax determined on form T691.

T2204 - Employee Overpayment of CPP Contributions and EI Premiums

T2204: Employee CPP and EI overpayment

Based on your entries on T4 slips, ProFile automatically calculates this form to determine if you overpaid into either the Canada Pension Plan or Employment Insurance.

Frequently Asked Questions

When can I no longer make CPP contributions?

You cannot make CPP contributions:

- before the month you turn 18,
- after the month you turn 70,
- after the month of death, or

- after the month that you start to collect CPP retirement or disability benefits.

The Canada Revenue Agency says... *T2204, Employee Overpayment of 2009 Canada Pension Plan Contributions and 2009 Employment Insurance Premiums*

To determine any overpayment of Canada Pension Plan (CPP) or Quebec Pension Plan (QPP) contributions made through employment if you had no self-employment earnings and you were not a resident of Quebec on December 31, 2009, complete Part 1. If you were a resident of Quebec on December 31, 2009, and you made CPP or QPP contributions, see your Quebec provincial income tax guide.

To determine any overpayment of Employment Insurance (EI) premiums, complete Part 2. To be refunded, the amount of the EI overpayment has to be more than $1. If you were a resident of Quebec on December 31, 2009, see your Quebec provincial income tax guide.

T2209 - Federal Foreign Tax Credits

T2209#: Federal foreign tax credits

Use this form to determine the amount you can claim as a deduction from federal tax and from the federal individual surtax for a taxation year if you were resident in Canada at any time in the taxation year, and you had to include, on your Canadian income tax return, income which originated in a foreign country for which you paid non-business or business taxes to that foreign country.

Attach a completed copy of this form to your income tax return.

ProFile will automatically calculate this form if you enter foreign income or tax paid in other forms (such as the T5).

Note:

As of the 2007 tax season, the CRA requires taxpayers to file a single copy of form T2209. Previously, taxpayers had to file a separate T2209 for each country to which they paid taxes in the year.

In ProFile, form T2209S will act as a summary of all the individual T2209 forms that you create. This is the form that will print along with your return or be included in the return that you file electronically.

Since the calculation of the Foreign Tax Credit differs for each country, you will still be required to create separate T2209 forms for each country for which you are making a claim (ex: T2209#1, T2209#2).

The total of the foreign taxes you paid to all foreign countries will flow to the T2209S, which should then be submitted with your return.

The Canada Revenue Agency says...

This credit is for foreign income or profits taxes you paid on income you received from outside Canada and reported on your Canadian tax return. Complete Form T2209, Federal Foreign Tax Credits, to calculate your credit and enter the amount from line 10 on line 405 of Schedule 1.

Note: You may have deducted an amount on line 256 for income that is not taxable in Canada under a tax treaty. In that case, do not include that income, or any tax withheld from it, in your foreign tax credit calculation.

If you paid tax to more than one foreign country, and the total non-business income tax you paid to all foreign countries is more than $200, you have to do a separate calculation for each country for which you claim a foreign tax credit. In that case, enter the total of your allowable federal foreign tax credit on Form T2209.

You also have to do a separate calculation for business income taxes paid to each foreign country. In that case, use this form to calculate your credit for both non-business income taxes and the business income taxes paid to each foreign country. For tax years ending before March 23, 2004, you can carry unclaimed foreign business income taxes back three years and forward seven years. For tax years ending after March 22, 2004, the carry forward period is 10 years.

In most cases, the foreign tax credit you can claim for each foreign country is whichever of the following two amounts is lower:

- the foreign income tax you actually paid; or
- the tax due in Canada on your net income from that country.

Note: If you paid tax on income from foreign property (other than real property), your foreign tax credit for the income from that property cannot be more than 15% of your net income from that property. However, you may be able to deduct on line 232 of your return the part of the foreign taxes you paid over 15%.

Beginning in 2004, your contribution to a foreign public pension plan is considered as a non-business income tax for foreign tax credit purposes where the following two conditions apply:

- you are required to make the contribution under the legislation of the foreign country; and
- it is reasonable to conclude that you will not be eligible for any financial benefit from your contribution considering that the employment in the foreign country was temporary and for a short period of time.

Note: U.S. FICA payments qualify for this credit.

Chapter 6

T1 Jacket & Schedules

2009 Tax Year

T1 Elective return identification

Use this field at the top of the T1 jacket to indicate that the taxpayer is filing an elective return. ProFile completes this field automatically for bankruptcy returns based on information you supply on the Bankruptcy worksheet.

T1 Identification

In ProFile, identifying data flows from the Info form to the Identification areas of the T1 jacket.

Complete the Info worksheet when you begin work on a new file.

T1 Province of residence

ProFile uses the Province of Residence selected on the Info form, to determine key tax calculations in this file. Provincial tax forms become available in the Form Explorer only after you have selected the province of residence.

T1 Province of self-employment

Enter the name of the province of self-employment for any taxpayer with income from self-employment.

T1 Date of entry or departure

A date of entry or departure into Canada is used to prorate credits a taxpayer may be eligible to receive.

T1 Date of death

The date of death for a deceased taxpayer transfers from the Info worksheet. For more information on preparing returns for deceased persons, see Completing a deceased taxpayer's return.

T1 Marital status

Spousal information transfers to the T1 jacket from the Info worksheet.

T1 Elections Canada

ProFile provides an active audit message to remind you to select "Yes" or "No" for the question, "Do you authorize the CRA to provide you name, address and date of birth to Elections Canada to update your information on the National Register of Electors?"

T1 GST/HST credit application

ProFile automatically determines eligibility for the GST/HST credit application, and selects "Yes" or "No" depending on client data. The GST/HST worksheet calculates the credit the taxpayer can expect to receive.

T1 Foreign property question

Each return that you file must have a response to the foreign property question on the T1 jacket. ProFile provides an audit message to alert you to this requirement.

T1 Guide: Line 101 - Employment income - Line 101

T1 Line 101: Employment income

Amounts that you enter on the T4 slips automatically flow to line 101 of the T1 jacket.

The Canada Revenue Agency says... *General Income Tax and Benefit Guide*

Enter the total of amounts shown in box 14 of all your T4 slips. If you have not received your slip by early April, or if you have any questions about an amount on a slip, contact your employer. For more information see What if you are missing information?

If you have employment expenses, see line 229 for more information.

Note:

- If you reported employment income on line 101, you can claim the Canada employment amount on line 363.
- If you received a housing allowance as a member of the clergy, the allowance may be included in box 14 of your T4 slip. If so, subtract the amount of the allowance from the amount shown in box 14, and include the difference on line 101. Include the allowance on line 104.
- If you have employment income from another country, report it on line 104 of your return.
- You may be able to make CPP contributions on certain employment income for which no contribution was made (for example, tips that were not included on your T4 slip) or extra contributions on T4 income if you had more than one employer in the year. For more information, see "Making additional CPP contributions" in line 308.

Tip: Your contributions to the Canada Pension Plan or Quebec Pension Plan (box 16 or 17 of your T4 slips and any amount on line 421) determine the amount of benefits you will receive under either of these plans. If there are no contributions shown in box 16 or 17 of your T4 slips, or if you have any questions about the amount of your contributions, contact your employer.

Emergency volunteers

In 2009, you may have received a payment from a government, municipality, or other public authority for your work as a volunteer ambulance technician, firefighter, or search, rescue, or other emergency worker. If so, the T4 slip issued by such an authority generally will show only the taxable part of the payment, which is the part that is more than $1,000. However, if that authority employed you (other than as a volunteer) for the same or similar duties, the whole payment will be taxable.

Security option benefits (stock options)

You may have to report taxable benefits you received in (or carried forward to) 2009 on certain security options you exercised. If you report any taxable benefits, see line 249for more information. However, you may be able to choose to defer reporting these benefits if you have not yet disposed of those securities.

For this to apply, you have to confirm certain information in writing with your employer and file Form T1212, Statement of Deferred Security Options Benefits, with your paper return each year. For more information, see Guide T4037, Capital Gains, or contact us. Your notice of assessment or notice of reassessment will show the remaining balance of your deferred amounts.

Commissions (box 42)

Enter on line 102 the total commissions shown in box 42 on all your T4 slips you received as an employee. This amount is already included in your income on line 101, so do not add it again when you calculate your total income on line 150. If you have commission expenses, see line 229 for more information.

If you are a self-employed commission salesperson, see Guide T4002, Business and Professional Income, to determine how to report your commission income and claim your expenses.

T1 Guide: Line 102 - Commissions

T1 Line 102: Commissions

Commissions that you enter on the T4 slips automatically flow to line 102 of the T1 jacket.

 The Canada Revenue Agency says... *General Income Tax and Benefit Guide*

Commissions (box 42)

Enter on line 102 the total commissions shown in box 42 on all your T4 slips you received as an employee. This amount is already included in your income on line 101, so do not add it again when you calculate your total income on line 150. If you have commission expenses, see line 229 for more information.

If you are a self-employed commission salesperson, see Guide T4002, Business and Professional Income, to determine how to report your commission income and claim your expenses.

T1 Guide: Line 104 - Other employment income

T1 Line 104: Other employment income

Enter other employment income amounts on the Other Income form. These amounts will flow to line 104 of the T1 jacket.

Frequently Asked Questions

Do I have to report my tips?

Why do I need to report tips not shown on a T-slip?

You should report all of your tip income, even if it isn't shown on a T-slip. Reporting this income gives you more RRSP contribution room and increases your CPP pensionable earnings. It may also increase your GST/HST credit.

The CRA has been known to audit employers and employees in the hospitality industry to look for unreported tip income.

What are occasional earnings?

Occasional earnings are income earned on a non-regular basis, and income from casual employment.

 The Canada Revenue Agency says... *General Income Tax and Benefit Guide*

Report on this line the total of the following amounts:

Employment income not reported on a T4 slip

> Include amounts such as tips and occasional earnings.
>
> Note
>
> If you reported employment income on line 104 you cam claim the Canada employment amount on line 363.

Net research grants

> Subtract your expenses from the grant you received and include the net amount on this line. Your expenses cannot be more than your grant. Attach to your paper return a list of your expenses. For more information, see Research Grants or get Interpretation Bulletin IT-75, Scholarships, Fellowships, Bursaries, Prizes, Research Grants and Financial Assistance

Clergy's housing allowance

> Include the amount shown in box 30 on your T4 slip. You may be entitled to claim a deduction on line 231. If your allowance is included in box 14 of your T4 slip, see line 101.

Foreign employment income

> Report your earnings in Canadian dollars. The amount on your United States W-2 slip may have been reduced by such contributions to a "401(k), 457 or 403(b) plan, US Medicare and Federal Insurance Contributions Act (FICA)." If this is the case, you must add these contributions to your foreign employment income at line 104 on your Canadian return. Based on the new Protocol between Canada and the United-States, these contributions may be deductible. For more information, see line 207.

Income-maintenance insurance plans (wage-loss replacement plans)

> Box 28 of your T4A slip includes the payments you received from such a plan. There also should be a note on the slip identifying the amount. You may not have to report the full amount on your return. Report the amount you received, minus contributions you made to the plan after 1967, if you did not use them on a previous year's return to calculate the amount to report. For more information, see Interpretation Bulletin IT-428, Wage Loss Replacement Plans.

Veterans' benefits

> Include the amount shown in box 28 of your T4A slip.

Certain GST/HST and QST (Quebec sales tax) rebates

> If you are an employee who paid and deducted employment expenses in 2008 or earlier, you may have received a GST/HST or QST rebate in 2009 for those expenses. If so, include on line 104 the rebate you received. However, a rebate on which you can claim capital cost allowances

treated differently. For more information, see Guide T4044, Employment Expenses. Guide T4044, Employment Expenses, contains instructions on how to report such rebates, and information about capital cost allowance.

Royalties

Include these amounts on this line if you received them for a work or invention of yours. Report other royalties (other than those included on line 135) on line 121.

Amounts you received under a supplementary unemployment benefit plan (a guaranteed annual wage)

Taxable benefit for premiums paid to cover you under a group term life-insurance plan

Include the amount shown in box 28 of your T4A slip.

Employee profit-sharing plan

Include the amount shown in box 35 of your T4PS slip.

Medical premium benefits

Include the amount shown in box 28 of your T4A slip.

Wage earners protection plan

Include the amount shown in box 28 of your T4A slip.

Note: Other income (employment) that is reported on line 104 is used when determining your RRSP deduction limit. Other income (miscellaneous) reported on line 130 is not used.

T1 Guide: Line 113 - Old Age Security Pension

T1 Line 113: Old Age Security (OAS) Pension

Old age security pension that you enter on the T4A(OAS) slip automatically flows to line 113 of the T1 jacket.

The maximum benefit of the OAS pension increases to $6,082.23.

The Canada Revenue Agency says... *General Income Tax and Benefit Guide*

Enter the amount shown in box 18 of your T4A(OAS) slip. For more information on how to report the amount shown in box 21, see line 146. If you do not have your T4A(OAS) slip, visit the Service Canada website at www.servicecanada.gc.ca (E-Services), or call 1 800 277-9914.

Note:

If your net income before adjustments on line 234 of your return, minus the amounts reported on lines 117 and 125, plus the amount deducted on line 213 and/or for a repayment of registered disability savings plans income included on line 232, is more than $66,335, see line 235 for information about repaying OAS benefits.

If, at any time in 2009, you were a non-resident of Canada receiving OAS pension, you also may have to complete Form T1136, Old Age Security Return of Income.

T1 Guide: Line 114 - Canada or Québec Pension Plan benefits

T1 Line 114: CPP or QPP benefits

Enter Canada Pension Plan (CPP) or Quebec Pension Plan (QPP) benefits on the T4A(P) slips.

The Canada Revenue Agency says... *General Income Tax and Benefit Guide*

Enter the total Canada Pension Plan (CPP) or Québec Pension Plan (QPP) benefits shown in box 20 of your T4A(P) slip. This amount is the total of the amounts shown in boxes 14 to 18. If your T4A (P) slip has an amount shown in box 16, 17, or 18, read whichever of the following sections apply to you. If you do not have your T4A(P) slip, visit the Service Canada website at www.servicecanada.gc.ca (E-Services), or call 1-800-277-9914.

Lump-sum benefits

> If you received a lump-sum CPP or QPP payment in 2009, parts of which were for previous years, you have to include the whole payment on line 114 of your return for 2009. We will not reassess the returns for the previous years to include this income. However, if the total of the parts that relate to previous years is $300 or more, we will calculate the tax payable on those parts as if you received them in those years only if the result is better for you. If you received a letter from Service Canada showing amounts that apply to previous years attach it to your paper return and we will tell you the results on your Notice of Assessment or Notice of Reassessment.

CPP or QPP disability benefit (box 16)

> Enter on line 152 (located below and to the left of line 114) the amount of your CPP or QPP disability benefits from box 16. This amount is already included in your income on line 114, so do not add it again when you calculate your total income on line 150.

CPP or QPP child benefit (box 17)

> Include a child benefit only if you received it because you were the child of a deceased or disabled contributor. Any benefits paid for your children are their income, even if you received the payment.

CPP or QPP death benefit (box 18)

> If you received this amount and you are a beneficiary of the deceased person's estate, you can choose to include it either on line 114 of your own return or on a T3, Trust Income Tax and Information Return, for the estate. Do not report it on the deceased person's individual return. The taxes payable may be different, depending on which return you use. For more information, see Guide T4013, Trust Guide.

T1 Guide: Line 115 - Other pensions or superannuation

T1 Line 115: Other pensions or superannuation

Line 115 includes other pensions and superannuation that may originate on any of several different forms.

Enter these amounts on the related ProFile slip or form: Other Income, T4A, T4RIF, T5, Foreign or T3. ProFile totals amounts from all these sources on line 115 of the T1 jacket.

Frequently Asked Questions

What amounts transfer to Line 115?

Line 115 includes these amounts:

T3 - Statement of Trust Income	**Box 31** - Eligible pension income
T4A - Statement of Pension, Retirement, Annuity and Other Income	**Box 16** - Pension or superannuation Income

Only if the taxpayer is 65 years or older or the amount was received due to the death of a spouse or common-law partner:

T4A - Statement of Pension, Retirement, Annuity and Other Income	**Box 24** – Annuities
T4RIF - Statement of Income Out of a Registered Retirement Income Fund	**Box 16** - Amounts taxable Box 20 - Deemed receipt by Annuitant
T5 - Statement of investment income	**Box 19** - Accrued income annuities

 The Canada Revenue Agency says... *General Income Tax and Benefit Guide*

Include on this line any other pensions or superannuation you received, such as amounts shown in box 16 of your T4A slip and box 31 of your T3 slips. Report on line 130 any amount shown in box 18 of your T4A slip or box 22 of your T3 slip.

You may also have to report on this line other amounts that you received. Read the following sections that apply to you.

Annuity and registered retirement income fund (RRIF) including life income fund payments

Report the amount from box 24 or the variable pension benefits from box 28 of your T4A slip, box 16 or 20 of your T4RIF slip, or box 19 of your T5 slip amounts as follows:

- If you were 65 years of age or older on December 31, 2009, include it on line 115.
- Regardless of your age, if you indicated that you received it because your spouse or common-law partner died, include it on line 115.

- Otherwise, report on line 130 the amount shown on box 24 or the variable pension benefits shown in box 28 of your T4A slip, or box 16 or 20 of your T4RIF slip, and shown on line 121 the amount for box 19 of your T5 slip.

 Note: If there is an amount in box 18 or 22 of your T4RIF slip, see the instructions on the back of the slip.

Tip:

If you have to report your pension or annuity payments on line 115, you may be able to claim the pension income amount (see line 314).

Also, you may be able to jointly elect with your spouse or common-law partner to split your pension, annuity, and RRIF (including life income fund) payments that you reported on line 115 if both of the following apply:

- you were both residents of Canada on December 31, 2009 (or were residents of Canada on the date of death); and
- you and your spouse or common-law partner were not, because of a breakdown in your marriage or common-law relationship, living separate and apart from each other at the end of the year and for a period of 90 days commencing in the year.

To make this election, you and your spouse or common-law partner must complete Form T1032, Joint Election to Split Pension Income.

Note: If you elected to split your pension, superannuation, annuity, and RRIF (including life income fund) payments with your spouse or common-law partner, you (the pensioner) must still report the full amount on line 115, but you can claim a deduction for the elected split-pension amount. For more information, see line 210 for details.

Pensions from a foreign country

In Canadian dollars the gross amount of your foreign pension income in 2009. Attach a note to your paper return identifying the type of pension you received and the country it came from. In some cases, amounts you receive may not be considered pension income and you may have to report them elsewhere on your return. (See Federal foreign tax credit calculation.)

 Tip:

You can claim a deduction on line 256 for the part of your foreign pension income that is tax-free in Canada because of a tax treaty. If you do not know whether any part of your foreign pension is tax-free in Canada, contact us.

U.S. individual retirement account (IRA)

If, during 2009, you received amounts from an IRA or converted the IRA to a "Roth" IRA, contact us..

U.S. social security

Include on line 115 the full amount, in Canadian dollars, of your U.S. Social Security benefits and U.S. Medicare premiums paid on your behalf. You can claim a deduction for part of this income. For more information, see line 256

Benefits paid for your children are their income, even if you received the payments.

T1 Guide: Line 119 - Employment Insurance Benefits

T1 Line 119: Employment Insurance benefits

Enter employment insurance and other benefits on the T4E slips. These amounts will flow to line 119 of the T1 jacket.

The Canada Revenue Agency says... *General Income Tax and Benefit Guide*

Enter the amount shown in box 14 of your T4E slip, minus any amount shown in box 18. If you already repaid excess benefits you received directly to the payer of your benefits, you may be able to claim a deduction. For more information, see line 232 for details.

Note: If your net income before adjustments on line 234 of your return, minus the amounts on lines 117 and 125, plus the amount deducted on line 213 and/or for a repayment of registered disability savings plan income included on line 232, is more than $52,875, you may have to repay some of the benefits you received. For more information, see line 235.

T1 Guide: Line 120 - Taxable amount of dividends (eligible and other than eligible) from taxable Canadian corporations

T1 Line 120: Taxable amount of dividends from taxable Canadian corporations

Enter the amount of taxable dividends from a Canadian corporation according to which slip reports the income: T5, T3, T5013, T4PS. ProFile totals the taxable dividends from all these slips and posts the result on line 120 of the T1 jacket.

The Canada Revenue Agency says... *General Income Tax and Benefit Guide*

There are two types of dividends, eligible and other than eligible dividends, you may have received from taxable Canadian corporations.

Calculate the taxable amount of eligible dividends by multiplying the actual amount of eligible dividends you received by 145%.

For dividends other than eligible dividends, calculate the taxable amount by multiplying the actual amount of dividends (other than eligible) you received by 125%.

If you require additional information on the type of dividends you received, contact the payer of your dividends.

How to report dividends

Enter on line 180 the taxable amount of dividends (other than eligible dividends) as shown in box 11 on T5 slips, box 25 on T4PS slips, box 32 on T3 slips, and box 51-1 on T5013 or T5013A slips.

Enter on line 120 the taxable amount of all dividends from taxable Canadian corporations, as shown in boxes 11 and 25 on T5 slips, boxes 25 and 31 on T4PS slips, boxes 32 and 50 on T3 slips and boxes 51-1 and 52-1 on T5013 or T5013A slips.

If you did not receive an information slip, you must calculate the taxable amount of other than eligible dividends by multiplying the actual amount of dividends (other than eligible) you received by 125% and reporting the result on line 180. You must also calculate the taxable amount of eligible dividends by multiplying the actual amount of eligible dividends you received by 145%. Report the combined total of eligible and other than eligible dividends on line 120.

Dividends received from taxable Canadian corporations qualify for the federal dividend tax credit, which can reduce the amount of tax you pay. You can claim this credit when you calculate your federal and provincial or territorial taxes. For more information, see line 425.

Report on line 121 any foreign dividends you received.

Notes:

Income from property

> Special rules apply for income from property (including shares) one family member lends or transfers to another. For more information, see "Loans and transfers of property" in Total income.

If a child is born in 1992or later

> If a child who was born in 1992 or later is reporting certain dividends, see Split income of a child under 18.

Tip: In some cases, it may be better for you to report all the taxable dividends your spouse or common-law partner received from taxable Canadian corporations. You can do this only if, by including the dividends in your income, you will be able to claim or increase your claim for the spouse or common-law partner amount (see line 303).

If you use this option, you may be able to take better advantage of the dividend tax credit. Do not include these dividends in your spouse's or common-law partner's income when you calculate claims such as the spousal or common-law partner amount on line 303 or amounts transferred from your spouse or common-law partner on Schedule 2.

T1 Guide: Line 121 - Interest and other investment income

T1 Line 121: Interest and other investment income

Enter interest from investment income according to the type of slip that reported the income. Use one of these ProFile slips or forms: S4, T5, T3, T5008, T5013, T4PS. ProFile posts the total of all interest from investment income to line 121 of the T1 jacket.

The Canada Revenue Agency says... *General Income Tax and Benefit Guide*

What to report

The amounts you report for the year depend on the type of investment and when you made it. Include on this line amounts you received minus any part of those amounts that you reported in previous years. Also include amounts that were credited to you but that you did not receive, such as amounts that were reinvested.

The amounts to report include those shown in boxes 13, 14, and 15 on T5 slips, box 25 on T3 slips, and boxes 50 and 55 of your T5013 or T5013A slips. You also have to report the interest on any tax refund you received in 2009, which is shown on your Notice of Assessment or Notice of Reassessment.

If you received foreign interest and dividend income, make sure you report it in Canadian dollars.

If you own an interest in a foreign investment entity or an interest in a foreign insurance policy, you may have to report investment income. For more information, contact the Canada Revenue Agency.

If, as a shareholder in a foreign corporation, you received certain shares in another foreign corporation, you may not have to include any amount in income for receiving those shares. For more information, get Form T1135, Foreign Income Verification Statement, or contact us.

 Note:

- Special rules apply for income from most property (including money) one family member lends or transfers to another. For more information, see Loans and transfers of property for more information.
- Generally, when you invest your money in your child's name, you have to report the income from those investments. However, if you deposited Canada Child Tax Benefit or Universal Child Care Benefit payments into a bank account or trust in your child's name, the interest earned on those payments is your child's income.
- If a child who was born in 1992 or later is reporting certain investment income, see Split income of a child under 18.

How to report

Enter a list of your investments in Part II of Schedule 4.

Generally, you report your share of interest from a joint investment based on how much you contributed to it.

For example: Sally and Roger received a T5 slip from their joint bank account showing the $400 interest they earned in 2009. Sally had deposited $4,000 and Roger had deposited $1,000 into the account.

Roger reports $80 interest calculated as follows:

$1,000 (his share) x $400 (total interest) = $80 $5,000 (total)

Sally reports $320 interest, calculated as follows:

$4,000 (her share) x $400 (total interest) = $320 $5,000 (total)

Bank accounts

Report interest paid or credited to you in 2009 even if you did not receive an information slip. You may not receive a T5 slip for amounts under $50.

Term deposits, guaranteed income certificates (GICs), and similar investments

On these investments, interest builds up over a period of time, usually longer than one year. Generally, you do not receive the interest until the investment matures, or you cash it in. For more information on Canada Savings Bonds, see Canada Savings Bonds (CSBs) below.

The amount of income you report is based on the interest you earned during each complete investment year. For example, if you made a long-term investment on July 1, 2008, report on your return for 2009 the interest that accumulated to the end of June 2009, even if you do not receive a T5 slip. Report the interest from July 2009 to June 2010 on your 2010 return.

Note: Your investment agreement may specify a different interest rate each year. If so, report the amount on your T5 slip, even if it is different from what the agreement specifies or what you received. The issuer of your investment can tell you how this amount was calculated.

For most investments you made in 1990 or later, you have to report the interest each year, as you earn it. For information about reporting methods for investments (including CSBs) made in 1989 or earlier, or see Interpretation Bulletin IT-396, Interest Income.

Canada Savings Bonds (CSBs)

Interest on a regular interest ("R") bond is paid annually until the bond matures, or you cash it in. Interest on a compound interest ("C") bond is not paid until you cash it in. For both kinds of bonds, enter the amount shown on your T5 slip.

Treasury bills (T-Bills)

If you disposed of a T-Bill at maturity in 2009, you have to report as interest the difference between the price you paid and the proceeds of disposition shown on your T5008 slip or account statement.

If you disposed of a T-Bill before maturity in 2009, you may also have to report a capital gain or loss. For more information, see Guide T4037, Capital Gains for information on reporting Tbills on Schedule 3.

Earnings on life insurance policies

Report the earnings that have accumulated on certain life insurance policies in the same way as you do for other investments. In all cases, your insurance company will send you a T5 slip. For policies bought before 1990, you can choose to report accumulated earnings annually by telling your insurer in writing that you choose to do so.

T1 Guide: Line 122 - Net partnership income (limited or non-active partners only)

T1 Line 122: Net partnership income (limited or non-active partners only)

Enter net partnership income for limited or non-active partners on the ProFile S4 or the T5013. These amounts flow automatically to line 122 of the T1 jacket.

The Canada Revenue Agency says... *General Income Tax and Benefit Guide*

What to report

Enter on line 122 your share of the net income or loss from a partnership if the partnership did not include a rental or farming operation and you were either:

- a limited partner; or
- not actively involved in the partnership and not otherwise involved in a business or profession similar to that carried on by the partnership.

Report your net rental income or loss from a partnership on line 126. Report your net farming income or loss from a partnership on line 141.

If none of the above apply to you, enter your share of the partnership's net income or loss on the applicable self-employment line of your return (see lines 135 to 143).

 Note:

- If the partnership has a loss, the amount you can claim could be limited. For more information, contact us.
- If a child who was born in 1992or later is reporting certain limited or non-active partnership income, see Split income of a child under 18.

Tax shelters

To claim deductions, losses or credits from tax shelter investments, attach to your paper return any applicable T5003 slip and a completed Form T5004 Claim for tax shelter Loss or Deduction. Also, if applicable, attach any T5013 slip. Make sure your form shows the tax shelter identification number.

How to report this income

- Complete Part III of Schedule 4.
- Attach to your paper return a T5013 or T5013A slip. If you did not receive one, attach a copy of the partnership's financial statement. For more information, see lines 135 to 143 for more details.

Note: You may have to make Canada Pension Plan contributions on the net income you report on line 122. For more information, see line 222 for details.

T1 Guide: Line 125 - Registered disability savings plan (RDSP) income

T1 Line 125: Registered disability savings plan income

Enter income from Registered Disability Savings Plan (RDSP) on the T4A slip. The amount flows automatically to line 125 of the T1 jacket.

 The Canada Revenue Agency says... *General Income Tax and Benefit Guide*

If you have received income from an RDSP in 2009, enter the amount shown in box 28 of your T4A slip. For more information, see Information Sheet RC4460, Registered Disability Savings Plan (RDSP).

Note: The RDSP income you report will not be included in the calculation of your GST/HST credit, your CCTB payments (including those from certain related provincial or territorial programs), the social benefits repayment (line 235), the refundable medical expense supplement (line 452), or the Working Income Tax Benefit (WITB) (line 453).

T1 Guide - Lines 126 and 160: Rental income

T1 Line 126: Rental Income

Provide details of rental income on one of these ProFile forms: T776#, Rental# or on a T5013 slip, as required. Net amounts from these three forms flow to line 126 of the T1 jacket. Gross amounts flow to line 160.

The Canada Revenue Agency says... *General Income Tax and Benefit Guide*

Enter your gross rental income on line 160 and your net rental income or loss on line 126. If you have a loss, show the amount in brackets. If you were a member of a partnership, you should also include any amount shown in box 23 and of your T5013 or T5013A slips, or any amount the partnership allocated to you in its financial statements.

You have to include with your paper return a statement (you can use Form T776, Statement of Real Estate Rentals) showing your rental income and expenses for the year. If it applies, also include either your T5013 slip or a copy of the partnership's financial statement.

For more information about rental activities see Guide T4036 Rental Income which includes Form T776.

Guide T4036, Rental Income includes Form T776 and more information about rental activities.

Tax Shelters

To claim deductions, losses or credits from tax shelter investments, attach to your paper return any applicable T5003 slip and a completed Form T5004 Claim for tax shelter Loss or Deduction. Also, if applicable, attach any T5013 slip. Make sure your form shows the tax shelter identification number.

T1 Guide: Line 127 - Taxable capital gains

T1 Line 127: Taxable capital gains

The following ProFile slips and forms may include taxable capital gains: S3, T3, T5, T4PS, T5013. Enter amounts on these forms and ProFile will automatically post the total to line 127 of the T1 jacket.

The Canada Revenue Agency says... *General Income Tax and Benefit Guide*

When do you have a capital gain or loss?

You may have a capital gain or loss when you sell or dispose of property, such as real estate or shares (including those in mutual funds). Generally, if the total of your gains for the year is more than the total of your losses, you have to include 50% of the difference in your income. However, if the total of your losses for the year is more than the total of your gains, you cannot claim a deduction for the difference. See "How to report" below.

If you have a capital gain or loss from selling or redeeming your mutual fund units or shares, get Information Sheet RC4169, Tax Treatment of Mutual Funds for Individuals, for more information.

Capital gains from a mortgage foreclosure or conditional sales repossession

> If you realized a capital gain as a result of a mortgage foreclosure or conditional sales repossession, this gain is not included in income when calculating your GST/HST credit, your Canada Child Tax Benefit payments, your Child Disability Benefit payments, the social benefits repayment (line 235), the age amount (line 301), the refundable medical expenses supplement (line 452), or the Working Income Tax Benefit (WITB) (line 453), British Columbia sales tax credit, or Prince Edward Island, Nova Scotia, New Brunswick or Newfoundland and Labrador tax reductions. If this applies to you, contact us for more information.

Donations of capital property to a charity

> When you donate capital property to a registered charity, the CRA considers you to have disposed of the property at its fair market value. As a result, you may have to report a capital gain or loss for that property. There are special rules for donations of certain property. For more information, see Guide T4037, Capital Gains and Losses and Pamphlet P113, Gifts and Income Tax.
>
> For donations of publicly traded securities the inclusion rate of zero has been extended to any capital gain realized on the exchange of shares of the capital stock of a corporation for those publicly listed securities donated. This treatment is subject to certain conditions. In cases where the exchanged securities are partnership interests a special calculation is required to determine the capital gain to be reported. For more information on exchangeable securities. For more information, see Pamphlet P113, Gifts and Income Tax.

How to report

Complete Schedule 3, and attach it to your paper return. Generally, if all of your gains or losses are shown on T4PS, T5, or T5013 or T5013A slips, enter the total of amounts on line 174 on Schedule 3, and if they are shown on T3 slips, enter the total of amounts on line 176. Also attach these documents to your paper return. If your securities transactions are shown on an account statement or a T5008 slip, use the information on these documents to help you complete Schedule 3. For more information about these and other capital dispositions, see Guide T4037, Capital Gains and Losses.

If the result on line 199 on Schedule 3 is positive (a gain) enter the amount on line 127 of your return. If it is negative (a loss), do not claim the amount on line 127 of your return. We will register it in our system. Keep track of this loss, which you can use to reduce your taxable capital gains of other years. The following Notes explain how to do this.

Note:

- You may have incurred a net capital loss in 2009 that you want to apply against taxable capital gains you reported on your 2006, 2007, or 2008 return. For more information and to carry back the loss, get Form T1A, Request for Loss Carry back, and Guide T4037 Capital Gains. Attach a

completed copy of Form T1A to your paper return or send one to the CRA separately. Do not file an amended return for the year or years to which you want to apply the loss.
- If you are completing a return for a person who died in 2009, see Guide T4011, Preparing Returns for Deceased Persons, for more information about special rules that apply to claiming these losses.

Tip: You may be able to claim a deduction for your capital gains. For more information, see line 254.

T1 Guide - Lines 128 and 156: Support payments received

T1 Line 128: Support payments received

Use the ProFile worksheet called Support to enter support payments received. ProFile will automatically transfer amounts to lines 128 and 156 of the T1 jacket.

The Canada Revenue Agency says... *General Income Tax and Benefit Guide*

Enter on line 156 the total of all taxable and not taxable support payments for yourself and/or for a child that you received (or, if you are the payer, the payments that were repaid to you under a court order) in 2009. Enter on line 128 only the taxable amount.

Note:

Most child support payments received according to a written agreement or court order dated after April 1997, are not taxable. For more information, see Guide P102, Support Payments.

Tip: You may be able to claim a deduction on line 256 for the part of the payments you received from a resident of another country that is tax-free in Canada because of a tax treaty. If you do not know whether any part of the payments is tax-free, contact us.

You may be able to claim a deduction on line 220 for support income you repaid under a court order. For more information, see Guide P102, Support Payments.

T1 Guide: Line 129 - Registered retirement savings plan (RRSP) income

T1 Line 129: Registered retirement savings plan (RRSP) income

Enter RSP income on the T4RSP slips. ProFile also includes a worksheet called RRSP for tracking RRSP contributions, Home Buyer's Plan and Lifelong Learning Plan repayments, and the current deduction limit. Amounts from these forms flow to line 129 of the T1 jacket.

Frequently Asked Questions

What if my RRSP or RRIF has been deregistered?

If in 2009 your RRSP was changed and it no longer satisfies the rules under which it was registered, it is no longer an RRSP. It is now an amended plan or fund. In such a case, the CRA considers you to have received in 2009 an amount that equals the fair market value of all the property the plan or fund held at the time it ceased being an RRSP or a RRIF. This amount is reported on a T4RSP shown in box 26.

 Note: If the RRSP from which you receive the amount is a spousal or common-law partner RRSP and your spouse or common-law partner made contributions to any of your RRSPs in 2007, 2008, or 2009, your spouse or common-law partner may have to include in income all or part of the amount received. see "Amounts from a spousal or common-law partner RRSP or RRIF."

What if I inherited an RRSP from someone who died?

If your spouse or common-law partner died during the tax year and you were the beneficiary of his or her matured RRSP:

- the RRSP becomes yours free of taxes, so do not report the total amount of the RRSP as income on your tax return.
- however, when you receive annuity payments from the RRSP, you must report the payment amounts on line 129.

When should I not report RRSP income here?

Do not report RRSP income on line 129 if the amount you received is a periodic annuity payment from an RRSP reported on a T4A slip. This income is reported on line 115.

 The Canada Revenue Agency says...

Enter on line 129 the total of amounts shown in boxes 16, 18, 28, and 34 of all your T4RSP slips.

Also include amounts shown in boxes 20, 22, and 26, unless your spouse or common-law partner made a contribution to your RRSP. For more information, see RRSPs for spouse or common-law partner in the next section.

Tip:

If unused RRSP contributions you made after 1990 were refunded to you or your spouse or common-law partner in 2009, you may be able to claim a deduction on line 232.

RRSP annuity payments that you report on line 129 (shown in box 16 of your T4RSP slip) qualify for the pension income amount if you were 65 years of age or older on December 31, 2009, or if you received the payments because of the death of your spouse or common-law partner. For more information, see line 314.

Also, you may be able to jointly elect with your spouse or common-law partner to split your RRSP annuity payments that you reported on line 129 if you meet all of the following conditions:

- you were 65 years of age or older on December 31, or you received the payments because of the death of your spouse or common-law partner;
- you were both residents of Canada on December 31 (or were residents of Canada on the date of death); and

- you and your spouse or common-law partner were not, because of a breakdown in your marriage or common-law relationship, living separate and apart from each other at the end of the year and for a period of 90 days commencing in the year.

To make this election, you and your spouse or common-law partner must complete Form T1032, Joint Election to Split Pension Income.

Note: If you elected to split your RRSP annuity payments with your spouse or common-law partner, you (the pensioner) must still report the full amount on line 129, but you can claim a deduction for the elected split-pension amount. For more information, see line 210 for details.

RRSPs for spouse or common-law partner

Your spouse or common-law partner may have to report some or all of the RRSP income shown in box 20, 22, or 26 of your T4RSP slips if he or she contributed to any of your RRSPs in 2007, 2008, or 2009. In that case, your T4RSP slip should have "Yes" ticked in box 24, and your spouse's or common-law partner's social insurance number in box 36.

To calculate the amount from an RRSP for a spouse or common-law partner that each of you has to report, complete Form T2205, Amounts from a Spousal or Common-Law Partner RRSP or RRIF to Include in Income. Both you and your spouse or common-law partner should include Form T2205 with your paper returns. However, only the person shown as the annuitant on the T4RSP slip can claim the income tax deducted (box 30) and should attach the slip to his or her paper return.

Note: If you and your spouse or common-law partner were living apart because of a breakdown in the relationship when you withdrew funds from your RRSP, you have to report the whole amount shown on your T4RSP slips.

For more information on RRSP income, get Guide T4040, RRSPs and Other Registered Plans for Retirement.

Repayments under the Home Buyers' Plan (HBP) and the Lifelong Learning Plan (LLP)

If, in previous years, you withdrew funds from your RRSP under the HBP or the LLP, you may have to make a repayment for 2009. The minimum repayment is shown on your Notice of Assessment or Notice of Reassessment for 2008. To make a repayment, you have to contribute to your RRSP from January 1, 2009, to March 1, 2010, and designate your contribution as a repayment on line 6 or 7 of Schedule 7. **Do not make the repayment to the CRA.**

If you repay less than the minimum amount for 2009, you have to include the difference as RRSP income on line 129 of your return.

> **Example**
>
> Kevin withdrew funds under the HBP in 2004. His minimum required prepayment for 2009 was $800. The only RRSP contribution he made from January 1, 2009, to March 1, 2010, was for $500 on June 18, 2009. He designated it on line 6 of Schedule 7 as a repayment under the HBP, and included $300 in his income on line 129 ($800 minimum required repayment minus $500 repaid and designated).

For more information, including the rules that apply when the person who made the withdrawal dies, turns 71 years of age, or becomes a non-resident. For more information, see Guide RC4135, Home Buyers' Plan (HBP) or Guide RC4112, Lifelong Learning Plan (LLP).

T1 Guide: Line 130 - Other income

T1 Line 130: Other income Enter the income in ProFile according to the slip(s) that the taxpayer received. The ProFile worksheet, Other Income, accumulates amounts from various forms and slips. The total for line 130 flows from Other Income automatically.

 The Canada Revenue Agency says... *General Income Tax and Benefit Guide*

Use this line to report taxable income that is not reported anywhere else on the return. To find out if an amount is taxable, contact the CRA. Make sure the amount you are reporting at line 130 is not a type of income that should have been reported at lines 101 to 129. In the space to the left of line 130, specify the type of income you are reporting. If you have more than one type of income, attach a note to your paper return giving the details.

Note: Special rules apply for income from property one family member lends or transfers to another. or more information, see "Loans and transfers of property" in Total income.

Scholarships, fellowships, bursaries, and artists' project grants

Post-secondary school scholarships, fellowships, or bursaries are not taxable if you received them for your enrolment in a program that entitles you to claim the education amount in 2008, 2009, or 2010. If this is not the case, enter on line 130 the part of the post-secondary scholarships, fellowships or bursaries you received in the year that is more than $500.

If you received an artists' project grant, see Interpretation Bulletin IT-75, Scholarships, Fellowships, Bursaries, Prizes, Research Grants and Financial Assistance.

Report prizes and awards you received as a benefit from your employment or in connection with a business. However, these are not eligible for the $500 tax-free amount. If you received a research grant, see line 104.

For more information, see Interpretation Bulletin IT-75.

Apprenticeship completion grant

If you received on apprenticeship completion grant in 2009, include the amount from box 28 of your T4A slip on line 130

Lump-sum payments

Include lump-sum payments from pensions and deferred profit-sharing plans (box 18 of your T4A slips and box 22 of your T3 slips) received when leaving a plan.

If, in 2009, you received a lump-sum payment that included amounts you earned in previous years, you have to include the whole payment on line 130 of your return for 2009. However, you can ask us to apply a reduced tax rate to the part that relates to amounts you earned before 1972. To ask us to apply this special rate, attach a note to your paper return. We will tell you the results on your Notice of Assessment or Notice of Reassessment.

Retiring allowances (severance pay)

A retiring allowance includes an amount paid as severance pay. Include the amount shown in boxes 26 and 27 of your T4A slips.

Also, report any retiring allowance included in the amount in box 26 of your T3 slips. Details regarding the retiring allowance will be shown in box 36 and in the footnotes area of the slips.

Note: You may be able to deduct legal fees you paid to get a retiring allowance. For more information, see line 232.

Tip: You may be able to transfer part or all of your retiring allowances to your RRSP. For more information, see "Line 11 - Transfers".

Death benefits (other than Canada Pension Plan or Quebec Pension Plan death benefits)

A death benefit is an amount you receive after a person's death for that person's employment service. It is shown in box 28 of your T4A slips or box 26 of your T3 slips.

You may not have to pay tax on up to $10,000 of the benefit you received. If you are the only one to receive a death benefit, report the amount you receive that is more than $10,000. Even if you do not receive all of the death benefit in one year, the total tax-free amount for all years cannot be more than $10,000. To find out what to report if anyone else also received a death benefit for the same person, or see Interpretation Bulletin IT-508, Death Benefits.

Attach to your paper return a note stating the amount of death benefits you received but did not include in your income.

Other kinds of income

Also include the following income amounts on line 130:

- amounts distributed from a retirement compensation arrangement shown on your T4ARCA Slip (for more information, see the back of your T4A-RCA slip);
- training allowances, Saskatchewan Pension Plan payments, or any other amount shown in box 28 of your T4A slips (other than amounts already mentioned for this line and line 104), 115 and 125;
- payments from a trust shown in box 26 of your T3 slips;
- payments from a registered education savings plan (RESP) shown in box 40 (see also line 418) or 42 of your T4A slips; and
- certain annuity payments (see line 115) and
- payments from a Tax-Free Savings Account shown in box 28 of your T4A slips.

T1 Guide: Lines 135 and 162 - Self-employment income - Business income

T1 line 135 and line 162 - Self-employment income - Business income

Enter business income on the ProFile forms: T2125#, Self Employ or T5013, according to how the income is reported. ProFile automatically transfers gross business income to line 162 and net income to line 135 of the T1 jacket.

 The Canada Revenue Agency says... *General Income Tax and Benefit Guide*

Enter on the appropriate line your gross and net income or loss from self-employment. If you have a loss, show it in brackets. Include with your paper return a statement showing your income and expenses.

You have to file Form T1139, Reconciliation of 2009 Business Income for Tax Purposes, with your return for 2009 if you want to keep a year-end that does not finish on December 31, 2009. However, if you filed Form T1139 with your return for 2008 you may have to complete the version of this form for 2009. For more information, see guide RC4015, Reconciliation of Business Income for Tax Purposes.

Note:

- You may have to make Canada Pension Plan contributions on your self-employment earnings. See line 222.
- If a child who was born in 1992 or later is reporting certain self-employment income, see Split income of a child under 18.

The following guides contain more information and forms you may need to help you calculate your self-employment income:

- Guide T4002, Business and Professional Income, (Form T2125, Statement of Business or Professional Activities);
- Guide T4004, Fishing Income, which includes Form T2121, Statement of Fishing Activities;
- Guide T4003, Farming Income,(Form T2042, Statement of Farming Activities;
- RC4060, Farming Income and the AgriStability and AgriInvest Programs Guide (Form T1163, Statement A - AgriStability and AgriInvest Programs Information and Statement of Farming Activities for Individuals , and Form T1164, Statement B - AgriStability and AgriInvest Programs Information and Statement of Farming Activities for Additional Farming Operations);
- RC4408,Farming Income and the AgriStability and AgriInvest Programs Harmonized Guide
- (Form T1273, Statement A - Harmonized AgriStability and AgriInvest Programs Information and Statement of Farming Activities for Individuals, and Form T1274, Statement B Harmonized AgriStability and AgriInvest Programs Information and Statement of Farming Activities for Additional Farming Operations).

Note:

- If you are participating in the AgriStability and AgriInvest Programs, and you are filing a paper return, use the envelope contained in your Guide RC4060 or Forms Book RC4408-2.
- If you use your home for day care, see Pamphlet P134, Using Your Home for Day Care, for more information.

Generally, if you were a limited or non-active partner, you enter your net income or loss on line 122. However, if your net income or loss is from a rental operation, enter the amount on line 126. If it is from a farming operation, enter it on line 141.

If you were an active partner and received a T5013, or T5013A slip, report the amount from boxes 20, 21, 35, 37, 39, 41, and 43 on the applicable line of your return. This is your share of the partnership's income or loss. Also report the partnership's gross income as shown in boxes 162, 164, 166, 168, and 170. Attach the T5013 or T5013A slip to your paper return. If you did not receive this slip, you should attach the applicable self-employment form indicated above, or a copy of the partnership's financial statement.

T1 Guide: Lines 137 and 164 - Self-employment income - Professional income

T1 line 137 and line 164: Self-employment income - Professional income

Enter professional income on the ProFile forms T2125#, Self Employ, T5013. ProFile automatically transfers the gross professional income to line 164 and the net income to line 137 of the T1 jacket.

 The Canada Revenue Agency says... *General Income Tax and Benefit Guide*

Enter on the appropriate line your gross and net income or loss from self-employment. If you have a loss, show it in brackets. Include with your paper return a statement showing your income and expenses.

You have to file Form T1139, Reconciliation of 2009 Business Income for Tax Purposes, with your return for 2009 if you want to keep a year-end that does not finish on December 31, 2009. However, if you filed Form T1139 with your return for 2008 you may have to complete the version of this form for 2009. For more information, see guide RC4015, Reconciliation of Business Income for Tax Purposes.

Note:
- You may have to make Canada Pension Plan contributions on your self-employment earnings. See line 222.
- If a child who was born in 1992 or later is reporting certain self-employment income, see Split income of a child under 18.

The following guides contain more information and forms you may need to help you calculate your self-employment income:

- Guide T4002, Business and Professional Income, (Form T2125, Statement of Business or Professional Activities);
- Guide T4004, Fishing Income, which includes Form T2121, Statement of Fishing Activities;
- Guide T4003, Farming Income,(Form T2042, Statement of Farming Activities;
- RC4060, Farming Income and the AgriStability and AgriInvest Programs Guide (Form T1163, Statement A - AgriStability and AgriInvest Programs Information and Statement of Farming Activities for Individuals, and Form T1164, Statement B - AgriStability and AgriInvest Programs Information and Statement of Farming Activities for Additional Farming Operations);
- RC4408, Farming Income and the AgriStability and AgriInvest Programs Harmonized Guide (Form T1273, Statement A - Harmonized AgriStability and AgriInvest Programs Information and

Statement of Farming Activities for Individuals, and Form T1274, Statement B Harmonized AgriStability and AgriInvest Programs Information and Statement of Farming Activities for Additional Farming Operations).

Note:

- If you are participating in the AgriStability and AgriInvest Programs, and you are filing a paper return, use the envelope contained in your Guide RC4060 or Forms Book RC4408-2.
- If you use your home for day care, see Pamphlet P134, Using Your Home for Day Care, for more information.

Generally, if you were a limited or non-active partner, you enter your net income or loss on line 122. However, if your net income or loss is from a rental operation, enter the amount on line 126. If it is from a farming operation, enter it on line 141.

If you were an active partner and received a T5013, or T5013A slip, report the amount from boxes 20, 21, 35, 37, 39, 41, and 43 on the applicable line of your return. This is your share of the partnership's income or loss. Also report the partnership's gross income as shown in boxes 162, 164, 166, 168, and 170. Attach the T5013 or T5013A slip to your paper return. If you did not receive this slip, you should attach the applicable self-employment form indicated above, or a copy of the partnership's financial statement.

T1 Guide: Lines 139 and 166 - Self-employment income - Commission income

T1 line 139 and line 166: Self-employment income - Commission income

Enter commission income on the ProFile forms: T2125#, Self Employ or T5013, according to how the income is reported. ProFile automatically transfers gross commission income to line 166 and net income to line 139 of the T1 jacket.

The Canada Revenue Agency says... *General Income Tax and Benefit Guide*

Enter on the appropriate line your gross and net income or loss from self-employment. If you have a loss, show it in brackets. Include with your paper return a statement showing your income and expenses.

You have to file Form T1139, Reconciliation of 2009 Business Income for Tax Purposes, with your return for 2009 if you want to keep a year-end that does not finish on December 31, 2009. However, if you filed Form T1139 with your return for 2008 you may have to complete the version of this form for 2009. For more information, see guide RC4015, Reconciliation of Business Income for Tax Purposes.

Note:

- You may have to make Canada Pension Plan contributions on your self-employment earnings. See line 222.
- If a child who was born in 1992 or later is reporting certain self-employment income, see Split income of a child under 18.

The following guides contain more information and forms you may need to help you calculate your self-employment income:

- Guide T4002, Business and Professional Income, (Form T2125, Statement of Business or Professional Activities);
- Guide T4004, Fishing Income, which includes Form T2121, Statement of Fishing Activities;
- Guide T4003, Farming Income,(Form T2042, Statement of Farming Activities;
- RC4060, Farming Income and the AgriStability and AgriInvest Programs Guide (Form T1163, Statement A - AgriStability and AgriInvest Programs Information and Statement of Farming Activities for Individuals , and Form T1164, Statement B - AgriStability and AgriInvest Programs Information and Statement of Farming Activities for Additional Farming Operations);
- RC4408, Farming Income and the AgriStability and AgriInvest Programs Harmonized Guide (Form T1273, Statement A - Harmonized AgriStability and AgriInvest Programs Information and Statement of Farming Activities for Individuals, and Form T1274, Statement B Harmonized AgriStability and AgriInvest Programs Information and Statement of Farming Activities for Additional Farming Operations).

Note:

- If you are participating in the AgriStability and AgriInvest Programs, and you are filing a paper return, use the envelope contained in your Guide RC4060 or Forms Book RC4408-2.
- If you use your home for day care, see Pamphlet P134, Using Your Home for Day Care, for more information.

Generally, if you were a limited or non-active partner, you enter your net income or loss on line 122. However, if your net income or loss is from a rental operation, enter the amount on line 126. If it is from a farming operation, enter it on line 141.

If you were an active partner and received a T5013, or T5013A slip, report the amount from boxes 20, 21, 35, 37, 39, 41, and 43 on the applicable line of your return. This is your share of the partnership's income or loss. Also report the partnership's gross income as shown in boxes 162, 164, 166, 168, and 170. Attach the T5013 or T5013A slip to your paper return. If you did not receive this slip, you should attach the applicable self-employment form indicated above, or a copy of the partnership's financial statement.

T1 Guide: Lines 141 and 168 - Self-employment income - Farming income

T1 line 141 and line 168: Self-employment income - Farming income

Enter farming income on the ProFile forms T2042#, T1164, Self Employ or T5013, according to how the income is reported. ProFile automatically transfers gross farming income to line 168 and net income to line 141 of the T1 jacket.

 The Canada Revenue Agency says... *General Income Tax and Benefit Guide*

Enter on the appropriate line your gross and net income or loss from self-employment. If you have a loss, show it in brackets. Include with your paper return a statement showing your income and expenses.

You have to file Form T1139, Reconciliation of 2009 Business Income for Tax Purposes, with your return for 2009 if you want to keep a year-end that does not finish on December 31, 2009. However, if you filed

Form T1139 with your return for 2008 you may have to complete the version of this form for 2009. For more information, see guide RC4015, Reconciliation of Business Income for Tax Purposes.

Note:

- You may have to make Canada Pension Plan contributions on your self-employment earnings. See line 222.
- If a child who was born in 1992 or later is reporting certain self-employment income, see Split income of a child under 18.

The following guides contain more information and forms you may need to help you calculate your self-employment income: Guide T4002, Business and Professional Income, (Form T2125, Statement of Business or Professional Activities);

- Guide T4004, Fishing Income, which includes Form T2121, Statement of Fishing Activities;
- Guide T4003, Farming Income, (Form T2042, Statement of Farming Activities;
- RC4060, Farming Income and the AgriStability and AgriInvest Programs Guide (Form T1163, Statement A - AgriStability and AgriInvest Programs Information and Statement of Farming Activities for Individuals, and Form T1164, Statement B - AgriStability and AgriInvest Programs Information and Statement of Farming Activities for Additional Farming Operations);
- RC4408, Farming Income and the AgriStability and AgriInvest Programs Harmonized Guide (Form T1273, Statement A - Harmonized AgriStability and AgriInvest Programs Information and Statement of Farming Activities for Individuals, and Form T1274, Statement B Harmonized AgriStability and AgriInvest Programs Information and Statement of Farming Activities for Additional Farming Operations).

Note:

- If you are participating in the AgriStability and AgriInvest Programs, and you are filing a paper return, use the envelope contained in your Guide RC4060 or Forms Book RC4408-2.
- If you use your home for day care, see Pamphlet P134, Using Your Home for Day Care, for more information.

Generally, if you were a limited or non-active partner, you enter your net income or loss on line 122. However, if your net income or loss is from a rental operation, enter the amount on line 126. If it is from a farming operation, enter it on line 141.

If you were an active partner and received a T5013, or T5013A slip, report the amount from boxes 20, 21, 35, 37, 39, 41, and 43 on the applicable line of your return. This is your share of the partnership's income or loss. Also report the partnership's gross income as shown in boxes 162, 164, 166, 168, and 170. Attach the T5013 or T5013A slip to your paper return. If you did not receive this slip, you should attach the applicable self-employment form indicated above, or a copy of the partnership's financial statement.

T1 Guide: Lines 135 to 143 - Self-employment income

T1 Lines 143 and 170: Self-employment income - Fishing income

Enter fishing income on the ProFile forms: T2121#, Self Employ or T5013, according to how the income is reported. ProFile automatically transfers gross fishing income to line 170 and net income to line 143 of the T1 jacket.

 The Canada Revenue Agency says... *General Income Tax and Benefit Guide*

Enter on the appropriate line your gross and net income or loss from self-employment. If you have a loss, show it in brackets. Include with your paper return a statement showing your income and expenses.

You have to file Form T1139, Reconciliation of 2009 Business Income for Tax Purposes, with your return for 2009 if you want to keep a year-end that does not finish on December 31, 2009. However, if you filed Form T1139 with your return for 2008 you may have to complete the version of this form for 2009. For more information, see guide RC4015, Reconciliation of Business Income for Tax Purposes.

Note:
- You may have to make Canada Pension Plan contributions on your self-employment earnings. See line 222.
- If a child who was born in 1992 or later is reporting certain self-employment income, see Split income of a child under 18.

The following guides contain more information and forms you may need to help you calculate your self-employment income:

- Guide T4002, Business and Professional Income, (Form T2125, Statement of Business or Professional Activities);
- Guide T4004, Fishing Income, which includes Form T2121, Statement of Fishing Activities;
- Guide T4003, Farming Income,(Form T2042, Statement of Farming Activities;
- RC4060, Farming Income and the AgriStability and AgriInvest Programs Guide (Form T1163, Statement A - AgriStability and AgriInvest Programs Information and Statement of Farming Activities for Individuals , and Form T1164, Statement B - AgriStability and AgriInvest Programs Information and Statement of Farming Activities for Additional Farming Operations);
- RC4408, Farming Income and the AgriStability and AgriInvest Programs Harmonized Guide (Form T1273, Statement A - Harmonized AgriStability and AgriInvest Programs Information and Statement of Farming Activities for Individuals , and Form T1274, Statement B Harmonized AgriStability and AgriInvest Programs Information and Statement of Farming Activities for Additional Farming Operations).

Note:
- If you are participating in the AgriStability and AgriInvest Programs, and you are filing a paper return, use the envelope contained in your Guide RC4060 or Forms Book RC4408-2.
- If you use your home for day care, see Pamphlet P134, Using Your Home for Day Care, for more information.

Generally, if you were a limited or non-active partner, you enter your net income or loss on line 122. However, if your net income or loss is from a rental operation, enter the amount on line 126. If it is from a farming operation, enter it on line 141.

If you were an active partner and received a T5013, or T5013A slip, report the amount from boxes 20, 21, 35, 37, 39, 41, and 43 on the applicable line of your return. This is your share of the partnership's income or loss. Also report the partnership's gross income as shown in boxes 162, 164, 166, 168, and 170. Attach the T5013 or T5013A slip to your paper return. If you did not receive this slip, you should attach the applicable self-employment form indicated above, or a copy of the partnership's financial statement.

T1 Guide: Line 144 - Workers' Compensation benefits

T1 Line 144: Workers' Compensation benefits

Enter workers' compensation benefits on the T5007 slips. These amounts will flow to line 144 of the T1 jacket.

 The Canada Revenue Agency says... *General Income Tax and Benefit Guide*

Enter the amount shown in box 10 of your T5007 slip. Claim a deduction on line 250 for the benefits you entered on line 144.

Note: In 2009, you may have repaid salary or wages originally paid to you by your employer in a previous year, in anticipation of workers' compensation benefits you would receive. This amount should be shown in box 77 of your T4 slip. In that case, you may be able to claim a deduction on line 229. For more information, contact the CRA.

T1 Guide: Line 145 - Social assistance payments

T1 Line 145: Social assistance payments

Enter social assistance payments on the T5007 slip. These amounts will flow to line 145 of the T1 jacket.

 The Canada Revenue Agency says...

Generally, you enter the amount shown in box 11 of your T5007 slip or the federal part of your Québec Relevé 5 slip. However, if you lived with your spouse or common-law partner when the payments were made, the one of you who has the higher net income on line 236 (not including these payments or the deductions on line 214 or line 235) has to report all the payments, no matter whose name is on the slip. If this amount is the same for both of you, the person whose name is on the T5007 slip (or the prestataire on the federal part of the Relevé 5 slip) has to report them.

 Note:

- You do not have to include certain social assistance payments you or your spouse or common-law partner received for being a foster parent or for caring for a disabled adult who lived with you. For more information, contact the CRA. However, if the payments are for caring for your

spouse, your common-law partner, or an individual related to either of you, whoever has the higher net income will have to include those payments in income.
- If you repay an amount that was reported on a T5007 slip or a Relevé 5 in a previous year, the return for that year may be adjusted based on the amended slip provided. For more information, see "How do you change a return?"

Claim a deduction on line 250 for the social assistance payments you entered on line 145.

T1 Guide: Line 146 - Net federal supplements

T1 Line 146: Net federal supplements

Enter net federal supplements on the T4A(OAS) slip. This amount will flow to line 146 of the T1 jacket.

The Canada Revenue Agency says... *General Income Tax and Benefit Guide*

Enter the amount shown in box 21 of your T4A(OAS) slip.

If your net income before adjustments (line 234) is $66,335 or less, claim a deduction on line 250 for the net federal supplements you entered on line 146. If the amount on line 234 of your return is more than $66,335, contact the CRA to find out how much you can deduct on line 250.

Note: Note However, your net income before adjustments on line 234 of your return will be reduced by the amounts entered on line 117 and line 125, and increased by any amount deducted on line 213, and/or for a repayment of the registered disability savings plans income included, on line 232, if required.

T1 Line 147: Net federal supplements

This line is a summary of amounts on lines 144 to 146. For more detail on this amount see the help specific to those forms that are used to calculate the totals added to this line. You may also find additional help for those lines on the T1 jacket.

T1 Line 150: Total income

Line 150 represents the total income entered for this return. For more detail on this amount see the help specific to those forms that are used to calculate the totals added to this line. You may also find additional help for those lines on the T1 jacket.

T1 Guide: Line 152 - Disability benefits included on line 114

T1 Line 152: Disability benefits included on line 114

Enter CPP or QPP disability benefits on the T4A(P) slip. These amounts flow to line 152 of the T1 jacket.

The Canada Revenue Agency says... *General Income Tax and Benefit Guide*

Enter on line 152 (located below and to the left of line 114) the amount of your CPP or QPP disability benefits from box 16 of your T4A(P) slip. This amount is already included in your total CPP or QPP benefits on line 114, and should not be added again when calculating your total income on line 150.

The CRA uses the disability benefit portion of CPP or QPP benefits in calculating your RRSP deduction limit.

T1 Guide: Line 206 - Pension adjustment

T1 Line 206: Pension adjustment

ProFile calculates this amount using data from other forms and worksheets. To jump to a related form, right click on the field and select from the list of forms in the context-sensitive menu. You can also press <F6> when your cursor is in the field to jump to the first source form.

The Canada Revenue Agency says... *General Income Tax and Benefit Guide*

Enter on line 206 the total of all amounts shown in box 52 of your T4 slips, or box 34 of your T4A slips. Generally, this total represents the value of the benefits you earned in 2009 under a registered pension plan (RPP) or a deferred profit-sharing plan (DPSP).

Do not include the pension adjustment (PA) amount in your income, and do not deduct it on your return. Enter this amount on line 206. We will use it to calculate your registered retirement savings plan (RRSP) deduction limit for 2010, which we will show on your Notice of Assessment or Notice of Reassessment for 2009 or on Form T1028. For more information, see line 208.

If you have any questions about how your PA was calculated, ask your employer.

Note: If you live in Canada and participated in a foreign pension plan in 2009, you may have to enter an amount on this line.

If you contributed to a foreign employer-sponsored pension plan or to a Social Arrangement (other than a United States (U.S.) Arrangement), see Form RC269, Contributions to a Foreign Employer Sponsored Pension Plan or to a Social Security Arrangement (other than a United States Arrangement). If you were a U.S. resident working in Canada and contributed to a U.S. employer sponsored retirement plan, see Form RC276, Contributions to a United States Employer-Sponsored Retirement Plan. If you are a commuter from Canada and contributed to a U.S. retirement plan, see Form RC268, Contributions to a United States Retirement Plan by a Commuter from Canada.

T1 Guide - Line 207: Registered pension plan (RPP) deduction

T1 Line 207: Registered pension plan (RPP) deduction

ProFile calculates this amount using data from other forms and worksheets. To jump to a related form, right click on the field and select from the list of forms in the context-sensitive menu. You can also press <F6> when your cursor is in the field to jump to the first source form.

The Canada Revenue Agency says... *General Income Tax and Benefit Guide*

Generally, you can deduct the total of all amounts shown in box 20 of your T4 slips, in box 32 of your T4A slips, or on your union or RPP receipts. Contact us or see Guide T4040, RRSPs and Other Registered Plans for Retirement, to find out how much you can deduct if any of the following apply:

- the total is more than $3,500 and your information slip shows a past-service amount for service before 1990;
- you contributed in a previous year and could not deduct part of the contributions; or
- you made contributions to a pension plan in a foreign country.

Note: If you contributed to a foreign employer-sponsored pension plan or to a Social Security Arrangement (other than a United States (U.S.) Arrangement), see Form RC269, Contributions to a Foreign Employer- Sponsored Pension Plan or to a Social Security Arrangement (other than a United States Arrangement). If you were a U.S. resident working in Canada and contributed to a U.S. employer-sponsored retirement plan, see Form RC267, Contributions to a United States Employer-Sponsored Retirement Plan by a Commuter from Canada.

T1 Guide: Line 208 - RRSP deduction

T1 Line 208: RRSP deduction

In 2009, the RRSP dollar limit increases to $21,000, when calculating the limit based on 18% of the 2008 earned income.

ProFile calculates this amount using data from other forms and worksheets. To jump to a related form, right click on the field and select from the list of forms in the context-sensitive menu. You can also press <F6> when your cursor is in the field to jump to the first source form.

The Canada Revenue Agency says... *General Income Tax and Benefit Guide*

This section gives general information on registered retirement savings plans (RRSPs). If you need more information after reading this section, see Guide T4040, RRSPs and Other Registered Plans for Retirement. See "Schedule 7" (below) for more information about completing Schedule 7. To view your RRSP information, go to My Account on our website.

Receipts

If you are filing a paper return, include your official receipts for all amounts you contributed from March 3, 2009, to March 1, 2010, including those you are not deducting on your return for 2009 and those you are designating as HBP or LLP repayments. For more information about HBP and LLP repayments, see "Lines 6 and 7". If you contributed to your spouse's or common-law partner's plan, the receipt has to show your name as the contributor and your spouse's or common-law partner's name as the annuitant. Also attach Schedule 7 if you have to complete it.

If you are filing electronically, keep all of your documents in case we ask to see them.

Maximum contributions you can deduct

The maximum you can deduct on line 208 is whichever of the following amounts is least:

- the unused RRSP contributions shown on line B of your Notice of Assessment for 2008 or on Form T1028, Your RRSP Information for 2009 plus the total of your RRSP contributions made from March 3, 2009, to March 1, 2010 (not including amounts you designate as HBP or LLP repayments, see Repayments under the HBP and LLP); or
- your RRSP deduction limit for 2009 plus amounts you transfer to your RRSP on or before March 1, 2010.

Note:

- After the end of the year you turn 71 years of age, you or your spouse or common-law partner cannot contribute to an RRSP under which you are the annuitant. However, you still can contribute to your spouse's or common-law partner's RRSP until the end of the year he or she turns 71 years of age, and you can deduct those contributions as long as you still have an unused RRSP deduction limit.
- If you contribute more to an RRSP than you can deduct, you may have to pay a special tax of 1% per month. To pay this tax you must file a T1-OVP, Individual Tax Return for RRSP Excess Contributions, for each applicable tax year.

T1 Guide: Line 209 - Saskatchewan Pension Plan (SPP) deduction

T1 Line 209: Saskatchewan Pension Plan (SPP) deduction

ProFile calculates this amount using data from other forms and worksheets. To jump to a related form, right click on the field and select from the list of forms in the context-sensitive menu. You can also press <F6> when your cursor is in the field to jump to the first source form.

Saskatchewan Pension Plan (SPP) deduction

Enter the contributions you made to a SPP on the Other Deduct form.

Undeducted contributions to a Saskatchewan Pension Plan cannot be carried forward. However, contributions made in the first 60 days of the year may be deducted on the previous year's tax return or in the year the contribution was made.

If you made contributions in the first 60 days of the year and these amounts were reported on your previous year's tax return but were not deducted, ProFile will carry forward these amounts in order to claim a deduction in the current year.

The Canada Revenue Agency says... *General Income Tax and Benefit Guide*

You can deduct contributions to the SPP for 2009, up to whichever of the following three amounts is least:

- $600;
- your 2009 RRSP deduction limit minus your RRSP deduction from line 208 (not including transfers to your RRSP); or
- the total amount you contributed to the SPP for yourself or your spouse or common-law partner from January 1, 2009, to March 1, March 1, 2010, not including any contributions that you deducted on your 2008 return.

T1 Guide: Line 210 - Deduction for elected split-pension amount

Frequently Asked Questions

When should you consider Pension Income Splitting?

Consider splitting pension income in the following situations:

- If the transfer of pension income reduces the total taxes payable for a married or common-law couple.
- If one spouse is in a higher tax bracket (page 2 of Federal Schedule 1). At a minimum, you will save the difference in the tax rates between each spouse's tax bracket.
- If one spouse is not fully using the Pension credit amount (line 314).
- If the spouse with the pension income to be transferred has OAS claw back (line 235) or a reduced age credit amount (line 301).
- If one spouse is paying Provincial surtax.

When will Pension Income Splitting not benefit you?

If both spouses have eligible pension income, are fully using the Pension income amount, and are in the same tax bracket, there may be no benefit to pension splitting.

If neither spouse is taxable, pension splitting will not be beneficial.

Other points to consider

The amount of pension income that can be split is indicated on the transferor's T1032.

Pension income does not have to be split equally (50/50). You can choose the most beneficial amount to transfer to your spouse, as long as it does not exceed 50% of your eligible pension income.

Pension splitting can impact other tax credits and calculations. You should review these claims before and after transferring pension income:

- Age amount (line 301)
- Medical expenses (line 330)
- Donations and gifts (line 349)
- Social benefits repayment (OAS claw back) (line 235)
- Spouse or common-law partner credit (line 303)
- Pension income amount (line 314)
- Amounts transferred from your spouse or common-law partner (line 326)

More information for Québec residents

Electing to split pension income

> Starting with the 2007 taxation year, spouses may jointly decide to include a portion of one spouse's retirement income in the calculation of the other spouse's income. Up to half of a taxpayer's eligible retirement income may be transferred to his or her spouse. For Québec purposes, you can elect (Schedule Q) to split a different amount than your federal tax return (T1032).

The amount included in your income, on line 123 of your Québec TP1, may be deducted on line 250 of your spouse's TP1.

Your spouse must also complete Schedule Q and enclose it with his or her return. If you agree on such a transfer, your spouse must also allocate to you the Québec income tax withheld from the eligible retirement income, in the same proportion as the retirement income is transferred. On line 451.3 of your TP1, enter the amount your spouse indicated on line 58 of Schedule Q. This amount must also be deducted on line 451.1 of your spouse's TP1.

Retirement income transferred by your spouse (line 123)

Income transferred by your spouse (line 123) If your spouse is 65 or over, his or her eligible retirement income may include the income reported on line 122 as:

- life annuity payments under a pension plan or a pension fund;
- payments from a registered retirement savings plan (RRSP);
- payments from a deferred profit-sharing plan (DPSP);
- payments from a registered retirement income fund (RRIF); or
- income from an income-averaging annuity or ordinary annuity, or income accrued under certain life insurance policies.

If your spouse is under 65, his or her eligible retirement income may include the income reported on line 122 as:

- life annuity payments under a pension plan or a pension fund;
- payments received further to the death of a spouse from a registered retirement savings plan (RRSP), a deferred profit-sharing plan (DPSP), a registered retirement income fund (RRIF) or an annuity.

Note: The old age security pension (line 114) and pensions paid under the Québec Pension Plan or the Canada Pension Plan (line 119) are not eligible retirement income.

Non-refundable tax credit for eligible retirement income (line 361)

The eligible retirement income that a taxpayer transfers to his or her spouse may entitle the spouse to a non-refundable tax credit up to $1,500. You may claim this credit if you entered an amount on line 122 or line 123 of your TP1.

Instalment payments

Instalment payments of pensioners who split their pension income will not be reduced.

Your spouse was resident in Canada, outside Québec

If your spouse was resident in Canada, outside Québec, you must include on line 123 of your TP1 the amount your spouse deducted on line 210 in his or her federal income tax return as "Deduction for elected split-pension amount."

The Canada Revenue Agency says... *General Income Tax and Benefit Guide*

If you and your spouse or common-law partner have jointly elected to split your eligible pension income by completing Form T1032, Joint Election to Split Pension Income, you (the pensioner) can deduct on this line the elected split-pension amount from line E of Form T1032.

Form T1032 is to be filed by your filing due date for the year. This form must be attached to both your and your spouse's or common-law partner's paper returns. The information provided on the forms must be the same. If you are filing electronically, keep your election form in case we ask to see it.

Note: Only one joint election can be made for a tax year. If both you and your spouse or common-law partner have eligible pension income, you will have to decide if you are splitting your pension income or your spouse's or common-law partner's pension income.

T1 Guide: Line 212 - Annual union, professional, or like dues

T1 Line 212: Annual union, professional, or like dues

Enter union dues on the forms T4Slip and Other Deduct. Any dues paid that are not detailed specifically on a T4 should be entered on the Other deductions worksheet. To jump to one of these related forms, right click on the field and select from the list of forms in the context-sensitive menu. You can also press <F6> when your cursor is in the field to jump to the first source form.

The Canada Revenue Agency says...

Enter the total of the following amounts related to your employment that you paid (or that were paid for you and included in your income) in the year:

- annual dues for membership in a trade union or an association of public servants;
- professions board dues required under provincial or territorial law;
- professional or malpractice liability insurance premiums or professional membership dues required to keep a professional status recognized by law; and
- parity or advisory committee (or similar body) dues required under provincial or territorial law.

Annual membership dues do not include initiation fees, licences, special assessments, or charges for anything other than the organization's ordinary operating costs. You cannot claim charges for pension plans as membership dues, even if your receipts show them as dues.

For more information, see Interpretation Bulletins IT-103, Dues paid to a union or to a parity or advisory committee, and IT-158, Employees' professional membership dues.

The amount shown in box 44 of your T4 slip, or on your receipts, includes any GST/HST you paid.

Tip: You may be eligible for a rebate of any GST/HST you paid as part of your dues (see line 457).

T1 Guide: Line 213 - Universal Child Care Benefit (UCCB) repayment

The Canada Revenue Agency says... *General Income Tax and Benefit Guide*

In 2009, you or your spouse or common-law partner may have repaid an amount that was included in your or your spouse's or common-law partner's income for 2008.

The person who reported the UCCB income in the previous year may deduct the related repayment amount on line 213. The amount of the UCCB repayment to deduct is shown in box 12 of the RC62 slip.

T1 Guide: Line 214 - Child care expenses

T1 Line 214: Child care expenses

ProFile calculates this T1 jacket amount from form T778. The first step in claiming this amount should be to complete ProFile's Dependant worksheet that updates the T778 schedule for you as applicable. The allowable claim then calculated on T778 automatically flows to line 214 of the T1 jacket. Keep in mind that the amounts calculated on the T778 are dependant on the income entered into the return. As a result, incomplete or incorrect entry of income will affect this claim amount.

To jump to a related form, right click on the field and select from the list of forms in the context-sensitive menu. You can also press <F6> when your cursor is in the field to jump to the first source form.

The Canada Revenue Agency says... *General Income Tax and Benefit Guide*

You or your spouse or common-law partner may have paid for someone to look after your child so one of you could earn income, go to school, or conduct research in 2009. The expenses are deductible only if, at some time in 2009, the child was under 16 years of age or had a mental or physical impairment. Generally, only the spouse or common-law partner with the lower net income (even if it is zero) can claim these expenses.

Note: You may have paid an amount that would qualify to be claimed as child care expenses and the children's fitness amount (line 365). If this is the case, you must first claim this amount as child care expenses. Any unused part can be claimed for the children's fitness amount as long as the requirements are met.

For more information, and to make your claim, get Form T778, Child Care Expenses Deduction for 2009. If you claimed child care expenses on your 2008 return, the tax package we mailed to you should include this form.

Tip: You may be able to claim payments you made to a boarding school, sports school, or camp. For more information, see Form T778.

Tip: If your child needs special attendant care or care in an establishment, see Guide RC4064, Medical and Disability-Related Information, for more information about different amounts you may be able to claim.

T1 Guide: Line 215 - Disability supports deduction

T1 Line 215: Disability supports deduction

ProFile calculates this amount using data from other forms and worksheets. To jump to a related form, right click on the field and select from the list of forms in the context-sensitive menu. You can also press <F6> when your cursor is in the field to jump to the first source form.

 The Canada Revenue Agency says... *General Income Tax and Benefit Guide*

You can claim expenses you paid for personal attendant care and other disability supports expenses that allowed you to go to school or to earn certain income. This includes income from employment or self-employment and a grant you received for conducting research.

For a complete list of allowable expenses, see Form T929, Disability Supports Deduction.

You cannot claim these expenses on this line if you or someone else will be claiming them as medical expenses on line 330 or 331.

To calculate your claim, complete Form T929, Disability Supports Deduction. For more information, see Form T929.

T1 Guide: Line 217 and line 228 - Business investment loss

T1 Line 217 (and 228) - Business Investment Loss

ProFile calculates this amount using data from other forms and worksheets. To jump to a related form, right click on the field and select from the list of forms in the context-sensitive menu. You can also press <F6> when your cursor is in the field to jump to the first source form.

 The Canada Revenue Agency says... *General Income Tax and Benefit Guide*

A business investment loss is a special type of capital loss. Such a loss can occur, for example, when you dispose of shares or certain debts of a small business corporation. For more information, and to find out how to complete lines 217 and 228 (to the left of line 217), see Guide T4037, Capital Gains.

If you have a tax shelter, see Tax Shelters.

T1 Guide: Line 219 - Moving expenses

T1 Line 219: Moving expenses

ProFile calculates this amount using data from other forms and worksheets. To jump to a related form, right click on the field and select from the list of forms in the context-sensitive menu. You can also press <F6> when your cursor is in the field to jump to the first source form.

Frequently Asked Questions

What expenses can I claim?

You can deduct reasonable amounts that you paid for moving yourself, your family, and your household effects. Not all members of your household have to travel together or at the same time.

Eligible moving expenses include:

- transportation and storage costs (such as packing, hauling, in-transit storage, and insurance) for household effects, including items such as boats and trailers;
- travelling expenses, including vehicle expenses, meals, and accommodation, to move you and members of your household to your new residence (you can choose to claim vehicle and meal expenses using the simplified method (see the note below);
- costs for up to 15 days for meals and temporary accommodation near either residence for you and the members of your household (you can choose to claim meal expenses using the using the simplified method (see the note below); and
- the cost of cancelling a lease for your old residence, except any rental payment for the period during which you occupied the residence.

When your old residence is sold as a result of your move, eligible moving expenses also include:

- legal or notaries fees for the purchase of the new residence, as well as any taxes paid (other than GST/HST or property taxes) for the transfer or registration of title to the new residence, if you or your spouse or common-law partner sold the old residence; and
- the cost of selling your old residence, including advertising, notaries or legal fees, real estate commission, and mortgage penalty when the mortgage is paid off before maturity.

If you moved after 1997, and your moving expenses were paid in a year after the year of your move, you may be able to claim them on your return for the year you paid them against employment or self-employment income earned at the new location. The same possibility is also extended to students reporting a taxable amount of scholarships, fellowships, bursaries, certain prizes, and research grants. You can carry forward any unused amounts and deduct them only against such income earned at the new location in the following years.

This may apply if your old residence did not sell until after the year of your move. If this is the case, you may be asked to submit this form with the receipts and explain the delay in selling your home.

If this affects how you would have filed your return for a previous year, you can ask us to change it.

See How do you change a return?

Be sure to keep receipts and documents supporting your claim.

Note:

Instead of claiming your actual expenses (the detailed method), you can choose the simplified method of claiming vehicle and meal expenses. Although you do not have to submit detailed receipts for actual expenses if you choose to use the simplified method, we may still ask you to provide some documentation to establish the duration of temporary lodging.

Incidental costs related to the move

> You can claim the cost of changing your address on legal documents, replacing driving licences and non-commercial vehicle permits (not including insurance), and utility hook-ups and disconnections.

Costs to maintain your old residence when vacant

You can claim, to a maximum of $5,000, the cost for interest, property taxes, insurance premiums, and heat and utilities expenses you paid to maintain your old residence when it was vacant after you moved, and during a period when reasonable efforts were made to sell the home.

The costs must have been incurred when your old residence was not ordinarily occupied by you or any other person who ordinarily resided with you at the old residence just before the move. You cannot deduct these costs during a period when the old residence was rented.

Are there expenses that I cannot claim?

Moving expenses that you cannot deduct include:

- expenses for work done to make your former residence more saleable;
- any loss from the sale of your home;
- expenses for house hunting trips before you move;
- the value of items movers refused to take, such as plants, frozen food, ammunition, paint, and cleaning products;
- expenses for job hunting in another city (such as travelling expenses);
- expenses to clean or repair a rented residence to meet the landlord's standards;
- expenses to replace personal-use items such as tool sheds, firewood, drapes, and carpets;
- mail-forwarding costs (such as with Canada Post);
- costs of transformers or adaptors for household appliances; and
- costs incurred in the sale of your old home if you delayed selling for investment purposes or until the real estate market improved.

Generally, you cannot deduct the cost of moving a mobile home. However, if you have personal effects in a mobile home when it is moved, you can deduct the amount it would have cost to move those personal effects separately.

How is the 40 km measured?

Distance of a move (Interview)

You can claim moving expenses when your new home is at least 40 kilometres closer (in one direction) to your new employer, business, or school, provided you meet all the conditions outlined in Moving expenses - who can claim?. This distance is measured by the shortest public route, not "as the crow flies."

What's the simplified method for travel and meal expenses?

Simplified method for travel expenses

 The Canada Revenue Agency says...

Meal and vehicle rates used to calculate travel expense

Meal expenses

If you choose the detailed method to calculate meal expenses, you have to keep your receipts.

If you choose the simplified method, you may claim a flat rate of $17 per meal, to a maximum of $51 per day, without receipts.

Vehicle expenses

If you choose the detailed method to calculate vehicle expenses, you must keep all receipts and records for the vehicle expenses you incurred for moving expenses and northern residents deductions during the tax year, or during the 12-month period you choose for medical expenses.

If you choose the simplified method of calculating vehicle expenses, you do not need to keep receipts. Instead, you must keep track of the number of kilometres driven during the tax year for your trips relating to northern residents deductions and moving expenses, or the 12-month period you choose for medical expenses. To determine the amount you can claim for vehicle expenses, multiply the number of kilometres by the cents/km rate from the chart below for the province or territory in which the travel begins.

The rates listed below are the 2008 rates.

Province or Territory	Cents/kilometre
Alberta	53.0
British Columbia	54.0
Manitoba	50.5
New Brunswick	52.0
Newfoundland and Labrador	55.5
Northwest Territories	64.5
Nova Scotia	52.5
Nunavut	64.0
Ontario	55.5
Prince Edward Island	52.5
Québec	58.0
Saskatchewan	49.5
Yukon	66.0

For example, if you moved from Ottawa to Montréal, you would have travelled about 200 km. The vehicle expense claim would be 200 km multiplied by the rate of 55.5 cents for Ontario, for a total of $111.

Long distance medical travel

If you or a family member has to travel to get medical treatment that is not available where you live, you may be able to claim transportation or travel costs for the patient as a medical expense. If you have a letter from a medical practitioner certifying that the person receiving the treatment cannot travel without the help of an attendant, you may also claim the transportation or travel costs of the person who accompanied the patient. To claim transportation costs, the place where the treatment is received must be at least 40 kilometres from where the patient lives. To claim additional travel costs such as meals and lodging, the place where the treatment is received must be at least 80 kilometres from where the patient lives.

The Canada Revenue Agency says... *General Income Tax and Benefit Guide*

Generally, you can deduct moving expenses you paid in 2009 if both of the following apply:

- You moved to work or run a business, or to study full-time at an educational institution that offers post-secondary courses.
- You moved at least 40 kilometres closer to your new work or school.

Note:

If you moved before 2009 but could not claim all your expenses on your return for that year or later, you may be able to claim the remaining expenses on your return for 2009.

In addition, if you pay expenses after the year of your move, you may be able to claim them on your return for the year you pay them. You may carry forward unused amounts until you have enough income to claim them.

Your deduction is limited to the amount of eligible income you earned at the new location. Also, you cannot deduct moving expenses against certain non-taxable scholarship, fellowship, and bursary income. For more information, and to calculate how much you can deduct, get Form T1-M, Moving Expenses Deduction. Make sure you tell us your new address.

T1 Guide: Line 220 and 230 - Support payments made

T1 Line 220 (and 230): Support payments made

Use the ProFile worksheet called Support to enter support payments made. ProFile will automatically post amounts to lines 220 and 230 of the T1 jacket.

The Canada Revenue Agency says... *General Income Tax and Benefit Guide*

Enter on line 230 the total of all deductible and non-deductible support payments for a spouse or common-law partner, or for a child, that you made (or, if you are the payee, that you repaid under a court order) in 2009. Claim on line 220 only the deductible amount.

Note: Most child support payments paid according to a written agreement or court order dated after April 1997, are not deductible. For more information, see Guide P102, Support Payments.

To avoid you claim being delayed or disallowed, you should register your written agreement or court order (including any amendments) with us by completing and sending us Form T1158, Registration of Family Support Payments.

T1 Guide: Line 221 - Carrying charges and interest expenses

T1 Line 221: Carrying charges and interest expenses

ProFile calculates this amount using data from other forms and worksheets. To jump to a related form, right click on the field and select from the list of forms in the context-sensitive menu. You can also press <F6> when your cursor is in the field to jump to the first source form.

The Canada Revenue Agency says... *General Income Tax and Benefit Guide*

You can claim the following carrying charges and interest you paid to earn income from investments:

- fees to manage or take care of your investments (other than administration fees you paid for your registered retirement savings plan or registered retirement income fund), including safety deposit box charges;
- fees for certain investment advice (see Interpretation Bulletin IT-238, Fees Paid to Investment Counsel) or for recording investment income;
- fees to have someone complete your return, but only if you have income from a business or property, accounting is a usual part of the operations of your business or property, and you did not use the amounts claimed to reduce the business or property income you reported (see Interpretation Bulletin IT-99 , Legal and Accounting Fees); and most interest you pay on money you borrow for investment purposes, but generally only as long as you use it to try to earn investment income, including interest and dividends. However, if the only earnings your investment can produce are capital gains, you cannot claim the interest you paid. For more information, contact us.

You **cannot** deduct on line 221 any of the following amounts:

- the interest you paid on money you borrowed to contribute to a registered retirement savings plan, a registered education savings plan, or a registered disability savings plan, or a Tax-Free Savings Account;
- the interest part of your student loan repayments (although you may be able to claim a credit on line 319 on Schedule 1 for this amount);
- subscription fees paid for financial newspapers, magazines, or newsletters; and
- brokerage fees or commissions you paid when you bought or sold securities. Instead, you use these costs when you calculate your capital gain or capital loss. For more information, see Guide T4037, Capital Gains, and Interpretation Bulletin IT-238, Fees Paid to Investment Counsel.

Policy loan interest

To claim interest paid during 2009 on a policy loan made to earn income, have your insurer complete Form T2210, Verification of Policy Loan Interest by the Insurer, on or before the date your return is due.

Refund interest

If we paid you interest on an income tax refund, you have to report the interest in the year you receive it, as we explain at line 121 in this guide. If we then reassessed your return and you repaid any of the refund interest in 2009, you can deduct the amount you repaid, up to the amount you had included in your income.

Carrying charges for foreign income

If you have carrying charges for Canadian and foreign investment income, identify them separately on Schedule 4, according to the percentage that applies to each investment.

T1 Guide: Line 222 - Deduction for CPP or QPP contributions on self-employment and other earnings

T1 Line 222: Deduction for CPP or QPP contributions on self-employment and other earnings

ProFile calculates this amount using data from other forms and worksheets. To jump to a related form, right click on the field and select from the list of forms in the context-sensitive menu. You can also press <F6> when your cursor is in the field to jump to the first source form.

The Canada Revenue Agency says... *General Income Tax and Benefit Guide*

You can claim half of the total of your Canada Pension Plan (CPP) or Quebec Pension Plan (QPP) contributions, if any, from Schedule 8. You also can claim, on line 310 on Schedule 1, an amount for the other half.

You can claim contributions you:

- have to make on self-employment and limited or non-active partnership income;
- choose to make on certain employment income (see "Making additional CPP contributions" in line 308); and
- choose to make on your provincial income tax return for Quebec on certain employment income (see your Quebec provincial guide).

The amount of CPP or QPP contributions that you have to make, or choose to make, will depend on how much you have already contributed to the CPP or QPP as an employee, as shown in boxes 16 and 17 of your T4 slips.

Making additional CPP contributions

You may be able to make CPP contributions on certain employment income for which no contribution was made (for example, tips that were not included on a T4 slip) or additional contributions on T4 income if you had more than one employer in the year and the total CPP contributions on all T4 slips is less than the required amount.

For more information, see "Making additional CPP contributions" in line 308.

How to calculate your contributions

Complete Schedule 8 to calculate your CPP or QPP contributions, and attach it to your paper return. If you were a member of a partnership, make sure you include on line 1 of Schedule 8 only your share of the net profit. You cannot use self-employment or partnership losses to reduce the CPP or QPP contributions that you paid on your employment earnings.

If you were not a resident of Quebec on December 31, 2009, enter on lines 222 and 310, in dollars and cents, the amount from line 11 of Schedule 8.

Enter on line 421 the amount from line 10 of Schedule 8.

If you were a resident of Quebec on December 31, 2009, enter on lines 222 and 310, in dollars and cents, the amount from line 10 of Schedule 8. Line 421 does not apply to you.

Note: We will prorate your CPP or QPP contribution and show the correct amount on your notice of assessment in certain situations, such as if, in 2009, you:

- were a CPP participant and either turned 18 or 70 years of age or received a CPP retirement or disability pension; or
- were a QPP participant and either turned 18 years of age or received a QPP disability pension.

If you are filing a return for a person who died in 2009, we will also prorate the CPP or QPP.

Request for refund of CPP contributions

Under the Canada Pension Plan, all requests for a refund of CPP over-contributions must be made within four years after the end of the year for which the request is being made.

T1 Guide: Line 223 - Deduction for provincial parental insurance plan (PPIP) premiums on self-employment income

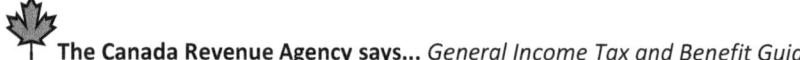
The Canada Revenue Agency says... *General Income Tax and Benefit Guide*

If you were a resident of Quebec on December 31, 2009, you have to pay PPIP premiums if any of the following conditions apply:

- your net self-employment income on lines 135 to 143 of your return is $2,000 or more; or
- the total of your employment income (including employment income from outside Canada) and your net self-employment income is $2,000 or more.

Complete Schedule 10 to calculate your PPIP premiums and attach it to your paper return. Under proposed changes, you can claim, on this line, 43.721% of the total of your PPIP premiums. Enter on this line, in dollars and cents, the amount from line 7 of Schedule 10. Also, enter the same amount on your provincial income tax return for Quebec.

T1 Guide: Line 224 - Exploration and development expenses

T1 Line 224: Exploration and development expenses

ProFile calculates this amount using data from other forms and worksheets. To jump to a related form, right click on the field and select from the list of forms in the context-sensitive menu. You can also press <F6> when your cursor is in the field to jump to the first source form.

 **The Canada Revenue Agency says...** *General Income Tax and Benefit Guide*

If you invested in a petroleum, natural gas, or mining venture in 2009, but did not participate actively, you can deduct your expenses on this line. If you participated actively, follow the instructions for line 135.

How to claim

Complete Form T1229, Statement of Exploration and Development Expenses and Depletion Allowance, using the information that the principals of the venture give you, such as T5, T101, T5013 or T5013A slips. Read the instructions on the back of these slips.

Claim your exploration and development expenses (including renounced resource expenses) and your resource allowances on line 224. Claim your depletion allowances on line 232.

Attach Form T1229 and your T5, T101, T5013 and T5013A slips to your paper return. If you do not have these slips, attach a statement that identifies you as a participant in the venture. The statement has to show your allocation (the number of units you own, the percentage assigned to you, or the ratio of your units to those of the whole partnership) and give the name and address of the fund.

T1 Guide: Line 229 - Other employment expenses

T1 Line 229: Other employment expenses

Enter employment expenses on form T777, TL2#, T4PS or Other Deduct. Those flow to line 229 of the jacket.

 **The Canada Revenue Agency says...** *General Income Tax and Benefit Guide*

You can deduct certain expenses (including any GST/HST) you paid to earn employment income if the following two conditions apply:

- your employment contract required you to pay them, and
- you did not receive an allowance for the expenses, or the allowance you received is included in your income.

 Note: Most employees cannot claim employment expenses. You cannot deduct the cost of travel to and from work or other expenses, such as clothing.

Attach to your paper return a completed Form T777, Statement of Employment Expenses, to give us details of your expenses and to calculate how much you can deduct. Guide T4044, Employment Expenses, contains Form T777 and other forms you will need. The guide also explains the limits and conditions that apply when you claim these expenses.

Repayment of salary or wages

You can deduct salary or wages you included in income for 2009 or a previous year, if you repaid them in 2009. This includes amounts you repaid for a period when you were entitled to receive wage-loss replacement benefits or workers' compensation benefits. However, you cannot deduct more than the income you received when you did not perform the duties of your employment.

Legal fees

Under proposed changes, you can deduct legal fees you paid to collect or establish a right to salary or wages. It is not necessary for you to be successful; however, the amount sought must be for salary or wages owed. You must reduce your claim by any amount awarded to you in respect of those fees, or any reimbursement you received for your legal expenses.

Under proposed legislation, you can deduct legal fees you paid to collect or establish a right to collect other amounts that must be included in employment income even if they are not directly paid by your employer.

Tip: You may be eligible for a rebate of any GST/HST you paid as part of your expenses (see line 457).

T1 Guide: Line 231 - Clergy residence deduction

T1 Line 231 - Clergy residence deduction

Use this line to claim a deduction for the resident of a cleric. Amounts in this field flow from form T1223#: Clergy residence deduction.

The Canada Revenue Agency says... *General Income Tax and Benefit Guide*

If you are a member of the clergy, use this line to claim a deduction for your residence. Your employer has to certify that you qualify for this deduction. Complete Form T1223, Clergy Residence Deduction, to find out what you can deduct.

T1 Guide: Line 232 - Other deductions

T1 Line 232: Other deductions

ProFile calculates this amount using data from other forms and worksheets. To jump to a related form, right click on the field and select from the list of forms in the context-sensitive menu. You can also press <F6> when your cursor is in the field to jump to the first source form.

The Canada Revenue Agency says... *General Income Tax and Benefit Guide*

Use this line to claim allowable amounts not deducted anywhere else on this return. For clarification of your request, specify the deduction you are claiming in the space to the left of line 232. If you have more than one amount, or you want to explain your deduction more fully, attach a note to your paper return.

Note: A child who was born in 1992 or later can claim a deduction for certain income he or she reports. For more information, see Split income of a child under 18.

Tax shelters

Income amounts paid back

In 2009, you may have paid back amounts that you received and included in income (other than salary or wages) for 2009 or a previous year. If this applies to you, you can deduct most of these amounts on line 232 of your return for 2009. However, if you repaid, under a court order, support payments that you included on line 128, deduct the repayment on line 220.

In 2009, you may have repaid an amount you received from a registered disability savings plan and declared as income in 2009 or a previous year. If so, you can deduct the amount on line 232. For more information, see Information Sheet RC4460, Registered Disability Savings Plan (RDSP).

Note:

- If you had an OAS repayment for 2008, tax may have been withheld from your OAS benefits for2009. The amount deducted is included in box 22 of your T4A(OAS) slip for 2009. Do not deduct it on line 232. Claim it on line 437. To calculate your OAS repayment, if any, for 2009, see line 235 and complete the chart for line 235 on the Federal Worksheet you will find in the forms book.
- If you paid back employment income, see "Repayment of salary or wages" under line 229. If you paid back income tax refund interest, see "Refund interest" under line 221.

Employment Insurance (EI) benefits

You may have received more benefits than you should have and already paid them back to the payer of your benefits. For example:

- The payer of your benefits may have reduced your EI benefits after discovering the mistake. In this case, your T4E slip will show only the net amount you received, so you cannot claim a deduction.
- You may have repaid excess benefits you received directly to the payer of your benefits. If so, box 30 of your T4E slip will show the amount you paid back. Include this amount on line 232. This is not the same as repaying a social benefit as explained under line 235.

Legal fees

You can deduct your expenses in any of the following situations:

- You paid fees (including any related accounting fees) for advice or assistance in responding to us when we reviewed your income, deductions, or credits for a year or in objecting to or appealing an assessment or decision under the Income Tax Act, the Unemployment Insurance Act, the Employment Insurance Act, the Canada Pension Plan Act, or the Quebec Pension Plan.
- You paid fees to collect (or establish a right to) a retiring allowance or pension benefit. However, you can only claim up to the amount of retiring allowance or pension income you received in the year, minus any part of these amounts transferred to a registered retirement savings plan or registered pension plan. You can carry forward, for up to seven years, legal fees that you cannot claim in the year.
- You paid fees to collect (or establish a right to) salary or wages. It is not necessary for you to be successful; however, the amount sought must be for salary or wages owed. You must reduce

your claim by any amount awarded to you in respect of those fees or any reimbursement you received for your legal expenses. (These fees must be deducted on line 229.) Under proposed changes, you can deduct legal fees you paid to collect or establish a right to collect other amounts that must be included in employment income even if they are not directly paid by your employer. (These fees must be deducted on line 229.)
- You incurred certain fees relating to support payments that your current or former spouse or common-law partner, or the natural parent of your child, will have to pay to you. You cannot claim legal fees you incurred to get a separation or divorce or to establish custody or visitation arrangements of a child. For more information, see Guide P102, Support Payments.

You have to reduce your claim by any award or reimbursements you received for these expenses. If you are awarded the cost of your deductible legal fees in a future year, you will have to include that amount in your income for that year.

For more information of other legal fees you may be able to deduct, see Interpretation Bulletin IT-99, Legal and Accounting Fees.

Other deductible amounts

The following are examples of other amounts that can be deducted on line 232:

- depletion allowances (attach to your paper return a completed Form T1229, Statement of Exploration and Development Expenses and Depletion Allowance);
- certain unused RRSP contributions you made after 1990 that were refunded to you or your spouse or common-law partner in 2009 (attach to your paper return an approved Form T3012A, Tax Deduction Waiver on the Refund of Your Unused RRSP Contributions, or Form T746, Calculating Your Deduction for Refund of Unused RRSP Contributions); and
- the excess part of a direct transfer of a lump-sum payment from your RPP to an RRSP or registered retirement income fund (RRIF) that you withdrew and are including on line 129 or 130 of your return for 2009. You can use Form T1043, Deduction for Excess Registered Pension Plan Transfers You Withdrew From an RRSP or RRIF , to calculate the deductible amount.

T1 Line 233

ProFile calculates this T1 jacket amount by totalling data from the other lines in the Net Income section of the T1 jacket.

T1 Guide: Line 234 - Net income before adjustments

T1 Line 234: Net income before adjustments ProFile calculates this T1 jacket amount by subtracting Line 233 from Line 150. Negative amounts show as zero.

 The Canada Revenue Agency says...

Net income before adjustments is your total income from all sources minus these deductions:

- Line 206 - Pension adjustment
- Line 207 - Registered pension plan (RPP) deduction
- Line 208 - RRSP deduction
- Line 209 - Saskatchewan Pension Plan (SPP) adjustment

- Line 210 - Deduction for elected split-pension amount
- Line 212 - Annual union, professional, or like dues
- Line 213 - Universal Child Care Benefit (UCCB) repayment
- Line 214 - Child care expenses
- Line 215 - Disability supports deduction
- Line 217 - Business investment loss
- Line 219 - Moving expenses
- Line 220 - Support payments made
- Line 221 - Carrying charges and interest expenses
- Line 222 - Deduction for CPP or QPP contributions on self-employment and other earnings
- Line 224 - Exploration and development expenses
- Line 229 - Other employment expenses
- Line 231 - Clergy residence deduction
- Line 232 - Other deductions, such as certain legal fees, repayments of income from some government programs, and refunds in special RRSP and RPP situations.

Net income before adjustments does not include the line 235 - Social benefits repayment deduction.

If you repaid social benefits, deduct the amount repaid to find your line 236 - net income.

T1 Guide: Line 235 - Social benefits repayment

T1 Line 235: Social benefits repayment

ProFile calculates this amount using data from other forms and worksheets. To jump to a related form, right click on the field and select from the list of forms in the context-sensitive menu. You can also press <F6> when your cursor is in the field to jump to the first source form.

The Canada Revenue Agency says... *General Income Tax and Benefit Guide*

Employment Insurance (EI) benefits

You have to repay part of the EI benefits (line 119) you received in 2009 if:

- there is an amount shown in box 15 of your T4E slip,
- the rate shown in box 7 is 30%, and
- your net income before adjustments on line 234 of your return, minus any amounts on lines 117 and 125, plus any deduction on line 213 and/or for a repayment of registered disability savings plans income included on line 232, is more than $52,875.

Complete the chart on your T4E slip to calculate how much of your EI benefits you have to repay. If you also have to repay Old Age Security (OAS) benefits you received (see next section), enter the EI benefits that you have to repay on lines 7 and 20 of the chart for line 235 on the Federal Worksheet in the forms book.

Old Age Security (OAS) benefits

You may have to repay all or a part of your OAS pension (line 113) or net federal supplements (line 146) if your net income before adjustments on line 234 of your return, minus the amounts on lines 117 and 125, plus any deduction on line 213 and/or for a repayment of registered disability savings plans income included on line 232, is more than $66,335. Complete the chart for line 235 on the Federal Worksheet in the forms book to calculate how much you have to repay, even if tax was withheld by Service Canada.

Note: If you had an OAS repayment for 2008, tax may have been withheld from your monthly OAS pension for 2009. The amount deducted is included in box 22 of your T4A(OAS) slip for 2009. Claim it on line 437. Similarly, if you have an OAS repayment for 2009, tax may be withheld starting with your July 2010 OAS payment. For more information, contact us.

T1 Guide: Line 236 - Net incomes

T1 Line 236: Net income

ProFile calculates this T1 jacket amount by subtracting Line 235 from Line 234.

The Canada Revenue Agency says... *General Income Tax and Benefit Guide*

We use this amount for certain calculation such as the Canada Child Tax Benefit, the GST/HST credit, the social benefits repayment, and certain tax credits.

Note:

- Make sure you enter, if it applies, your spouse's or common-law partner's net income in the "Information about your spouse or common-law partner" area on page 1 of your return. Enter this amount even if it is zero. See Spouse or common-law partner's net income for instructions on how to enter this amount.
- If the amount you calculate for line 236 is negative, you may have a non-capital loss. To find out, use Form T1A, Request for Loss Carry back. If you have a loss for 2009, you may want to carry it back to your 2006, 2007, or 2008 return. To do this, attach a completed Form T1A to your paper return (or send it to the CRA separately). Do not file an amended return for the year or years to which you want to apply the loss.

Amounts that make up Net income

T1 Guide: Line 244 - Canadian Forces personnel and police deduction

T1 Line 244: Canadian Forces personnel and police deduction

Certain members can claim this deduction under certain conditions.

For certain members of the Canadian Forces and Canadian police services, an amount will be shown in box 43 only if you were deployed outside Canada on a high-risk or current moderate-risk operational mission. For more information, contact your employer.

ProFile calculates this amount using data from other forms and worksheets. To jump to a related form, right click on the field and select from the list of forms in the context-sensitive menu. You can also press <F6> when your cursor is in the field to jump to the first source form.

The Canada Revenue Agency says... *General Income Tax and Benefit Guide*

Enter the total of amounts shown in box 43 of all your T4 slips.

T1 Guide: Line 248 - Employee home relocation loan deduction

T1 Line 248: Employee home relocation loan deduction

ProFile calculates this amount using data from other forms and worksheets. To jump to a related form, right click on the field and select from the list of forms in the context-sensitive menu. You can also press <F6> when your cursor is in the field to jump to the first source form.

 The Canada Revenue Agency says... *General Income Tax and Benefit Guide*

Enter the total of amounts shown in box 37 of all your T4 slips.

T1 Guide: Line 249 - Security options deductions

T1 Line 249: Security options deductions

ProFile calculates this amount using data from other forms and worksheets. To jump to a related form, right click on the field and select from the list of forms in the context-sensitive menu. You can also press <F6> when your cursor is in the field to jump to the first source form.

 The Canada Revenue Agency says... *General Income Tax and Benefit Guide*

Enter the total of the amounts shown in boxes 39 and 41 of your T4 slips. In addition, if you disposed of securities for which you had previously deferred the taxable benefit (see Reporting income from stock options and ESPP), claim 50% of the amount from line 4 of Form T1212, Statement of Deferred Security Option Benefits.

You may be able to claim a deduction for donating securities you acquired through your employer's security options plan.

For more information, see Gifts of securities acquired under a security option plan in Pamphlet P113, Gifts and Income Tax.

T1 Guide: Line 250 - Other payments deduction

T1 Line 250: Other payments deduction

ProFile calculates this amount using data from other forms and worksheets. To jump to a related form, right click on the field and select from the list of forms in the context-sensitive menu. You can also press <F6> when your cursor is in the field to jump to the first source form.

 The Canada Revenue Agency says... *General Income Tax and Benefit Guide*

Generally, you can deduct the amount from line 147 of your return. This is the total of the workers' compensation payments, social assistance payments, and net federal supplements you entered on lines 144, 145, and 146.

Note: If your net income on line 234, minus the amounts on line 117 and line 125, plus any deduction on line 213 and/or for a repayment of registered disability savings plans income included on line 232, is more than $66,335 and you reported net federal supplements on line 146, you may not be entitled to claim the whole amount from line 147.

T1 Guide: Line 251- Limited partnership losses of other years

T1 Line 251: Limited partnership losses of other years

ProFile calculates this T1 jacket amount using data from the Non-capital losses worksheet. If you have carried amounts forward from a previous year they will already be entered in the Non-capital losses worksheet. If you have not carried the return forward enter the previous year's losses into the schedule. ProFile will claim these losses automatically on Line 251 after you indicate the income amount that losses are eligible to be applied against.

The Canada Revenue Agency says... *General Income Tax and Benefit Guide*

If you had limited partnership losses in previous years that you have not already deducted, you may be able to claim part of these losses this year. For more information, contact us.

You can carry forward limited partnership losses indefinitely. If you claim these losses, attach to your paper return a statement showing a breakdown of your total losses, the year of each loss, and the amounts deducted in previous years. You cannot use the amount shown in box 24 of your T5013 or T5013A slip for 2009 on your return for 2009.

T1 Guide: Line 252 - Non-capital losses of other years

T1 Line 252: Non-capital losses of other years

ProFile calculates this T1 jacket amount using data from the Non-capital losses worksheet. If you have carried amounts forward from a previous year they will already be entered in the Non-capital losses worksheet. If you have not carried the return forward enter the previous year's losses into the schedule. ProFile will claim these losses automatically on Line 252 against eligible income as applicable. ProFile's claim is optimized to avoid as much as possible the expiry of losses from previous years.

The Canada Revenue Agency says... *General Income Tax and Benefit Guide*

In 2009, enter the amount of the unapplied non-capital losses you reported on your 2002 to 2008 returns that you want to apply. For non-capital losses incurred in tax years ending after March 22, 2004, and before January 1, 2006, the loss carry-forward period is 10 years.

For non-capital losses incurred in tax years after December 31, 2005, the loss carry-forward period is 20 years.

Also, enter any unapplied farming and fishing losses you reported on your 1999 to 2008 returns that you want to apply in 2009. Your available losses are shown on your notice of assessment or notice of reassessment for 2008.

There are restrictions on the amount of certain farm losses that you can deduct each year. If you have a farming or fishing business, see Guide T4003, Farming Income, Guide RC4060, Farming Income and the AgriStability and AgriInvest Programs Guide, Guide RC4408, Farming Income and the AgriStability and AgriInvest Programs Harmonized Guide , or Guide T4004, Fishing Income, for more information.

If you need more information on losses, see Interpretation Bulletin IT-232, Losses - Their Deductibility in the Loss Year or in Other Years.

T1 Guide: Line 253 - Net capital losses of other years

T1 Line 253: Net capital losses of other years

ProFile calculates this T1 jacket amount using data from Net capital losses worksheet. If you have carried amounts forward from a previous year they will already be entered in the Net capital losses worksheet. If you have not carried the return forward enter the previous year's losses into the schedule. ProFile will claim these losses automatically on Line 253 against eligible income as applicable.

The Canada Revenue Agency says...

Within certain limits, you can deduct your net capital losses of previous years that you have not already claimed. Your available losses are shown on your Notice of Assessment or Notice of Reassessment for 2008. You probably will have to adjust any losses you incurred after 1987 and before 2001. For more information, see Guide T4037, Capital Gains.

T1 Guide: Line 254 - Capital gains deduction

T1 Line 254: Capital gains deduction

ProFile calculates this T1 jacket amount using data from the T657 form. Review form T657 for the detailed calculations ProFile used to arrive at this number.

To jump to the related form, right click on the field and select the form from the context-sensitive menu. You can also press <F6> when your cursor is in the field to jump to the source form.

The Canada Revenue Agency says... *General Income Tax and Benefit Guide*

You may be able to claim a capital gains deduction for gains realized on the disposition of qualified small business corporation shares, qualified farm property and disposition of qualified fishing property.

For more information, see Guide T4037, Capital Gains.

T1 Guide: Line 255 - Northern resident's deductions

T1 Line 255: Northern resident's deductions

ProFile calculates this amount using data from other forms and worksheets. To jump to a related form, right click on the field and select from the list of forms in the context-sensitive menu. You can also press <F6> when your cursor is in the field to jump to the first source form.

 The Canada Revenue Agency says... *General Income Tax and Benefit Guide*

To make your claim, use Form T2222, Northern Residents Deductions. Residents of the Northwest Territories, Nunavut, and Yukon will find this form in their forms book. You can also get a copy by going to Forms and Publications on our Web cite. For a list of the areas that qualify, see Publication T4039, Northern Residents Deductions - Places in Prescribed Zones.

The residency deduction has increased to $8.25 per day if you are entitled to only the basic residency amount, or $16.50 per day if you are entitled to both the basic and the additional residency amounts. For more information, see Form T2222.

Include a completed Form T2222 when paper filing your return.

T1 Guide: Line 256 - Additional deductions

T1 Line 256: Additional deductions

ProFile calculates this amount using data from other forms and worksheets. To jump to a related form, right click on the field and select from the list of forms in the context-sensitive menu. You can also press <F6> when your cursor is in the field to jump to the first source form.

 The Canada Revenue Agency says... *General Income Tax and Benefit Guide*

In the space to the left of line 256, specify the deduction you are claiming. If you have more than one amount, or you want to explain your deduction more fully, attach a note to your paper return.

Income exempt under a tax treaty

If you included foreign income on your return (such as support payments you received from a resident of another country and reported on line 128) that is tax-free in Canada because of a tax treaty, you can claim a deduction for it.

Note: Under the Canada-U.S. tax treaty, you can claim a deduction equal to 15% of the U.S. social security benefits, including U.S. Medicare premiums, that you included in your income on line 115.

Vow of perpetual poverty

If you have taken a vow of perpetual poverty as a member of a religious order, you can deduct the amount of earned income and pension benefits that you have given to the order. Attach to your paper return a letter from your order or your employer stating that you have taken a vow of perpetual poverty. For more information, see Interpretation Bulletin IT-86, Vow of Perpetual Poverty.

Adult basic education tuition assistance

You may have received (and included in your income) assistance to cover all or part of the tuition fees you paid for courses at a primary or secondary school level. If so, you can claim a deduction for the amount of qualifying assistance shown in box 21 of your T4E slip.

Note: You may have received taxable tuition assistance shown in box 20 of the T4E slip for post-secondary level courses or courses that provide or improve skills in an occupation. If so, these amounts are not deducted on line 256, but you may be eligible for the tuition, education, and textbook amounts (see line 323).

Employees of prescribed international organizations

If, in 2009, you were employed by a prescribed international organization, such as the United Nations, you can claim a deduction for net employment income you report from that organization. Net employment income is your employment income minus the related employment expenses that you are claiming.

T1 Line 257

ProFile calculates this T1 jacket amount by adding data from Lines 248 to 256 immediately above it.

T1 Line 260: Taxable income

ProFile calculates Line 260 by subtracting Line 256 from Line 236 to arrive at the taxable income.

T1 Guide: Line 421 - CPP contributions payable on self-employment and other earnings

T1 Line 421: CPP contributions payable on self-employment earnings

ProFile calculates this amount using data from other forms and worksheets. To jump to a related form, right click on the field and select from the list of forms in the context-sensitive menu. You can also press <F6> when your cursor is in the field to jump to the first source form.

The Canada Revenue Agency says... *General Income Tax and Benefit Guide*

If you were not a resident of Quebec on December 31, 2009, enter the Canada Pension Plan (CPP) contributions you have to pay from line 10 on Schedule 8.

If you were a resident of Quebec on December 31, 2009, this line does not apply to you. Enter the Québec Pension Plan contributions you have to pay on your provincial income tax return for Quebec.

T1 Guide: Line 422 - Social benefits repayment

T1 Line 422: Social benefits repayment

ProFile calculates this amount using data from other forms and worksheets. To jump to a related form, right click on the field and select from the list of forms in the context-sensitive menu. You can also press <F6> when your cursor is in the field to jump to the first source form.

The Canada Revenue Agency says... *General Income Tax and Benefit Guide*

Enter the amount of social benefits you have to repay, from line 235 of your return.

T1 Guide: Line 428: Provincial or territorial tax

T1 Line 428: Provincial or territorial tax

ProFile calculates this amount using data from other forms and worksheets. To jump to a related form, right click on the field and select from the list of forms in the context-sensitive menu. You can also press <F6> when your cursor is in the field to jump to the first source form.

 The Canada Revenue Agency says... *General Income Tax and Benefit Guide*

If you were not a resident of Quebec on December 31, 2009, use Form 428 in the forms book to calculate your provincial or territorial tax. Attach a copy to your paper return.

If you were a resident of Quebec on December 31, 2009, this line applies to you only if you had a business with a permanent establishment outside Quebec. In that case, use Form T2203, Provincial and Territorial Taxes for 2009 - Multiple Jurisdictions, to calculate your tax for provinces and territories other than Quebec. Attach a copy to your paper return. To calculate your tax for Quebec, you have to file a provincial income tax return for Quebec.

T1 Line 435: Total payable

Line 435 on the Jacket represents the total tax calculated and payable before tax credits are applied.

T1 Guide: Line 437 - Total income tax deducted

T1 Line 437: Total income tax deducted

ProFile calculates this amount using data from other forms and worksheets. To jump to a related form, right click on the field and select from the list of forms in the context-sensitive menu. You can also press <F6> when your cursor is in the field to jump to the first source form.

 The Canada Revenue Agency says... *General Income Tax and Benefit Guide*

Enter the total of all of the amounts shown in the "Income tax deducted" box from all of your Canadian information slips.

If you were not a resident of Quebec on December 31, 2009, but you had Quebec provincial income tax withheld from your income, also include those amounts on this line and attach your provincial information slips to your paper return.

If you were a resident of Quebec on December 31, 2009, do not include on this return any of your Quebec provincial income tax deducted. If you and your spouse or common-law partner elected to split pension income, follow the instructions at Step 5 on Form T1032, Joint Election to Split Pension Income, to calculate the amount to enter on line 437 of your and your spouse's or common-law partner's returns.

 Note: If you paid tax by instalments in 2009, claim them on line 476.

If you paid foreign taxes, do not claim these amounts on this line. However, you may be able to claim a foreign tax credit. For more information see Form T2209, Federal foreign Tax Credits.

T1 Guide: Line 438 - Tax transfer for residents of Québec

T1 Line 438: Tax transfer for residents of Québec

The transfer for residents of Quebec flows from the ProFile worksheet called Other Credits. You can double-click at line 438 to jump to the source field directly.

The Canada Revenue Agency says... *General Income Tax and Benefit Guide*

If you were a resident of Québec on December 31, 2009, you may have earned income, such as employment income, outside Québec during 2009. In that case, tax may have been deducted for a province or territory other than Québec.

You can transfer, to the Province of Québec, up to 45% of the income tax shown on information slips issued to you by payers outside Québec.

Note: If you or your spouse or common-law partner elected to split pension income, and you are the pension transferee, be sure to include in the calculation of the transfer the part of the income tax added on line 437 that relates only to the split-pension amount. If you are the pensioner, do not include the part of the income tax subtracted on line 437 that relates to the split-pension amount.

Enter on line 438 of your federal return and on line 454 of your provincial income tax return for Québec the amount you want to transfer (up to the maximum). If the taxable income on your provincial income tax return for Quebec is zero, no transfer is necessary.

T1 Line 439

This is the result of the total income tax deducted from all slips (line 437) minus the tax transfer for residents for Quebec (line 438). This line only appears on the T1 jacket if the taxpayer is a resident of Quebec, a deemed resident or a non-resident.

T1 Guide: Line 440: Refundable Québec abatement

T1 Line 440: Refundable Québec abatement

ProFile calculates this amount using data from other forms and worksheets. To jump to a related form, right click on the field and select from the list of forms in the context-sensitive menu. You can also press <F6> when your cursor is in the field to jump to the first source form.

The Canada Revenue Agency says... *General Income Tax and Benefit Guide*

The Québec abatement is provided under the federal-provincial fiscal arrangement, in place of direct cost-sharing by the federal government. It reduces your balance owing and may even give you a refund.

If you were a resident of Québec on December 31, 2009, and you did not have a business with a permanent establishment outside Québec, your refundable Québec abatement is 16.5% of the basic federal tax on line 46 of Schedule 1.

If you had a business with a permanent establishment outside Québec, or you were not a resident of Québec on December 31, 2009, and you had a business with a permanent establishment in Québec, use Form T2203, Provincial and Territorial Taxes for 2009 - Multiple Jurisdictions, to calculate your abatement.

T1 Guide: Line 448 - CPP overpayment

T1 Line 448: CPP overpayment

ProFile calculates this amount using data from other forms and worksheets. To jump to a related form, right click on the field and select from the list of forms in the context-sensitive menu. You can also press <F6> when your cursor is in the field to jump to the first source form.

 The Canada Revenue Agency says... *General Income Tax and Benefit Guide*

If you were not a resident of Quebec on December 31, 2009, and you contributed more to the Canada Pension Plan (CPP) than you had to (see line 308), enter the difference on this line. We will refund the excess contributions to you or use them to reduce your balance owing.

If you were a resident of Quebec on December 31, 2009, this line does not apply to you. Claim the excess amount on your provincial income tax return for Quebec.

T1 Guide: Line 450: Employment insurance overpayment

T1 Line 450: Employment Insurance overpayment

ProFile calculates this amount using data from other forms and worksheets. To jump to a related form, right click on the field and select from the list of forms in the context-sensitive menu. You can also press <F6> when your cursor is in the field to jump to the first source form.

 The Canada Revenue Agency says... *General Income Tax and Benefit Guide*

If you were not a resident of Quebec on December 31, 2009, and contributed more than you had to (see line 312), enter the difference on line 450. We will refund the excess amount to you or use it to reduce your balance owing. If the difference is $1 or less, you will not receive a refund.

Note: If you repaid some of the Employment Insurance benefits you received, do not claim the repayment on this line. You may be able to claim a deduction on line 232 for the benefits you repaid.

Under proposed changes, if you were a resident of Quebec on December 31, 2009, and contributed more than you had to (see line 312), enter the difference on line 450. If you completed Schedule 10, enter, in dollars and cents, the amount from line 21 on line 450.

The excess amount on line 450 is reduced by the provincial parental insurance plan (PPIP) premiums that you have to pay (line 376 on Schedule 1). The part of the excess amount used will be transferred directly to Revenu Québec. We will refund the unused excess amount to you or use it to reduce your balance owing. If the difference is $1 or less, you will not receive a refund.

Note: If you repaid some of the Employment Insurance benefits you received, do not claim the repayment on this line. You may be able to claim a deduction on line 232 for the benefits you repaid.

T1 Guide: Line 452 - Refundable medical expense supplement

T1 Line 452: Refundable medical expense supplement

ProFile calculates this amount using data from other forms and worksheets. To jump to a related form, right click on the field and select from the list of forms in the context-sensitive menu. You can also press <F6> when your cursor is in the field to jump to the first source form.

The Canada Revenue Agency says... *General Income Tax and Benefit Guide*

You may be able to claim a credit of up to $1,067 if all of the following apply:

- you have an amount on line 215 on your return or on line 332 of Schedule 1:
- you were resident in Canada throughout 2009; and
- you were 18 of age or older at the end of 2009.

In addition, the total of the following two amounts has to be $3,040 or more:

- your employment income on lines 101 and 104 (other than amounts received from a wage-loss replacement plan) minus the amounts on lines 207, 212, 229, and 231 (but if the result is negative, use "0"); and
- your net self-employment income (not including losses) from lines 135 to 143.

You cannot claim this credit if the total of your net income (line 236) and your spouse or common-law partner's net income (line 236 of his or her return, or the amount that it would be if he or she filed a return), minus any amount reported by you or your spouse or common-law partner on lines 117 and 125, is $44,973 or more. In addition, if you or your spouse or common-law partner deducted an amount on line 213, and/or an amount for a repayment of registered disability savings plan income included on line 232, we will add these amounts to your or your spouse's or common-law partner's net income when calculating this credit.

Note:

If you or your spouse or common-law partner deducted a UCCB repayment (on line 213), you do not have to include your spouse's or common-law partner's net income. However, if you were separated because of a breakdown in your relationship for a period of 90 days or more that included December 31, 2009, you do not have to include your spouse or common-law partner's income when calculating this credit.

Make sure you enter, in the Identification area on page 1 of your return, your marital status and, if it applies, the information concerning your spouse or common-law partner. This includes his or her net income, even if it is zero and, if applicable, the UCCB income on line 117 included in his or her net income and/or the UCCB repayment entered on line 213 of his or her return.

Complete the chart for line 452 on the Federal Worksheet in the forms book to calculate your claim. You can claim this credit for the same medical expenses that you claimed on line 215 of your return and line 332 on Schedule 1.

T1 Guide: Line 453 - Working income tax benefit (WITB)

The Canada Revenue Agency says... *General Income Tax and Benefit Guide*

The WITB is for low-income individuals and families who have earned income from employment or business.

The WITB consists of a basic amount and a disability supplement. Complete Schedule 6 to calculate the basic WITB and, if applicable, the WITB disability supplement to which you may be entitled.

Enter on line 453 the amount calculated on Schedule 6 and attach a copy of this schedule to your paper return.

If you had an eligible spouse, only one of you can claim the basic WITB.

Note: The person who receives the WITB advance payments is the person who must claim the basic WITB for the year.

If you had an eligible dependant, you and another person cannot both claim the basic WITB for that same eligible dependant.

If you had an eligible spouse, and one of you qualifies for the disability amount, that person should claim both the basic WITB and the WITB disability supplement.

If you had an eligible spouse and both of you qualify for the disability amount, only one of you can claim the basic WITB. However, each of you must claim the WITB disability supplement on a separate Schedule 6.

For the purpose of the WITB, an eligible spouse is a person who meets all the following conditions:

- was your spouse or common-law partner on December 31, 2009;
- was a resident of Canada throughout 2009;
- was not enrolled as a full-time student at a designated educational institution for a total of more than 13 weeks in the year, unless he or she had an eligible dependant at the end of the year; and
- was not confined to a prison or similar institution for a period of 90 days or more during the year.

For the purpose of the Working Income Tax Benefit (WITB), an eligible dependant is a person who meets all of the following conditions:

- was your or your spouse's or common-law partner's child;
- was under 19 years of age and lived with you on December 31, 2009; and
- was not eligible for the WITB for 2009.

Note:

For the purpose of calculating working income on line 385 and line 386 of Schedule 6, you must include the tax-exempt part of employment income, other employment income, business income (excluding losses), and scholarship income, earned/received reserve. Also include on these lines the tax-exempt part of allowances received as an emergency volunteer.

For the purpose of calculating adjusted family net income on line 388 and line 389 of Schedule 6, you must include the tax-exempt part of all income earned on a reserve. For example, if you were a status Indian and you received Employment Insurance benefits included in box 18 of a T4E, you must include this amount on line 388. Also include on these lines the tax-exempt part of allowances received as an emergency volunteer.

For more information, see Pamphlet RC4227, Working Income Tax Benefit.

T1 Guide: Line 454 - Refund of investment tax credit

T1 Line 454: Refund of investment tax credit

ProFile calculates this amount using data from other forms and worksheets. To jump to a related form, right click on the field and select from the list of forms in the context-sensitive menu. You can also press <F6> when your cursor is in the field to jump to the first source form.

 The Canada Revenue Agency says... *General Income Tax and Benefit Guide*

If you are eligible for an investment tax credit (line 412 on Schedule 1) based on expenditures made in 2009, you may be able to claim a refund of your unused investment tax credit. This refund will reduce the amount of credit available to you for other years.

Calculate the refundable part of your investment tax credit on Form T2038(IND), Investment Tax Credit (Individuals) . Attach a completed copy of the form to your paper return.

T1 Guide: Line 456 - Part XII.2 trust tax credit

T1 Line 456: Part XII.2 trust tax credit

ProFile calculates this amount using data from other forms and worksheets. To jump to a related form, right click on the field and select from the list of forms in the context-sensitive menu. You can also press <F6> when your cursor is in the field to jump to the first source form.

 The Canada Revenue Agency says... *General Income Tax and Benefit Guide*

Enter the total of amounts shown in box 38 of all your T3 slips.

Line 457: Employee and partner GST/HST 370 rebate

T1 Line 457: Employee and partner GST/HST 370 rebate

ProFile calculates this amount using data from other forms and worksheets. To jump to a related form, right click on the field and select from the list of forms in the context-sensitive menu. You can also press <F6> when your cursor is in the field to jump to the first source form.

The Canada Revenue Agency says... *General Income Tax and Benefit Guide*

If you deducted expenses from your income as an employee (line 212 or 229) or as a partner (lines 135 to 143), you may be eligible for a rebate of the GST/HST you paid on those expenses.

Generally, you can claim this rebate if either of the following apply:

- your employer is a GST/HST registrant, other than a listed financial institution; or
- you are a member of a GST/HST-registered partnership, and you have reported on your return your share of the income from that partnership.

To claim this rebate, if you incurred the expenses as an employee, use Guide T4044, Employee Expenses. If you incurred the expenses as a member of a partnership, use Guide RC4091, GST/HST Rebate for Partners. These guides list the expenses that qualify. They also include Form GST370, Employee and Partner GST/HST Rebate Application, which you will need to make your claim. Attach a completed copy of this form to your paper return, and enter on line 457 the rebate you are claiming.

 Note:

- Generally, you have to include in income any GST/HST rebate you receive on the return for the year in which you receive it. For example, you may claim a rebate on your return for 2009. If we allow your claim, and assess that return in 2010, you must report the rebate on your return for 2010.
- You may have received a GST/HST rebate in 2009. If you did, and you were an employee, see line 104. If you are a partner, contact our Business Enquiries service. See "Contacting us".

T1 Line 460: Direct deposit

Complete the direct deposit section of the T1 jacket only to start direct deposits or to change information. Alternately, attach a void cheque to the tax return.

Enter the bank branch number on this line.

T1 Line 461: Direct deposit

Complete the direct deposit section of the T1 jacket only to start direct deposits or to change information. Alternately, attach a void cheque to the tax return.

Enter the bank institution number on this line.

T1 Line 462: Direct deposit

Complete the direct deposit section of the T1 jacket only to start direct deposits or to change information. Alternately, attach a void cheque to the tax return.

Enter the taxpayer's account number on this line.

T1 Line 463: Direct deposit

Complete the direct deposit section of the T1 jacket only to start direct deposits or to change information. Alternately, attach a void cheque to the tax return.

Select this checkbox for direct deposit of the Canadian Child Tax Benefit and certain related provincial or territorial payments.

T1 Line 465: Donation to the Ontario Opportunities Fund

T1 Guide: Line 476 - Tax paid by instalments

ProFile calculates this amount using data from other forms and worksheets. To jump to a related form, right click on the field and select from the list of forms in the context-sensitive menu. You can also press <F6> when your cursor is in the field to jump to the first source form.

The Canada Revenue Agency says... *General Income Tax and Benefit Guide*

Enter the total instalment payments you made for your taxes for 2009.

In February 2010, we will issue you Form INNS1, Instalment Reminder, or Form INNS2, Instalment Payment Summary, which shows your total instalment payments for 2009 that we have on record. To view your instalment account, go to My Account on our website.

If you made an instalment payment for your taxes for 2009 that does not appear on this reminder or summary, also include that amount on line 476.

Note: If tax was withheld from your income, claim on line 437 the amounts shown on your information slips.

T1 Guide: Line 479 - Provincial or territorial credits

T1 Line 479: Provincial or territorial credits

ProFile calculates this amount using data from other forms and worksheets. To jump to a related form, right click on the field and select from the list of forms in the context-sensitive menu. You can also press <F6> when your cursor is in the field to jump to the first source form.

The Canada Revenue Agency says...

If you were a resident of Ontario, Manitoba, Saskatchewan, British Columbia, Yukon, the Northwest Territories, or Nunavut on December 31, 2009, use Form 479 to calculate your provincial or territorial credits. Attach a copy to your paper return. If you were a resident of Nova Scotia, use Form 428 to claim the Nova Scotia volunteer firefighters and ground search and rescue tax credit, and enter the amount on line 479 of your return. If you were not a resident of any of those provinces and territories, Form 479 does not apply to you.

Residents of Newfoundland and Labrador, Prince Edward Island, Nova Scotia, New Brunswick, Saskatchewan, and Alberta claim their provincial credits on Form 428 and use them to reduce their provincial taxes payable on line 428.

Québec residents claim their provincial credits on their provincial income tax returns for Québec.

T1 Line 482: Total credits

These are the total tax credits entered into the return to be applied against provincial and federal taxes payable.

T1 Refund or balance owing

This line subtracts total credits from total tax payable. If the amount is negative, the taxpayer is entitled to a refund. If the amount is positive, there is a balance owing. CRA does not charge or refund amounts that are less than $2.

T1 Guide: Line 484 - Reimbursement

T1 Line 484: Refund

ProFile calculates this amount using data from other forms and worksheets. To jump to a related form, right click on the field and select from the list of forms in the context-sensitive menu. You can also press <F6> when your cursor is in the field to jump to the first source form.

 The Canada Revenue Agency says... *General Income Tax and Benefit Guide*

If your total payable (line 435) is less than your total credits (line 482), enter the difference on line 484. This amount is your refund. Generally, if the difference is $2 or less for 2009, you will not receive a refund.

Note: One person's refund cannot be transferred to pay another person's balance owing. Although you may be entitled to a refund for 2009, we may keep some or all of it to:

- apply against any amount you owe us or are about to owe us;
- satisfy a garnishment order under the Family Orders and Agreements Enforcement Assistance Act ; or
- apply against certain other outstanding federal, provincial, or territorial government debts, such as student loans, Employment Insurance and social assistance benefit overpayments, immigration loans, and training allowance overpayments.

If you pay your taxes by instalments, you can attach a note to your paper return to ask us to transfer your refund to your instalment account for 2010. We will transfer your full refund and consider such a payment to have been received on the date that we assess your return.

T1 Guide: Line 485 - Balance owing

T1 Line 485: Balance owing

Line 485 is the balance of taxes owing, if there are any.

 The Canada Revenue Agency says... *General Income Tax and Benefit Guide*

If your total payable (line 435) is more than your total credits (line 482), the difference (on line 485) is your balance owing. This amount is due no later than April 30, 2010. Generally, if the difference is $2 or less for 2009, you do not have to make a payment.

Note: When a due date falls on a Saturday, a Sunday, or a holiday recognized by the CRA, we consider your return to be filed on time or your payment to be made on time if we receive it or it is postmarked on the next business day.

Filing a paper return

Whether you file a paper return or file electronically, you can make your payment in several different ways:

- **My Payment** is a new payment option that allows individuals and businesses to make payments online using the CRA's Web site from an account at a participating Canadian financial institution.
- You may be able to pay electronically using your financial institution's Internet or telephone banking services. Most financial institutions allow you to schedule future-dated payments.
- You can make your payment at your Canadian financial institution free of charge. To do so, you have to use the remittance form in your personalized tax package (if you received one) or Form T7DR(A), EFILE Remittance Form which you can get from us.
- You can attach to the front of your paper return a cheque or money order made out to the Receiver General. Enter the payment amount on line 486.
- You can send us a cheque or money order with the remittance form in your personalized tax package (if you received one) or with Form T7DR(A), which you can get from us.
    Mail the form and your cheque or money order to:
    Canada Revenue Agency,
    875 Heron Road
    Ottawa ON, K1A 1B1

Note: If you are making a payment by cheque or money order, write your social insurance number on the back to help us process your payment correctly. For more information, see Social insurance number.

Do not mail us cash or include it with your return.

You can file your return early and make a post-dated payment as late as April 30. In that case, if we process your return before the date of the payment, your payment will appear on your Notice of Assessment, but it will not reduce your balance owing. We will credit your account on the date of the payment and then send you a revised statement of your account.

If you make a payment with a cheque that your financial institution does not honour (including a cheque on which you put a "stop-payment"), we will charge you a fee.

Making a payment arrangement

If you cannot pay your balance owing on or before April 30, 2010, we will accept a payment arrangement only after you have reasonably tried to obtain the necessary funds by borrowing or re-arranging your financial affairs. If you cannot pay the balance in full, you may be able to make a preauthorized debit payment arrangement by using our My Account service. Go to My Account on our website.

You may also make a payment arrangement using a touch-tone telephone through our TeleArrangement service by calling our toll-free number at 1-866-256-1141. To use this service you will need to provide your social insurance number, your date of birth, and the amount you entered on line 150 from your last return for which you received a Notice of Assessment. TeleArrangement is available Monday to Friday, 7:00 a.m. to 8:00 p.m., EST.

In addition, you can also make a payment arrangement by calling one of our agents at 1-888-863-8657. This service is available Monday to Friday (except holidays) from 8:00 a.m. to 8:00 p.m. (local time).

We will still charge daily compound interest on any outstanding balance starting May 1, 2010, until you pay it in full.

Your failure to proceed with timely action to resolve your tax arrears can lead to serious measures by CRA including legal action such as garnisheeing your income or your bank account or initializing other legal action such as seizing and selling your assets.

Tip: Even if you cannot pay all of your balance owing right away, you should still file your return on time. Then you will not have to pay a penalty for filing your return after the due date. See What penalties and interest do we charge? for more information.

T1 Guide: Line 486 - Amount enclosed

T1 Line 486: Amount enclosed

Line 486 is the amount enclosed with the return upon submission to the CRA.

The Canada Revenue Agency says... *General Income Tax and Benefit Guide*

If you have a balance owing and you are filing a paper return (instead of filing electronically, enter on this line the amount that you are submitting to the CRA with your return. For information about other ways to pay your balance owing, see line 485.

T1 Line 490: Preparer information

ProFile calculates this amount using data from other forms and worksheets. To jump to a related form, right click on the field and select from the list of forms in the context-sensitive menu. You can also press <F6> when your cursor is in the field to jump to the first source form.

Schedule 1 - Federal tax and non-refundable tax credits

S1: Federal tax calculation

ProFile uses Schedule 1 to automatically calculate your federal tax and non-refundable tax credits.

For 2009, The federal income tax bracket levels change as follows:

- On income under $40,726: 15%
- $40,726 to $81,452: 22%

- $81,452 to $126,264: 26%
- Over $126,264: 29%

If you have to pay minimum tax, or if you are claiming an overseas employment tax credit, you will need to complete form T691: Calculation of minimum tax or form T626: Overseas employment tax credit, whichever applies, before completing Schedule 1.

The Canada Revenue Agency says... *General Income Tax and Benefit Guide*

These credits reduce your federal tax. However, if the total of these credits is more than your federal tax, you will not get a refund for the difference. If, after you have read the information in this guide, you need more details about claiming the amounts on lines 300 to 306, get Interpretation Bulletin IT-513, Personal Tax Credits.

Schedule 1: Line 300 - Basic personal amount

Schedule 1 - Line 300: Basic personal amount

ProFile calculates this amount using data from other forms and worksheets. To jump to a related form, right click on the field and select from the list of forms in the context-sensitive menu. You can also press <F6> when your cursor is in the field to jump to the first source form.

The Canada Revenue Agency says... *General Income Tax and Benefit Guide*

Claim $10,320.

Schedule 1: Line 301 - Age amount

Schedule 1 - Line 301: Age amount

ProFile calculates this amount using data from other forms and worksheets. To jump to a related form, right click on the field and select from the list of forms in the context-sensitive menu. You can also press <F6> when your cursor is in the field to jump to the first source form.

The Canada Revenue Agency says... *General Income Tax and Benefit Guide*

If you were 65 years of age or older on December 31, 2009, and your net income (line 236 of your return) was:

- $32,312 or less, enter $6,408 on line 301;
- more than $32,312, but less than $75,032, complete the chart for line 301 on the Federal Worksheet in the CRA forms book to calculate your claim; or
- $75,032 or more, you cannot claim the age amount.

Make sure you enter your date of birth in the "Information about you" area on page 1 of your return.

 Tip: You may be able to transfer all or part of your age amount to your spouse or common-law partner or to claim all or part of his or her age amount. For more information, see line 326.

Schedule 1: Line 303 - Spouse or common-law partner amount

Schedule 1 - Line 303: Spouse or common-law partner amount

ProFile calculates the net spousal amount by subtracting the spouses' income, if any, from the base spousal amount. If the client and spouse returns have been coupled, ProFile will automatically enter the income for you. If the returns are not coupled, you must override the income amount for the spouse.

Ensure that the client is indicated as married or common-law on the Info form to allow the spousal amount to be claimed. In addition, if the spouse has no income, indicate this on the Info form of the client file, in the Spousal information section, if the returns are not coupled.

The Canada Revenue Agency says... *General Income Tax and Benefit Guide*

You can claim this amount if, at any time in the year, you supported your spouse or common-law partner and his or her net income (line 236 of his or her return, or the amount that it would be if he or she filed a return) was less than $10,320. Calculate your amount on line 303 of your Schedule 1.

Make sure you enter the information concerning your spouse or common-law partner in the Identification area on page 1 of your return if you were married or living common law on December 31, 2009. In certain situations, the net income of your spouse or common-law partner must be indicated even if your marital status has changed. See "Net income of spouse or common-law partner" in the next section. Both of you cannot claim this amount for each other for the same year.

If you were required to make support payments to your current or former spouse or common-law partner, and you were separated for only part of 2009 because of a breakdown in your relationship, you have a choice. You can claim either the deductible support amounts paid in the year to your spouse or common-law partner on line 220 or an amount on line 303 for your spouse or common-law partner, whichever is better for you. If you reconciled with your spouse or common-law partner before the end of 2009, you can claim an amount on line 303 and any allowable amounts on line 326.

Net income of spouse or common-law partner

This is the amount on line 236 of your spouse's or common-law partner's return, or the amount that it would be if he or she filed a return.

If you were living with your spouse or common-law partner on December 31, 2009, use his or her net income for the whole year. This applies even if you got married or back together with your spouse in 2009, or you became a common-law partner or started to live with your common-law partner again.

If you separated in 2009 because of a breakdown in your relationship and were not back together on December 31, 2009, reduce your claim only by your spouse's or common-law partner's net income before the separation. In all cases, enter in the "Information about your spouse or common-law partner" area on page 1 of your return, the amount you use to calculate your claim, even if it is zero.

Tip: If you cannot claim the amount on line 303 (or you have to reduce your claim) because of dividends your spouse or common-law partner received from taxable Canadian corporations, you may be able to reduce your tax if you report all of your spouse's or common-law partner's dividends. For more information, see line 120.

Schedule 1: Line 305 - Amount for an eligible dependant

Schedule 1 - Line 305: Amount for an eligible dependant

ProFile calculates this amount using data from other forms and worksheets. To jump to a related form, right click on the field and select from the list of forms in the context-sensitive menu. You can also press <F6> when your cursor is in the field to jump to the first source form. Attention: The Amount for an eligible dependant was previously known as the equivalent-to-spouse amount.

The Canada Revenue Agency says... *General Income Tax and Benefit Guide*

You may be able to claim this amount if, at any time in the year, you met all of the following conditions at once:

- you did not have a spouse or common-law partner or, if you did, you were not living with, supporting, or being supported by that person;
- you supported a dependant in 2009; and
- you lived with the dependant (in most cases in Canada) in a home that you maintained. You cannot claim this amount for a person who was only visiting you.

In addition, at the time you met the above conditions, the dependant also must have been either:

- your parent or grandparent by blood, marriage, common-law partnership, or adoption; or
- your child, grandchild, brother, or sister by blood, marriage, common-law partnership, or adoption and either under 18 years of age, or mentally or physically impaired.

Note:

- Your dependant may live away from home while attending school. If the dependant ordinarily lived with you when not in school, we consider that dependant to live with you for the purposes of this amount.
- For the purposes of this claim, your child is not required to have lived in Canada but still must have lived with you. This would be possible, for example, if you were a deemed resident living in another country with your child.

Even if all of the preceding conditions have been met, you cannot claim this amount if any of the following apply:

- You are claiming a spouse or common-law partner amount (see line 303).
- The person for whom you want to claim this amount is your common-law partner. However, you may be able to claim the amount on line 303.
- Someone else in your household is making this claim. Each household is allowed only one claim for this amount, even if there is more than one dependant in the household.
- The claim is for a child for whom you were required to make support payments for 2009. However, if you were separated from your spouse or common-law partner for only part of 2009 due to a breakdown in your relationship, you can still claim an amount for that child on line 305 (plus any allowable amounts on lines 306, 315, and 318) as long as you do not claim any support amounts paid to your spouse or common-law partner on line 220. You can claim whichever is better for you.

Note: If you and another person were required to make support payments for the child for 2009 and, as a result, no one would be entitled to claim the amount for an eligible dependant for the child, you can still claim this amount provided you and the other person(s) paying support agree you will be the one making the claim. If you cannot agree who will claim this amount for the child, neither of you can make the claim.

How to claim

You can claim this amount if your dependant's net income (line 236 of his or her return, or the amount that it would be if he or she filed a return) was less than $10,320. Calculate your amount on line 305 of your Schedule 1.

Complete the appropriate part of Schedule 5, and attach it to your paper return.

Note:

- You cannot split this amount with another person. Once you claim this amount for a dependant, no one else can claim this amount or an amount on line 306 for that dependant.
- If you and another person both can claim this amount for the same dependant (such as shared custody of a child) but cannot agree who will claim the amount, neither of you can make the claim.

Tip:

If the dependant has an impairment, see guide RC4064, Medical and Disability-Related Information, for more information about different amounts you may be able to claim.

Schedule 1: Line 306 - Amounts for infirm dependants age 18 or older

Schedule 1 - Line 306: Amounts for infirm dependants age 18 or older

ProFile calculates this amount using data from other forms and worksheets. To jump to a related form, right click on the field and select from the list of forms in the context-sensitive menu. You can also press <F6> when your cursor is in the field to jump to the first source form.

The Canada Revenue Agency says... *General Income Tax and Benefit Guide*

You can claim an amount up to a maximum of $4,198 for each of your or your spouse's or common-law partner's dependent children or grandchildren only if that child or grandchild had an impairment in physical or mental functions and was born in 1991 or earlier.

You can also claim an amount for more than one person as long as each one meets all of the following conditions. The person must have been:

- your or your spouse's or common-law partner's parent, grandparent, brother, sister, aunt, uncle, niece, or nephew;
- born in 1991 or earlier and had an impairment in physical or mental functions;

- dependent on you, or on you and others, for support; and
- a resident of Canada at any time in the year. You cannot claim this amount for a person who was only visiting you.

Note:
- A parent includes someone on whom you were completely dependent and who had custody and control of you when you were under 19 years of age.
- A child can include someone older than you who has become dependent on you.

If, for a particular dependant, anyone other than you is claiming an amount on line 305, or anyone (including you) can claim an amount on line 315, you cannot claim an amount on line 306 for that dependant. If you are claiming an amount on line 305 for a dependant who has an impairment and is 18 years of age or older, you also may be able to claim a part of the amount on line 306 for that dependant.

You can claim an amount only if the dependant's net income (line 236 of his or her return, or the amount that it would be if he or she filed a return) is less than $10,154.

If you were required to make support payments for that child, you cannot claim an amount on line 306 for that child. However, if you were separated from your spouse or common-law partner for only part of 2009 due to a breakdown in your relationship, you can still claim an amount for that child on line 306 (plus any allowable amounts on lines 305 and 318) as long as you do not claim any support amounts paid to your spouse or common-law partner on line 220. You can claim whichever is better for you.

How to claim

- For each of your dependants, calculate his or her net income (line 236 of his or her return, or the amount that it would be if he or she filed a return). Complete the chart for line 306 on the Federal Worksheet in the forms book to calculate your claim.
- Complete the appropriate part of Schedule 5, and attach it to your paper return. You also should have a signed statement from a medical doctor that gives the nature, commencement, and duration of the dependant's impairment. Keep the statement in case we ask to see it.

Claims made by more than one person

If you and another person support the same dependant, you can split the claim for that dependant. However, the total of your claim and the other person's claim cannot be more than the maximum amount allowed for that dependant.

Tip:

For more information about different amounts you may be able to claim, see RC4064, Medical and Disability-Related Information.

Schedule 1: Line 308 - CPP or QPP contributions through employment

Schedule 1 - Line 308: CPP or QPP contributions through employment

ProFile calculates this amount using data from other forms and worksheets. To jump to a related form, right click on the field and select from the list of forms in the context-sensitive menu. You can also press <F6> when your cursor is in the field to jump to the first source form.

 The Canada Revenue Agency says... *General Income Tax and Benefit Guide*

Claim, in dollars and cents, the total of the Canada Pension Plan (CPP) or Quebec Pension Plan (QPP) contributions shown in boxes 16 and 17 of your T4 slips. Do not enter more than $2,118.60.

If you contributed to the QPP in 2009 but resided outside Quebec on December 31, 2009, treat those contributions as if you made them to the CPP. Attach to your paper return the RL-1 slip your employer sent you.

 Note: If you contributed to a foreign employer-sponsored pension plan or to a Social Security Arrangement (other than a United States Arrangement); for more information, see Form RC269 Contributions to a foreign Employer-Sponsored Pension Plan or to a Social Security Arrangement (other than a United States Arrangement.) You can get this form by going to Forms and publications on our Web site or by contacting us.

If you contributed more than $2,118.60, enter the excess amount on line 448 of your return. We will refund this overpayment to you or use it to reduce your balance owing. However, if you were a resident of Quebec on December 31, 2009, and contributed more than $2,118.60, claim the overpayment on your provincial income tax return for Quebec.

You may have an overpayment, even if you contributed $2,118.60 or less. For example:

- In 2009, you may have been a CPP participant and either turned 18 or 70 years of age, or received a CPP retirement or disability pension.

 Note:

If you were also a QPP participant and either turned 70 years of age or received a CPP or QPP retirement pension you may not have an overpayment.

- In 2009, you may have been a QPP participant and either turned 18 years of age or received a QPP disability pension.
- From all your T4 slips for 2009, the total of amounts shown in box 14 may be more than the total of amounts shown in box 26. If box 26 of one of the slips is blank, use the amount shown in box 14.

You can calculate your overpayment, if any, using Form T2204, Employee Overpayment of 2009 Canada Pension Plan Contributions and 2009 Employment Insurance Premiums .

Request for refund of CPP contributions

Under the Canada Pension Plan, a request for a refund of CPP over-contributions must be made within four years after the end of the year for which the request is being made.

Tax-exempt employment income earned by a registered Indian

If you are a registered Indian with tax-exempt employment income, and there is no amount shown in box 16 or 17 of your T4 slip, you may also be able to contribute to the CPP on this income.

Making additional CPP or QPP contributions

You may not have contributed to the CPP for certain income you earned through employment, or you may have contributed less than you were required. This can happen if any of the following apply:

- You had more than one employer in 2009.
- You had income, such as tips, from which your employer did not have to withhold contributions.
- You were in a type of employment that was not covered under CPP rules, such as casual employment.

Generally, if the total of your CPP and QPP contributions through employment, as shown in boxes 16 and 17 of your T4 slips, is less than $2,118.60, you can contribute 9.9% on any part of the income on which you have not already made contributions. The maximum income for 2009 for which you can contribute to the CPP is $46,300. Making additional contributions may increase the pension you receive later.

To make additional CPP contributions for 2009, complete Schedule 8 and Form CPT20, Election to Pay Canada Pension Plan Contributions to calculate the amount of the additional contributions and claim the appropriate amounts at lines 222 and 310. Attach a copy of Schedule 8 and form CPT20 to your paper return, or send Form CPT20 to us separately on or before June 15, 2011. Form CPT20 lists the eligible employment income on which you can make additional CPP contributions.

Schedule 1: Line 310 - CPP or QPP contributions on self-employment and other earnings

Schedule 1 - Line 310: CPP or QPP contributions on self-employment and other earnings

ProFile calculates this amount using data from other forms and worksheets. To jump to a related form, right click on the field and select from the list of forms in the context-sensitive menu. You can also press <F6> when your cursor is in the field to jump to the first source form.

 The Canada Revenue Agency says... *General Income Tax and Benefit Guide*

Claim, in dollars and cents, the same amount you claimed on line 222 of your return.

Schedule 1: Line 312 - Employment Insurance premiums

Schedule 1 - Line 312: Employment Insurance premiums

ProFile calculates this amount using data from other forms and worksheets. To jump to a related form, right click on the field and select from the list of forms in the context-sensitive menu. You can also press <F6> when your cursor is in the field to jump to the first source form.

In 2009, the rates and amounts used in the calculation of EI premiums are:

- Maximum insurable earnings: $42,300
- Premium rate: 1.73%
- Maximum premiums: $731.79

The Canada Revenue Agency says... *General Income Tax and Benefit Guide*

If you were not a resident of Quebec on December 31, 2009, claim, in dollars and cents, the total of the amount shown in box 18 of all your T4 slips. If you contributed to a provincial parental insurance plan (PPIP) in 2009, also include the total of the amount shown in box 55 of all your T4 slips on this line. Do not enter more than $731.79. Attach to your paper return the RL-1 slip your employer sent you.

If you contributed more than $731.79, enter the excess amount on line 450 of your return. We will refund this overpayment to you or use it to reduce your balance owing.

Under proposed changes, if you were a resident of Quebec on December 31, 2009 and worked only in Quebec during the year, claim, in dollars and cents, the total of the amount shown in box 18 of all your T4 slips. Do not enter more than $583.74 If you contributed more than $583.74, enter, in dollars and cents, the excess amount on line 450 of your return. We will refund this overpayment to you or use it to reduce your balance.

If, during the year, you were a resident of Quebec, worked outside Quebec and your employment income is $2,000 or more, you must complete Schedule 10 and attach it to your paper return. Claim, on this line, in dollars and cents, the amount of your Employment Insurance premiums from line 18 or line 19 (whichever is less) of Schedule 10.

Insurable earnings

This is the total of all earnings on which you pay Employment Insurance premiums. These amounts are shown in box 24 of your T4 slips for 2009 (or box 14 if box 24 is blank).

You may have an overpayment of your premiums even if the total is $731.79 or less (if you were not a resident of Quebec) or $583.74 or less if you were a resident of Quebec. This can happen when your insurable earnings are less than the total of all amounts shown in box 14 of all your T4 slips. You can calculate your overpayment, if any, using Form T2204, Employee Overpayment of 2009 Canada Pension Plan Contributions and 2009 Employment Insurance Premiums . If you were a resident of Quebec and had to complete Schedule 10 because you worked outside Quebec, do not use Form T2204. You will calculate the overpayment on Schedule 10.

If your insurable earnings are $2,000 or less, we will refund all of your premiums to you or use them to reduce your balance owing. In this case, do not enter any premiums on this line. Instead, enter the total on line 450.

Request for refund of EI contributions

You may have an overpayment if your insurable earnings are more than $2,000 and less than $2,035. You can calculate your overpayment, if any, using Form T2204. Under the Employment Insurance Act, a request for refund of EI overpayment must be made within three years after the end of the year for which the request is being made.

Schedule 1: Line 313 - Adoption expenses

Schedule 1 - Line 313: Adoption expenses

Complete the data entry for adoption expenses on the Other Credits worksheet. From there, the adoption expenses will transfer to line 313 of the federal Schedule 1 and corresponding provincial form 428.

Provinces that allow the adoption expenses claim on their respective 428 forms are:

- Alberta
- British Columbia
- Manitoba
- Newfoundland and Labrador
- Ontario
- Yukon Territory

The Canada Revenue Agency says... *General Income Tax and Benefit Guide*

You can claim an amount for eligible adoption expenses related to the adoption of a child who is under 18 years of age. The maximum claim for each child is $10,909.

The claim for eligible expenses can be split between two adoptive parents as long as the combined total claim is not more than the amount before the split.

Parents can claim these incurred expenses in the tax year that includes the end of the adoption period in respect of the child. The adoption period:

- begins at the earlier of the time that the eligible child's adoption file is opened with a provincial or territorial ministry responsible for adoption (or with an adoption agency licensed by a provincial or territorial government) and the time, if any, that an application related to the adoption is made to a Canadian court; and
- ends at the later of the time an adoption order is issued by, or recognized by, a government in Canada in respect of that child and the time that the child first begins to reside permanently with you.

Eligible adoption expenses

Eligible adoption expenses that you can claim are:

- fees paid to an adoption agency licensed by a provincial or territorial government (an "adoption agency");
- court costs and legal and administrative expenses related to an adoption order in respect of the child;
- reasonable and necessary travel and living expenses of the child and the adoptive parents;
- document translation fees;
- mandatory fees paid to a foreign institution;
- mandatory expenses paid in respect of the immigration of that child; and
- any other reasonable expenses related to the adoption that are required by a provincial or territorial government or an adoption agency.

Reimbursement of an eligible expense - You must reduce your eligible expenses by any reimbursements or other forms of assistance that you received.

Schedule 1: Line 314 - Pension income amount

Schedule 1 - Line 314: Pension income amount

ProFile calculates this amount using data from other forms and worksheets. To jump to a related form, right click on the field and select from the list of forms in the context-sensitive menu. You can also press <F6> when your cursor is in the field to jump to the first source form.

The Canada Revenue Agency says... *General Income Tax and Benefit Guide*

You may be able to claim up to $2,000 if you reported eligible pension, superannuation, or annuity payments on lines 115, 116, and/or 129 of your return.

Make sure you have reported your pension or annuity income correctly. To calculate your claim, complete the chart for line 314 on the Federal Worksheet in the forms book.

If you and your spouse or common-law partner elected to split pension income, follow the instructions at Step 4 on Form T1032, Joint Election to Split Pension Income, to calculate the amount to enter on line 314 of your and your spouse's or common-law partner's Schedule 1.

Note: Amounts such as Old Age Security benefits, Canada Pension Plan benefits, Quebec Pension Plan benefits, Saskatchewan Pension Plan benefits, death benefits, retiring allowances, excess amounts from RRIF transferred to an RRSP, another RRIF or annuity, and amounts shown in boxes 18, 20, 22, 26, 28, and 34 of your T4RSP slip, and amounts distributed from a retirement compensation arrangement shown on your T4A-RCA slip do not qualify.

Tip: You may be able to transfer all or part of your pension income amount to your spouse or common-law partner or to claim all or part of his or her pension income amount. For more information, see line 326.

Non-Residents

This credit as well as many other credits is not available to a non-resident unless all or substantially all (90%) of income is from business, employment, scholarships, bursaries or grants from Canada and is not protected by treaty.

Non-residents and non-residents electing under section 217

If this amount applies to you, complete Schedule A, Statement of World Income, and Schedule B, Allowable Amount of Non-Refundable Tax Credits, to determine the amount you can claim. Attach Schedule A to your return.

Schedule 1: Line 315 - Caregiver amount

Schedule 1 - Line 315: Caregiver amount

ProFile calculates this amount using data from other forms and worksheets. To jump to a related form, right click on the field and select from the list of forms in the context-sensitive menu. You can also press <F6> when your cursor is in the field to jump to the first source form.

The Canada Revenue Agency says... *General Income Tax and Benefit Guide*

If, at any time in 2009, you (either alone or with another person) maintained a dwelling where you and one or more of your dependants lived, you may be able to claim a maximum amount of $4,198 for each dependant. Each dependant must have been one of the following individuals:

- your or your spouse's or common-law partner's child or grandchild; or
- your or your spouse's or common-law partner's brother, sister, niece, nephew, aunt, uncle, parent, or grandparent who was resident in Canada. You cannot claim this amount for a person who was only visiting you.

In addition, each dependant must meet all of the following conditions. The person must have:

- been 18 years of age or over at the time he or she lived with you;
- had a net income in 2009(line 236 of his or her return, or the amount that it would be if he or she filed a return) of less than $18,534; and
- been dependent on you due to mental or physical impairment or, if he or she is your or your spouse's or common-law partner's parent or grandparent, born in 1944 or earlier.

If you were required to make support payments for a child, you cannot claim an amount on line 315 for that child. However, if you were separated from your spouse or common-law partner for only part of 2009 due to a breakdown in your relationship, you can still claim an amount for that child on line 315 (plus any allowable amounts on lines 305 and 318) as long as you do not claim any support amounts paid to your spouse or common-law partner on line 220, You can claim whichever is better for you.

Complete the chart for line 315 on the Federal Worksheet in the forms book to calculate your claim. Complete the appropriate part of Schedule 5, and attach it to your paper return.

Claim made by more than one person

If you and another person support the same dependant, you can split the claim for that dependant. However, the total of your claim and the other person's claim cannot be more than the maximum amount allowed for that dependant.

If anyone (including you) can claim this amount for a dependant, no one can claim an amount on line 306 for that dependant. If anyone other than you claims an amount on line 305 for a dependant, you cannot claim an amount on line 315 for that dependant. For more information, see Guide RC4064, Medical and Disability-Related Information.

Schedule 1: Line 316 - Disability amount for self

Schedule 1 - Line 316: Disability amount

Answer the question Claim disability amount? on the Info form to have ProFile calculate the disability amount for the taxpayer.

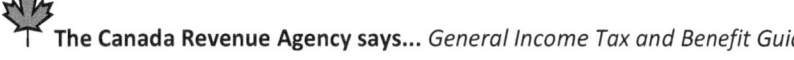
The Canada Revenue Agency says... *General Income Tax and Benefit Guide*

To claim this amount, you must have an impairment in physical or mental functions that is severe and prolonged during 2009. An impairment is prolonged if it has lasted, or is expected to last, for a continuous period of at least 12 months. You may be able to claim $7,196 if a qualified practitioner certifies, on Form T2201, Disability Tax Credit Certificate, that you meet certain conditions.

To view your disability tax credit information, go to My Account on our Web site. For more information, including details about different amounts you may be able to claim, see Guide RC4064, Medical and Disability-Related Information. That guide includes Form T2201.

Supplement for persons under 18

If you qualify for the disability amount and you were under 18 years of age at the end of the year, you can claim up to an additional $4,198. However, this supplement may be reduced if, in 2009, someone claimed child care expenses (line 214) or attendant care expenses (as a medical expense on line 330 or 331) for you. It will also be reduced if you claimed a disability supports deduction on line 215 or line 330 for yourself.

How to claim

- If this is a new application for this amount, you have to submit a completed (including Part A) Form T2201, Disability Tax Credit Certificate, certified by a qualified practitioner or your claim will be delayed. We will review your claim before we assess your return to determine if you qualify.
- If you qualified for this amount for 2008 and you still meet the eligibility requirements in 2009, you can claim this amount without sending us a new Form T2201. However, you have to send us one if the previous period of approval has ended before 2009, or we ask you to do so.
- If you were 18 years of age or over at the end of the year, claim $7,196. Otherwise, complete the chart for line 316 on the Federal Worksheet in the forms book to calculate your claim.

Tip: You may be able to transfer all or part of your disability amount (and, if it applies, the supplement) to your spouse or common-law partner (who would claim it on line 326) or to another supporting person (who would claim it on line 318).

You may be able to claim all or part of the disability amount (and, if it applies, the supplement) transferred from your spouse or common-law partner on line 326 or from another dependant on line 318.

Also, you may be able to claim a Working Income Tax Benefit disability supplement. For more information, see line 453.

Schedule 1: Line 318 - Disability amount transferred from a dependant

Schedule 1 - Line 318: Disability amount transferred from a dependant

ProFile calculates this amount using data from other forms and worksheets. To jump to a related form, right click on the field and select from the list of forms in the context-sensitive menu. You can also press <F6> when your cursor is in the field to jump to the first source form.

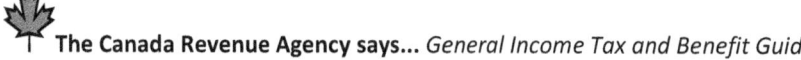**The Canada Revenue Agency says...** *General Income Tax and Benefit Guide*

You may be able to claim all or part of your dependant's disability amount (line 316) if he or she was resident in Canada at any time in 2009 and was dependent on you for all or some of the basic necessities of life (food, shelter, or clothing).

In addition, one of the following situations has to apply:

- You claimed an amount on line 305 for that dependant, or you could have if you did not have a spouse or common-law partner and if the dependant did not have any income. See line 305 for conditions.
- The dependant was your or your spouse's or common-law partner's parent, grandparent, child, grandchild, brother, sister, aunt, uncle, niece, or nephew, and you claimed an amount on line 306 or 315 for that dependant, or you could have if he or she had no income and had been 18 years of age or older in 2009.

If you are required to make support payments for your child, you cannot claim a transfer of that child's disability amount. However, if you were separated from your spouse or common-law partner for only part of 2009 due to a breakdown in your relationship, you can still claim an amount for that child on line 318 (plus any allowable amounts on lines 305, 306, and 315) as long as you do not claim any support amounts paid to your spouse or common-law partner on line 220. You may claim whichever is better for you.

Note:

- You cannot claim this credit if the spouse or common-law partner of the person with a disability is already claiming the disability amount or any other non-refundable tax credit (other than medical expenses) for the person with a disability.
- If you are splitting this claim with another individual, attach a note to your paper return including the name and social insurance number of the other individual who is making this claim. The total claimed for that dependant cannot be more than the maximum amount allowed for that dependant.
- If you or anyone else paid for an attendant, or for care in an establishment, special rules may apply. For more information, see Guide RC4064, Medical and Disability-Related Information. To view your disability tax credit information, go to My Account on our Web site.

How to claim

- If this is a new application for the disability amount, you have to submit a completed and certified Form T2201, Disability Tax Credit Certificate. We will review your claim before we assess your return to determine if your dependant qualifies.
- If your dependant qualified for the disability amount for 2008 and still met the eligibility requirements in 2009, you can claim this amount without sending us a new Form T2201. However, you have to send us one if the previous period of approval ended before 2009 or we ask you to. If you are not attaching a Form T2201 for a dependant, attach to your paper return a note stating the dependant's name, social insurance number, and relationship to you.
- If your dependant was under 18 years of age at the end of the year, first complete the chart for line 316 on the Federal Worksheet in the forms book to calculate the supplement that dependant may be able to claim.
- Complete the chart for line 318 on the Federal Worksheet in the forms book to calculate your claim for each dependant.

Tip:

If you can claim this amount, you also may be able to claim an amount on line 315 for the same dependant. See Guide RC4064, Medical and Disability-Related Information, for details about different amounts you may be able to claim.

Schedule 1: Line 319 - Interest paid on your student loans

Schedule 1 - Line 319: Interest paid on your student loans

ProFile calculates this amount using data from other forms and worksheets. To jump to a related form, right click on the field and select from the list of forms in the context-sensitive menu. You can also press <F6> when your cursor is in the field to jump to the first source form.

The Canada Revenue Agency says... *General Income Tax and Benefit Guide*

A loan may have been made to you under the Canada Student Loans Act, the Canada Student Financial Assistance Act, or similar provincial or territorial government laws for post-secondary education. If so, only you can claim an amount for the interest you, or a person related to you, paid on that loan in 2009 and / or the preceding five years.

You can claim an amount only for interest you have not previously claimed. If you have no tax payable for the year the interest is paid, it is to your advantage not to claim it on your tax return. You can carry the interest forward and apply it on your return for any of the next five years.

Note:

You cannot claim interest paid on any other kind of loan or on a student loan that has been combined with another kind of loan. If you renegotiated your student loan with a bank or financial institution, or included it in an arrangement to consolidate your loans, the interest on the new loan does not qualify for this tax credit.

In addition, you cannot claim interest paid in respect of a judgment obtained after you failed to pay back a student loan.

Schedule 1: Line 323 - Tuition, education, and textbook amounts

Schedule 1 - Line 323: Tuition and education amounts

ProFile calculates this amount using data from other forms and worksheets. To jump to a related form, right click on the field and select from the list of forms in the context-sensitive menu. You can also press <F6> when your cursor is in the field to jump to the first source form.

The Canada Revenue Agency says... *General Income Tax and Benefit Guide*

Complete Schedule 11 to report your total eligible tuition, education, and textbook amounts for 2009, and any unused amounts carried forward from previous years that are shown on your Notice of assessment or Notice of reassessment for 2008. For more information, see "Transferring and carrying forward amounts" or see Pamphlet P105, Students and Income Tax.

Tip:

Even if you have no tax to pay and you are transferring part of your tuition, education, and textbook amounts, you should file your return and attach a completed Schedule 11 so we can update our records with your unused tuition, education, and textbook amounts available for carry forward to other years.

If you are transferring an amount to another person, do not transfer more than the person can use. That way, you can carry forward as much as possible to use in a future year.

You may be able to claim all or part of your spouse's or common-law partner's tuition, education, and textbook amounts on line 326, and/or your child or grandchild's tuition, education, and textbook amounts on line 324.

Eligible tuition fees

Generally, a course qualifies if it was taken at the post-secondary level or (for individuals aged 16 years of age or over at the end of the year) it develops or improves skills in an occupation and the educational institution has been certified by Human Resources and Skills Development Canada. In addition, you must have taken the course in 2009.

Not all fees can be claimed. To qualify, the fees you paid to attend a Canadian educational institution must be more than $100. For fees paid to an educational institution outside Canada, see Pamphlet P105 and Information Sheet RC192, Information for Students - Educational Institutions Outside Canada. In addition, you cannot include in your claim the amounts paid for other expenses, such as board and lodging, students' association fees, or textbooks.

If the fees were paid or reimbursed by your employer, or an employer of one of your parents, you can claim them only if the payment or reimbursement was included in your or your parent's income.

Forms

- For you to claim tuition fees paid to an educational institution in Canada, your institution has to give you either an official tax receipt or a completed Form T2202A, Tuition, Education, and Textbook Amounts Certificate.
- For you to claim tuition fees paid to an educational institution outside Canada, your institution has to complete and give you either, Form TL11A, Tuition, Education, and Textbook Amounts Certificate - University Outside Canada, or Form TL11C, Tuition, Education, and Textbook Amounts Certificate - Commuter to the United States, whichever applies.
- For you to claim tuition fees paid to a flying school or club in Canada, your school or club has to give you a completed Form TL11B, Tuition, Education, and Textbook Amounts Certificate - Flying School or Club.

You can get these forms from us. You also can get Form TL11B from your flying school or club.

Education amount

You can claim this amount for each whole or part month in 2009 in which you were enrolled in a qualifying educational program. If you were under 16 years of age at the end of the year, you can claim this amount only for courses you took at the post-secondary level.

Generally, you cannot claim this amount for a program for which you received a benefit, a grant, an allowance, or a reimbursement of your tuition fees.

However, you can claim this amount even if you received salary or wages from a job that is related to your program of study, certain other kinds of payments, such as scholarships and student loans, or if you received and included in your income any financial assistance provided under **either:**

- Part II of the Employment Insurance Act (and shown in box 20 of your T4E slip) or a labour-market development agreement as part of a similar provincial or territorial program; or
- a program developed under the authority of the Department of Human Resources and Skills Development Act. .

Your educational institution has to complete and give you either Form T2202, Education Amount Certificate , Form T2202A, Tuition, Education, and Textbook Amounts Certificate, Form TL11A, Tuition, Education, and Textbook Amounts Certificate - University Outside Canada , Form TL11B, Tuition, Education, and Textbook Amounts Certificate - Flying School or Club, or Form TL11C, Tuition, Education, and Textbook Amounts Certificate - Commuter to the United States , whichever applies, to confirm the period in which you were enrolled in a qualifying program.

The following amounts apply for each month in which you were enrolled:

- If you were enrolled full-time, you can claim $400 per month.
- If you attended only part-time and you can claim the disability amount on line 316, you can claim $400 per month.
- If you could attend only part-time because you had an impairment that restricted you in one of the activities listed in Guide RC4064, Medical and Disability-Related Information, but your condition was not severe and prolonged, you can claim $400 per month. In that case, have an authorized person either complete Part 3 of Form T2202 or give you a signed letter certifying your impairment.
- If you were enrolled part-time, you can claim $120 per month.

You cannot claim more than one education amount for a particular month.

Textbook amount

You can claim this amount only if you are entitled to claim the education amount. The amount is:

- $65 for each month you qualify for the full-time education amount; and
- $20 for each month you qualify for the part-time education amount.

Transferring and carrying forward amounts

You have to claim your tuition, education, and textbook amounts first on your own return, even if someone else paid your fees. However, you may be able to transfer the unused part of these amounts to your spouse's or common-law partner (who would claim it on line 326 of his or her Schedule 1) or to your or your spouse or common-law partner's parent or grandparent (who would claim it on line 324 of his or her Schedule 1).

Complete Schedule 11 (particularly line 327) to calculate this transfer and Forms T2202, T2202A or TL11A, TL11B, or TL11C to designate it. Attach Schedule 11 to your return even if you are transferring your total tuition, education, and textbook amounts.

You can carry forward and claim in a future year the part of your tuition, education, and textbook amounts you cannot use (and do not transfer) for the year. However, if you carry forward an amount, you will not be able to transfer it to anyone. You have to claim your carry forward amount in the first year that you have to pay federal tax. Calculate the carry-forward amount on Schedule 11.

To view your carry-forward amounts, go to My Account on our Web site.

Schedule 1: Line 324 - Tuition, education, and textbook amounts transferred from a child

Schedule 1 - Line 324: Tuition and education amounts transferred from a child

ProFile calculates this amount using data from other forms and worksheets. To jump to a related form, right click on the field and select from the list of forms in the context-sensitive menu. You can also press <F6> when your cursor is in the field to jump to the first source form.

The Canada Revenue Agency says... *General Income Tax and Benefit Guide*

You may be the parent or grandparent of a student or his or her spouse or common-law partner. If so, the student may be able to transfer to you all or part of his or her tuition, education, and textbook amounts for 2009. The maximum tuition, education, and textbook amounts transferred from a child (or from each child) is $5,000 minus the amounts that he or she uses even if there is still an unclaimed part.

Note: The student cannot transfer to you any tuition, education, or textbook amounts carried forward from a previous year.

How to claim

The student has to complete Schedule 11 (particularly line 327) and attach it to his or her return, to calculate the transfer amount. The student must also complete any of the following applicable forms: Form T2202, Education and Textbook Amounts Certificate, Form T2202A, Tuition, Education, and Textbook Amounts Certificate, Form TL11A, Tuition, Education, and Textbook Amounts Certificate - University Outside Canada, Form TL11B, Tuition, Education, and Textbook Amounts Certificate - Flying School or Club , or TL11C, Tuition, Education, and Textbook Amounts Certificate - Commuter to the United States, to designate you as the person who can claim it. If the tuition fees being transferred to you are not shown on these forms, you should have a copy of the student's official tuition fee receipt.

Amounts claimed by student's spouse or common-law partner

If a student's spouse or common-law partner claims an amount on line 303 or 326 for the student, you cannot claim an amount on line 324 for that student. However, the student's spouse or common-law partner can include the transfer on line 326.

No amounts claimed by student's spouse or common-law partner

If the student's spouse or common-law partner does not claim an amount on line 303 or 326 for the student, or if the student does not have a spouse or common-law partner, the student can choose which parent or grandparent will claim an amount on line 324.

Only one person can claim this transfer from the student. However, it does not have to be the same parent or grandparent that claims an amount on line 305 or 306 for the student.

Schedule 1: Line 326 - Amounts transferred from your spouse or common-law partner

Schedule 1 - Line 326: Amounts transferred from your spouse or common-law partner

ProFile calculates this amount using data from other forms and worksheets. To jump to a related form, right click on the field and select from the list of forms in the context-sensitive menu. You can also press <F6> when your cursor is in the field to jump to the first source form.

The Canada Revenue Agency says... *General Income Tax and Benefit Guide*

You may be able to claim all or part of the following amounts for which your spouse or common-law partner qualifies:

- the age amount (line 301) if your spouse or common-law partner was 65 years of age or older;
- the amount for children born in 1992 or later (line 367);
- the pension income amount (line 314);
- the disability amount (line 316); and
- tuition, education, and textbook amounts (line 323) for 2009 that your spouse or common-law partner designates. The maximum amount that your spouse or common-law partner can transfer is $5,000 minus the amounts that he or she uses, even if there is still an unused part.

Note: Your spouse or common-law partner cannot transfer to you to any tuition, education, or textbook amounts carried forward from a previous year. In addition, he or she cannot transfer any unused amounts to you if you were separated because of a breakdown in your relationship for a period of 90 days or more that included December 31, 2009.

How to claim

Complete Schedule 2 to calculate your claim. Make sure you enter your marital status and the information concerning your spouse or common-law partner (including his or her net income, even if it is zero) in the Identification area on page 1 of your return.

If the amount on this line includes a new application for the disability amount, also attach a completed and certified Form T2201, Disability Tax Credit Certificate. We will review your claim before we assess your return to determine if your spouse or common-law partner qualifies. If he or she qualified for the disability amount for 2008 and still met the eligibility requirements in 2009, you can claim this amount without sending us a new Form T2201. However, you have to send us one if the previous period of approval ended before 2009 or we ask you to do so.

Schedule 1: Line 330 - Medical expenses for self, spouse or common-law partner, and your dependent children

Schedule 1 - Line 330: Medical expenses for self, spouse or common-law partner, and your dependent children born in 1988 or later

ProFile calculates this amount using data from Medical worksheet. Enter medical expenses on the Medical worksheet and ProFile will calculate for you the allowable portion of these claims. The Medical worksheet contains optimization for medical expense claims and allows for carry forwards of unclaimed expenses.

To jump to the related form, right click on the field and select the form in the context-sensitive menu. You can also press <F6> when your cursor is in the field to jump to the source form.

Frequently Asked Questions

What are examples of allowable medical expenses?

Eligible medical expenses

Your total expenses must be more than either 3% of your net income or $2,011, whichever is less.

This is a list of the more common medical expenses that you can claim, provided you were not reimbursed for them. If your employer or a private insurance or drug plan paid a percentage of the expenses, you can claim the remaining portion that you paid (see examples below).

- payments to a medical doctor, dentist, nurse, or certain other medical professionals, or to a public or licensed private hospital;
- payments for prescription medicines and drugs;
- dental services (including x-rays, fillings, extractions, oral surgery, dentures, and tooth straightening);
- prescription eyeglasses, prescription contact lenses, laser eye surgery, ;
- ambulance charges to or from hospital;
- premiums paid to private or non-government health services plans (other than those paid by an employer);
- artificial limbs, aids, and other devices and equipment (including artificial eyes and limbs, iron lung, a rocking bed for poliomyelitis victims, wheelchairs, crutches, spinal braces, a brace for a limb, ileostomy or colostomy pads, a truss for a hernia, laryngeal speaking aids, hearing aids, pacemakers, an artificial kidney machine, and certain prescription medical devices;
- repairs to and replacement batteries for the above;
- laboratory tests;
- hospital services (including anaesthesia, oxygen masks/tents, vaccines, and x-rays);
- amounts paid for attendant care, or care in an establishment, provided no one claimed the disability amount for the person receiving the care;
- devices designed to assist in daily living (for example, to enter or leave a bathtub or shower);
- special telephone devices to help people who are hearing-impaired.
- expenses relating to guide and hearing-ear dogs;
- cost of diabetic testing supplies;
- incremental cost of gluten-free food (compared to the cost of non-gluten-free food) if required due to Celica disease; and
- reasonable travel expenses (such as meals and accommodation), if medical treatment was not available locally.

Note: You cannot claim payments to a provincial health insurance plan (e.g., Ontario Health Insurance Plan (OHIP), Alberta Health Care Insurance Plan (AHCIP), and BC Medical Services Plan (MSP)).

Examples

Your medication cost $400. Your insurance paid 80% ($320) and you paid the remaining 20% ($80). You can claim the $80 that you paid.

> Your son's new braces cost $1,600 for the first consultation and $2,000 more over the next 10 months, for a total of $3,600. Your insurance plan covered 50% of the cost to a maximum of $1,500 and you paid the rest. You can claim the $2,100 that you paid.
>
> Your new glasses cost $375. Your insurance company paid their maximum of $250; your spouse's insurance paid the remaining $125. You cannot claim any of the expense, because you were fully reimbursed.

For a complete list of what you can claim as medical expenses, CRA publication IT519, Medical Expense and Disability Tax Credits and Attendant Care Expense Deduction.

What if I paid medical expenses for people other than my spouse or me?

Can I claim medical expenses for people other than my spouse or me?

In addition to being able to claim medical expenses for yourself and your spouse or common-law partner, you can also claim medical expenses that were paid for:

- you or your spouse or common-law partner's children or grandchildren who were dependent on you for support; and
- you or your spouse or common-law partner's parent, grandparent, brother, sister, uncle, aunt, niece, or nephew who lived in Canada and who were dependent on you for support.

Medical expenses for your spouse and dependant children 18 and under are claimed at line 330. The allowable amount of medical expenses for other dependants is claimed at line 331, and is subject to a maximum of $10,000.

 The Canada Revenue Agency says... *General Income Tax and Benefit Guide*

You can claim on line 330 the total eligible medical expenses you or your spouse or common-law partner paid for:

- yourself;
- your spouse or common-law partner; or
- you or your spouse's or common-law partner's child born in 1992 or later and who depended on you for support. Medical expenses for other dependants must be claimed on line 331.

You can claim medical expenses paid in any 12-month period ending in 2009 and not claimed for 2008. Generally, you can claim all amounts paid, even if they were not paid in Canada. Your total expenses have to be more than either 3% of your net income (line 236) or $2,011, whichever is less.

 Note:

- On the return for a person who died in 2009, a claim can be made for expenses paid in any 24month period that includes the date of death, if they were not claimed for any other year.
- If you are claiming expenses paid for a dependant who died in the year, these amounts can be claimed for any 24-month period that includes the date of death, if they were not claimed for any other year.

Tip: There is a refundable tax credit for working individuals with low incomes and high medical expenses. See line 452 for details.

Eligible medical expenses

Some eligible medical expenses that you can claim are:

- payments to a medical doctor, dentist, nurse, or certain other medical professionals, or to a public or licensed private hospital;
- premiums paid to private health services plans (other than those paid by an employer, such as the amount shown in box J of your Quebec Relevé 1 slip);
- premiums paid under a provincial or territorial prescription drug plan such as the Quebec Prescription Drug Insurance Plan and the Nova Scotia Seniors' Pharmacare Program (amounts or premiums paid to provincial or territorial government medical or hospitalization plans are not eligible);
- payments for artificial limbs, wheelchairs, crutches, hearing aids, prescription eyeglasses or contact lenses, dentures, pacemakers, prescription drugs, and certain prescription medical devices.

Tip: Alterations made to your dwelling to make it more accessible may also qualify for the home renovation expenses amount. For more information, see line 368. Home renovation expenses and Interpretation Bulletin IT-519 Medical Expense and Disability tax Credits and Attendant care Expense Deduction.

Under proposed changes, new eligible medical expenses include amounts paid to purchase, operate, and maintain the following devices if prescribed by a medical practitioner:

- altered auditory feedback devices for the treatment of a speech disorder;
- electrotherapy devices for the treatment of a medical condition or a severe mobility impairment;
- standing devices for standing therapy in the treatment of a severe mobility impairment; and
- pressure pulse therapy devices for the treatment of a balance disorder.

You can also claim amounts paid to purchase, care for and maintain a service animal specially trained to assist an individual who is severely affected by autism or epilepsy. Reasonable travel expenses incurred for the individual to attend a school, institution or other place that trains the individual in the handling of the service animal are also eligible.

See Guide RC4064, Medical and Disability-Related Information, for more information.

Reimbursement of an eligible expense

You can only claim the part of an expense for which you have not been or will not be reimbursed. However, you can claim all of the expense if the reimbursement is included in your income, such as a benefit shown on a T4 slip, and you did not deduct the reimbursement anywhere else on your return.

Travel expenses

If medical treatment is not available to you within 40 kilometres of your home, you may be able to claim the cost of travelling to get the treatment somewhere else. You can choose to simplify the way you calculate this amount. If you use the simplified method, you can find the rate per kilometre for each province or territory by going to travel expenses our website.

If you had to travel at least 80 kilometres from your home, you can deduct accommodation and meal expenses in addition to your travelling expenses.

For more information on medical expenses, see Guide RC4064, Medical and Disability-Related Information, and Interpretation Bulletin IT-519, Medical Expense and Disability Tax Credits and Attendant Care Expense Deduction.

Tip: Compare the result with the amount your spouse or common-law partner would be allowed. It may be better for the one of you with the lower net income (line 236) to claim the allowable medical expenses. You can make whichever claim you prefer.

How to calculate your claim (example)

Rick and his wife Paula have reviewed their medical bills and decided that the 12-month period ending in 2009 for which they will calculate their claim is July 1, 2008, through June 30, 2009. They incurred the following expenses:

Rick	$1,500
Paula	$1,000
Jenny (their 16-year-old daughter)	$1,800
Kyle (their 19-year-old son)	$1,000
Total medical expenses	**$5,300**

The total allowable expenses for 2009 are $4,300 which will be entered on line 330. As Kyle is over 18 years of age, his expenses will be reported on line 331.

Paula's net income on line 236 of her return is $32,000. She calculates 3% of that amount as $960. Because the result is less than $2,011, she enters $960 on the line below line 330 on Schedule 1 and subtracts it from $4,300. The difference is $3,340, which is the amount (A) above line 331.

Rick's net income on line 236 of his return is $48,000. He calculates 3% of that amount as $1,440. Because the result is less than $2,011, he enters $1,440 on the line below line 330, and subtracts it from $4,300. The difference is $2,860.

In this case, Paula and Rick have found it better for Paula to claim all the expenses for them and their daughter Jenny.

Disability-related expenses

You may be claiming expenses that would be allowable only for a patient who qualified for the disability amount on line 316. To qualify for the disability amount, a qualified practitioner must certify Form T2201, Disability Tax Credit Certificate, that an individual has a severe and prolonged mental or physical impairment. We must receive and approve this form before you can claim the expenses.

Schedule 1: Line 331- Allowable amount of medical expenses for other dependants

Schedule 1 - Line 331: Allowable amount of medical expenses for other dependants

ProFile calculates this T1 jacket amount using data from Medical worksheet.

To jump to the related form, right click on the field and select the form in the context-sensitive menu. You can also press <F6> when your cursor is in the field to jump to the source form.

 The Canada Revenue Agency says... *General Income Tax and Benefit Guide*

Claim the part of eligible medical expenses you or your spouse or common-law partner paid for the following persons who depended on you for support on line 331:

- your or your spouse's or common-law partner's child who was born in 1991 or earlier, or grandchild; or
- you or your spouse's or common-law partner's parent, grandparent, brother, sister, aunt, uncle, niece, or nephew who was a resident of Canada at any time in the year.

The expenses must meet the criteria in the section called "Eligible medical expenses" at line 330. Also, the claim must be for the same 12-month period that was determined under line 330.

For more information, see Guide RC4064, Medical and Disability-Related Information. This guide includes Form T2201.

You have to calculate, for each dependant, the medical expenses that you are claiming on this line. The total of these expenses must exceed the lesser of $2,011 and 3% of the dependant's net income for the year (line 236), up to a maximum of $10,000.

Other dependant's medical expenses	
Less: $2,011 or 3% of line 236 of that dependant (whichever is less)	-
Subtotal	=
Allowable medical expenses (maximum $10,000)	

Enter on line 331 the total of all allowable amounts in respect of each dependant.

Complete the appropriate part of Schedule 5 for each dependant and attach it to your paper return.

Example:

Dan has two dependant children, Marc, who is 19 years of age and has a net income of $6,000, and Ross, who is 21 years of age and has a net income of $8,000. Dan has paid $2,000 in medical expenses for Marc and $11,000 in medical expenses for Ross. Dan's calculations are:

Other dependant's medical expenses (Marc)	$2,000
Less: $2,011 or 3% of line 236 for Marc (whichever is less)	- $180
Subtotal	= $1,820
Allowable medical expenses for Marc (maximum $10,000)	**$1,820**
Other dependant's medical expenses (Ross)	$11,000
Less: $2,011 or 3% of line 236 for Ross (whichever is less)	- $240
Subtotal	= $10,760
Allowable medical expenses for Ross (maximum $10,000)	**$10,000**

> Dan has to complete Schedule 5 and claim $11,820 ($1,820 for Marc and $10,000 for Ross) at line 331.

Schedule 1 - Line 332: Allowable amount of medical expenses

Line 332 is the allowable portion of medical expenses. Enter medical claims on the Medical worksheet and ProFile will automatically calculate the allowable portion of these claims. The Medical worksheet contains optimization for medical expense claims and allows for carry forwards of unclaimed expenses.

Schedule 1 - Line 335: Non-refundable tax credit calculation

ProFile calculates this amount using data from other lines on the Schedule 1 in the Non-refundable tax credits section.

Schedule 1 - Line 338: Non-refundable tax credit calculation

This line represents non-refundable tax credits before claims for donations and gifts.

Schedule 1: Line 349 - Donations and gifts

Schedule 1 - Line 349: Donations and gifts

ProFile calculates this amount using data from other forms and worksheets. To jump to a related form, right click on the field and select from the list of forms in the context-sensitive menu. You can also press <F6> when your cursor is in the field to jump to the first source form.

The Canada Revenue Agency says... *General Income Tax and Benefit Guide*

You can claim donations either you or your spouse or common-law partner made. Enter your claim from the calculation on Schedule 9. See Pamphlet P113, Gifts and Income Tax, for more information about donations and gifts, or if you donated any of the following:

- gifts of property other than cash;
- gifts to organizations outside Canada; or
- gifts to Canada, a province, or a territory made after 1997 and agreed to in writing before February 19, 1997.

Note:

- These gifts do not include contributions to political parties. If you contributed to a federal political party, see lines 409 and 410 to find out about claiming a credit. If you contributed to a provincial or territorial political party, see the provincial or territorial forms in the forms book to find out about claiming a credit. If you are a resident of Quebec, refer to your provincial guide.
- Gifts to Canada include monetary gifts made directly to the federal Debt Servicing and Reduction Account. If you made such a gift, which will be used only to service the public debt, you should have received a tax receipt.
- To make a gift to this account, which should be made payable to the Receiver General, send it, along with a note asking that we apply it to this account, to:
    Place du Portage, Phase III

11 Laurier Street
Gatineau QC K1A 0S5

If you need more information about official receipts, see Interpretation Bulletin IT-110, Gifts and Official Donation Receipts.

Allowable charitable donations and government gifts (line 340 of Schedule 9)

Add up all of the eligible amounts of your donations made in 2009 plus any donations made in any of the previous five years that have not been claimed before. This includes unclaimed gifts to Canada, a province, or a territory made after 2003. However, if the gift was agreed to in writing before February 19, 1997, include it on line 342 of Schedule 9.

The eligible amount is the amount by which the fair market value of your gift or monetary contribution exceeds any advantage that you received or will receive for making the donation or gift. Generally, an advantage includes the value of certain property, service, compensation, use or any other benefit. This proposed change applies to any donations or gifts made after December 20, 2002. For more information, see Pamphlet P113, Gifts and Income Tax.

Generally, you can claim on line 340 all or part of this amount, up to a limit of 75% of your net income (line 236). For the year a person dies and the year before that, this limit is 100% of the person's net income.

Note: If you have taken a vow of perpetual poverty as a member of a religious order, this limit does not apply. Claim your donations on line 256.

Tip: You do not have to claim, on your return for 2009, the donations you made in 2009. It may be more beneficial for you not to claim them for 2009, but to carry them forward and claim them on your return for any of the next five years. No matter how you claim them, you can claim them only once.

Qualified donees

Generally, you can claim only amounts you gave to registered charities and other qualified donees. For a list of the types of donees that qualify, see Pamphlet P113, Gifts and Income Tax.

Cultural and ecological gifts (line 342 of Schedule 9)

Unlike other donations, your total eligible amount claimed for these types of gifts is not limited to a percentage of net income. You can choose the part you want to claim in 2009 and carry forward any unused parts for up to five years. For more information about the amount to claim for these gifts, see Pamphlet P113, Gifts and Income Tax.

Schedule 1 - Line 350: Total non-refundable tax credits

This line represents the total non-refundable tax credits including claims for donations and gifts.

Schedule 1: Line 363 - Canada employment amount

Schedule 1 - Line 363: Canada employment amount

This credit is implemented in recognition of work-related expenses incurred by employees. All employees are eligible to claim this employment amount.

 The Canada Revenue Agency says... *General Income Tax and Benefit Guide*

Claim the lesser of:

- $1,044; and
- the total of the employment income you reported on lines 101 and line 104 of your return.

Schedule 1: Line 364 - Public transit amount

Schedule 1 - Line 364: Public transit passes amount

Consult the CRA guide information below for details regarding this line.

 Frequently Asked Questions

Common questions about the public transit pass credit

Can I claim daily or weekly costs?

Not usually. The CRA only allows you to claim passes for monthly or longer duration.

For exceptions, see line 364, Public transit amount.

Can I claim taxi fare?

No. The credit applies only to monthly (or longer) passes for commuting on buses, streetcars, subways, commuter trains and local ferries.

Can I claim a transit credit if I purchased a U-pass as part of my university tuition?

Yes. Your university should issue you a separate U-pass receipt along with your T2202A slip. Use this to claim the transit credit for the applicable months.

 The Canada Revenue Agency says... *General Income Tax and Benefit Guide*

You can claim the cost of monthly public transit passes or passes of longer duration such as an annual pass for travel within Canada on public transit during the year. These passes must permit unlimited travel on local buses, streetcars, subways, commuter trains or buses, and local ferries.

You can also claim the cost of shorter duration passes if each pass entitles you to unlimited travel for an uninterrupted period of at least 5 days and you purchase enough of these passes so that you are entitled to unlimited travel for at least 20 days in any 28-day period.

You can claim the cost of electronic payment cards when used to make at least 32 one-way trips during an uninterrupted period not exceeding 31 days.

Only you or your spouse or common-law partner can claim the cost of transit passes (to the extent that these amounts have not already been claimed) for:

- yourself;

- your spouse's or common-law partner; and
- you or your spouse's or common-law partner's children who are under 19 years of age on December 31.

Reimbursement of an eligible expense

You can only claim the part of the amount for which you have not been or will not be reimbursed. However, you can claim all the amount if the reimbursement is included in your income (such as a benefit shown on a T4 slip) and you did not deduct the reimbursement anywhere else on your return.

Schedule 1: Line 365 - Children's fitness amount

Schedule 1 - Line 365: Children's fitness amount

ProFile calculates this amount based on the fitness amounts entered for children in the Dependant worksheet.

To jump to a related form, right click on the field and select from the list of forms in the context-sensitive menu. You can also press <F6> when your cursor is in the field to jump to the first source form.

 The Canada Revenue Agency says... *General Income Tax and Benefit Guide*

You can claim to a maximum of $500 per child, the fees paid in 2009 that relate to the cost of registering your or your spouse's or common-law partner's child in a prescribed program of physical activity. The child must have been under 16 years of age or under 18 years of age if eligible for the disability amount at the beginning of the year in which an eligible fitness expense was paid.

You can claim this amount provided that another person has not already claimed the same fees and that the total claimed is not more than the maximum amount that would be allowed if only one of you were claiming the amount.

Children with disabilities

If the child qualifies for the disability amount and is under 18 years of age at the beginning of the year, an additional amount of $500 can be claimed provided that a minimum of $100 is paid on registration or membership fees for a prescribed program of physical activity.

Note: You may have paid an amount that would qualify to be claimed as child care expenses (line 214) and the children's fitness amount. If this is the case, you must first claim this amount as child care expenses. Any unused part can be claimed for the children's fitness amount as long as the requirements are met.

Prescribed program

To qualify for this amount, a program **must**:

- be ongoing (either a minimum of eight weeks duration with a minimum of one session per week or, in the case of children's camps, five consecutive days);
- be supervised;
- be suitable for children; and

- require significant physical activity (generally, most of the activities must include a significant amount of physical activity that contributes to cardio respiratory endurance plus muscular strength, muscular endurance, flexibility and/or balance).

Note:

For a child who qualifies for the disability amount, the requirement for significant physical activity is met if the activities result in movement and in an observable use of energy in a recreational context.

Physical activity includes horseback riding, but does not include activities where, as an essential component, a child rides on or in a motorized vehicle.

Reimbursement of an eligible expense

You can only claim the part of the amount for which you have not been or will not be reimbursed. However, you can claim all of the amount if the reimbursement is included in your income (such as a benefit shown on a T4 slip), and you did not deduct the reimbursement anywhere else on your return.

Schedule 1: Line 367 - Amount for children born in 1992 or later

The Canada Revenue Agency says... *General Income Tax and Benefit Guide*

You can claim $2,089 for each of your or your spouse's or common-law partner's children who are under 18 years of age at the end of the year if the child resided with both of you throughout the year.

The full amount can be claimed in the year of the child's birth, death, or adoption.

Note:

- If you are making this claim for more than one child, either you or your spouse or common-law partner must make the claim for all children under 18 years of age at the end of the year and who resided with both of you throughout the year.
- If you have shared custody of the child throughout the year but cannot agree who will claim the amount, no one can make the claim for that child.

If the child **did not reside** with both parents throughout the year, the parent or the spouse or common-law partner who claims the amount for an eligible dependant (see line 305) for that child can make the claim.

Note:

You can still claim this amount for the child if you were unable to claim for an eligible dependant because:

- the child's net income was more than $10,320; or
- you are already claiming the amount for an eligible dependant for another child.

If you have shared custody of the child throughout the year but cannot agree who will claim the amount, no one can make the claim for that child.

If you and another person were required to make support payments for the child in 2009 and, as a result, no one would be entitled to claim either this amount or the amount for an eligible dependant for the child, you can still claim this amount provided you and the other person(s) paying support agree you will be the one making the claim. If you cannot agree who will claim this amount for the child, no one can make the claim for that child.

  Tip: You may be able to transfer all or part of this amount to your spouse or common-law partner or to claim all or part of his or her amount. For more information, see line 326.

T1 Guide: Line 405 - Federal foreign tax credit

The Canada Revenue Agency says... *General Income Tax and Benefit Guide*

This credit is for foreign income or profits taxes you paid on income you received from outside Canada and reported on your Canadian tax return. Complete Form T2209, Federal Foreign Tax Credits, to calculate your credit and enter the amount from line 10 on line 405 of Schedule 1.

Note: You may have deducted an amount on line 256 for income that is not taxable in Canada under a tax treaty. In that case, do not include that income, or any tax withheld from it, in your foreign tax credit calculation.

Receipts

If you are filing a paper return, include your completed Form T2209 and documents, such as official receipts, that show the foreign taxes you paid. If you paid taxes to the United States, attach your W-2 information slip, U.S. 1040 return, and any other supporting documents that apply. If you are filing electronically, keep all of your documents in case we ask to see them.

Schedule 1: Lines 409 and 410 - Federal political

Schedule 1 - Lines 409 and 410: Federal political contribution tax credit

ProFile calculates this amount using data from other forms and worksheets. To jump to a related form, right click on the field and select from the list of forms in the context-sensitive menu. You can also press <F6> when your cursor is in the field to jump to the first source form.

The Canada Revenue Agency says... *General Income Tax and Benefit Guide*

Enter on line 409 the total you and your spouse or common-law partner contributed during 2009 to a registered federal political party or a candidate for election to the House of Commons.

The **eligible amount** is the amount by which the fair market value of your gift or monetary contribution exceeds any advantage that you received or will receive for making it. Generally, an advantage includes the value of certain property, service, compensation, use, or any other benefit. This applies to any contribution made after December 20, 2002.

Complete the chart for line 410 on the Federal Worksheet in the forms book to calculate your credit. However, if your total political contributions are $1,275 or more, enter $650 on line 410.

Schedule 1: Line 412 - Investment tax credit

Schedule 1 - Line 412: Investment tax credit

ProFile calculates this amount using data from other forms and worksheets. To jump to a related form, right click on the field and select from the list of forms in the context-sensitive menu. You can also press <F6> when your cursor is in the field to jump to the first source form.

The Canada Revenue Agency says... *General Income Tax and Benefit Guide*

You may be eligible for this credit if any of the following apply. You:

- bought certain new buildings, machinery, or equipment and they were used in certain areas of Canada in qualifying activities such as farming, fishing, logging, manufacturing, or processing;
- have unclaimed credits from the purchase of qualified property after 1998;
- have an amount shown in box 41 of your T3 slip;
- have an amount shown in box 107 or 128 of your T5013 or T5013A slip;
- have an amount shown in box 128 of your T101 slip;
- have a partnership statement that allocates to you an amount that qualifies for this credit; or
- have an investment in a mining operation that allocates certain exploration expenditures to you; or
- employ an eligible apprentice in your business.

You can claim an investment tax credit if you carry on a business and create one or more new child care spaces for children of your employees and other children. For more information, see Form T2038(IND), Investment Tax Credit (Individuals).

For investment tax credits earned in a year after 2005, the carry-forward period is 20 years.

The deadline to claim the mineral exploration tax credit on qualifying expenses renounced under flow-through share agreements has been extended to March 31, 2010.

How to claim

Attach to your paper return a completed copy of Form T2038(IND), Investment Tax Credit (Individuals). For more information on the investment tax credit, see the information sheet attached to Form T2038(IND).

The time to submit Form T2038(IND) for a qualifying expenditure is limited. To be able to claim a credit for such an expenditure, you have to send the form to us no later than 12 months after the due date of your return for the year the expenditure arises.

 Tip: You may be able to claim a refund of your unused investment tax credit (see line 454).

Schedule 1: Lines 413 and 414 - Labour-sponsored funds tax credit

Schedule 1 - Lines 413 and 414: Labour-sponsored funds tax credit

ProFile calculates this amount using data from other forms and worksheets. To jump to a related form, right click on the field and select from the list of forms in the context-sensitive menu. You can also press <F6> when your cursor is in the field to jump to the first source form.

The Canada Revenue Agency says... *General Income Tax and Benefit Guide*

You may be able to claim this credit if you became the first registered holder to acquire, or irrevocably subscribe to and pay for, an approved share of the capital stock of a prescribed labour sponsored venture capital corporation (LSVCC) from January 1, 2009, to March 1, 2010.

Under proposed changes, if you bought shares after 2003 of a provincial or territorial registered LSVCC (that is not a federally registered LSVCC), you can only claim the federal labour-sponsored funds tax credit in respect of those shares if a provincial or territorial income tax credit is also available to be claimed for them.

If you became the first registered holder of an approved share from January 1, 2009, to March 2, 2009, and did not claim the whole credit for it on your 2008 return, you can claim the unused part on your 2009 return.

If you became the first registered holder of an approved share from January 1, 2010, to March 1, 2010, you can claim any part of the credit for that share on your return for 2009 and the unused part on your return for 2010.

Enter your net cost on line 413. Net cost is the amount you paid for your shares, minus any government assistance (other than federal or provincial tax credits) on the shares. Enter the amount of the credit on line 414. The allowable credit cannot be more than 15% of the net cost, to a maximum of $750.

Note: If the first registered holder of the share is an RRSP for spouse or common-law partner, either the RRSP contributor or the annuitant can claim this credit for that share.

Tip: Your province or territory may offer a similar tax credit. For details, see the provincial or territorial forms in the forms book, unless you were a resident of Quebec on December 31, 2009. In that case, see the guide for your provincial income tax return for Quebec.

Schedule 1: Line 415 - Working Income Tax Benefit (WITB) advance payments

Schedule 1 - Line 415: Working Income Tax Benefit advance payments

ProFile calculates this amount using data from the RC210 slip.

To jump to the related form, right click on the field and select the form in the context-sensitive menu. You can also press <F6> when your cursor is in the field to jump to the source form.

The Canada Revenue Agency says... *General Income Tax and Benefit Guide*

If you received WITB advance payments in 2009, enter the amount from box 10 of your RC210 slip. To view your RC210 slip online, go to My Account on our Web site. For more information, visit our Web site or see Pamphlet RC4227, Working Income Tax Benefit.

Note: If you can claim the WITB for 2009, complete Schedule 6 to calculate the amount to which you may be entitled.

T1 Guide: Line 418 - Additional tax on RESP accumulated income payments

Schedule 1 - Line 418: Additional tax on RESP accumulated income payments

ProFile calculates this amount using data from other forms and worksheets. To jump to a related form, right click on the field and select from the list of forms in the context-sensitive menu. You can also press <F6> when your cursor is in the field to jump to the first source form.

The Canada Revenue Agency says... *General Income Tax and Benefit Guide*

You may have received an accumulated income payment from a registered education savings plan (RESP) in 2009. If so, you may have to pay an additional tax on all or part of the amount shown in box 40 of your T4A slip.

Enter the amount from line 10, 13, or 16 (whichever applies) on Form T1172, Additional Tax on Accumulated Income Payments from RESPs.

For more information, see Guide RC4092, Registered Education Savings Plans (RESPs).

Schedule 1 - Line 420: Net federal tax

Line 420 is the net federal tax calculated before provincial tax and tax credits are applied.

T1 Guide: Line 424 - Federal tax on split income

Schedule 1 - Line 424: Federal tax on split income

ProFile carries this amount from Line 5 of form T1206 - Tax on split income.

To jump to a related form, right click on the field and select from the list of forms in the context sensitive menu. You can also press <F6> when your cursor is in the field to jump to the first source form.

The Canada Revenue Agency says... *General Income Tax and Benefit Guide*

Certain income of a child who was born in 1992or later is treated differently. This income is not subject to the rules discussed in "Loans and transfers of property" in Total income. It is subject to a special tax, but also qualifies for a deduction. This applies to the following amounts received either directly or through a trust (other than a mutual fund trust) or partnership:

- dividends from shares (not including those in a mutual fund corporation or listed on a designated stock exchange); and
- shareholder benefits that relate to shares that are not listed on a prescribed stock exchange.

The above also applies to income from a trust (other than a mutual fund trust) or partnership for providing property or services to (or in support of) a business operated by:

- someone related to the child at any time in the year;
- a corporation that has a specified shareholder who is related to the child at any time in the year; or
- a professional corporation that has a shareholder who is related to the child at any time in the year.

The special tax and deduction do not apply if:

- the income is from property that the child inherits from a parent;
- the income is from property inherited by the child from anyone else and, during the year, he or she either is enrolled full-time in a post-secondary institution or qualifies for the disability amount (line 316 on Schedule 1);
- the child was a non-resident of Canada at any time in the year; or
- neither of the child's parents were residents of Canada at any time in the year.

How to report

The child still reports the income on the appropriate lines of his or her return. However, he or she can claim a deduction on line 232 for this income. The special tax is included in the calculation of his or her federal and provincial or territorial taxes.

If this tax applies, calculate it on Form T1206, Tax on Split Income, and enter the amount from line 5 on line 424 on Schedule 1.

Attach a completed copy to the child's paper return.

Schedule 1: Line 425 - Federal dividend tax credit

Schedule 1 - Line 425: Federal dividend tax credit

ProFile calculates this amount based on the dividends reported on Line 120 or Line 180 of the T1 return.

To jump to a related form, right click on the field and select from the list of forms in the context sensitive menu. You can also press <F6> when your cursor is in the field to jump to the first source form.

The Canada Revenue Agency says... *General Income Tax and Benefit Guide*

If you reported dividends on line 120, enter on line 425 of Schedule 1 the total of the dividend tax credits from taxable Canadian corporations shown on your information slips.

If you received eligible dividends, the federal dividend tax credit is 18.9655% of your taxable amount of eligible dividends included on line 120.

If you received dividends (other than eligible), the federal dividend tax credit is 13.3333% of your taxable amount of dividends reported on line 180.

For explanations on eligible and other than eligible dividends, see line 120 of this guide.

Note: Foreign dividends do not qualify for this credit.

Schedule 1: Line 426 - Overseas employment tax credit

Schedule 1 - Line 426: Overseas employment tax credit

ProFile carries this amount from Line 6774 of form T626 - Overseas Employment Tax Credit.

To jump to a related form, right click on the field and select from the list of forms in the context-sensitive menu. You can also press <F6> when your cursor is in the field to jump to the first source form.

The Canada Revenue Agency says... *General Income Tax and Benefit Guide*

You may be able to claim this credit if both of the following apply for 2009:

- you were a resident or deemed resident of Canada at any time in the year; and
- you have employment income from certain kinds of work you did in another country.

To make your claim, use Form T626 Overseas Employment Tax Credit, and mail it with your tax return to the

International Tax Services Office

2204 Walkley Road

Ottawa, ON, K1A 1A8

For more information, see Interpretation Bulletin It-497, Overseas Employment Tax Credit, and Form T626.

Schedule 1: Line 427 - Minimum Tax Carryover

Schedule 1 - Line 427: Minimum tax carryover

If the taxpayer paid minimum tax on previous returns, but does not have to pay minimum tax for the current year, credits might be claimable for all or part of the minimum tax paid in previous years. ProFile automatically carries the amount for Line 427 from form T691 - Alternative Minimum Tax.

To jump to a related form, right click on the field and select from the list of forms in the context-sensitive menu. You can also press <F6> when your cursor is in the field to jump to the first source form.

The Canada Revenue Agency says... *General Income Tax and Benefit Guide*

If you paid minimum tax on any of your 2002 to 2008 returns, but you do not have to pay minimum tax for 2009, you may be able to claim credits against your taxes for 2009 for all or part of the minimum tax you paid in those years.

To calculate your claim, complete the parts of Form T691, Alternative Minimum Tax, that apply. Attach the form to your paper return.

Schedule 2 - Federal Amounts Transferred From Your Spouse or Common-Law Partner

S2: Amounts transferred from your spouse

If you are processing the spousal returns together (i.e. coupled tax returns), ProFile will automatically claim these amounts on Schedule 2 where applicable.

T1 jacket line number

The calculation on Schedule 2 transfers automatically to line 326, Amounts transferred from your spouse.

The Canada Revenue Agency says... *Schedule 2, Federal Amounts Transferred From Your Spouse or Common-law Partner*

Complete this schedule to claim a transfer of the unused amount from your spouse or common-law partner's age amount, amount for children born in 1992 or later, pension income amount, disability amount, and tuition, education, and textbook amounts.

If your spouse or common-law partner is not filing a return, use the amounts that he or she would enter on his or her return, schedules, and worksheet if filing a return. Attach his or her information slips but do not attach the return or schedules.

Attach a copy of this schedule to your return. See Line 326 - Amounts transferred from your spouse or common-Law partner for more information.

Eligible federal amounts that can be transferred include:

- the age amount from line 301 if your spouse or common-law partner was 65 or older in 2009 and his or her net income was $31,524 or less, enter $5,276; otherwise, enter his or her amount on line 301;
- the amount for children born in 1991 or later;
- the pension income amount from line 314;
- the disability amount from line 316; and
- the tuition, education, and textbook amounts (line 323) from the current tax year as designated in your name on the back of his or her T2202, T2202A, TL11A, TL11B, or TL11C.

Note: Your spouse or common-law partner cannot transfer any unused amounts to you if you were separated because of a breakdown in your relationship for a period of 90 days or more that included December 31, 2009.

Receipts

Attach to your paper return the completed Schedule 2. If your spouse or common-law partner is not filing a return, also attach his or her information slips (but not his or her return or schedules).

Do not include any receipts or forms, other than your own Schedule 2, for your spouse or common-law partner's tuition, education, and textbook amounts, but keep them in case we ask to see them.

If you are filing electronically, keep all of your documents.

Non-Residents

This credit is not available to a non-resident unless all or substantially all (90%) of income is from business, employment, scholarships, bursaries, or grants from Canada and is not protected by treaty. For further details, see Non-residents.

Schedule 3 - Capital gains (or losses)

S3: Capital gains (or losses)

A capital gain or a capital loss usually occurs when you sell or dispose of property, such as real estate or shares. The taxable part of a capital gain is a percentage of the net amount of your capital gains minus your capital losses for the year. If you have gains or losses shown on T3, T4PS, T5 or T5013 slips, ProFile automatically enters the total on line 174 of Schedule 3. Enter other capital gains on the S3Details worksheet.

ProFile uses Schedule 3 to calculate your taxable capital gains or allowable capital losses and attach the completed schedule to your return. ProFile uses expandable tables for the Capital Gains (Losses) on Schedule 3. As you enter each amount, ProFile adds a new line to the table for your next entry. If you enter enough data into this form, ProFile will print it in multiple pages -- therefore, there is no need for "supplementary schedules." This multiple page format is acceptable for submission to CRA.

If your securities transactions are indicated on an account statement or a T5008 slip, use the information on these documents to help you complete Schedule 3.

ProFile transfers taxable capital gains from Schedule 3 to line 127 of the T1 jacket. If you have a net capital loss, this amount transfers to form T1A. You can use the loss to reduce your taxable capital gains of other years.

 The Canada Revenue Agency says... *Capital Gains Guide (T4037)*

This form provides a summary of your capital dispositions for the year.

Completing the form

For more information on specific lines of the form, see the following topics:

- Line 107 - Qualified small business corporation shares
- Line 110 - Qualified farm property
- Line 110 - Qualified fish property
- Line 132 - Mutual funds and other shares
- Line 138 - Real estate and depreciable property
- Line 153 - Bonds, debentures, promissory notes and other properties
- Line 155 - Other mortgage foreclosures and conditional sales repossessions
- Line 158 - Personal-use property
- Line 159 - Listed personal property
- Line 161 - Capital gains deferral for investment in small business
- Line 173 - Eligible farming and fishing income

Calculating your capital gain or loss

To calculate any capital gain or loss, you need to know the following three amounts:

- the proceeds of disposition
- the adjusted cost base (ACB)
- the outlays and expenses you incurred when selling your property

To calculate your capital gain or loss, subtract the total of your property's ACB, and any outlays and expenses incurred to sell your property, from the proceeds of disposition.

You have a capital gain when you sell, or are considered to have sold, a capital property for more than the total of its ACB and the outlays and expenses incurred to sell the property.

For more information see the CRA's guide T4037, Capital Gains.

Schedule 3 - Line 199 - Capital losses

If you have a net capital loss, it is calculated on line 199 of Schedule 3, but you cannot claim it on line 127 of your T1 General. You can only use it to reduce your taxable capital gains of other years. If you incurred a net capital loss in 2009, and you want to apply it against taxable capital gains you reported on one of your previous 3 years' returns, complete Form T1A, Request for Loss Carry back. Include this form with your 2009 return. Do not file an amended return for the year or years to which you want to apply the loss.

Did you file a capital gains election in 1994?

If you are reporting a capital gain from the disposition of property for which you filed (in a previous year) Form T664, Election to Report a Capital Gain on Property Owned at the End of February 22, 1994, you may be able to reduce all or part of the gain.

If you filed Form T664 for your shares of, or interest in a flow through entity, and the proceeds of disposition you indicated on the form for your investment were more than its fair market value, the adjusted cost base (ACB) of your investment may be affected.

Property bought before 1972

If you are reporting a capital gain on property that you bought before 1972, you have to apply a special set of rules. You apply these rules because you did not have to pay tax on capital gains before 1972. For further details see Property bought before 1972.

Capital gains deduction

The capital gains deduction is available in 2009 for the following dispositions only:

- Qualified farm property
- Qualified small business corporation shares

Business investment losses

Do not use Schedule 3 to claim an allowable business investment loss (ABIL) from disposing of shares or debts of a small business corporation. For more information, see Business investment losses - Line 217.

What other forms do you complete?

You may have to complete one or more of the following related forms:

- T657 - Capital Gains Deduction Calculation
- T936 - Cumulative Net Investment Loss (CNIL)
- T2017 - Reserves on Dispositions of Capital Property
- T1A

Schedule 4 - Statement of Investment Income

S4: Statement of investment income

Use this form to enter your investment income that does not have supporting slips. ProFile will expand the entry tables as required. ProFile also transfers any amounts you enter on the various information slip forms (T3, T5, etc) to Schedule 4.

If you enter a % share to spouse on a T5 slip, ProFile automatically calculates the value and posts only the taxpayer's amount to Schedule 4 with a description of the calculation (e.g. (Royal Bank 45% of 1000)). If you are processing coupled returns, the spousal percentage will also transfer automatically to the spouse's Schedule 4.

ProFile uses expandable tables for the Investment Information on Schedule 4. As you enter each amount, ProFile adds a new line to the table for your next entry. If you enter enough data into this form, ProFile will print it in multiple pages -- therefore, there is no need for "supplementary schedules." This multiple page format is acceptable for submission to CRA.

Values calculated on Schedule 4 flow to the corresponding lines of the T1 jacket.

 The Canada Revenue Agency says...

State the names of the payers and attach any information slips you received. Attach a separate sheet of paper if you need more space. Attach a copy of this schedule to your return.

Schedule 5 - Details of Dependant

S5: Details of dependant

Based on the information you provide on the Dependant worksheet, ProFile automatically calculates the claim on Schedule 5. The calculation takes into account the age of the dependant, dependant net income and infirmity.

Equivalent to spouse

ProFile will automatically complete the line 305 calculation on Schedule 5 if you answer "Yes" to the question "Claim as equivalent to spouse?" on the Dependant worksheet.

Amount for infirm dependants age 18 or older

ProFile will complete this Schedule 5 claim automatically if you indicate an infirmity on the Dependant worksheet and answer "Yes" to the question "Qualify for the disability amount?". On the Dependant worksheet, you must also enter a percentage amount for the Schedule 5 claim you would like to make. Depending on the dependant's net income, ProFile will automatically select the correct claim for either this amount or the caregiver amount.

Caregiver Amount

Based on the information you provide on the Dependant worksheet, ProFile automatically completes Schedule 5 to claim the caregiver amount. You may be able to claim this amount for the taxation year if you maintained a dwelling where you and a dependant lived. ProFile automatically transfers the details concerning your dependants from the Dependant worksheet to Schedule 5. Depending on the dependant's net income, ProFile will automatically select the correct claim for either this amount or the disability amount.

🍁 **The Canada Revenue Agency says...** *Schedule 5 - Details of Dependant*

If you are making a claim for a dependant on Line 305 - Amount for an eligible dependant, Line 306 - Amounts for infirm dependants, Line 315 - Caregiver amount, or Line 331 - Allowable amount of medical expenses for other dependants, the CRA requires information about your dependants on Schedule 5.

See each line number below for details on entering this information.

Schedule 6 - Working Income Tax Benefit

S6: Working Income Tax Benefit

Complete this schedule for a taxpayer who is eligible for the Working Income Tax Benefit (WITB).

The WITB is a refundable tax credit, payable to low-income earning individuals with employment or business income, for 2007 and subsequent taxation years.

Schedule 6 allows you to :

- calculate the basic WITB
- calculate the supplementary WITB for individuals entitled to the disability tax credit

Schedule 6 is province or territory specific. As such, four versions of Schedule 6 are available, each with different rates and base amounts. ProFile will automatically select which version of Schedule 6 is opened, based on the taxpayer's province of residence (as entered on the Info form).

The chart below describes which form version of Schedule 6 will be used to calculate the WITB, for each province and territory. If applicable, ProFile will transfer the WITB credit from Schedule 6 to line 453 of the T1 jacket.

Provinces and Territories	Form Version
AB, MB, NB, NL, NS, ON, PE, SK, NT, YT	5000
BC	5010
QC	5005
NU	5014

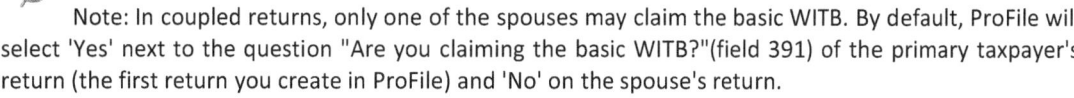

Note: In coupled returns, only one of the spouses may claim the basic WITB. By default, ProFile will select 'Yes' next to the question "Are you claiming the basic WITB?"(field 391) of the primary taxpayer's return (the first return you create in ProFile) and 'No' on the spouse's return.

Who should claim

- If you had an eligible spouse, the one with the higher working income should claim the basic WITB.
- If you had an eligible spouse, and one of you qualified for the disability amount and has sufficient working income, that person should claim both the basic WITB and the WITB disability supplement regardless of who has the higher working income.

- If you had an eligible spouse, and both of you qualified for the disability amount and have sufficient working income, the one with the higher working income should claim the basic WITB. However, each of you must claim the WITB disability supplement on a separate Schedule 6.

The Canada Revenue Agency says... *Schedule 6 - Working Income Tax Benefit*

Complete this schedule and attach a copy of it to your return to claim the working income tax benefit (WITB) if:

	AB, MB, NB, NL, NS, NT, PE, SK, YT	BC	NU	QC	ON
you were single with no eligible dependants and your adjusted family net income (Step 1, Part B) is less than	$17,733	$18,265	$34,500	$18,373.99	$16,667
or you had an eligible spouse eligible spouse or an eligible dependant and your adjusted family net income (Step 1, Part B) is less than	$25,100	$26,235	$40,000	$28,298.34	$25,700

Note: If you were married or living in a common-law relationship but did not have an eligible spouse or an eligible dependants, complete this schedule using the instructions as if you were single.

You must also meet all of the following conditions in 2009:

- you were a resident of Canada throughout the year;
- you earned income from employment or business;
- at the end of the year, you were 19 years of age or older, or you had an eligible spouse, or you had an eligible dependant.

You cannot claim the WITB if in 2009:

- you were enrolled as a full-time student at a designated educational institution for more than 13 weeks in the year, unless you had an eligible dependant at the end of the year;
- you were confined to a prison or similar institution for a period of 90 days or more during the year.

Note: If you are completing a final return for a deceased person who met the above conditions, you can claim the WITB for that person if the date of death was after June 30, 2009.

Calculating your basic WITB

If you have an eligible spouse, only one of you can claim the basic WITB. If you have an eligible dependant, you and another person cannot both claim the basic WITB for that same eligible dependant.

Calculating your WITB disability supplement

If you were single with no eligible dependants, you qualify for the disability amount and the amount on line 15 in Step 1 is less than $14,777*, complete Step 3 to calculate your WITB disability supplement. Otherwise, enter the amount from line 28 on line 453 of your return.

If you qualify for the disability amount, you had an eligible spouse or an eligible dependant, and the amount on line 15 in Step 1 is less than $23,269**, complete Step 3 to calculate your WITB disability supplement. Otherwise, enter the amount from line 28 on line 453 of your return.

If you had an eligible spouse, both of you qualify for the disability amount, and the amount on line 15 in Step 1 is less than $24,969***, complete Step 3 to calculate your WITB disability supplement. Your eligible spouse must complete Step 1 and Step 3 on a separate Schedule 6 to calculate his or her WITB disability supplement. Otherwise, enter the amount from line 28 on line 453 of your return.

CONTENT	AB, MB, NB, NL, NS, NT, PE, SK, YT	BC	NU	QC	ON
*	$20,817	$21,294	$36,433	$20,977.09	$19,750
**	$28,183	$29,264	$41,933	$23,377.09	$28,783
***	$31,267	$32,294	$43,867	$25,777.09	$31,867

Schedule 7 - RRSP Unused Contributions, Transfers and HBP or LPP Activities

S7: RRSP unclaimed contributions

Complete this schedule if any of the following situations applies to you:

- You will not be deducting on this return all of the contributions you made to your own or your spouse's RRSP from March 2, 2009 to March 1, 2010. Include all of these contributions on line 2, even if you are not going to deduct them this year. This will enable CRA to correctly show on your Notice of Assessment, your un-deducted contributions (contributions made but not yet deducted) available to deduct on your 2009 return.
- You claimed a deduction on line 208 for eligible income you reported on line 115, 129 or 130 of your return and transferred to your RRSP.
- You want to designate all or part of your RRSP contributions as a Home Buyers' Plan (HBP) or Life Long Learning Plan (LLP) repayment.

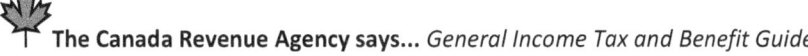
The Canada Revenue Agency says... *General Income Tax and Benefit Guide*

You may not have to complete Schedule 7. To find out, read the information at the top of the schedule. If you do have to complete it, you will find information below about lines 1, 2, 3, 6, 7, 10, 11, and 15 to 18.

Line 1 - Unused RRSP contributions

These are amounts you contributed to your own RRSP or to an RRSP for your spouse or common-law partner after 1990, but did not deduct on line 208 of any previous return or designate as an HBP or LLP repayment. The total of these amounts is shown on your Notice of Assessment or Notice of Reassessment for 2008 or on Form T1028, Your RRSP Information for 2009, if you showed them on a previous year's Schedule 7.

If you do not have your notice, you can find out if you have unused RRSP contributions by using RRSP deduction limit, by going to My Account on our website..

Note:

- If you have unused RRSP contributions that you made from March 2, 2008, to March 2, 2009, you should have filed a completed Schedule 7 with your 2008 paper return. If you did not, you should submit your receipts and a completed copy of a 2008 Schedule 7 to your tax centre, but not with your return for 2009.

See How do you change a return? for details.

- If you have unused contributions that you made from January 1, 1991, to March 2, 2008, but did not show on a Schedule 7 for 2007 or earlier, contact us.

More about unused RRSP contributions

Lines 2 and 3 - Total RRSP contributions

This total includes amounts you:

- contributed to your own RRSP or an RRSP for your spouse or common-law partner from March 3, 2009, to March 1, 2010;
- transferred to your own RRSP (see "Line 11 -Transfers" below); and
- designate as Home Buyers' Plan (HBP) or Lifelong Learning Plan (LLP) repayments (see "Lines 6 and 7 - Repayments under the HBP and LLP" in the next section).

Make sure you include on these lines all contributions you made from January 1, 2010, to March 1, 2010, even if you are not deducting or designating them on your return for 2009. Otherwise, we may reduce or disallow your claim for these contributions on your return for a future year.

Tip: If you have made deductible RRSP contributions for 2009 (other than transfers) from March 3, 2009, to March 1, 2010, you do not have to claim the full amount on line 208 of your 2009 return. Depending on your federal and provincial or territorial rates of tax for 2009, and your expected rates of tax for future years, it may be more beneficial for you to claim, if applicable, only part of your contributions on line 10 of Schedule 7 and on line 208 of your 2009 return. The contributions you do not claim for 2009 will then be available for you to carry forward and claim for future years when your federal and provincial or territorial rates of tax are higher.

Remember, in either case, you must record the total contributions you made from March 3, 2009, to March 1, 2010, on either line 2 or 3 and line 245 of your 2009 Schedule 7.

Do not include the following amounts:

- Any unused RRSP contributions you made after March 2, 2009, that were refunded to you or your spouse or common-law partner in 2009. Report the refund on line 129 of your return for 2009. You may be able to claim a deduction on line 232.
- Part or all of the contributions you made to your RRSP or an RRSP for your spouse or common-law partner less than 90 days before either of you withdrew funds from that RRSP under the HBP or LLP. For more details, see Home Buyers' Plan (HBP) or Lifelong Learning Plan (LLP).
- Any payments directly transferred to your RRSP if you did not receive an information slip for it or if it is shown in box 35 of your T4RSP or T4RIF slip.
- The part of an RRSP withdrawal that you recontributed to your RRSP and deducted on line 232. This would have happened if, in error, you withdrew more RRSP funds than necessary to obtain past-service benefits under a registered pension plan (RPP).
- The excess part of a direct transfer of a lump-sum payment from your RPP to an RRSP or registered retirement income fund (RRIF) that you withdrew and are including on line 129 or 130 of your return for 2009, and deducting on line 232.

Lines 6 and 7 - Repayments under the HBP and LLP

If you withdrew funds from your RRSP under the Home Buyer's Plan (HBP) before 2008, you have to make a repayment for 2009. If you withdrew funds from your RRSP under the Lifelong Learning Plan (LLP) before 2008, you may have to make a repayment for 2009. In either case, the minimum amount you have to repay for the year is indicated on your Notice of Assessment or Notice of Reassessment for 2008 or on Form T1028, Your RRSP Information for 2009.

To make a repayment for 2009, contribute to your own RRSP from January 1, 2009, to March 1, 2010, and designate your contribution as a repayment on line 6 or 7 of Schedule 7. Do not include an amount you deducted or designated as a repayment on your 2008 return, or that was refunded to you. Do not make your repayment to us. You cannot deduct any RRSP contribution you designate as an HBP or LLP repayment on Schedule 7.

Note: If you repay less than the minimum amount for 2009, you have to include the difference on line 129 of your return.

Line 10 - RRSP contributions you are deducting for 2009

Your RRSP deduction limit for 2009 is shown on your Notice of Assessment or Notice of Reassessment for 2008, or, if we sent you one, on Form T1028, Your RRSP Information for 2009 . You can carry forward indefinitely any part of your RRSP deduction limit accumulated after 1990 that you do not use.

If you would like to calculate your RRSP deduction limit for 2009, get Guide T4040, RRSPs and Other Registered Plans for Retirement.

Note: In a previous year, you may have received income for which you could contribute to an RRSP, but you may not have filed a return for that year. If you want to keep your RRSP deduction limit up to date, you have to file a return for that year.

Line 11 - Transfers

You may have reported income on line 115, 129, or 130 of your return for 2009. If you contributed certain types of this income to your own RRSP on or before March 1, 2010, you can deduct this contribution, called a transfer, in addition to any RRSP contribution you make based on your RRSP deduction limit for 2009.

For example, if you received a retiring allowance in 2009, you would report it on line 130 of your return. You can contribute to your RRSP up to the eligible part of that income (box 26 of your T4A slip or box 47 of your T3 slip) and deduct it as a transfer. Include the amounts you transfer on lines 2 or 3 and 11 of Schedule 7.

For more information about the amounts you can transfer, see Transfers to registered plans or funds and annuities or get the CRA guide T4040, RRSPs and Other Registered Plans for Retirement.

Line 14 - RRSP unused contributions available to carry forward

This is the portion of your RRSP that you are not using on this year's return. You can carry this amount forward and claim it in a future tax year.

Lines 15 to 18 - 2009 withdrawals under HBP and the LLP

On line 15, enter the total of your HBP withdrawals for 2009 from box 27 of your T4RSP slips. In addition, check the box at line 16 if the address of the home you acquired with these withdrawals is the same as the address on page 1 of your return.

On line 17, enter the total of your LLP withdrawals for 2009 from box 25 of your T4RSP slips. In addition, you can check the box at line 18 to designate that your spouse or common-law partner was the student for whom the funds were withdrawn. If you do not check the box, you will be considered to be the student for LLP purposes. You can change the person you designate as the student only on the return for the year you make your first withdrawal.

The topics Home Buyers' Plan (HBP) and Lifelong Learning Plan include more information about:

- when you have to make your repayments; and
- the rules that apply when the person who made the withdrawal dies, turns 71, or becomes a non-resident.

Schedule 8 - CPP contributions on self-employment and other earnings

S8: CPP on self-employment and other earnings

Consult the CRA guide information below for details regarding this form.

Frequently Asked Questions

When can I not make CPP contributions?

You cannot make CPP contributions:

- before the month you turn 18,
- after the month you turn 70,
- after the month of death, or
- after the month that you start to collect CPP retirement or disability benefits.

The Canada Revenue Agency says... *Schedule 8 - CPP contributions on self-employment and other earnings*

Complete this schedule to determine the amount of your Canada Pension Plan (CPP) contributions if:

- you reported self-employment income on lines 135 to 143 of your return;
- you reported business or professional income from a partnership on line 122 of your return; or
- you made an election on Form CPT20 to pay additional CPP contributions on other earnings.

Attach a copy of this schedule to your return. See line 222 for more information.

Note: Québec residents, see Québec Schedule 8 instead.

Quebec Schedule 8 - QPP Contributions on Self-Employment and Other Earnings

S8Q: QPP on self-employment and other earnings

Complete Schedule S8Q to calculate your Quebec Pension Plan contributions payable. If you were a member of a partnership, make sure you include only your share of the net profit or loss.

The calculation on Schedule 8 depends on amounts from the Quebec provincial return.

The CRA Provincial Guide says... *QPP Contributions on Self-Employment and Other Earnings (Schedule 8 - Quebec)*

Complete this schedule to determine the amount of your Quebec Pension Plan (QPP) contributions if you reported net business income on line 164 of your income tax return for Quebec.

Also use this schedule to calculate your optional QPP contributions.

Attach a copy of this schedule to your return. See line 222 for more information.

Schedule 9 - Donations and Gifts

S9: Donations and gifts

Schedule 9 summarizes all your charitable donations and gifts and calculates your allowable deduction. ProFile completes this schedule automatically based on amounts from the Donations worksheet and from T5013 slips.

The Canada Revenue Agency says... *Gifts and Income Tax Guide (P113)*

Calculating your increased donation limit

If you donate cash or other property to a registered charity or other qualified donee in the year, your total donations limit will be 75% of your net income for the year. However, you can increase your total donations limit if you donate capital property in the year. If you received an advantage in respect of the donation of the property include, in your calculations, only the portion of taxable capital gains and recapture of depreciation that related to the gift portion of your donation.

To do so, complete Chart 1, and enter the result on Schedule 9, Donations and Gifts. Your donations limit cannot exceed your net income for the year.

Did you have a recapture of depreciation?

You can also increase your total donations limit if you have to include a recapture of depreciation on your current year return as a result of donating the property.

To do so, complete Chart 2, and enter the result on Schedule 9. Your total donations limit cannot exceed your net income for the year.

Schedule 10 - Employment Insurance (EI) and Provincial Parental Insurance Plan (PPIP) Premiums

S10: Employment Insurance (EI) and Provincial Parental Insurance Plan (PPIP) Premiums

Consult the CRA guide information below for details regarding this form.

The Canada Revenue Agency says... *Form Schedule 10, Employment Insurance (EI) and Provincial Parental Insurance Plan (PPIP) Premiums*

Complete this schedule to determine EI and PPIP premium amounts if:

- you reported employment income (including employment income from outside Canada) of more than $2,000 and one of your T4 slips has a province of employment other than Québec in box 10; or
- you reported net self-employment income of more than $2,000 on lines 135 to 143 of your return; or
- the total of employment income (including employment income from outside Canada) and net self-employment income you reported is more than $2,000.

Schedule 11 - Federal Tuition, Education, and Textbook Amounts

S11: Tuition and education amounts

Students claiming tuition fees and education amounts must complete Schedule 11, Tuition and Education Amounts. Even if someone else paid the tuition fees, the student must claim these amounts to reduce tax payable to zero before transferring any unused balance.

To qualify for the education amount, courses must have been taken at a designated educational institution

If I attended more than one institution in the same month, can I claim the equivalent of two months of education amount?

You can claim only one education amount for each calendar month you are registered, regardless of how many programs or educational institutions you attend in that month.

If you attended two qualifying institutions during the same month, you can only claim the education amount for one institution/program. If you attended two sequential programs that overlapped, claim each calendar month that you attended.

> **Example:**
> Your T2202 from College A shows 4 part-time months (from January through April). Your T2202 from College B shows 3 part-time months (from April through June). Claim 6 months total, one for each calendar month you attended. You cannot claim 2 months for April.

Note: Although you can only claim the education amount for one program taken during the same month, you can claim the tuition fees for both programs.

Full-time students

$400 per month

The student must have been enrolled in a qualifying educational program. Such a program must last at least 3 consecutive weeks and requires each student to spend at least 10 hours per week on courses or work in the program (exclusive of study time). A disabled student who is enrolled on a part-time basis in such a program can also claim the education amount of $400 per month.

Part-time students

$120 per month

The student must have been enrolled in a specified educational program. Such a program lasts at least 3 consecutive weeks and involves a minimum of 12 hours on courses in the program per month.

Co-operative students

$400 per month

If you are a co-operative student who attends an educational institution for an academic period and then you work for a similar period in a business or industry that relates to your academic studies, you are considered a full-time student only during the months you attend the educational institution.

Textbook amount

You can claim this amount only if you are entitled to claim the education amount.

The amount is:

- $65 for each month you qualify for the full-time education amount; and
- $20 for each month you qualify for the part-time education amount.

The Canada Revenue Agency says... *Schedule 11 - Tuition, Education, and Textbook Amounts*

Only the student must complete this schedule. Use it to:

- calculate your federal tuition, education, and textbook amounts;
- determine the federal amount available to transfer to a designated individual; and
- determine the unused federal amount, if any, available for you to carry forward to a future year.

Attach a copy of this schedule to your return. If you do not file a return, keep this schedule for your records. The person claiming the transfer should not attach this schedule to his or her return.

Note: If your taxable income (Line 260 of the T1 General) exceeds the lowest federal tax bracket ($ 37,885.00), Line 11 of the Schedule 11 is calculated as: Line 35 of the Schedule 1 divided by the lowest tax rate (15%).

If you qualify for the education and textbook amounts, you should have received Form T2202, Education and Textbook Amounts Certificate, T2202A, Tuition, Education, and Textbook Amounts Certificate, TL11A, Tuition, Education, and Textbook Amounts Certificate - University Outside Canada, TL11B, Tuition Fees Certificate - Flying School or Club, or TL11C, Tuition, Education, and Textbook Amounts Certificate - Commuter to the United States. See Line 323 for more information on eligible tuition, education, and textbook amounts.

Transfers

You can transfer all or part of the amount on line 23 to your spouse or common-law partner, or to your or your spouse's or common-law partner's parent or grandparent. To do this, you have to designate the individual on your Form T2202, T2202A, TL11A, TL11B or TL11C and specify the federal amount that you are transferring to him or her. Enter the amount you are transferring on line 24.

Note:

If your spouse or common-law partner is claiming an amount for you on line 303 or line 326 of his or her Schedule 1, you cannot transfer an amount to your or your spouse's or common-law partner's parent or grandparent.

Carry forward

You can carry forward and claim in a future year the part of your tuition and education amounts you do not need to use (and do not transfer) for the year.

The person claiming the transfer should not attach this schedule to his or her return.

Eligible tuition fees and educational institutions

Qualifying courses

Generally, a course qualifies if it was taken in the calendar year, and:

- it was taken at the post-secondary level or
- it develops or improves skills in an occupation, you were 16 or over at the end of the year, and the educational institution has been certified by Human Resources and Social Development Canada.

Tuition fees paid to any one institution have to be more than $100 in a calendar year.

If your employer or your parent's employer paid your tuition fees, you can only claim them if the amount paid is included in your income or your parent's income. If your tuition fees are paid by a federal or provincial job training program, and no related amount is included in your income, the fees do not qualify for this credit.

If your fees are paid (or you are entitled to be reimbursed for them) under a federal program to assist athletes, you cannot claim the fees unless the payment or reimbursement has been included in your income.

Schools and educational institutions

Designated educational institutions include:

- Canadian universities, colleges, and other educational institutions providing courses at a postsecondary school level;
- Canadian educational institutions certified by Human Resources and Social Development Canada providing courses that develop or improve skills in an occupation, other than courses designed for university credit;
- universities outside Canada where the student is enrolled in a course that lasts at least 13 consecutive weeks and leads to a degree at the bachelor level or higher; and
- universities, colleges, or other educational institutions in the United States that give courses at the post-secondary school level if the student is living in Canada (near the border) throughout the year and commutes to that institution.

Note: To claim tuition fees paid to an educational institution outside Canada, the institution has to complete and provide the student with either Form TL11A, Tuition Fees Certificate - University Outside Canada, or Form TL11C, Tuition Fees Certificate - Commuter to the United States, whichever applies.

To claim tuition fees paid to a flying school or club in Canada, the school or club has to complete and provide the student with form TL11B, Tuition Fees Certificate - Flying School or Club.

Things you can claim

The following are eligible tuition fees and expenses:

- admission fees;
- charges for laboratory or library facilities;
- examination fees;
- application fees (but only if you later enrol in the institution);
- charges for a certificate, diploma, or degree;
- mandatory computer service fees;
- academic fees;
- the cost of any books that are included in the total fees for a correspondence course taken through a post secondary educational institution in Canada; and
- fees, such as athletic and health services fees, paid to a university, college, or other educational institution in addition to your tuition for post-secondary courses, when such fees are required to be paid by all students. The amount of eligible fees is limited to $250 if the fees do not have to be paid by all students.

Things you can't claim

The following fees and expenses are not eligible tuition expenses. You cannot claim:

- cost of books (other than books that are included in the total fees for a correspondence course). However, you may be entitled to the textbook amount.
- student association fees;
- medical expenses;
- transportation and parking;
- meals and lodging.
- goods of lasting value that you will keep, such as a computer, microscope, uniform, or an academic gown;
- initiation or entrance fees to a professional organization;
- private elementary or secondary school tuition (e.g., grade 1 through grade 12), pre-school, play school, or camp fees (although you might be able to claim these as a child care expense;
- high school upgrade courses as a prerequisite to university or college entrance;
- private tutoring;
- summer school programs (unless they are part of a post-secondary program, such as a college summer semester);
- music, art, drama, or dance lessons (unless in conjunction with a post-secondary educational program, such as a Bachelor of Fine Arts or teaching certificate);
- driver's education.

Schedule 12 - Home renovation expenses

S12: Home Renovation Expenses

Use the new Schedule 12 to claim the **Home Renovation Tax Credit (HRTC).**

Under proposed legislation, taxpayers can claim amounts for eligible renovation expenses incurred for work performed or goods acquired after January 27, 2009 and before February 1, 2010 on eligible dwellings (including the land that forms part of the eligible dwelling). Expenses must have been made under agreements entered into after January 27, 2009.

The HRTC amount consists of 15% of eligible expenses above $1,000 up to $10,000 (for a maximum credit of $1,350).

For a dwelling or housing unit to be considered eligible:

- The taxpayer (either alone or jointly with another person) must have owned it at the time of the renovation or alteration, and
- The taxpayer (or a current or former spouse, common-law partner, or the spouse's or common-law partner's children) ordinarily inhabited the dwelling some time during the eligibility period.

In general, taxpayers who own multiple eligible dwellings can claim expenses for both dwellings. Taxpayers can also claim expenses for dwellings that were sold and purchased during the eligibility period. However, the maximum total expenses that can be claimed (over all dwellings) is $10,000 per family. The claim can be split among eligible family members, as long as the total claim does not exceed the maximum.

For dwellings that are also used for rental or business income, expenses can be claimed only for those incurred on personal-use areas of the dwelling, or on personal-use portions of common areas.

To claim this credit, type "S12" in the Form Explorer. Enter the expenses to be claimed in the form; the table will expand as needed. If the dwelling is also used for rental or business income, enter the rental or business portion in line 2. Enter amounts claimed by other family members on line 6. ProFile calculates the final home renovation expense amount and carries it to line 368 on Schedule 1.

Note: This tax credit is available only for the 2009 tax year.

Tip: Eligible expenses are not reduced by government tax credits or grants, such as grants made under the ecoENERGY - Retrofit Homes program. Credits for both can be claimed for the same expense.

The Canada Revenue Agency says... *Schedule 12*

Complete this schedule if you had eligible home renovation expenses and you are claiming the Home Renovation Tax Credit (HRTC). For more information, see line 368 - Home renovation expenses.

Attach a copy of this schedule to your return. Do not include receipts, but keep them in case we ask to see them.

Eligible expenses are those incurred after January 27, 2009 and before February 1, 2010, under an agreement entered into after January 27, 2009, for work performed or goods acquired in respect of an eligible dwelling.

Schedule A - Statement of World Income

SA: Statement of world income

This schedule is used only in determining your allowable non-refundable tax credits on Schedule B.

Note: Be sure to report all income in Canadian dollars.

The Canada Revenue Agency says... *General Income Tax and Benefit Guide for Non-Residents and Deemed Residents of Canada (5013g)*

Schedule A is used to report your world income. World income is income from all sources, both inside and outside Canada. Complete this schedule, and attach it to your return if you were a non-resident of Canada or a deemed non-resident of Canada for all of 2009, including non-residents, and deemed non-residents electing under section 217 and/or section 216.1 of the Income Tax Act.

Section 217 Election

Election Canadian payers have to withhold non-resident tax on certain types of income they paid or credited to you as a non-resident of Canada. The tax withheld is usually your final tax obligation to Canada on this income.

However, you can choose to file a Canadian return and report types of Canadian-source income. By doing this, you will pay tax on this income using an alternative taxing method and may receive a refund of some or all of the non-resident tax withheld.

Choosing to send us this return is called "electing under section 217 of the Income Tax Act."

Is a section 217 election beneficial?

You will benefit from filing a return under section 217 of the Income Tax Act if the tax you have to pay on your 2009 tax return by making this election is less than the tax you would otherwise pay if you did not make this election. Use this form to determine the tax you will pay if you elect under section 217, and to determine the tax you would otherwise pay.

What types of income are eligible for a section 217 election?

The section 217 election applies to the following types of Canadian-source income:

- Old Age Security pension;
- Canada Pension Plan and Québec Pension Plan benefits;
- superannuation and pension benefits;
- registered retirement savings plan payments;
- registered retirement income fund payments;
- death benefits;
- Employment Insurance benefits;
- retiring allowances;
- registered supplementary unemployment benefit plan payments;
- deferred profit-sharing plan payments;
- registered retirement income fund payments; and
- amounts received from a retirement compensation arrangement, or the purchase price of an interest in a retirement compensation arrangement;
- prescribed benefits under a government assistance program; and
- Auto Pact benefits.

When is your section 217 return due?

Your 2009 section 217 return has to be filed on or before June 30, 2010.

However, if you have a balance owing for 2009, you have to pay it by April 30, 2010, to avoid interest charges.

If you send us your return late, your section 217 election will be invalid. If the required amount of non-resident tax was withheld on your eligible 217 income, we consider that to be the final tax liability. If the required amount was not withheld, we will send you a non-resident tax assessment.

 Note: The due date for filing your return may be different if you report on the return Canadian-source income, such as employment or business income, net Canadian partnership income if you are a limited or non-active partner, or taxable capital gains from disposing of taxable Canadian property. For the exceptions, see the section called "What date is your return for 2009 due?" in the for Non-Residents and Deemed Residents of Canada.

Your taxable income for calculating federal tax on Schedule 1 is the greater of the following two amounts:

- the taxable income reported on line 260 of your return; or
- your adjusted net world income from line 16 on Schedule A, Statement of World Income.

If your federal tax is based on your adjusted net world income, you will be entitled to a tax adjustment to reduce your federal tax. See line 445 in the General Income Tax Guide for Non-Residents and Deemed residents of Canada for details on how to calculate this tax adjustment.

Section 216 Election

Election As a non-resident of Canada you may have received one of the following in 2009:

If so, you can file a separate return to report this income for the year. Choosing to send this separate return is called "electing under section 216 of the Income Tax Act". You cannot use section 216 if your rental income is from carrying on a business in Canada.

When you receive rental income from Canada, the payer has to withhold non-resident tax usually at the rate of 25% (unless reduced by a tax treaty) on the gross rental income paid or credited to you, and then send it to CRA. This tax is usually your final tax obligation to Canada on the rental income. However, you may be able to save tax by making an election under section 216 as explained below.

What is the benefit of electing under section 216?

> Electing under section 216 allows you to pay tax on your net Canadian-source rental income instead of on the gross amount. If the non-resident tax withheld by the payer is more than the amount of tax payable calculated on your section 216 return, we will refund the excess to you.

When is your section 216 return due?

> Generally, you have to send us your section 216 return within two years from the end of the year in which the rental income was paid or credited to you. For exceptions to this filing date, obtain the guide Income Tax Guide for Electing Under Section 216.

> Tip: You may also want to consider having non-resident tax withheld on the net rental income instead of the gross amount. For details, see "Withholding on net rental income (Form NR6)."

Section 216.1 Election

As a non-resident actor providing acting services in Canada in a film or video production, you are subject to a 23% non-resident tax. The 23% tax is your final tax liability on the acting income.

If the acting income is your only source of Canadian income, you are not required to file a tax return. However, you may be able to reduce your tax obligation by electing to file a return. This means that, under section 216.1 of the Income Tax Act, you choose to report the acting income on a Canadian tax return.

What income does the 23% tax apply to?

> The 23% tax applies to all amounts paid or credited to you, or to a related corporation, for acting services that you provide in Canada on a film or video production, including payments of residuals and contingent compensation.

> The tax applies to fees for acting services provided in Canada, per diem payments for days in Canada, amounts paid on your behalf to third parties, and similar benefits. However, withholding of 23% is not required from the following amounts: reasonable travel expenses (airfare, hotels)

paid directly to third parties on your behalf, and reasonable travel expenses reimbursed to you provided they are adequately supported by vouchers from the payer.

Note: Receipts are not required for reimbursement of meals, including incidentals, to a maximum of CAN $100/day. For more details, see Per diems for non-resident actors providing acting services in Canada.

The 23% tax does not apply to other income earned in Canada (for services as a producer or director, for example).

The person paying you for the services (your payer), whether a Canadian or a non-resident, has to withhold this tax and remit it to the CRA on your behalf. Your payer is also required to report, on an NR4 slip, the amount of income and any taxes withheld and remitted to us. Your payer will give you a copy of this slip for your records.

Where to send your return

Send your completed return to the International Tax Services Office.

Schedule B - Allowable amount of non-refundable tax credits

SB: Allowable amount of non-refundable tax credits

Consult the CRA guide information below for details regarding this form.

**The Canada Revenue Agency says...**

This form calculates the allowable amount of non-refundable tax credits for non-residents. Complete Schedule B if you are a Non-resident or a Non-resident making a Section 217 election.

- Complete Box A if you were a non-resident of Canada.
- Complete Box B if you were a non-resident of Canada and you are electing under section 217 of the Income Tax Act.

Schedule C - Electing Under Section 217 of the Income Tax Act

SC: Electing under Section 217 of the Income Tax Act

Use this form only if you were a non-resident of Canada for all of the year and you are electing under section 217 of the Income Tax Act.

For more information on completing non-resident returns in ProFile, see Completing returns for non-residents.

The Canada Revenue Agency says... *5013-SC: Schedule C - Electing Under Section 217 of the Income Tax Act for Non-Resident and Deemed Residents of Canada*

Complete this schedule and attach it to your return if you were a non-resident of Canada for all 2009 and you are electing under section 217 of the Income Tax Act.

Part 1 - Eligible section 217 income

Check that the lines that apply to you are complete.

Part 2 - Non-resident tax required to be withheld

Complete section 1 or section 2 below, but not both, to calculate the amount of non-resident tax required to be withheld on your eligible section 217 income.

Note: The amount you calculate may be different than the non-resident tax withheld on your eligible section 217 income. This would be the case if the payer did not withhold the correct amount of tax, or if we approved a reduction in the amount of tax to be withheld as a result of the 2009 NR5 form you submitted.

If you were a resident of a country that Canada has signed a tax treaty with, complete section 1. If you were a resident of a country that Canada has not signed a tax treaty with, complete section 2.

Part 3 - Section 217 tax adjustment

Complete this section only if the amount that you entered on line 30 of Schedule 1 is the same as the "net world income after adjustments" from line 16 of Schedule A.

SD: Information about your residency status

Use this form if you are filing a provincial or territorial tax return, and if for the entire year you were one of the following:

A non-resident of Canada

You were a non-resident for tax purposes if you did not have residential ties in Canada, and:

- you stayed in Canada for less than 183 days in the tax year (including the days you arrived and left); or
- you lived outside Canada throughout the tax year (except if you were a deemed resident).

A deemed non-resident of Canada

You may be a deemed non-resident for tax purposes if you're otherwise a deemed resident of Canada who, under a tax treaty, is considered a resident of another country.

A factual resident of Canada

You're considered a factual resident of Canada for tax purposes if you keep residential ties with Canada while travelling or living abroad. The term factual resident means that although you're not in Canada, you're still considered a resident of Canada for income tax purposes.

You may be a factual resident for tax purposes if you:

- work temporarily outside Canada
- teach or attend school in another country
- commute daily or weekly to the United States to work
- vacation outside Canada.

If you're conducting missionary work in another country and you meet certain requirements, you may choose to be a factual resident even if you don't keep residential ties with Canada.

If you also establish residential ties in a country with which Canada has a tax treaty and you're considered to be a resident of that country for the purposes of that tax treaty, you may be considered a deemed non-resident of Canada for tax purposes.

In either of these cases, contact the International Tax Services Office for more information.

Chapter 7

Filing

2009 Tax Year

Bankruptcy: Bankruptcy information

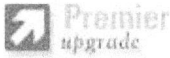

Complete this form when you are preparing a return for a taxpayer who has filed for bankruptcy.

If you complete this form for a new file, before you save the return for the first time, ProFile will automatically include the bankruptcy return type in the filename. This makes it easy to distinguish between pre- and post-bankruptcy returns prepared for the same taxpayer in the same year.

The bankruptcy type also flows to a field at the top of the T1 jacket, page 1. This alerts CRA that the return is of a special type.

If you indicate a pre-bankruptcy return, the Post-bankruptcy column become active. Likewise, if you indicate that you are preparing a post-bankruptcy return, the pre-bankruptcy column becomes active. Enter the details from the related bankruptcy return, since the two separate files do not share data.

Bankruptcy returns require some manual calculation. For both pre- and post-bankruptcy returns, you must calculate the applicable portion of income and deductions, based on the portion of the calendar year covered by each return.

For example, you do not enter the complete T5 information for the year. Rather, enter the portion of that income attributed to the pre- and post bankruptcy return. ProFile then calculates the non-refundable tax credits based on those amounts.

DC905: Bankruptcy identification form

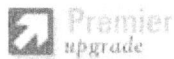

File this form when you are preparing a return for a taxpayer who has filed for bankruptcy.

RC59: Business consent form

To authorize or cancel a representative for an individual taxpayer, complete the T1013.

RC59 is the business consent form that authorizes CRA to release confidential client information to a designated third-party representative in matters pertaining to applicable legislation.

Complete a separate RC59 for each representative who may have access to confidential information.

The authorization is valid until the client or authorized signing person cancels it in writing. Complete part 3 of this form to cancel consent.

RC71: Statement of discounting transaction

The RC71 is the Statement of Discounting Transaction. The RC71I form is the accompanying information and instructions. ProFile includes these forms so you can print them for your clients.

You can suppress the instructions form (or any other form) if you do not wish to print it when you print your complete client files. Select Options > Form selection from the main ProFile menu. Customize the print jobs you use to make sure there is no checkmark beside the RC71 form.

If you are resident of a province that has the harmonized sales tax (HST), you must enter that province name under Options > Environment > Preparer if you want the RC71 to use the HST amount rather than the GST amount in Area D.

RC72: Notice of the actual amount of the refund of tax

Discounters use this form when they receive payment from CRA on discounted returns. The form advises the taxpayer of the actual refund received and handles any discrepancy between the estimated and actual refund amounts.

ProFile automatically transfers the estimated refund amount to the RC72, so the discounter needs to enter only the actual amount of the refund payment.

To complete and close a discounted client file, use the refund cheque information fields on the File details window (File menu).

RC210: Working Income Tax Benefit advance payment received

To maximize the effectiveness of the WITB, an advance payment option became available in January 2008, when taxpayers were able to start applying for WITB advance payments. Taxpayers who qualify for the WITB can opt to receive advance payments of up to 50% of their refundable tax credit (including the WITB disability supplement). Advance payments received will reduce the refund amount of a taxpayer's tax return.

Any taxpayer who received WITB advance payments during the year must file a tax return. In box 10 of the RC210 worksheet, enter the amount of WITB advance payments received in the year. The amount will flow to line 415 of Schedule 1.

If a client is eligible to claim the WITB for 2009, complete Schedule 6 to calculate the amount to which they are entitled.

T1A - Request for Loss Carry back

T1A: Request for loss carry back

If, in the taxation year, you incurred a net capital loss, a non-capital loss, a listed personal property loss, a farming or fishing loss or a restricted farm loss, use this form to apply it against taxable capital gains you reported on your return(s) for any of the three previous taxation years.

Attach a completed copy to your return. Do not file an amended return for the year or years to which you want to apply the loss.

ProFile will automatically transfer current year amounts to this form. However, you must manually enter the amounts you wish to carry back in the applicable area of the form.

Form T1A can be used to carry back the following types of losses:

- Non-Capital losses (including fishing and farming losses)
- Net Capital losses
- Listed Personal Property losses
- Restricted farm losses

The Canada Revenue Agency says... *Form T1A, Request for Loss Carry back*

- Use this form to ask for the application of a loss from 2009 to any of the three previous tax years. Attach the completed form to your 2009 income tax return or to your request for an adjustment and send it to your tax centre.
- Complete only the sections that apply to you, and sign the certification section.
- You cannot carry back a loss to reduce any late-filing penalty for the year to which the loss is being applied.
- You can apply the refund arising from the loss carry back adjustment(s) to outstanding taxes owing for any tax year.
- You cannot carry back losses of a limited partnership.
- The lines we mention on this form refer to the Income Tax and Benefit Return.

Section I - Non-capital loss for carry back

The following amounts will reduce the income or increase the loss (as appropriate) from the source(s) to which they relate: capital cost allowance relating to investment in Canadian motion picture films (see line 232); deductions allowed under subsections 20(11) and 20(12) of the Income Tax Act (for more information, see Interpretation Bulletin IT-506, Foreign Income Taxes as a Deduction From Income); and repayments of a shareholder's loans.

If you have an amount on line 224 of your income tax return, deduct the amount against either your investment income or loss, or your partnership (limited or non-active partners) income or loss, whichever applies. Do not deduct the amount twice.

For more information, see the CRA Guide T4011, Preparing returns for deceased persons.

Section III - Net capital loss for carry back

Use this section to apply 2009 net capital losses only. For more information, see Chapter 5 in the CRA Guide T4037, Capital Gains.

You can only apply 2009 net capital losses against taxable capital gains.

Applying a net capital loss carry back will result in a reduction of the capital gains deduction, if claimed, in the year(s) of the loss application. It may also reduce capital gains deductions you claimed in the following years.

T1ADJ - T1 Adjustment Request

Frequently Asked Questions

If I submit an adjustment request form, what do I include with it?

To request an adjustment by mail, send one of the following plus any supporting documents (T-slips, receipts, etc.) to your tax centre:

- a completed Form T1-ADJ, T1 Adjustment Request, or
- a letter providing all the details, including your social insurance number, address, a telephone number where CRA can reach you during the day, and the taxation years you want them to adjust.

It will take longer for the CRA to process your request if you send a letter instead of Form T1ADJ.

For more information, visit the CRA's Web site.

 The Canada Revenue Agency says... *General Income Tax and Benefit Guide*

If you need to make a change to any return you have sent us, do not file another return for that year. You should wait until you receive your Notice of Assessment before requesting any change to a return that has not been processed. You can change your return by going to My Account on our Wed site or by sending both of the following to your tax centre:

- a completed Form T1-ADJ, Adjustment Request, or a signed letter providing the details of your request (including the years of the return(s) you want to change), your social insurance number, your address, and a telephone number where we can reach you during the day; and
- supporting documents for the changes you want to make and, if you have not sent them to us before, supporting documents for your original claim.

 Note: Send your Form T1-ADJ or letter separately from your return for 2009.

Only requests relating to tax years ending in any of the 10 calendar years before the year you make the request will be considered. For example, a request made in 2010 must relate to the 2000 or a subsequent tax year to be considered.

It usually takes eight weeks before we complete the adjustment and mail you a Notice of Reassessment.

Direct deposit

T1DD: Direct deposit request

Use this form to start direct deposit of:

- your income tax return refund
- Goods and Services Tax / Harmonized sales tax credit (GST/HST), including certain related provincial payments
- Working Income Tax Benefit (WITB) advance payment
- Child Tax Benefit payment

Submit this form to change the direct deposit information you already gave CRA.

Do not complete this form if you already use the direct deposit service and your banking information has not changed.

Your direct deposit request will stay in effect until you change the information or cancel the service.

 The Canada Revenue Agency says... *General Income Tax and Benefit Guide*

You can have your income tax refund, as well as your goods and services tax/harmonized sales tax (GST/HST) credit, (including those from certain related provincial payments), Universal Child Care Benefit (UCCB) payments, and Canada Child Tax Benefit (CCTB) payments (including those from certain related provincial or territorial programs), and Working Income Tax Benefit (WITB) advance payments and any other deemed overpayment of tax to which you are entitled or to which you may become entitled, deposited directly into your account at a financial institution in Canada.

To start direct deposit, or to change information you already gave us, complete the "Direct deposit Start or change" section on page 4 of your return. You do not have to complete this area if you already have direct deposit service and the information you already gave us has not changed. Your direct deposit request will stay in effect until you change the information or cancel the service.

If you want your UCCB and/or CCTB payments deposited into a different account, you will have to send us, either with your paper return or separately, a completed Form T1-DD(1), Direct Deposit Request - Individuals.

If you are changing the account into which we deposit a payment, do not close the old account before we deposit the payment into the new account.

If your financial institution advises us that you have a new account, we may deposit your payments into the new account.

If, for any reason, we cannot deposit a payment into your account, we will mail a cheque to you at the address we have on file.

T7DRA: Payment form

Every taxpayer whose uses EFILE and has tax payable must take the T7DRA form to a bank to process the payment (before April 30 to avoid penalties).

It is essential to use the form that CRA provides for this purpose. The T7DRA in ProFile formats client information to print directly on the pre-printed CRA T7DRA form.

T183: Information return for electronic filing

The T183 is the Information Return for Electronic Filing. ProFile includes this form in case you wish to print it for your client.

You can suppress the instructions form (or any other form) if you do not wish to print it when you print your complete client files. Select Options > Form selection from the ProFile main menu.

The T183 contains information from the taxpayer's tax return. The taxpayer should therefore sign the T183 after you have completed the return.

T1013: Consent form

Attention: To authorize or cancel a representative for a business number account, complete the RC59.

A taxpayer can complete and sign form T1013 to authorize a representative, including his or her spouse, to access the taxpayer's tax information through CRA.

CRA will only release information to a representative after they are satisfied that the taxpayer has provided authorization.

This authorization is valid until the taxpayer or authorized signing person cancels it in writing. A separate authorization form is required for each type of account, every time a taxpayer gives an authorization or cancels a previous authorization.

T1132: Alternative address authorization

Complete this form to authorize CRA to mail your Notice of Assessment and your refund cheque (if applicable) to an alternate address. Attach this form to your return.

This authorization is valid for the current tax year only. You will have to file a new, signed authorization each year you want to use this service.

CRA will not use this authorization to mail your Goods and Services Tax / Harmonized Sales Tax credit payments, Child Tax Benefits payments (including any related provincial credits and benefits), correspondence, or Notice of Reassessment, to an alternative address.

You cannot use this form if:

- you were bankrupt at any time during the year;
- a discounter is submitting your tax return;
- it is for a tax year other than the current year;
- you are a non-resident filing an Old Age Security Return of Income; or
- you are filing returns for other years at the same time as you are filing the current year return.

Your signed authorization removes from CRA any responsibility for the use or disclosure of information contained on your Notice of Assessment and for any misappropriation of your refund.

Form T1135 - Information Return Relating to a Foreign Property

T1135: Foreign income verification statement

The Identification options for corporation, trust and partnership have been reproduced from the CRA form. However, these options are not available in the ProFile T1 software, so you cannot select those checkboxes.

If you received income from the property throughout the year, you can use an average exchange rate.

 The Canada Revenue Agency says... *Foreign Income Verification Statement (T1135)*

Complete and file this statement with your tax return (or, if a partnership, with your partnership information return) if at any time in the year the total cost amount of all specified foreign property you owned or held a beneficial interest in was more than $100,000.

Filing this statement

File this statement with your tax return (or, if a partnership, with your partnership information return) if at any time in the year the total cost amount of all specified foreign property you owned or held a beneficial interest in was more that $100,000. If you do not have to file a tax return or a partnership information return, or you use NETFILE, send this statement separately to:

> *Ottawa Technology Centre*
>
> *Data Assessment and Evaluations Program,*
>
> *Foreign Reporting Unit,*
>
> *875 Heron Road,*

Ottawa, ON K1A 1A2

All legislative references below refer to the Income Tax Act (the Act). If the reporting taxpayer is a partnership, references to year or tax year should be read as fiscal period and references to taxpayer should be read as partnership.

Do you have to file this statement?

Canadian resident individuals, corporations, and trusts, as well as partnerships, who held certain property outside Canada with a total cost amount of more than $100,000 at any time in the tax year, have to file Form T1135, Foreign Income Verification Statement.

Non-resident discretionary trusts, as defined under section 94 of the Act, may also have to file this statement.

As an individual (other than a trust) you do not have to file this statement for the year in which you first become a resident of Canada.

You do not have to report information about property held for personal use. This includes vacation property used by you primarily as a personal residence, as well as listed personal property such as works of art, jewellery, rare folios, rare manuscripts, rare books, stamps, and coins. See the latest version of Interpretation Bulletin IT-332, Personal-Use Property, for more details about personal property. You also do not have to report property used or held by you exclusively in an active business.

You do not have to file this statement for the following entities:

Corporations

- mutual fund corporations;
- non-resident-owned investment corporations;
- corporations exempt from tax under Part I of the Act;
- a registered investment under section 204.4 of the Act;

Trusts

- mutual fund trusts;
- trusts described in paragraphs (a) to (e.1) of the definition of trust in subsection 108(1) of the Act;
- trusts exempt from tax under Part I of the Act;
- a registered investment under section 204.4 of the Act;
- a trust in which all persons beneficially interested are either corporations or trusts listed above;

Partnerships

- partnerships all the members of which are corporations or trusts referred to above;
- partnerships where the share of the partnership's income or loss for non-resident members is 90% or more of the income or loss of the partnership;

Persons* exempt from tax under Part I of the Act.

- Persons* other than corporations or trusts.

Examples

> Q. I am an individual who owns shares in a non-resident corporation with a cost amount of $75,000. I also have a bank account in the United States that has $35,000 on deposit. Since neither of the foreign properties that I own have a cost amount greater than $100,000, do I have to file Form T1135?
>
> A. Yes. In this case, the statement should be filed since the total cost amount of all foreign properties owned is $110,000. You should add up the cost amount of each foreign property that you own in the year to determine if, at any time in the year, the total of those cost amounts exceeded $100,000 (in Canadian dollars). Cost amount is defined in subsection 248(1) of the Act. You can also see the income tax guide called Capital Gains. If the $100,000 threshold is exceeded at any time in the year, you are required to file Form T1135.
>
> Q. How do I know the cost amount of foreign property that I acquired before immigrating to Canada?
>
> A. In determining the cost of foreign property acquired before becoming a resident of Canada, use the fair market value of the property at the time you became a resident.
>
> Q. How do I know the cost amount of foreign property acquired by way of gift or inheritance?
>
> A. Where foreign property is acquired by way of gift or inheritance, use the fair market value at the time the gift was received or at the time you received the inheritance.
>
> Q. I have a self-directed registered retirement savings plan (RRSP) which has over $100,000 in foreign securities. Does the trust (i.e., the RRSP) have to file Form T1135?
>
> A. A trust governed by a RRSP does not have to file Form T1135.
>
> Q. My husband and I have a joint foreign bank account and joint ownership of other foreign property. The total cost of the foreign property we own jointly is $180,000. Are we required to file Form T1135? If so, who has to file the form?
>
> A. The proportionate ownership of the foreign property is based on the amount contributed by each person. If the contribution by one person is more than $100,000, that person has to file Form T1135.

What property do you have to report?

You only have to report property that is specified foreign property. Specified foreign property **includes**:

- funds in foreign bank accounts;
- shares of Canadian corporations on deposit with a foreign broker;
- shares of non-resident corporations held by the resident filer or on deposit with a Canadian or foreign broker;
- land and buildings located outside Canada, such as a foreign rental property;
- precious metals, gold certificates, and futures held outside Canada;
- interests in mutual funds that are organized in a foreign jurisdiction;
- debts owed by non-resident persons, such as government or corporate bonds, debentures, mortgages, and notes receivable;
- an interest in or a right to any specified foreign property;
- property that is convertible or that can be exchanged for a right to acquire specified foreign property;
- an interest in a partnership where the share of income or loss of the partnership for non-resident members is 90% or more and the partnership holds specified foreign property;

- an interest in a non-resident trust or a non-resident trust deemed to be resident by section 94 of the Act (discretionary trust);
- patents, copyrights or trademarks held outside Canada; and
- an interest in, or a right with respect to, an entity that is non-resident.

Specified foreign property **does not include:**

- property used or held exclusively in the course of carrying on an active business;
- personal-use property (i.e., property used primarily for personal use and enjoyment, such as a vacation property used primarily as a personal residence);
- an interest in a U.S. Individual Retirement Account (IRA);
- shares of the capital stock, or indebtedness, of a non-resident corporation that is a foreign affiliate;
- an interest in, or indebtedness, of a non-resident trust that is a foreign affiliate;
- an interest in a non-resident trust that neither you nor a person related to you had to pay for in any way;
- an interest in a non-resident trust principally providing superannuation, pension, retirement or employee benefits primarily to non-resident beneficiaries, that does not pay income tax in the taxing jurisdiction where it is resident; or
- an interest in, or a right to acquire any of the above-noted excluded foreign property.

> **Examples**
>
> **I am an individual who owns shares in non-resident corporations with a total cost amount of $250,000. These shares are held by a Canadian stockbroker. Do I have to report these shares on Form T1135?**
>
> You must report all shares of non-resident corporations (other than foreign affiliates) regardless of whether the shares are physically held inside or outside Canada. Since the cost amount of your shares exceeds $100,000, you have to report the shares on Form T1135.
>
> **I am an individual who owns units in a mutual fund trust. The cost amount of the units is $150,000. The mutual fund invests entirely in foreign securities. Do I have to file Form T1135?**
>
> If the mutual fund trust is resident in Canada, you do not have to file Form T1135. If you had an interest in a non-resident trust you might have to file the form. The type of investment held by a mutual fund trust does not determine its residency status. This also applies to a mutual fund corporation.
>
> **I own a condominium in Florida that has a cost amount of $120,000. Am I required to file Form T1135 if the property is: (a) only for personal use? (b) rented out for eight months of the year with a reasonable expectation of profit and kept for personal use the other four months? (c) rented out year round with a reasonable expectation of profit?**
>
> If the property is personal use property (i.e., property owned by you that is used by you or someone related to you primarily for personal use and enjoyment) you do not have to report the property on Form T1135. As a result, in situation (a), you would not need to report the condominium since it is held primarily for personal use and enjoyment.
>
> In situations (b) and (c), the property is an income-earning investment property that is not held primarily for personal use and enjoyment. As a result, since the cost amount is more than $100,000, you have to file Form T1135.

> **My Canadian corporation has a warehouse in England which it uses to store its products for distribution. The cost amount of the warehouse is $900,000. Should the corporation report this property on Form T1135?**
>
> You do not have to report property that is used or held exclusively in an active business. Since the warehouse is used exclusively for storing inventory used in the corporation's business, it does not have to be reported on Form T1135.
>
> **I have $200,000 in U.S. treasury bills. Do I have to file Form T1135? What if I do not hold the treasury bills at the end of the year?**
>
> Yes. You should report indebtedness owed by a non-resident on Form T1135. Report the property even if you did not hold it at the end of the year, as long as you held at any time in the year.

Completing the form

Check the appropriate box to identify the type of taxpayer reporting and provide the name, address, and identification number of the reporting taxpayer. Provide the tax year for which this statement is being filed.

For each type of property, check the box which corresponds to the cost amount of the property at the end of the year. Report the property if you owned it at any time in the year, i.e., report the property even if you did not own it at the end of the year, but did at some time in the year. If you do not own the property at the end of the year, use its cost amount at the time of disposition.

1. Funds held outside Canada

    Funds outside Canada include money on deposit in foreign bank accounts and money held with a foreign depository for safekeeping or held by any other institution. For this reporting requirement, funds include negotiable instruments such as cheques and drafts. (Marketable securities such as notes, bonds, and debentures issued by non-residents should be reported under the section called "Indebtedness owed by non-residents".)

2. Shares of non-resident corporations, other than foreign affiliates

    Report shares of non-resident corporations whether or not they are listed on a stock exchange or are physically held inside or outside Canada. Do not report shares in a corporation that is your foreign affiliate.

    Generally, a foreign affiliate is a non-resident corporation (or certain non-resident trusts) in which you hold at least 1% of the shares individually and (either alone or with related persons) hold 10% or more of the shares. If this is the case, you should obtain Form T1134A, Information Return Relating to Foreign Affiliates that are not Controlled Foreign Affiliates, or Form T1134B, Information Return Relating to Controlled Foreign Affiliates.

3. Indebtedness owed by non-residents

    Report all amounts owed to you by a non-resident person. Include all promissory notes, bills, bonds, commercial paper, loans, mortgages, and indebtedness issued by a non-resident person. Do not include indebtedness owed to you by your foreign affiliate.

4. Interests in non-resident trusts

Report any interest in a non-resident trust (other than a trust that is your foreign affiliate), including a non-resident trust deemed to be a resident by section 94 of the Act. You do not have to report your interest in the following types of trusts:

- a trust that is governed by a U.S. Individual Retirement Account (IRA);
- a non-resident trust that neither you nor a person related to you had to pay for in any way; and
- a non-resident trust principally providing superannuation, pension, retirement or employee benefits primarily to non-resident beneficiaries, that does not pay income tax in the taxing jurisdiction where it is resident.

5. Real property outside Canada

Report any real estate holdings that you have outside of Canada, other than real estate used in an active business or for personal use. For example, if you have a rental property outside Canada it should be included in this area.

6. Other property outside Canada

Other property means the following:

- precious metals or bullion (e.g., gold and silver) situated outside Canada;
- precious stones situated outside Canada;
- shares in corporations resident in Canada held by you or for you outside of Canada;
- commodity or future contracts, options or derivatives that constitute a right to, a right to acquire, or an interest in, specified foreign property; and
- any other right to, right to acquire, or interest in, specified foreign property.

Total income reported

Report the total amount of income (or loss) earned on the reported assets in the year. Include any taxable capital gain or loss on the disposition of the asset.

Amounts should be rounded to the nearest dollar.

Certification

This area should be completed and signed by:

- the person filing Form T1135 in the case of an individual;
- an authorized officer in the case of a corporation;
- the trustee, executor or administrator if the person filing the statement is a trust; or
- an authorized partner in the case of a partnership.

Name of the person who completed this statement

If you are not the reporting taxpayer, and were paid to prepare this statement, give your name and address.

Due dates for filing this statement

The reporting requirements for specified foreign property apply to tax years that begin after 1997. Form T1135 must be filed annually on or before the due date of your income tax return, or the partnership information return in section 229 of the Regulations to the Act in the case of a partnership.

In no case is Form T1135 due before April 30, 1999.

Foreign currency conversion

When converting amounts (i.e., income received on foreign property or the cost amount of the property) into Canadian dollars from a foreign currency, you should use the exchange rate in effect at the time of the transaction (i.e., the time the income was received or the property was purchased). However, if you received income throughout the year, you can use an average rate for the year.

Penalties for non-reporting

There are substantial penalties for failing to complete and file Form T1135 by the due date.

Voluntary disclosures

To promote compliance with Canada's tax laws, we encourage you to voluntarily correct any deficiencies in your past tax affairs.

You can make a voluntary disclosure by contacting your tax services office. The address and telephone numbers are listed under "Canada Revenue Agency" in the Government of Canada section of your telephone book.

For more information, see Information Circular 85-1R2, Voluntary Disclosures.

T1141: Information return - transfers or loans to non-resident trust

You have to file a separate return for each non-resident trust. Give all amounts in Canadian dollars.

Form T1141 must be filed separately from your tax return. Send the original to:

Ottawa Tax Centre

Employer Services Division

Other Program Unit

875 Huron Road

Ottawa, Ontario K1A 1A2

T1142: Information return in respect of ... non-resident trust

The full name of this form is "Information return in respect of distributions from and indebtedness to a non-resident trust." You have to file a separate return for each non-resident trust.

Use this same form if you are reporting for a partnership. In that case, read all references to year or tax year as fiscal period and all references to taxpayer as partnership.

T1153: Consent and request form

Discounters must use this form to obtain consent from clients to access information on the System for Electronic Notification of Debt (SEND).

T1158#: Registration of family payments

Complete this form if:

- Your order or agreement was made in 2001 or a subsequent year, and it specifies support payments for a spouse or common-law partner. Starting in 2001, the term spouse applies only to a person to whom you are legally married; the term common-law partner is a person of the same or opposite sex who is not your spouse, and who meets certain conditions.
- Your order or agreement was made after April 1997 and before January 2001, and it specifies support payments for a spouse. For years before 2001, the term spouse applies to a person to whom you were legally married or a person of the opposite sex with whom you lived in a common-law relationship.
- Your order or agreement was made before May 1997, it specifies support payments for a spouse or clearly specifies separate amounts for a spouse and for a child, and:
    - you have filed Form T1157 Election for Child Support Payments; or
    - your order or agreement was changed after April 1997 to increase or decrease the amount of child support payable.

Complete a separate form for each court order or agreement you are registering.

Send the completed form (one for each court order or written agreement you are registering) and a copy of your court order or written agreement if applicable, to one of the offices listed on the form.

T1161: List of properties by an emigrant of Canada

Complete this form if you emigrated from Canada at any time during the year and the fair market value of all the property you owned at that time was more than $25,000.

T1162A: Pre-authorized payment plan

Complete this form to sign up for quarterly automatic bank withdrawals of your federal income tax instalment payments.

Choose between two options for these withdrawals. The amount withdrawn is either the amount in box 2 of the Install Reminder sent to you in February or an amount you specify.

T1243: Deemed disposition of property by an emigrant of Canada

Complete this form if you ceased to be a resident of Canada at any time during the year and you have property that you are deemed to have disposed of when you left Canada.

T1244: Election, under subsection 220(4.5) of the Income Tax Act, to defer the payment of tax on income relating to the deemed disposition of property

If the taxpayer elects under subsection 220(4.5) of the Income Tax Act to defer the payment of taxes related to deemed dispositions of property, the taxpayer still has to pay the taxes owing which were calculated when they prepared their return. CRA will notify the taxpayer if they are eligible for the election. If the taxpayer is eligible, CRA will issue a refund for the taxes paid which pertain to deemed dispositions of property.

TX19: Asking for a clearance certificate

Use this form if you are the legal representative for an estate, business or property and you are asking for a clearance certificate. A legal representative includes an executor, administrator, liquidator, trustee, or like person other than a trustee in bankruptcy.

Send this form to the Assistant Director, Verification and Enforcement Division, at your tax services office. Do not attach it to the return.

Do not submit this form until:

- you have filed and CRA has assessed all the required return(s); and
- all income taxes (including provincial or territorial taxes CRA administers), CPP contributions, EI premiums and any related interest and penalties have been received or secured.

Provide CRA with the following documents to avoid delay (attach any documents that apply to your situation):

- a copy of the will, including any codicils, renunciations, or disclaimers and all probate documents (if the taxpayer died intestate, also attach a copy of the document appointing an administrator and details of the proposed distribution of assets, including the name, address and SIN or account number of each beneficiary and relationship to the deceased);
- a copy of the trust document;
- a statement showing the properties and distribution plan including the date chosen for the distribution of properties, and a list of the recipients of each of the properties (for each property, provide a description, the adjusted cost base, and the fair market value at date of death or distribution);
- any other documents which are necessary to prove that you are the legal representative; and
- a letter of authorization that you signed if you want us to communicate with someone else.

Chapter 8

Clients

2009 Tax Year

Client

None of the forms in the Client category of the Form Explorer are CRA forms. These are all ProFile forms to facilitate your tax return processing or client interactions.

Billing

Based on information you have entered into the tax return, ProFile T1 calculates billing amounts using the pricing schedule found under Options > Pricing.

As you work on a tax return, the Billing form will show all the per form charges that apply (based on data you've entered and whether or not ProFile determines that the form is included in the tax return). The amounts on Billing are specific to the current return -- you can override these here without affecting other returns.

- At the top of the Billing form, you can override your default pricing options for a particular client.
- There is space at the bottom of this form to show disbursements.
- In the Description of services you can type free-form text that will merge with the template file to provide additional detail for this client.
- The templates Invoice and Invoice use the amounts from the Billing form. You can edit these templates for all clients, for example, to add your corporate logo.
- To edit the invoice for all clients or to personalize the invoice for one client, right click on the invoice in the Edit window and choose Edit template or Personalize.
- Preparer information automatically transfers from Options > Environment > Preparer.

You can edit the charges on the Billing form to change the invoice for a particular taxpayer. The software uses this information to produce the client invoice. You can select a Client or Joint Invoice from the Form Explorer, and view the results of your entries on the Billing form.

You can transfer invoicing information on the Billing worksheet to an invoice in QuickBooks. For more information on this function, see QuickBooks Integration.

Client letters and invoices

There are a number of client letters and invoices (Letter, JLetter, Invoice, JInvoice, User1, User2, etc.) that ProFile can automatically prepare based on information in the tax return.

You can edit these client letters and invoices with the built-in word processor. To make edits, right-click on the letter and select "Edit template" from the context-sensitive menu. Or, select Options > Templates from the main menu.

You can choose between joint or individual letters and invoices. Joint letters and invoices let you incorporate information from both taxpayers' returns in a single letter or invoice. To use the joint version of the templates, select the appropriate checkbox under Options > Module > General > Options.

CCTB: Canada Child tax benefit

By default, ProFile answers "Yes" to the question Are you eligible to receive the Child Tax Benefit? at the top of the Child Tax Benefit and Dependant forms. If the returns are coupled, ProFile automatically determines which of the two spousal returns should show the claim. Answer "No" if you do not wish for ProFile to calculate this amount.

Important: To receive the CCTB, you must apply for each child. Once you have applied (for example, when the child was born) you do not need to reapply for that child. However, you should apply even if your family income excludes you from actually receiving the CCTB. Most provincial family benefit programs depend on your child being registered for the CCTB. To receive these other benefits, your child must be registered for the CCTB, even if he or she does not receive it.

Estimation of the Canada Child Tax Benefit

ProFile will automatically calculate the estimated Child Tax Benefit that the taxpayers are entitled to receive in the coming year, based on information provided in the tax returns. (The CRA will send a CCTB Notice to the taxpayer once it calculates the exact benefit - if any is entitled.)

The estimate includes the federal benefit as determined by the CRA, as well as the provincial benefit (for most provinces and territories).

Note: The ProFile CCTB calculation feature is based on information we obtain from provincial budgets (some of which may not be available at time of a particular release).

ProFile posts the amount from the provincial CCTB form (for example, CCTB (BC)) on the federal CCTB form to show the estimated combined monthly payment.

More about the CCTB

If you are responsible for the care and upbringing of a child who is under 18 years of age, you can apply for the CCTB for that child. Submit a completed Form RC66, Canada Child Benefits Application, along with any other documents required, as soon as possible after the child is born or begins to live with you. This information is also used to apply for payments from certain related provincial or territorial programs. If you are a permanent resident, temporary resident, or protected person (refugee) as defined in the Immigration and Refugee Protection Act, you should apply as soon as possible after you and your child arrive in Canada.

In addition to the CCTB, you can also receive a Child Disability Benefit (CDB) if your child meets the criteria for the disability amount and the CRA has approved Form T2201, Disability Tax Credit Certificate for that child.

The CCTB and CDB are based on the net income (line 236) shown on your return and, if applicable, your return minus any amount you or your spouse's or common-law partner reported on lines 117 and 125. If you or your spouse or common-law partner deducted an amount on line 213, and/or an amount for a repayment of registered disability savings plan income included on line 232, we will add these amounts to your or your spouse's or common-law partner's net income. Therefore, to qualify for these benefits, you both have to file a return every year, even if there is no income to report.

To apply for the CCTB or to view your CCTB or CDB, see Pamphlet T4114, Canada Child Benefits.

GST/HST credit application

T1 GST/HST credit application

ProFile automatically determines eligibility for the GST/HST credit application, and selects "Yes" or "No" depending on client data. The GST/HST worksheet calculates the credit the taxpayer can expect to receive.

❓ Frequently Asked Questions

Why didn't I receive my credit?

The CRA may apply your GST/HST credit against certain outstanding federal, provincial, or territorial government debts, such as student loans, Employment Insurance and social assistance benefit overpayments, Immigration loans, and training allowance overpayments. They also may apply it to satisfy a garnishment order under the Family Orders and Agreements Enforcement Assistance Act.

Which spouse should claim the GST credit?

It really doesn't matter who claims the GST/HST credit, as long as only one member of a household claims it. It is a tax-free payment to help lower income individuals and families offset the cost of the GST/HST. It is based on the number of children you have and on your net family income (not including that of your children).

GST/HST credit payments are not considered income. You do not have to report them on next year's return.

 The Canada Revenue Agency says... *General Income Tax and Benefit Guide*

To receive this credit, including any related provincial credit, you have to apply for it, even if you received it last year. Complete the application area on page 1 of your return for 2009. Your credit is based on the number of children you have and your net income added to the net income of your spouse or common-law partner, if you have one, minus any amount you or your spouse or common-law partner reported on lines 117 and 125. If you or your spouse or common-law partner deducted an amount on line 213, and/or an amount for a repayment of registered disability savings plan income included on line 232, we will add those amounts to your or your spouse's or common-law partner's net income.

This information also is used to calculate any payments from certain related provincial programs. Net income is the amount on line 236 of a person's return, or the amount that it would be if the person filed a return.

Make sure you enter, in the Identification area of your return, your marital status and, if it applies, the information concerning your spouse or common-law partner (including his or her net income, even if it is zero. Otherwise, your application may be delayed. Either you or your spouse or common-law partner can receive the credit, but not both. No matter which one of you applies, the credit will be the same.

To view your GST/HST credit account, go to My Account on our website. For more information on the GST/HST credit, see Pamphlet RC4210, GST/HST Credit.

Paying Your Tax by Instalments (Instalment Worksheet)

Instalments

Use the Instalments worksheet to estimate instalments payable during the next taxation year.

CRA calculates instalments based on net tax owing from the taxation year that has just ended, and from the preceding tax year. This blend is used because the first two instalment payments are due in March and June, before the current year filing deadline for self-employed taxpayers.

By default, the ProFile calculation of the first two instalments is based on net tax owing from the preceding year's tax return. If you carried the return forward, required amounts appear automatically on the Instalment form. If you are creating a return for a new client and have a copy of the preceding year's tax return, you can enter relevant amounts on the Instalment form.

The third and fourth instalments are based on amounts that flow to the Instalments form from other sections of this tax return file. To determine the amounts for the third and fourth instalments, ProFile subtracts the first two instalment amounts from the total tax owing on this tax return. The balance of tax payable is split between the third and fourth instalments.

Note that if the net tax owing was lower in the preceding year, the first and second payments will be lower than the third and fourth.

If there are no amounts available for the preceding taxation year, the third and fourth instalment payments will equal the full tax owing. ProFile will assume that the taxpayer had no net tax owing in the preceding year. If instalments were required, but amounts are not available, you will need to override the payment option. Base the calculation on the amounts from this return only, to ensure that the taxpayer avoids interest and penalties.

Instalment payment options

When the net tax owing was greater for the preceding year than it is on the current return, ProFile will automatically base instalments on amounts from this return only.

If you estimate income and credits for the next taxation year, ProFile will automatically use those amounts to calculate instalments. This is to the taxpayer's advantage when income is certain to be lower in the current year. However, if the taxpayer has underestimated current year income, CRA will assess interest and penalties.

A taxpayer will never be subject to instalment interest or penalties when paying, by the due date, the instalments as they appear on CRA's instalment notices.

 **The Canada Revenue Agency says...** *Pamphlet P110, Paying Your Income Tax by Instalments*

What are instalments?

Instalments are periodic income tax payments that individuals have to pay to the Canada Revenue Agency (CRA) to cover tax that they would otherwise have to pay on April 30 of the following year. Instalments are not paid in advance; they are paid throughout the calendar year in which you are earning the taxable income.

Why do you have to pay tax by instalments?

Why do you have to pay tax by instalments? You have to pay tax by instalments for the same reason that an employee has to have tax deducted from his or her pay. If you receive income that has no tax withheld or does not have enough tax withheld for more than one year, you may have to pay tax by instalments.

This can happen if you receive rental, investment, or self-employment income, certain pension payments, or income from more than one job.

Who has to pay by instalments?

Who has to pay by instalments? You have to pay your income tax by instalments for 2010 if your net tax owing is more than $3,000:

- in 2010; and
- in either 2009 or 2008.

Quebec residents: If you live in Quebec on December 31 of a year, use a limit of $1,800 instead of $3,000 for that year.

Farmers and Fishers: Different rules apply if your main source of income in 2010 is self-employment income from farming or fishing. For details, see Farming and fishing.

Net tax owing - In general, this is the amount you owe on your tax return.

When are your payments due?

Your instalment payments for 2010 are due March 15, June 15, September 15, and December 15, 2010.

When a due date falls on a Saturday, a Sunday, or a holiday recognized by the CRA, we consider your payment to be paid on time if we receive it or if it is postmarked on the next business day. For a list of holidays, visit our Web site at Public holidays or call 1 800-959-8281.

Your payment will be considered paid on one of the following dates:

- Payments you make in person at your financial institution, are considered paid on the date stamped on your INNS3 receipt.
- Payments you send by mail are considered paid on the date you mail them.
- Payments you made through your financial institution's Internet or telephone banking services are considered paid when your financial institution credits us with your payment.
- Post-dated cheques and payments you make by pre-authorized debit are considered paid on the negotiable date.

Deceased person: If an individual who has to pay tax by instalments dies during the year, instalment payments due on or after the date of death do not have to be paid.

What is an instalment reminder?

Instalments reminders are issued to help you determine if you have to pay income tax by instalments. The reminder will suggest an amount to pay and list the payment options.

In February and August, we send instalment reminders to individuals who may have to pay tax by instalments. The February reminder is for the March and June payments, and the August reminder is for the September and December payments.

Note: If the only reminder we send you in 2010 is for the September and December due dates, see "Did you only get an instalment reminder for September and December 2009?"

Even if we send you an instalment reminder in 2010, you do not have to make instalment payments for 2010 if your net tax owing for 2010 will be $3,000 or less ($1,800 or less for residents of Quebec).

How and where do you make your instalment payments

Each instalment reminder package we send includes Form INNS3, Instalment Remittance Voucher . Form INNS3 includes two tear off voucher sections.

You can choose any of the following methods to make your payments.

Electronically: You cannot make electronic payments to us directly. You may be able to pay electronically through your financial institution's Internet or telephone banking services and you may be able to schedule post-dated payments.

At your financial institution: You can make your payment free of charge at your branch of a Canadian chartered bank, caisse populaire, or credit union. However, the institution will only accept your payment if you have Form INNS3 from the CRA. The teller will stamp Form INNS3 and give it to you as a receipt.

By pre-authorized debits: You can have your instalment payments debited from your bank account. To do this, use My Account on our Web site, or send us a completed Form T1162A-1, Pre-Authorized Payment Plan (Personal Quarterly Instalment Payments), by mail to:

> Canada Revenue Agency
>
> P.O. Box 9659, Station T
>
> Ottawa ON K1G 6L7

To cancel the pre-authorized debit plan or to change the amount of your payments, send a letter to the above address or a fax to 613 739-1147, or call 1 800-959-8281. Starting in February 2010, simple cancellation requests can be processed online. To do this, use My Account on our Web site.

To change your banking information, you have to send a letter to the above address or a fax to 613-739-1147.

 Note: Any change can take up to 30 days to process.

By mail: You can send a cheque (post-dated cheques accepted) or money order payable to the Receiver General, and a completed voucher section of Form INNS3, to:

> Canada Revenue Agency
>
> 875 Heron Road
>
> Ottawa ON K1A 1B1

Please write your social insurance number (SIN) on the back of your cheque or money order to help us process your payment correctly.

Installment interest

We charge installment interest if all of the following conditions apply:

- we send you an installment reminder in 2010 that shows an amount to pay;
- you are required to make installment payments in 2010; (see "Who has to pay by instalments?") and
- you do not make installment payments, or you make payments that are late or less than the required amount.

We calculate the interest on each installment that you should have paid using the payment option that calculates the least amount of interest. Then we calculate the interest on each installment you did pay. We charge the difference between these two amounts only if the difference is more than $25.

Installment interest is compounded daily at the prescribed interest rate. This rate can change every three months. To get the current interest rate

If you realize during 2010 that you paid less than your required installment payment, or that you did not pay it on time, you can reduce or eliminate an installment interest charge by overpaying your next 2010 installment payment or by paying it early.

Installment penalty

You may also have to pay a penalty if your installment payments are late or less than the required amount. We apply this penalty only if your installment interest charges for 2010 are more than $1,000.

To calculate the penalty, we determine which of the following amounts is higher:

- $1,000; or
- one-quarter of the installment interest that you would have had to pay if you had not made installment payments for 2010.

Then, we subtract the higher amount from your actual installment interest charges for 2010. Finally, we divide the difference by two and the result is your penalty.

For complete information about installments, get publication P110.

Notes

The notes page is a blank form in which you can enter text.

These notes automatically carry forward from year to year. This makes the Notes form a convenient place to leave reminders for yourself about how the return was prepared, or things to consider for next year.

ProFile does not currently offer any option to export notes from your client files, or to include them in your customized template letters.

Plan#: Tax planner

Use the tax planner to prepare a projection of the taxpayer's position for the next taxation year.

Plan is an unlimited form, so you can create many different scenarios for a single T1 file. When you create a new Plan (right-click on an existing Plan and choose New form), ProFile creates new T1 plans for the client and spouse, all in the same numbered set.

You can enter a description for a specific scenario in the Description field at the top of the form. This description then appears in the Form Explorer to help you quickly distinguish between the different scenarios you create.

Attention: Our Development team keeps the Tax Planner as current as possible with information from recent budget announcements. Depending on what rates were available at the time of the last software release, the Tax Planner may not include all federal and provincial changes for the year.

Create a T1 Plan

To save time entering data on a new plan, you can transfer amounts from the current year's tax return to get you started. Follow these steps:

1. Open a completed T1 client file.

2. Open the form Plan from the Client category of the Form Explorer.

3. Right-click in any field and select Copy T1 return.

Once you have the T1 return data in the plan, you can change any amounts to reflect your client's new projections for the year.

Data locking

Like the T1Adj form, the Plan form is not impacted by any data locking you apply to your completed client files. This means that you can continue to create new plans in a tax return file that is locked to prevent accidental changes to the current year return you have filed.

Updating a plan

ProFile does NOT update the Plan form(s) when you change amounts in the current year tax return. If you do make changes in the return and want to update a Plan, select "Copy T1 return" once again from the right-click menu. ProFile will update transfer amounts, but you won't lose any data you have entered as overrides.

Plans in the Form Explorer

In the Detail view of the Form Explorer, a plan is not "Used" until you enter an amount directly or copy data from the tax return.

Optimize - Split pension Income

The Split Pension Income optimization worksheet helps you determine the amount, if any, to enter on line E of the T1032 Joint Election to Split Pension Income. The suggested split-pension amount optimizes the combined total of tax payable for the current year (line 435).

To view the amount that ProFile recommends that the taxpayer transfer to his/her spouse or common law partner, right-click on the worksheet and select Optimize split-pension income.

The Calculation of the elected split-pension amount table automatically populates, illustrating pretransfer results in the Zero Transfer column, and post-transfer results using the recommended amount (displayed on the elected split-pension amount line) in the ProFile suggested column.

The Combined net benefit (cost) line shows the overall savings you will realize if you select to transfer the suggested split-pension amount.

Note: The Split-pension Income worksheet is designed to be used in the return of the taxpayer who is transferring pension income to a spouse or common-law partner. You must first select Pensioner in the checkbox at the top of form T1032 in order for the worksheet to calculate. Returns must also be "coupled returns" in ProFile.

Since this is a suggested amount only, and other considerations should be made when deciding to allocate part of a taxpayer's eligible income to a spouse or common-law partner, ProFile will not transfer the suggested amount unless you elect to do so.

If you choose to elect the ProFile suggested amount, right-click on the worksheet and select Elect split pension amount of $___. The amount will then automatically transfer to line E of form T1032.

Experimenting with different scenarios

The worksheet also provides a Calculator feature that enables you to experiment with different scenarios and view the effect that a custom split-pension amount would have on the return.

In the Calculator section of the table, simply enter the amount of your choice in the field provided on the first line and watch as ProFile calculates the combined net benefit for that scenario. You can experiment with as many different amounts as you wish.

If you choose to elect one of your custom split-pension amounts, enter the amount you wish to transfer on line E - Elected split-pension amount of the worksheet. The amount will automatically transfer to form T1032.

Summaries

ProFile offers these summary forms that present the tax return data in different ways:

- **Summary** - This form shows all the non-zero line items of a single taxpayer's T1 return (each field that contains data in the return).
- **T1Summary** - This form shows major items from the taxpayer's return.
- **T1/TP1 5-Year Summary** - This form shows the major items for a single taxpayer's last five years of tax returns.
- **T1/TP1 Comparative** - This form compares the major items from this year's tax return to last year's tax return for a single taxpayer. If you carried the return forward using ProFile, last year's amounts appear automatically on the comparative summary.
- **Comparative NRTC Summary** - This form compares the non-refundable tax credits on the federal and provincial tax returns.
- **T1 Review - ProFile Premier only** - Similar to the Comparative Tax Summary, the T1Review form compares the major items from this year's tax return to last year's tax return for a single taxpayer, with a special focus on review. The form uses default variance thresholds (as specified under Options > Module > Variance) to highlight significant changes from current and prior year returns; you can also set your own threshold on the form itself. The differences calculated automatically and are shown on the T1Review in dollar and/or percentage amounts.

    Note: If you wish to view the changes in excess of the variance threshold in the ProFile auditor, you can enable this preference on the T1Review form.
- **Audit** - In addition to these forms, there are also summaries based on information that appears in the Active Auditor (press <F9> to view the Active Auditor on screen). You can right-click on any tab in the Active auditor and select 'Print' to create a printout of diagnostics for your files. You can customize what is included in the Audit summary under Options > Environment > Audit > Audit Summary includes.

    Note: The Variance tab will contain information only for returns that you have carried forward and only if you enable variance diagnostics under Options > Module > Variance.

T1EFILE: EFILE information

The T1EFILE form allows you to review exclusions from EFILE before sending the return to CRA. Some of the questions ProFile answers automatically based on information in the taxpayer's return. Other question you must answer yourself as they apply. If the answer is "Yes" to any of the exclusions, you cannot EFILE the tax return. Instead, you must submit a paper return for the client.

Additional fields contain amounts that ProFile calculates for EFILE but does not show on any of the other forms. This gives you an opportunity to review these amounts before you EFILE the return.

There are a few fields (such as line 487 - Enter 1 if return is completed under the CRA volunteer program) that ProFile cannot determine and that you must enter manually.

Do you need more information?

Throughout this guide, we mention forms, pamphlets, interpretation bulletins, information circulars, and other guides that give more details on specific tax topics. You can get most of CRA publications, including the General guide and forms book, by visiting **Forms and publications** on the CRA Web site or by calling **1-800-959-2221** from 8:15 a.m. to 5:00 p.m. CRA Web site at http://www.cra.gc.ca

If you use a teletypewriter (TTY) because you have difficulty hearing or speaking, you can call CRA toll-free, bilingual TTY enquiry service to get information. The telephone number is 1-800-665-0354.

Your opinion counts!
We review our publications every year. If you have comments or suggestions that would help us improve them, we would like to hear from you. Please send your comments and suggestions on our publications to:
The Ford Group
PO Box 1123
Bradford, ON L3Z 2B5

Appendix

2009 Tax Year

 Canada Revenue Agency / Agence du revenu du Canada

Teaching Taxes Program
Student Workbook

2009

TIS17(E) Rev. 09

Community Volunteer Income Tax Program

What is it?

Since 1971, the Canada Revenue Agency (CRA) has worked with community volunteers to help people complete their income tax and benefit returns.

Help people in your community

Many people don't know how to complete their income tax and benefit return and cannot pay for assistance. We need volunteers like you to provide this important community service to taxpayers who have low incomes and simple tax situations. As a volunteer, we will ask you to respect the privacy of the taxpayer, decline any offers of monetary reward for your services, and return the completed income tax and benefit return and other personal documents to the taxpayer.

What do you get out of it?

As a volunteer, you will meet other people who, like yourself, want to lend a helping hand. You will also have the satisfaction of knowing that you are providing a service to those who need it most. Volunteering is easy and rewarding.

The CRA organizes free volunteer training sessions for individuals and community organizations across the country and provides a package that includes a handy reference kit. With the knowledge from the volunteer training session and the reference kit, you will be ready to help others in your community. Remember that the CRA is always available to help you if you have any questions.

How can you get involved?

If you want to help in your community, register online at **www.cra.gc.ca/volunteer**, or call us at **1-800-959-8281**.

You would be a welcome addition to our volunteer team!

Table of contents

	Page
Definitions	4
Introduction	6
Why should you learn about taxes?	6
What will you learn from the Teaching Taxes Program?	6
Additional information	6
Learning Sections	6
Section 1 – History of taxes in the world and Canada	6
Section 2 – Canada's tax system and the Taxpayer Bill of Rights	6
Section 3 – Your tax obligations when you start working	7
Social insurance number	7
Form TD1, *Personal Tax Credits Return*	7
What gets deducted from your salary or wages	7
Your statement of earnings (pay stub)	8
T4 information slip – *Statement of Remuneration Paid*	8
Section 4 – Income tax and benefit return	8
Calculating your income	9

	Page
Calculating federal and provincial or territorial taxes payable	9
Refund or Balance owing	10
Filing your return	10
Tax Scenarios	11
Example 1 – High school student	11
Example 2 – High school student (with Quebec as the province of employment)	13
Example 3 – Post-secondary student	15
Example 4 – Employed individual	18
Example 5 – Single-parent family	19
Example 6 – First nations Resident	22
Additional Information	24
Quick reference to box numbers on information slips and line numbers on a return	24
2009 Personal Tax Credits Return – TD1	25
Sample – Statement of Earnings (Pay Stub)	27
Sample – T4 – *Statement of Remuneration Paid*	28

Definitions

Canada Child Tax Benefit (CCTB) – a tax-free monthly payment made to eligible families to help them with the cost of raising children under age 18. The number of children, their age, and the family net income are all factors used to calculate the benefit.

Canada Pension Plan (CPP) – a pension plan designed to provide you with income for your retirement.

Child care expenses – amounts you or another person paid to have someone look after an eligible child, so that you or the other person could earn employment income, carry on a business, attend school, or conduct research.

EFILE – a method of filing an income tax and benefit return electronically through an EFILE service provider.

Employment Insurance (EI) premiums – employers deduct EI premiums from the salary or wages of their employees, and remit these amounts to the CRA. When an employee becomes unemployed, he or she may be entitled to EI benefits. Self-employed people are usually not covered under the *Employment Insurance Act*.

Goods and services tax/harmonized sales tax (GST/HST) credit – a tax-free quarterly payment that helps individuals and families with low and modest incomes offset all or part of the GST or HST that they pay.

Income tax and benefit returns – the five most common income tax and benefit returns are:

T1 General – this is the most detailed of all the returns and it covers all tax situations. It is the only income tax and benefit return available by going to **www.cra.gc.ca/forms**.

T1 Special – this is a less detailed version of the General return and is designed for non-business tax situations.

T1S-A – this return is for retired seniors with straightforward tax situations whose taxable income is $50,000 or less. It includes the most common types of retirement income and credits.

T1S-C – this return is for individuals who have certain types of income for which no taxes are being withheld and no taxes are payable. They use this return to apply for the GST/HST credit and to give the CRA the information needed to calculate any CCTB (and related provincial or territorial child benefits and credits) payments they may be entitled to receive.

T1S-D – this credit and benefit return is for Indians who are registered, or eligible to be registered, under the *Indian Act*.

Income tax deductions – employers deduct income tax from the salary or wages of their employees and remit these amounts to the CRA.

Information slips – forms that employers, trusts, and businesses use to tell the CRA and taxpayers how much income was earned and how much tax was deducted, if applicable. These include forms such as the T3, T4, and T5.

Instalment payments – taxpayers who receive income that has no tax withheld or not enough tax withheld may have to pay their taxes by instalments.

NETFILE – a method of filing a return electronically over the Internet. For more information, visit our Web site at **www.netfile.gc.ca**.

Net income – the amount left after certain allowable deductions have been subtracted from the **total income** calculated on an income tax and benefit return.

Non-refundable tax credits – these credits reduce the amount of income tax you owe. Federal non-refundable tax credits are used to reduce the amount of federal tax you owe. Provincial or territorial non-refundable tax credits are used to reduce the provincial or territorial tax you owe. However, if the total of these credits is more than the amount you owe, you will not get a refund for the difference. This is why they are called "non-refundable."

Notice of Assessment – a notice that the CRA sends to taxpayers after it processes their income tax and benefit returns. The notice tells taxpayers whether the CRA has made any corrections to their return and what the changes were. It also lets taxpayers know whether they owe more tax or what the amount of their refund will be, and gives them their registered retirement savings plan contribution limit for the following year.

Penalties – amounts taxpayers must pay if they fail to file an income tax and benefit return on time or try to evade paying tax by not filing a return. Individuals who make false statements or omissions on a return or who do not provide the information required on a prescribed form must also pay a penalty.

Quebec Pension Plan (QPP) – a pension plan maintained by the Province of Quebec, which is equivalent to the CPP.

Refund – the amount refunded to the taxpayer if the total credits on line 482 of the income tax and benefit return are more than the total payable on line 435.

Refundable tax credits – these credits reduce the amount of income tax you owe. If the total of these credits is more than the amount you owe, you may be entitled to a refund of the difference.

Registered education savings plan (RESP) – a plan that can help an individual save money for a child's post-secondary education. Contributions to a plan are not deductible from income, but a beneficiary has to include RESP educational assistance payments (income earned in the plan) in income.

Registered retirement savings plan (RRSP) – a retirement savings plan that an individual establishes and contributes to, and the CRA registers. Any income earned in an RRSP is generally exempt from tax until the individual receives payments from the plan.

Self-assessment – the foundation of the tax system, whereby taxpayers are required to report their income and calculate their income tax payable without the government having to formally request that they do so.

Statement of Remuneration Paid (T4 slip) – an information slip that shows the income and taxable benefits an employer paid to their employee in the past year. It also shows the total deductions for the year.

Taxation – the legislation (law and regulations) concerning consumption taxes and income tax.

Tax credits – amounts of money considered to have been paid towards an individual's tax payable. Governments give tax credits to reduce or redistribute taxes or to encourage certain types of activity or investment. Examples of these are provincial or territorial tax credits and the dividend tax credit.

Taxable income – the amount of income remaining after certain allowable deductions have been subtracted from **net income**.

Tax year – usually the calendar year, that is, the year that begins on January 1 and ends on December 31.

Taxpayer – an individual or business that is required to pay tax.

TELEFILE – a method of filing a return electronically. This system lets you file your completed return using a touch-tone telephone.

Universal Child Care Benefit (UCCB) – a taxable benefit designed to help Canadian families, as they try to balance work and family life, by supporting their child care choices through direct financial support.

Introduction

Why should you learn about taxes?

Taxes will affect you and your family both now and in the future. As individuals or businesses, Canadians have to deal with taxes, whether they file a return or claim a credit.

A basic knowledge and understanding of Canada's income tax system will allow you to deal effectively with taxes throughout your life. You will learn how to comply with the law and, at the same time, learn about all the federal, provincial, or territorial benefits and credits to which you may be entitled.

What will you learn from the Teaching Taxes Program?

The Teaching Taxes Program is made up of four sections that will introduce you to the world of taxes in Canada.

After completing the Tax Scenarios in this workbook, you will be able to prepare an income tax and benefit return with confidence, and you could help family members with their returns.

You could also join the **Community Volunteer Income Tax Program**. It is an excellent opportunity for you to get involved in your community and to deal with real-life tax situations. See page 2 for more information.

Additional information

This workbook also has a glossary, a quick reference guide to the box and line numbers you will find on the most common information slips and sample copies of some forms

Learning Sections

Section 1 – History of taxes in the world and Canada

Many people assume that taxes are a recent development and that our ancestors did not have to pay them. This is not the case.

Since the beginning of recorded history, some kind of tax system has existed in organized societies and governments. Over 3,500 years ago, the ancient Egyptians collected taxes and the Roman Empire had a highly evolved tax system.

In this section, you will learn the evolution of taxes from the early years of civilization to our present day. You will also have the opportunity to discover some of the milestones in Canada's tax system.

Your teacher can provide you with all the handouts and/or activities you will need to complete this section.

Section 2 – Canada's tax system and the Taxpayer Bill of Rights

This section will introduce you to the characteristics of a good tax system. It will also give you an overview of Canada's tax system, and you will learn about the principle upon which the tax system is founded. You will also take a closer look at your rights as a taxpayer by reviewing the Taxpayer Bill of Rights. It can be found by going to **www.cra.gc.ca/fairness**.

Your teacher can provide you with all the handouts and/or activities you will need to complete this section.

Section 3 – Your tax obligations when you start working

You will learn all you need to know about some of the documents and forms that will help you to meet your tax obligations, and be introduced to those you will most likely see when you start working. You will also be provided with information on completing Form TD1, *Personal Tax Credits Return,* and be introduced to the common deductions you will most likely see on your statement of earnings (pay stub). You will also learn how to read and understand the T4 information slips.

Social insurance number

The social insurance number (SIN) is a nine-digit number that you need to work in Canada and to have access to government programs and benefits.

For more information, or to get an application for a SIN, contact Service Canada at **1-800-206-7218**, or visit their Web site at **www.servicecanada.gc.ca**.

Form TD1, *Personal Tax Credits Return*

When you begin working, your employer will ask you to complete a Form TD1, *Personal Tax Credits Return.* This will enable your employer to calculate the correct amount of income tax to deduct from your income.

Depending on your income level and the province or territory in which you work, you may also have to complete a form for that province or territory.

Form TD1 outlines the non-refundable tax credits you can claim on the income tax and benefit return you file after the end of each year. Non-refundable tax credits are used to reduce the amount of tax withheld on your income, because they reduce the federal and provincial/territorial taxes you have to pay.

Generally, every taxpayer is eligible to claim the basic personal amount on line 1 of Form TD1. Depending on your situation when you complete Form TD1, you may be eligible for other non-refundable tax credits.

If you have **more than one** employer or payer at the same time and you have already claimed personal tax credit amounts on another Form TD1, you should not claim them again. If you do, your non-refundable tax credits will be counted twice, and you will have taxes owing at the end of the year when you file your income tax and benefit return. To choose this option, you would enter "0" on line 13 and not complete lines 2 to 12.

The amount of tax withheld by your employer during the year will build a credit (total income tax deducted) that you will apply against your total taxes payable when you complete your income tax and benefit return. See a copy of Form TD1 on page 25.

What gets deducted from your salary or wages

Your employer will make deductions from your salary or wages. The most common deductions are Canada Pension Plan (CPP) or Quebec Pension Plan (QPP) contributions, Employment Insurance (EI) premiums, and income tax.

Canada Pension Plan (CPP) or Quebec Pension Plan (QPP) contributions

Once you turn 18, and until you turn 70, you have to make CPP or QPP contributions based on your pensionable employment income. Your employer is responsible for deducting these contributions and sending them to the CRA.

If you worked in the province of Quebec, your employer will deduct QPP contributions instead of CPP contributions.

The amount of your contribution (deducted each pay period) is calculated on an estimate of your pensionable earnings, including an exemption of $3,500 up to a maximum of $46,300.

The result is then multiplied by the contribution rate. The contribution rate for CPP is 4.95% for 2009. The maximum amount that you can pay for the year is $2,118.60.

Employment Insurance (EI) premiums

There is no age limit for EI contributions. These are also a percentage of your insurable earnings (generally gross pay). The employee's EI rate for 2009 is 1.73%. The maximum premium you pay for the year is $731.79. Employees with Quebec employers pay EI premiums at the rate of 1.38% and the maximum premium payable for the year is $583.74.

Quebec Parental Insurance Plan (QPIP) premiums (only if province of employment is Quebec)

The QPIP is a plan to which employers and you as an employee contribute to provide for the payment of benefits to an employee whose regular income is interrupted as a result of taking maternity, paternity, parental, or adoption leave. All employees, regardless of their age, pay QPIP premiums. The employee rate for 2009 is 0.484% and the maximum premium payable for the year is $300.08.

Income tax deductions

Your employer or payer will determine the income tax to deduct based on your total claim amount on the Form TD1, *Personal Tax Credits Return* that you completed, and takes into account the CPP contributions and EI premiums deducted. There is no annual limit to the total amount of income tax your employer or payer can deduct in a year.

If you expect your total income for the year to be less than the total claim amount on Form TD1, you can ask your employer or payer not to deduct tax from your earnings. If you have multiple employers throughout the year, it is important that you complete Form TD1 for each employer.

Your statement of earnings (pay stub)

When you receive your first statement of earnings (pay stub), it will show how much income you have earned over a specified period. Most importantly, it will show what your employer deducted from your income such as CPP or QPP contributions, EI premiums, and income tax.

The rates for your contributions, premiums, and deductions are revised every year. See a sample of a pay stub on page 27.

T4 information slip – *Statement of Remuneration Paid*

You will receive your T4 slip from your employer by the end of February following the year in which you worked.

Your T4 slip will show your gross earnings for the year, CPP or QPP contributions, EI premiums, and income tax deducted at source. Use the amounts from your T4 slip to complete your income tax and benefit return. See a sample of a T4 slip on page 28.

Section 4 – Income tax and benefit return

This section will introduce you to the income tax and benefit return and the *General Income Tax and Benefit Guide – 2009*. You will learn how to use the General guide as a reference tool to complete an income tax and benefit return.

You will also learn the importance of filing a return every year and the various ways of filing a completed return.

You will use the General guide to complete simple returns using the examples of tax scenarios on pages 11-23 of this workbook. You will also learn about the deductions and credits that you are entitled to claim and which information slips and official receipts you must attach to your return before you file it. You may also find helpful the quick reference on page 24 of this workbook, which matches box numbers on information slips to line numbers on the return.

Take the time to read the "At your service" and "General information" sections of the General guide. To complete a return, read the line-by-line instructions, and enter the appropriate amounts on the corresponding lines of the return. All the information you need to complete your return is in the guide.

The return is set up in an easy-to-follow format with clearly defined areas called:

- Identification;
- Elections Canada;
- Goods and services tax/harmonized sales tax (GST/HST) credit application;
- Total income;
- Net income;
- Taxable income; and
- Refund or Balance owing.

Start with the "Identification" area and move through each area in the order they appear on the return. Use only the lines that apply to your situation. **Leave the other lines blank**.

For example, if you have no pension income, do not enter any information on the pension income line on the return. It is important to complete each area before going on to the next. Most importantly, do not miss any areas.

You may also have to complete one or more schedules, such as Schedule 1, *Federal Tax*.

Calculating your income

Most of the income you receive should be reported on your return.

Total income (line 150)

The most common types of income you may receive as a student include:

- employment income;
- tips and occasional earnings;
- Universal Child Care Benefit
- investment income;
- research grants;
- registered education savings plan income; and
- scholarships, fellowships, bursaries, study grants, and artists' project grants.

Note
The full amount of scholarships, fellowships, or bursaries that are received by you as a student with respect to your enrolment in a program that entitles you to claim the education amount are not taxable and are no longer reported as income on your return.

You do not have to include your GST/HST credit or Canada Child Tax Benefit (CCTB) payments, or those from related provincial or territorial programs, lottery winnings, or most gifts and inheritances.

Net income (line 236)

In this section, you reduce your total income with certain deductions such as registered retirement savings plan (RRSP) contributions, union dues, child care expenses, and moving expenses to determine your net income.

Net income is used to calculate certain federal and provincial or territorial credits. It is also used to calculate the CCTB and GST/HST credit.

Taxable income (line 260)

This is the amount left after all allowable deductions have been subtracted from your net income. This amount is used to calculate your federal and provincial or territorial taxes payable.

Calculating federal and provincial or territorial taxes payable

Your taxable income (line 260) is used to calculate both federal and provincial or territorial taxes. Use Schedule 1, *Federal Tax*, to calculate your net federal tax. Use Form 428 for the province (except Quebec) or territory where you lived on December 31, 2009, to calculate your net provincial or territorial tax.

Although your federal and provincial or territorial tax is calculated using a separate form, the method and structure are similar. Each province or territory has its own tax brackets and rates, which differ from the federal brackets and rates.

Federal and provincial or territorial non-refundable tax credits

Non-refundable tax credits reduce the amount of income tax you owe. However, even if the total of these credits is more than the amount you owe, you will not get a refund for the difference.

The eligibility criteria and rules for claiming provincial or territorial non-refundable tax credits are the same as the federal non-refundable tax credits.

However, the value and calculation of most provincial and territorial non-refundable tax credits are different from the corresponding federal credits. You may find it easier to calculate your net federal tax before you calculate your net provincial or territorial tax payable.

Refund or Balance owing

In this area, calculate all federal and provincial or territorial credits and taxes payable and determine if you will get a refund or have a balance owing.

Enter any federal and provincial or territorial tax payable on the applicable lines of the return, and follow the instructions on the return to calculate the total payable on line 435.

Add all the tax credits listed from lines 437 to 479, and enter the total on line 482. Unlike the non-refundable credits, we do refund the part of the total credits on line 482 that is more than the total payable on line 435.

The most common refundable credits that will apply to you are:

- total income tax deducted;
- CPP overpayment;
- EI overpayment; and
- provincial or territorial credits.

Once you have determined the total credits on line 482, subtract this amount from the total payable shown on line 435.

If the amount on line 435 is less than the amount on line 482, you are entitled to a refund of the difference. Enter the refund amount on line 484.

If the amount on line 435 is more than the amount on line 482, you owe the amount of the difference. Enter the balance owing on line 485. Even if you cannot pay all of your balance owing right away, you should still file your return on time. This way you will not have to pay a penalty for filing your return after the due date.

Filing your return

You can mail or deliver your income tax and benefit return, or you can file it electronically using EFILE, NETFILE, or TELEFILE. If you mail or deliver your return, you should attach all the required information slips, receipts, schedules, and statements to the return, as indicated in the *General Income Tax and Benefit Guide*, and sign your return.

If you file your return electronically, keep your documents in case we ask to see them at a later date. Generally, you should keep your supporting documents for six years.

Example 1 – High school student

- Samantha Valcourt is a single 17-year-old high school student (born November 13, 1992) who lives at home with her parents. During 2009, she worked part time at Dan's Vegan Emporium and Plaza Restaurant.
- In February 2010, her employers sent her the attached T4 information slips.
- In 2009, she earned $300.00 in tips (not indicated on T4) at the Plaza Restaurant.

Based on the information given, complete her 2009 *Income Tax and Benefit Return*.

To complete Samantha's return, you will need the following:

- T1 General – *Income Tax and Benefit Return*
- Schedule 1, *Federal Tax*
- (**if your province of residence is Quebec**) Schedule 10, *Employment Insurance (EI) and Provincial Parental Insurance Plan (PPIP) Premiums*

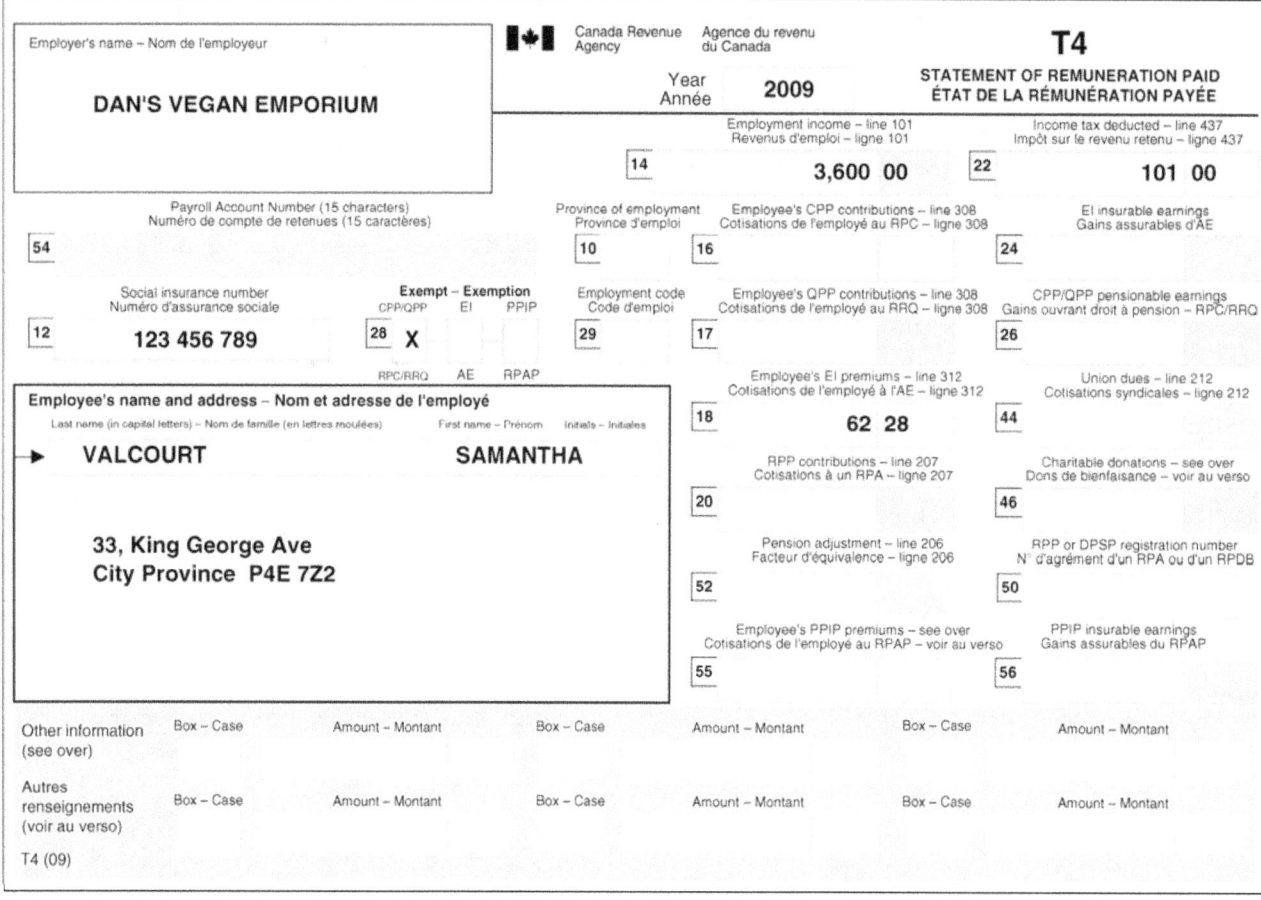

Employer's name – Nom de l'employeur

PLAZA RESTAURANT

Canada Revenue Agency / Agence du revenu du Canada

Year / Année: 2009

T4 — STATEMENT OF REMUNERATION PAID / ÉTAT DE LA RÉMUNÉRATION PAYÉE

Box	Description	Amount
14	Employment income – line 101 / Revenus d'emploi – ligne 101	2,600 00
22	Income tax deducted – line 437 / Impôt sur le revenu retenu – ligne 437	101 00
54	Payroll Account Number (15 characters) / Numéro de compte de retenues (15 caractères)	
10	Province of employment / Province d'emploi	
16	Employee's CPP contributions – line 308	
24	EI insurable earnings / Gains assurables d'AE	
12	Social insurance number / Numéro d'assurance sociale	123 456 789
28	Exempt – Exemption CPP/QPP EI PPIP	X
29	Employment code / Code d'emploi	
17	Employee's QPP contributions – line 308	
26	CPP/QPP pensionable earnings / Gains ouvrant droit à pension – RPC/RRQ	
18	Employee's EI premiums – line 312	44 98
44	Union dues – line 212 / Cotisations syndicales – ligne 212	
20	RPP contributions – line 207	
46	Charitable donations – see over / Dons de bienfaisance – voir au verso	
52	Pension adjustment – line 206 / Facteur d'équivalence – ligne 206	
50	RPP or DPSP registration number	
55	Employee's PPIP premiums – see over	
56	PPIP insurable earnings / Gains assurables du RPAP	

Employee's name and address – Nom et adresse de l'employé

Last name (in capital letters) / Nom de famille: VALCOURT
First name / Prénom: SAMANTHA
Initials / Initiales:

33, King George Ave
City Province P4E 7Z2

Other information (see over) / Autres renseignements (voir au verso)

Box – Case	Amount – Montant	Box – Case	Amount – Montant	Box – Case	Amount – Montant

T4 (09)

Example 2 – High school student (with Quebec as the province of employment)

- Marie-Chantal Gagnon is a single 17-year-old high school student (born November 13, 1992) who lives at home with her parents. During 2009, she worked part time at Librairie du Coin and Les Souliers de Sam.
- In February 2010, her employers sent her the attached T4 information slips.
- In 2009, she earned $300.00 (not indicated on T4) in tips at the Plaza Restaurant.

Based on the information given, complete Marie-Chantal's 2009 *Income Tax and Benefit Return*.

To complete this return, you will need the following:

- T1 General – *Income Tax and Benefit Return*
- Schedule 1, *Federal Tax*
- Schedule 10, *Employment Insurance (EI) and Provincial Parental Insurance Plan (PPIP) Premiums*

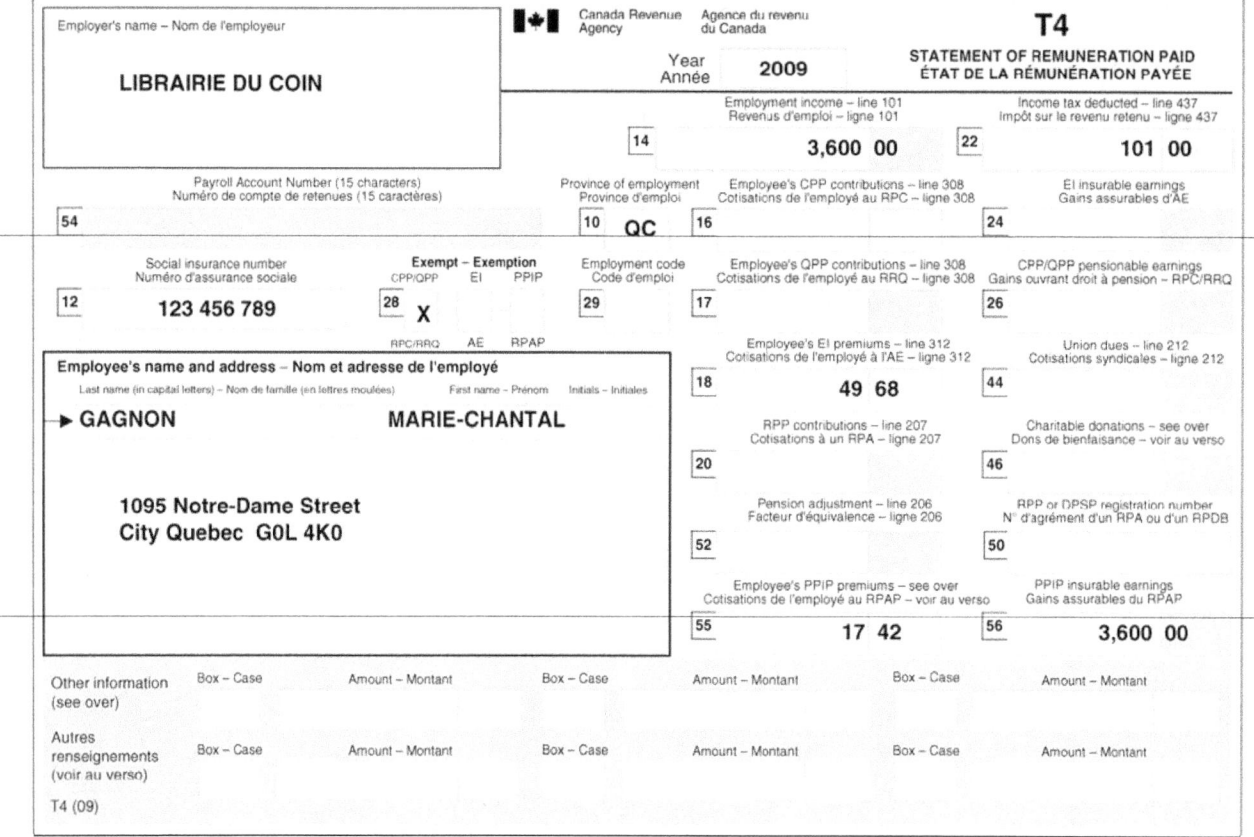

Employer's name – Nom de l'employeur

PLAZA RESTAURANT

Canada Revenue Agency / Agence du revenu du Canada

Year / Année: 2009

T4 – STATEMENT OF REMUNERATION PAID / ÉTAT DE LA RÉMUNÉRATION PAYÉE

Box	Description	Amount
14	Employment income – line 101 / Revenus d'emploi – ligne 101	2,600 00
22	Income tax deducted – line 437 / Impôt sur le revenu retenu – ligne 437	101 00
54	Payroll Account Number (15 characters) / Numéro de compte de retenues (15 caractères)	
10	Province of employment / Province d'emploi	QC
16	Employee's CPP contributions – line 308 / Cotisations de l'employé au RPC – ligne 308	
24	EI insurable earnings / Gains assurables d'AE	
12	Social insurance number / Numéro d'assurance sociale	123 456 789
28	Exempt – Exemption (CPP/QPP, EI, PPIP)	X (RPC/RRQ), AE, RPAP
29	Employment code / Code d'emploi	
17	Employee's QPP contributions – line 308 / Cotisations de l'employé au RRQ – ligne 308	
26	CPP/QPP pensionable earnings / Gains ouvrant droit à pension – RPC/RRQ	
18	Employee's EI premiums – line 312 / Cotisations de l'employé à l'AE – ligne 312	35 88
44	Union dues – line 212 / Cotisations syndicales – ligne 212	
20	RPP contributions – line 207 / Cotisations à un RPA – ligne 207	
46	Charitable donations – see over / Dons de bienfaisance – voir au verso	
52	Pension adjustment – line 206 / Facteur d'équivalence – ligne 206	
50	RPP or DPSP registration number / N° d'agrément d'un RPA ou d'un RPDB	
55	Employee's PPIP premiums – see over / Cotisations de l'employé au RPAP – voir au verso	12 58
56	PPIP insurable earnings / Gains assurables du RPAP	2,600 00

Employee's name and address – Nom et adresse de l'employé

GAGNON   MARIE-CHANTAL

1095 Notre-Dame Street
City Quebec G0L 4K0

Other information (see over) / Autres renseignements (voir au verso)

T4 (09)

Example 3 – Post-secondary student

- Sue attends a post-secondary institution. She was born on August 2, 1990 and is single.

- The attached T2202A information slip that the post-secondary institution gave her shows she paid tuition fees of $2,500 for the courses she took during 2009. According to the slip, she can claim the education and textbook amounts for eight months. She wants to carry forward any amount she cannot use this year.

- During the year, she received a scholarship of $3,500 from her post-secondary institution. This amount is shown on the attached T4A information slip.

- Sue moved to her parents' home for the summer months (a distance of 500 kilometres) and got a job there at Information. She completed Form T1-M, *Moving Expenses Deduction*, listing her expenses of $300 for the move, and determined that she can claim the expenses on her *Income Tax and Benefit Return*.

- She earned $12,300 at Information during the summer, and they sent her the attached T4 information slip.

- She received $52 interest from her savings account at the bank. This amount is shown on the attached T5 information slip that the bank sent her.

- In 2009, Sue paid $720.00 for her public transit passes ($60 a month).

Based on the information given, complete Sue's 2009 *Income Tax and Benefit Return*.

To complete this return, you will need the following:

- T1 General – *Income Tax and Benefit Return*
- Schedule 1, *Federal Tax*
- Schedule 11, *Tuition, Education, and Textbook Amounts*
- (**if your province of residence is Quebec**) Schedule 10, *Employment Insurance (EI) and Provincial Parental Insurance Plan (PPIP) Premiums*

T4 – STATEMENT OF REMUNERATION PAID

Employer's name: **INFORMATION**
Year: **2009**

Box	Description	Amount
14	Employment income – line 101	12,300 00
22	Income tax deducted – line 437	1,995 00
10	Province of employment	
16	Employee's CPP contributions – line 308	435 60
24	EI insurable earnings	
12	Social insurance number	123 456 789
28	Exempt CPP/QPP EI PPIP	
29	Employment code	
17	Employee's QPP contributions – line 308	
26	CPP/QPP pensionable earnings	
18	Employee's EI premiums – line 312	212 79
44	Union dues – line 212	
20	RPP contributions – line 207	
46	Charitable donations	
52	Pension adjustment – line 206	
50	RPP or DPSP registration number	
55	Employee's PPIP premiums	
56	PPIP insurable earnings	

Employee's name and address:
BROWN   SUE
55 Main St
Town Province Y2C 6Z4

T4 (09)

T4A — Statement of Pension, Retirement, Annuity, and Other Income (2009)

- Box 12 Social insurance number: 123 456 789
- Box 38 Footnote codes: 05
- Payer's name: Sue's post-secondary institution
- Recipient: BROWN SUE
- Scholarship: 3,500.00

T4A (09)

T5 — Statement of Investment Income (2009)

- Box 13 Interest from Canadian sources: 52.00
- Box 22 Recipient identification number: 123 456 789
- Recipient: BROWN SUE, 555 MAIN STREET, TOWN PROVINCE Y2C 6Z4
- Payer: SUE'S BANK

T5 (09)

Canada Revenue Agency / Agence du revenu du Canada

TUITION, EDUCATION, AND TEXTBOOK AMOUNTS CERTIFICATE
CERTIFICAT POUR FRAIS DE SCOLARITÉ, MONTANT RELATIF AUX ÉTUDES ET MONTANT POUR MANUELS

T2202A (09)

For student / Pour l'étudiant **1**

- Issue this certificate to a student who was enrolled during the calendar year in a qualifying educational program or a specified educational program at a post-secondary institution, such as a college or university, or at an institution certified by the Minister of Human Resources and Skills Development (HRSDC).
- Tuition fees paid in respect of the calendar year to any one institution have to be more than $100. Fees paid to a post-secondary institution have to be for courses taken at the post-secondary level. Fees paid to an institution certified by HRSDC have to be for courses taken to get or improve skills in an occupation, and the student has to be 16 years of age or older before the end of the year.
- **Do not enter the cost of textbooks on this form.** Students calculate the education **and textbook** amounts based on the number of months indicated in Box B or C below.

- Délivrez ce certificat à un étudiant qui était inscrit, au cours de l'année civile, à un programme de formation admissible ou à un programme de formation déterminé dans un établissement postsecondaire, comme un collège ou une université, ou dans un établissement reconnu par le ministre des Ressources humaines et du Développement des compétences Canada (RHDCC).
- Les frais de scolarité payés à un établissement postsecondaire doivent viser des cours de niveau postsecondaire. Les frais payés à un établissement reconnu par RHDCC doivent viser des cours suivis en vue d'acquérir ou d'améliorer des compétences professionnelles, et l'étudiant doit avoir 16 ans ou plus avant la fin de l'année.
- **N'inscrivez pas le coût des manuels sur ce formulaire.** L'étudiant calcule les montants relatifs aux études et aux manuels d'après le nombre de mois indiqué dans les cases B ou C ci-dessous.

Name of program or course – Nom du programme ou du cours					Student number – Numéro d'étudiant
COMPUTER SCIENCE					**12-345**

Name and address of student – Nom et adresse de l'étudiant	Session periods, part-time and full-time / Périodes d'études à temps partiel et à temps plein				A – Eligible tuition fees, part-time and full-time sessions / Frais de scolarité admissibles pour études à temps partiel et à temps plein	Number of months for: Nombre de mois à :	
	From – De		To – À			B Part-time / Temps partiel	C Full-time / Temps plein
	Y – A	M	Y – A	M			
BROWN SUE 555 Main St Town Province Y2C 6Z4	09	01	09	04	1,250.00		4
	09	09	09	12	1,250.00		4
				Totals / Totaux	2,500.00		8

Name and address of educational institution – Nom et adresse de l'établissement d'enseignement

Sue's post-secondary institution

Information for students: See the back of copy 1. If you want to transfer all or part of your tuition, education, and textbook amounts, complete the back of copy 2.
Renseignements pour les étudiants : Lisez le verso de la copie 1. Si vous désirez transférer une partie ou la totalité de vos frais de scolarité et de vos montants relatifs aux études et aux manuels, remplissez le verso de la copie 2.

Example 4 – Employed individual

- In 2009, Clément (single, born August 2, 1984) started a job as a graphic artist at TechnoDesigns. During the year, he earned $28,000, and in February 2010, TechnoDesigns sent him the attached T4 information slip.

- In December 2009, he contributed $1,180 to a registered retirement savings plan (RRSP) at his local bank. The bank gave him an official RRSP contribution slip showing this amount. Clément can claim the full amount as a deduction on his 2009 *Income Tax and Benefit Return*.

- Clément also received $22 interest from his savings account at the bank. He did not receive a T5 information slip for this amount.

Based on the information given, complete Clément's 2009 *Income Tax and Benefit Return*.

To complete this return, you will need the following:

- T1 General – *Income Tax and Benefit Return*
- Schedule 1, *Federal Tax*
- (**if your province of residence is Quebec**) Schedule 10, *Employment Insurance (EI) and Provincial Parental Insurance Plan (PPIP) Premiums*

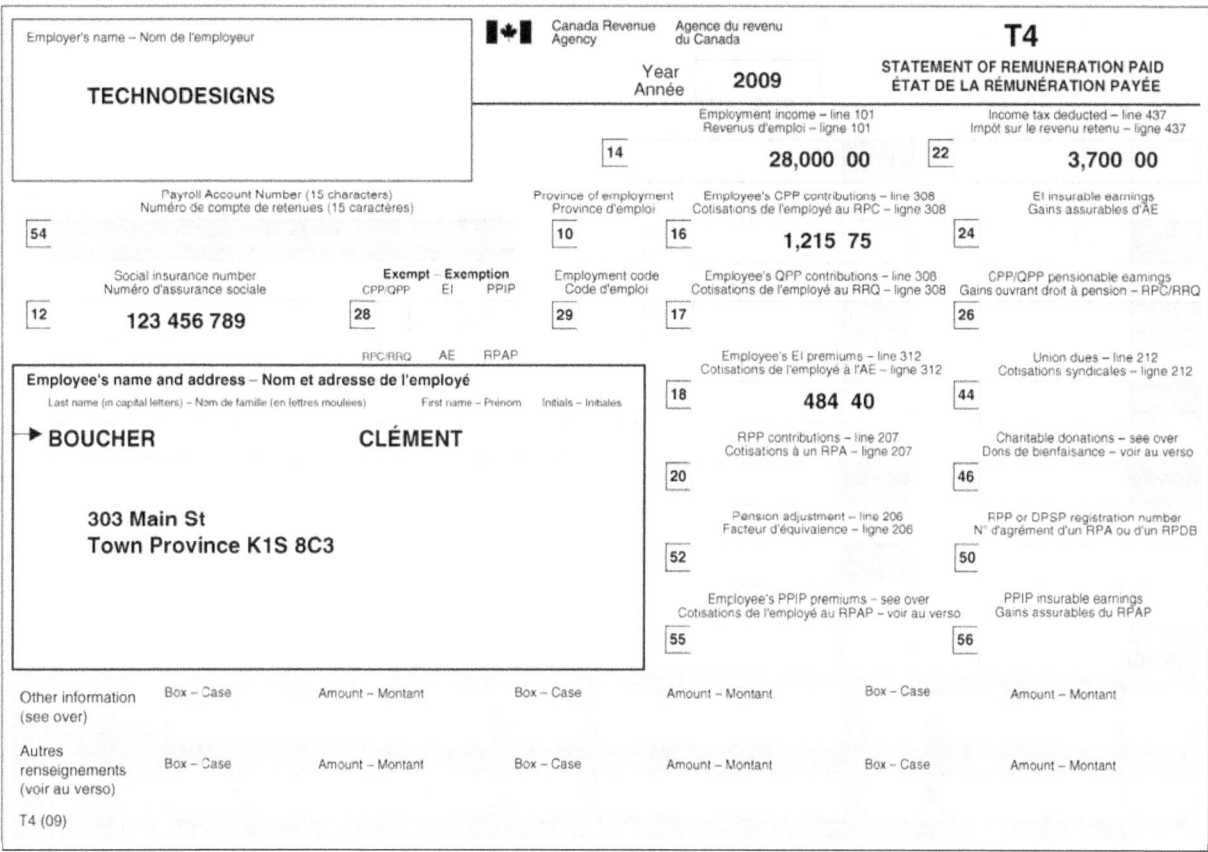

Example 5 – Single-parent family

- Karen is a single mother of a young child, Annie, born June 4, 2007. Karen's date of birth is May 15, 1976.

- During 2009, she worked for 40 weeks and earned $34,790. This income, plus other relevant information, is shown on the attached T4 information slips.

- She also received $850 in social assistance payments and $1,200 in Universal Child Care Benefit payments. These payments are shown on the attached information slips T5007, *Statement of Benefits*, and RC62, *Statement of Universal Child Care Benefit*.

- Karen sent her child to Sunny Nursery while she was working. Karen has partially completed the attached Form T778, *Child Care Expenses Deduction for 2009*, and has determined that she is entitled to claim $3,160 for child care expenses on her *Income Tax and Benefit Return*.

- Karen paid $9,000 in rent during 2009.

Based on the information given, complete Karen's 2009 *Income Tax and Benefit Return*.

To complete this return, you will need the following:

- T1 General – *Income Tax and Benefit Return*
- Schedule 1, *Federal Tax*
- Schedule 5, *Details of Dependant*
- Form T778, *Child Care Expenses Deduction for 2009* (You must finish the partially completed Form T778 included)
- (if your province of residence is Quebec) Schedule 10, *Employment Insurance (EI) and Provincial Parental Insurance Plan (PPIP) Premiums*

T4 – STATEMENT OF REMUNERATION PAID / ÉTAT DE LA RÉMUNÉRATION PAYÉE

Canada Revenue Agency / Agence du revenu du Canada

Employer's name – Nom de l'employeur: **ABC COMPANY**

Year / Année: **2009**

Box	Description	Amount
14	Employment income – line 101	34,790 00
22	Income tax deducted – line 437	5,250 00
54	Payroll Account Number (15 characters)	
10	Province of employment	
16	Employee's CPP contributions – line 308	1,548 85
24	EI insurable earnings	
12	Social insurance number	123 456 789
28	Exempt – Exemption (CPP/QPP, EI, PPIP)	
29	Employment code	
17	Employee's QPP contributions – line 308	
26	CPP/QPP pensionable earnings	
18	Employee's EI premiums – line 312	601 87
44	Union dues – line 212	165 00
20	RPP contributions – line 207	782 50
46	Charitable donations	
52	Pension adjustment – line 206	1,565 00
50	RPP or DPSP registration number	
55	Employee's PPIP premiums	
56	PPIP insurable earnings	

Employee's name and address – Nom et adresse de l'employé:
SINGH KAREN
83 Elm St
Bytown Province K1S 4F8

T4 (09)

Canada Revenue Agency / Agence du revenu du Canada

T5007 — STATEMENT OF BENEFITS / ÉTAT DES PRESTATIONS

Year / Année	10 Workers' compensation benefits / Indemnités pour accidents du travail	11 Social assistance payments or provincial or territorial supplements / Prestations d'assistance sociale ou supplément provincial ou territorial	12 Social insurance number / Numéro d'assurance sociale	13 Report code / Code de genre de feuillet
2009		950.00	123 456 789	

Recipient's name and address - Nom et adresse du bénéficiaire

Last name (please print) / Nom de famille (en lettres moulées)	First name / Prénom	Initials / Initiales
SINGH	KAREN	

Payer's name and address / Nom et adresse du payeur

PROVINCE

T5007(09)

Canada Revenue Agency / Agence du revenu du Canada

STATEMENT OF UNIVERSAL CHILD CARE BENEFIT — RC62
ÉTAT DE LA PRESTATION UNIVERSELLE POUR LA GARDE D'ENFANTS

Year / Année	Social insurance number / Numéro d'assurance sociale	10 Total benefit paid / Prestation totale versée	12 Repayment of previous-year benefits / Remboursement de prestations d'années précédentes
2009	123 456 789	1,200.00	

Issued by: Human Resources and Social Development Canada
Émis par : Ressources humaines et Développement social Canada

Year - Année	Amount - Montant

SINGH   KAREN
83 Elm St
Bytown Province K1S 4F8

Canada

RC62

Child Care Expenses Deduction for 2009

Canada Revenue Agency / Agence du revenu du Canada

Read the attached information sheet. On the sheet we define **child care expenses**, **eligible child**, **net income**, **earned income**, and **educational program**. For more details, see Interpretation Bulletin IT-495, *Child Care Expenses*.

Each person claiming the child care expenses deduction must attach a completed Form T778 to his or her return.
Do not include receipts, but keep them in case we ask to see them.

If you are the **only person** claiming child care expenses, complete parts A and B, and, if it applies, Part D.
If there is **another person** (as described under "Who can claim child care expenses?" on the attached sheet) and you are the one with the **lower net income**, complete parts A and B.
If there is **another person** (as described under "Who can claim child care expenses?" on the attached sheet) and you are the one with the **higher net income**, complete parts A, B, C, and, if it applies, Part D.

Part A – Total child care expenses

List the **first and last names** and the **dates of birth** of all your eligible children, even if you did not pay child care expenses for all of them.

Name	Year	Month	Day
Annie Singh	2007	06	04

First name of each child for whom payments were made	Child care expenses paid (see note below)	Name of the child care organization or the name and social insurance number of the individual who received the payments	Number of weeks for boarding schools or overnight camps
Annie	+ 3,160 00	Sunny Nursery	
	+		
	+		
	+		
Total	=		

Note: The maximum you can claim for expenses that relate to a stay in a boarding school (other than education costs) or an overnight camp (including an overnight sports school) is **$175 per week** for a child included on line 1 in Part B, **$250 per week** for a child included on line 2, and **$100 per week** for a child included on line 3.

Enter any child care expenses included above that were incurred in 2009 for a child who was 18 or older. **6795** _____

Part B – Basic limit for child care expenses

Number of eligible children:

Born in 2003 or later, for whom the disability amount cannot be claimed	× $7,000 =	1
Born in 2009 or earlier, for whom the disability amount can be claimed *	× $10,000 = **6796** +	2
Born in 1993 to 2002, (or born in 1992 or earlier, with a mental or physical infirmity, for whom the disability amount cannot be claimed)	× $4,000 = +	3
Add lines 1 to 3.	=	4

Enter your **total child care expenses** from Part A. _____ 5

Enter your **earned income**. _____ × 2/3 = _____ 6

Enter the amount from line 4, 5, or 6, whichever is **least**. _____ 7

If you are the person with the higher net income, go to Part C. Leave lines 8 and 9 blank.

Enter any child care expenses that the **other person** (as described under "Who can claim child care expenses?" on the attached sheet) with the higher net income deducted on line 214 of his or her 2009 return. − _____ 8

Line 7 minus line 8. If you attended school in 2009 and you are the only person making a claim, also go to Part D. Otherwise, enter this amount on line 214 of your return. **Your allowable deduction** = _____ 9

* Attach Form T2201, *Disability Tax Credit Certificate*. If this form has already been filed for the child, attach a note to your return showing the name and social insurance number of the person who filed the form and the tax year for which it was filed.

T778 E (09)   (Vous pouvez obtenir ce formulaire en français à www.arc.gc.ca ou au 1-800-959-3376.)   Canada

Example 6 – First Nations Resident

- John is a single, Status Indian, born on July 8, 1975. In 2009, he worked as a full-time administrator for a medical clinic located on a reserve. His employer, Big Isle Health Clinic, has elected to participate in the CPP.

- In 2009, John also worked part-time for an organization dedicated to developing social programs for local youth. The organization is located off reserve and all of John's work was carried out off reserve.

Based on the information given, complete John's 2009 *Income Tax and Benefit Return*.

To complete this return, you will need the following:

- T1 General – *Income Tax and Benefit Return*
- Schedule 1, *Federal Tax*
- (**if your province of residence is Quebec**) Schedule 10, *Employment Insurance (EI) and Provincial Parental Insurance Plan (PPIP) Premiums*
- For assistance in completing this return, go to www.cra.gc.ca/brgnls/gdlns-eng.html on our Web site.
- **Please note,** when electronically filing the tax return of a Status Indian who has a T4 indicating tax exempt income (box 71), it is important to key into the software the amounts from boxes 24 and 26, even if the employer did not complete these boxes.

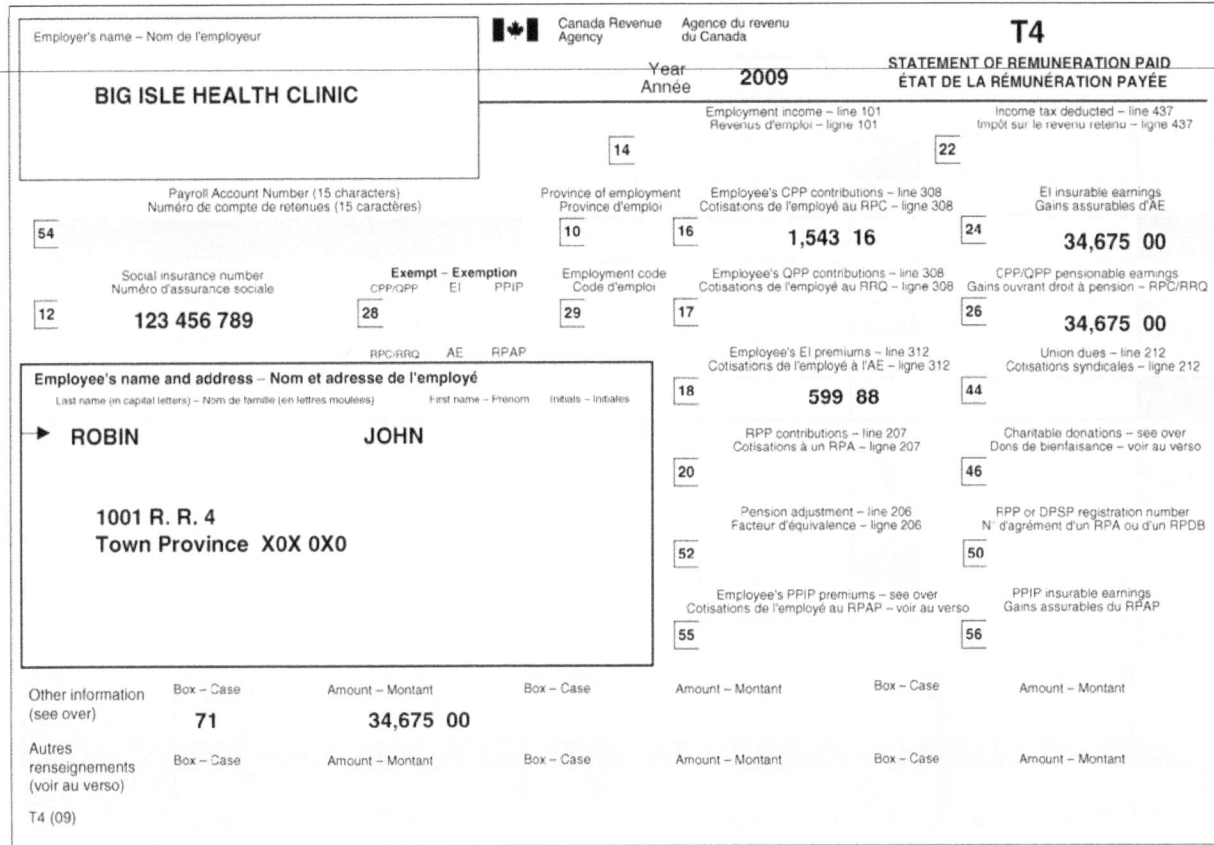

Employer's name – Nom de l'employeur

COMMUNITY CENTRE

Canada Revenue Agency / Agence du revenu du Canada

Year / Année: 2009

T4 – STATEMENT OF REMUNERATION PAID / ÉTAT DE LA RÉMUNÉRATION PAYÉE

Box	Description	Amount
14	Employment income – line 101 / Revenus d'emploi – ligne 101	5,500 00
22	Income tax deducted – line 437 / Impôt sur le revenu retenu – ligne 437	107 27
54	Payroll Account Number (15 characters) / Numéro de compte de retenues (15 caractères)	
10	Province of employment / Province d'emploi	
16	Employee's CPP contributions – line 308 / Cotisations de l'employé au RPC – ligne 308	99 00
24	EI insurable earnings / Gains assurables d'AE	5,500 00
12	Social insurance number / Numéro d'assurance sociale	123 456 789
28	Exempt – Exemption CPP/QPP, EI, PPIP / RPC/RRQ, AE, RPAP	
29	Employment code / Code d'emploi	
17	Employee's QPP contributions – line 308 / Cotisations de l'employé au RRQ – ligne 308	
26	CPP/QPP pensionable earnings / Gains ouvrant droit à pension – RPC/RRQ	5,500 00
18	Employee's EI premiums – line 312 / Cotisations de l'employé à l'AE – ligne 312	95 15
44	Union dues – line 212 / Cotisations syndicales – ligne 212	
20	RPP contributions – line 207 / Cotisations à un RPA – ligne 207	
46	Charitable donations – see over / Dons de bienfaisance – voir au verso	
52	Pension adjustment – line 206 / Facteur d'équivalence – ligne 206	
50	RPP or DPSP registration number / N° d'agrément d'un RPA ou d'un RPDB	
55	Employee's PPIP premiums – see over / Cotisations de l'employé au RPAP – voir au verso	
56	PPIP insurable earnings / Gains assurables du RPAP	

Employee's name and address – Nom et adresse de l'employé

ROBIN JOHN

1001 R. R. 4
Town Province X0X 0X0

Other information (see over) / Autres renseignements (voir au verso)

T4 (09)

Additional Information

Quick reference to box numbers on information slips and line numbers on an income tax and benefit return

Slip type	Box No.	Box title	Line on return
T4		**Statement of Remuneration Paid**	
	14	Employment income	101
	16	Employee's Canada Pension Plan contributions	308
	17	Employee's Quebec Pension Plan contributions	308
	18	Employee's Employment Insurance premiums	312
	20	Registered pension plan contributions	207
	22	Income tax deducted	437
	55	Employee's provincial parental insurance plan (PPIP) (if province of employment is Quebec)	375
T4A		**Statement of Pension, Retirement, Annuity, and Other Income**	
	16	Pension or superannuation	115 and 314
	18	Lump-sum payments	130
	20	Self-employed commissions	166 and 139
	22	Income tax deducted	437
	28	Other income	Miscellaneous
	40	RESP accumulated income payments	130 and 418
	42	RESP educational assistance payments	130
T5		**Statement of Investment Income**	
	25	Taxable amount of eligible dividends	120
	26	Dividend tax credit for eligible dividends	425
	11	Taxable amount of dividends other than eligible dividends	180 and 120
	12	Dividend tax credit for dividends other than eligible dividends	425
	13	Interest from Canadian sources	121
	14	Other income from Canadian sources	121
	15	Foreign income	121
T4E		**Statement of Employment Insurance and Other Benefits**	
	7	Repayment rate	235 and 422
	14	Total benefits paid	119
	20	Taxable tuition assistance	Not entered on return
	22	Income tax deducted	437
	23	Quebec income tax deducted	437 (if not a resident of Quebec)

2009 PERSONAL TAX CREDITS RETURN

TD1

Canada Revenue Agency / Agence du revenu du Canada

Read the back before completing this form. Complete this form based on the best estimate of your circumstances.
Sections 1, 3, 7, and 8 include changes proposed in the 2009 budget.

Last name	First name and initial(s)	Date of birth (YYYY/MM/DD)	Employee number

Address including postal code	For non-residents only – Country of permanent residence	Social insurance number

1. Basic personal amount – Every resident of Canada can claim this amount. If you will have more than one employer or payer at the same time in 2009, see "Completing Form TD1" on the next page. If you are a non-resident, see "Non-residents" on the next page. — **10,320**

2. Child amount – Either parent (but not both), may claim $2,089 for each child born in 1992 or later that resides with both parents throughout the year. Any unused portion can be transferred to that parent's spouse or common-law partner. If the child does not reside with both parents throughout the year, the parent who is entitled to claim the "Amount for an eligible dependant" on line 8 may also claim $2,089 for that same child.

3. Age amount – If you will be 65 or older on December 31, 2009, and your net income for the year from all sources will be $32,312 or less, enter $6,658. If your net income for the year will be between $32,312 and $76,699 and you want to calculate a partial claim, get the TD1-WS, *Worksheet for the 2009 Personal Tax Credits Return*, and complete the appropriate section.

4. Pension income amount – If you will receive regular pension payments from a pension plan or fund (excluding Canada Pension Plan, Quebec Pension Plan, Old Age Security, or Guaranteed Income Supplement payments), enter $2,000 or your estimated annual pension income, whichever is less.

5. Tuition, education, and textbook amounts (full time and part time) – If you are a student enrolled at a university or college, or an educational institution certified by Human Resources and Social Development Canada, and you will pay more than $100 per institution in tuition fees, complete this section. If you are enrolled full time, or if you have a mental or physical disability and are enrolled part time, enter the total of the tuition fees you will pay, plus $400 for each month that you will be enrolled, plus $65 per month for textbooks. If you are enrolled part time and do not have a mental or physical disability, enter the total of the tuition fees you will pay, plus $120 for each month that you will be enrolled part time, plus $20 per month for textbooks.

6. Disability amount – If you will claim the disability amount on your income tax return by using Form T2201, *Disability Tax Credit Certificate*, enter $7,196.

7. Spouse or common-law partner amount – If you are supporting your spouse or common-law partner who lives with you, and whose net income for the year will be less than $10,375, enter the difference between $10,375 and his or her estimated net income for the year. If your spouse's or common-law partner's net income for the year will be more than $10,375, you cannot claim this amount.

8. Amount for an eligible dependant – If you do not have a spouse or common-law partner and you support a dependent relative who lives with you, and whose net income for the year will be less than $10,375, enter the difference between $10,375 and his or her estimated net income. If your eligible dependant's net income for the year will be $10,375 or more, you cannot claim this amount.

9. Caregiver amount – If you are taking care of a dependant who lives with you, whose net income for the year will be $14,336 or less, and who is either your or your spouse's or common-law partner's:
- parent or grandparent (aged 65 or older), or
- relative (aged 18 or older) who is dependent on you because of an infirmity, enter $4,198.

If the dependant's net income for the year will be between $14,336 and $18,534 and you want to calculate a partial claim, get the TD1-WS, and complete the appropriate section.

10. Amount for infirm dependants age 18 or older – If you support an infirm dependant age 18 or older who is your or your spouse's or common-law partner's relative, who lives in Canada, and whose net income for the year will be $5,956 or less, enter $4,198. You cannot claim an amount for a dependant you claimed on line 9. If the dependant's net income for the year will be between $5,956 and $10,154 and you want to calculate a partial claim, get the TD1-WS, and complete the appropriate section.

11. Amounts transferred from your spouse or common-law partner – If your spouse or common-law partner will not use all of his or her age amount, pension income amount, tuition, education and textbook amounts, disability amount or child amount on his or her income tax return, enter the unused amount.

12. Amounts transferred from a dependant – If your dependant will not use all of his or her **disability amount** on his or her income tax return, enter the unused amount. If your or your spouse's or common-law partner's dependent child or grandchild will not use all of his or her **tuition, education, and textbook amounts** on his or her income tax return, enter the unused amount.

13. TOTAL CLAIM AMOUNT – Add lines 1 through 12.
Your employer or payer will use this amount to determine the amount of your tax deductions.

Continue on the next page ➔

TD1 E (09-04) (Vous pouvez obtenir ce formulaire en français à www.arc.gc.ca/formulaires ou au 1-800-959-3376.)

Canada

Completing Form TD1

Complete this form **only** if:
- you want to change amounts you previously claimed;
- you have a new employer or payer and you will receive salary, wages, commissions, pensions, Employment Insurance benefits, or any other remuneration;
- you want to claim the deduction for living in a prescribed zone; or
- you want to increase the amount of tax deducted at source.

Sign and date it and give it to your employer or payer.

☐ If you have more than one employer or payer at the same time and you have already claimed personal tax credit amounts on another TD1 form for 2009, you can choose not to claim them again. By doing this, you may not have to pay as much tax when you file your income tax return. **Check** the box to choose this option, enter "0" on line 13 on the front page and do not complete lines 2 to 12.

If you do not complete a TD1 form, your new employer or payer will deduct taxes after allowing the basic personal amount **only**.

Total income less than total claim amount

☐ Check this box if your total income for the year from all employers and payers will be less than your total claim amount on line 13. Then your employer or payer will not deduct tax from your earnings.

Non-residents

Are you a non-resident of Canada who will include 90% or more of your world income when determining your taxable income earned in Canada in 2009? If you are unsure of your residency status, call the International Tax Services Office at **1-800-267-5177**.

☐
- If **yes**, complete the previous page.
- If **no**, **check** the box, enter "0" on line 13 and do not complete lines 2 to 12, as you are not entitled to the personal tax credits.

Provincial or territorial personal tax credits return

If your claim amount on line 13 is more than $10,375, you also have to complete a provincial or territorial personal tax credit return. If you are an employee, use the TD1 form for your province or territory of employment. If you are a pensioner, use the TD1 form for your province or territory of residence. Your employer or payer will use both this federal form and your most recent provincial or territorial TD1 form to determine the amount of your tax deductions.

If you are claiming the basic personal amount **only** (your claim amount on line 13 is $10,375), your employer or payer will deduct provincial or territorial taxes after allowing the provincial or territorial basic personal amount.

Note: If you are a Saskatchewan resident supporting children under 18 at any time during 2009, you may be able to claim the child amount on Form TD1SK, *2009 Saskatchewan Personal Tax Credits Return*. Therefore, you may want to complete Form TD1SK even if you are **only** claiming the basic personal amount on this form.

Deduction for living in a prescribed zone

If you live in the Northwest Territories, Nunavut, Yukon, or another prescribed **northern** zone for more than six months in a row beginning or ending in 2009, you can claim:
- $8.25 for each day that you live in the prescribed northern zone, or
- $16.50 for each day that you live in the prescribed northern zone if, during that time, you live in a dwelling that you maintain, and you are the only person living in that dwelling who is claiming this deduction.

$ _____

Employees living in a prescribed **intermediate** zone can claim 50% of the total of the above amounts.

For more information, get Form T2222, *Northern Residents Deductions*, and the Publication T4039, *Northern Residents Deductions – Places in Prescribed Zones*.

Additional tax to be deducted

You may want to have more tax deducted from each payment, especially if you receive other income, including non-employment income such as CPP or QPP benefits, or Old Age Security pension. By doing this, you may not have to pay as much tax when you file your income tax return. To choose this option, state the amount of additional tax you want to have deducted from each payment. To change this deduction later, complete a new Form TD1.

$ _____

Reduction in tax deductions

You can ask to have less tax deducted if on your income tax return you are eligible for deductions or non-refundable tax credits that are not listed on this form (for example, periodic contributions to a Registered Retirement Savings Plan (RRSP), child care or employment expenses, and charitable donations). To make this request, complete Form T1213, *Request to Reduce Tax Deductions at Source*, to get a letter of authority from your tax services office. Give the letter of authority to your employer or payer. You do not need a letter of authority if your employer deducts RRSP contributions from your salary.

Certification

I certify that the information given in this return is, to the best of my knowledge, correct and complete.

Signature _____ Date _____

It is a serious offence to make a false return.

Sample – Statement of Earnings (Pay Stub)

YOUR NAME		Employee #	0032344589		Employer #	11 - 36	Pay from 2009 / 11 / 23		To 2009 / 12 / 04		Date 2009 / 12 / 09
STATEMENT OF EARNINGS							EMPLOYEE DEDUCTIONS AND EMPLOYER CONTRIBUTIONS				
TYPE	HOURS	RATE	AMOUNT	Y.T.D.	TYPE		CURRENT	Y.T.D.	TYPE	CURRENT	Y.T.D.
001 BASIC PAY	40.00	11.00/hr	440.00	440.00	EI CPP / QPP TAX		7.61 15.20 68.20	7.61 15.20 68.20	* QPIP	2.13	2.13

SUMMARY	GROSS PAY	DEDUCTIONS	NET PAY	NET PAY ALLOCATION
CURRENT	440.00	91.01	348.99	348.99 - CHEQUE
Year-to-date	440.00	91.01	348.99	

Canada Pension Plan / Quebec Pension Plan
Based on the earned income shown on this stub, the employer deducted $15.20 as CPP contributions. If the province of employment is Quebec, this contribution will be called QPP instead of CPP. The employer will also contribute $15.20 on the employee's behalf.

Employment Insurance (EI)
The EI premium on this stub is $7.61. It represents 1.73% of the insurable earnings. The employer will contribute its share of 1.4 times the premium deducted (1.4 x $7.61 = $10.65). If the province of employment is Quebec, the premium will be $6.07, representing 1.38% of the insurable earnings and the employer will contribute $8.50 on the employee's behalf (1.4 x $6.07).

*Quebec Parental Insurance Plan (QPIP)
Also if the province of employment is Quebec, a premium for QPIP will be deducted. Based on the earned income shown on this stub, the employer deducts $2.13 and will in turn contribute $2.98 on behalf of the employee.

Tax
By referring to the total claim amount on a Form TD1, *2009 Personal Tax Credits Return*, and using Canada Revenue Agency (CRA) approved calculation methods, the employer deducted $68.20 from the income.

Remittance to the CRA
The employer is responsible for regularly sending their contribution as well as the total employee contributions, premiums and deductions from the earned income on this pay stub to the CRA.

Sample *Statement of Remuneration Paid* – T4 information slip

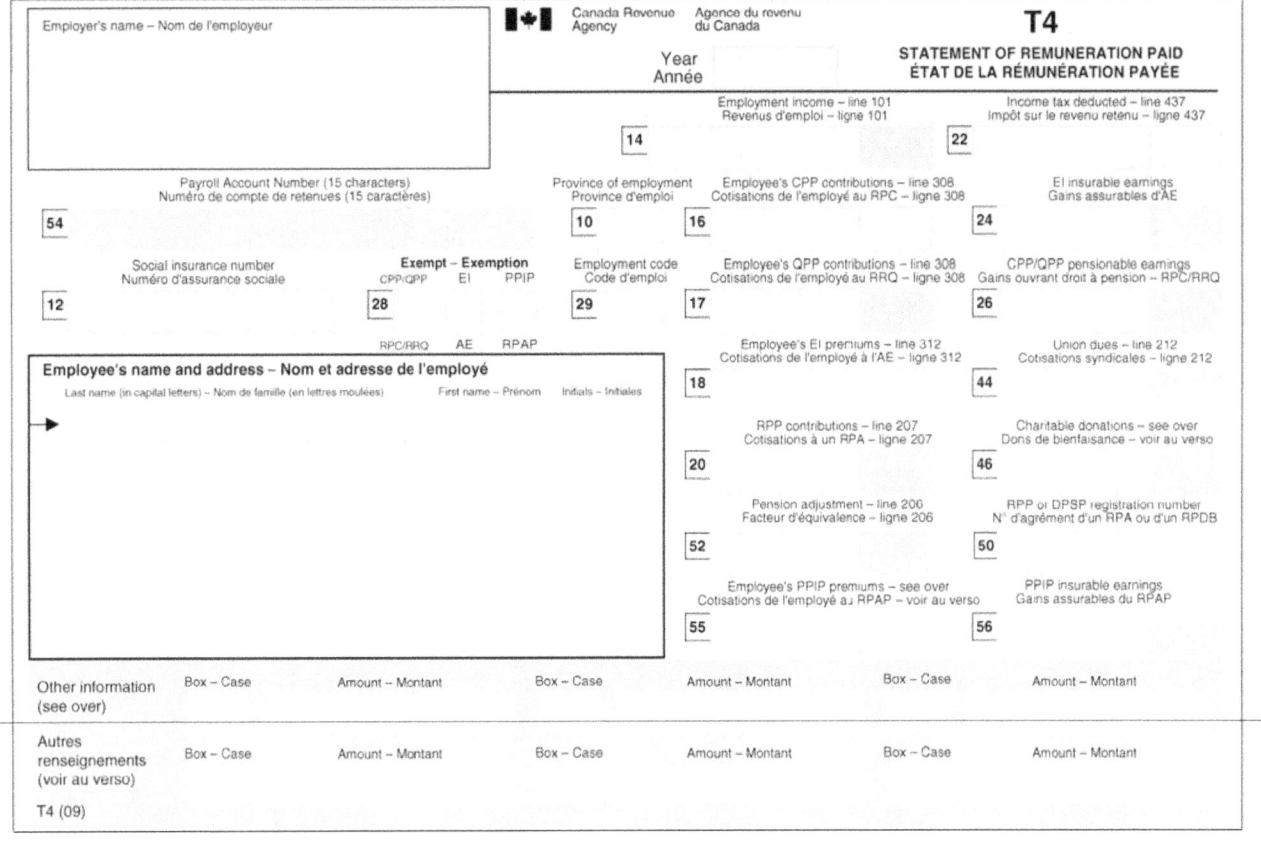

Report these amounts on your tax return

- **14** Employment income – Enter on line 101.
- **16** Employee's CPP contributions – See line 308 in your tax guide.
- **17** Employee's QPP contributions – See line 308 in your tax guide.
- **18** Employee's EI premiums – See line 312 in your tax guide.
- **20** RPP contributions – Includes past service contributions. See line 207 in your tax guide.
- **22** Income tax deducted – Enter on line 437.
- **37** Employee home-relocation loan deduction – Enter on line 248.
- **39** Security options deduction 110(1)(d) – Enter on line 249.
- **41** Security options deduction 110(1)(d.1) – Enter on line 249.
- **42** Employment commissions – Enter on line 102. This amount is already included in box 14.
- **43** Canadian Forces personnel & police deduction – Enter on line 244.
- **44** Union dues – Enter on line 212.
- **46** Charitable donations – See line 349 in your tax guide.
- **52** Pension adjustment – Enter on line 206.
- **53** Deferred security option benefits – See Form T1212.
- **55** Provincial Parental Insurance Plan (PPIP) Residents of Quebec, see line 375 in your tax guide. Residents of provinces or territories other than Quebec, see line 312 in your tax guide.
- **72** Section 122.3 income – Employment outside Canada – See Form T626.
- **73** Number of days outside Canada – See Form T626.
- **74** Past service contributions for 1989 or earlier years while a contributor
- **75** Past service contributions for 1989 or earlier years while not a contributor See line 207 in your tax guide.
- **77** Workers' compensation benefits repaid to the employer Enter on line 229.
- **78** Fishers gross earnings
- **79** Fishers net partnership amount
- **80** Fishers shareperson amount

See Form T2121. Do not enter on line 101.

- **81** Placement or employment agency workers
- **82** Drivers of taxis and other passenger-carrying vehicles
- **83** Barbers or hairdressers

Gross earnings. See Form T2125. Do not enter on line 101.

- **84** Public transit pass – See line 364 in your tax guide.
- **85** Employee-paid premiums for private health services plans See line 330 in your tax guide.

Your opinion counts

If you have any comments or suggestions that could help us improve our publications, we would like to hear from you. Please send your comments to:

Taxpayer Services Directorate
Canada Revenue Agency
750 Heron Road
Ottawa ON K1A 0L5

Email address: teachtax@cra.gc.ca

Canada Revenue Agency
Electronic Services

Take advantage of the quick, easy, secure electronic services that the Canada Revenue Agency offers all year long, right at your fingertips. File a return, change your return or your address, calculate your family benefits, view your client's information, get direct deposit, make electronic payments, and more!

Electronic services	www.cra.gc.ca/electronicservices
NETFILE	www.netfile.gc.ca
My Account	www.cra.gc.ca/myaccount
Quick Access	www.cra.gc.ca/quickaccess
Direct deposit	www.cra.gc.ca/dd-ind
Electronic payments	www.cra.gc.ca/electronicpayments
NETFILE Access Code online	www.netfile.gc.ca/netfilecode
Represent a client	www.cra.gc.ca/representatives
TELEFILE	www.cra.gc.ca/telefile
EFILE	www.cra.gc.ca/efile-individuals
My Business Account	www.cra.gc.ca/mybusinessaccount

Want tips on various tax-related topics? Go to **www.cra.gc.ca/taxtips**.

For more information, visit **www.cra.gc.ca**.

Think Recycling!

Printed in Canada

www.ingramcontent.com/pod-product-compliance
Lightning Source LLC
Chambersburg PA
CBHW081208230426
43666CB00015B/2678